D0138518

Spaces for Children

The Built Environment and Child Development

Spaces for Children

The Built Environment and Child Development

Edited by

CAROL SIMON WEINSTEIN

Graduate School of Education
Rutgers—The State University of New Jersey
New Brunswick, New Jersey

and

THOMAS G. DAVID

Bush Program in Child and Family Policy
University of California, Los Angeles
Los Angeles, California

Plenum Press • New York and London

Library of Congress Cataloging in Publication Data

Spaces for children.

Includes bibliographies and index.
1. Environment and children. 2. Dwellings—Psychological aspects. I. Weinstein, Carol Simon. II. David, Thomas G., 1949- . [DNLM: 1. Child Development. 2. Child Psychology. 3. Environment. 4. Facility Design and Construction. WS 105.5.E9 S732]
BF353.S68 1987 729′088054 87-14041
ISBN 0-306-42423-1

A Division of Plenum Publishing Corporation
233 Spring Street, New York, N.Y. 10013

Printed in the United States of America

To Neil, Rachel, and Laura
CSW

To Jane and Owen
TGD

Contributors

MICHAEL BAKOS The ARC Group, 1743 East 116th Place, Cleveland, Ohio

CAROL BALDASSARI Environmental Psychology Program, Graduate Center, City University of New York, New York, New York

RICHARD D. BARNES Department of Psychology, Randolph-Macon Woman's College, Lynchburg, Virginia

RICHARD BOZIC The ARC Group, 1743 East 116th Place, Cleveland, Ohio

DAVID CHAPIN The ARC Group, 1743 East 116th Place, Cleveland, Ohio, and Environmental Psychology Program, Graduate Center, City University of New York, New York, New York

THOMAS G. DAVID Bush Program in Child and Family Policy, University of California, Los Angeles, Los Angeles, California

ABBE K. FABIAN Graduate Center, City University of New York, New York, New York

ROGER A. HART Sub-Program in Environmental Psychology, Graduate Center, City University of New York, New York, New York

LAURA C. JOHNSON Social Planning Council of Metropolitan Toronto, 950 Yonge Street, Toronto, Ontario, Canada

SHEILA LEHMAN Environmental Psychology Program, Graduate Center, City University of New York, New York, New York

GARY T. MOORE School of Architecture and Urban Planning, University of Wisconsin–Milwaukee, Milwaukee, Wisconsin

ANITA RUI OLDS Anita Olds and Associates, Consultants, Environmental Facilities for Children, 10 Saville Street, Cambridge, Massachusetts, and Child Study Department, Tufts University, Medford, Massachusetts

ELIZABETH PRESCOTT Department of Human Development, Pacific Oaks College, Pasadena, California

HAROLD M. PROSHANSKY Graduate Center, City University of New York, New York, New York

LEANNE G. RIVLIN Environmental Psychology Program, Graduate Center, City University of New York, New York, New York

LELAND G. SHAW College of Architecture, University of Florida, Gainesville, Florida

THEODORE D. WACHS Department of Psychological Sciences, Purdue University, West Lafayette, Indiana

CAROL SIMON WEINSTEIN Graduate School of Education, Rutgers—The State University of New Jersey, New Brunswick, New Jersey

JOACHIM F. WOHLWILL Department of Individual and Family Studies, College of Human Development, Pennsylvania State University, University Park, Pennsylvania

MAXINE WOLFE Environmental Psychology Program, Graduate Center, City University of New York, New York, New York

CRAIG ZIMRING College of Architecture, Georgia Institute of Technology, Atlanta, Georgia

Foreword

As a developmental psychologist with a strong interest in children's response to the physical environment, I take particular pleasure in writing a foreword to the present volume. It provides impressive evidence of the concern that workers in environmental psychology and environmental design are displaying for the child as a user of the designed environment and indicates a recognition of the need to apply theory and findings from developmental and environmental psychology to the design of environments for children. This seems to me to mark a shift in focus and concern from the earlier days of the interaction between environmental designers and psychologists that occurred some two decades ago and provided the impetus for the establishment of environmental psychology as a subdiscipline. Whether because children—though they are consumers of designed environments—are not the architect's clients or because it seemed easier to work with adults who could be asked to make ratings of environmental spaces and comment on them at length, a focus on the child in interaction with environments was comparatively slow in developing in the field of environment and behavior.

As the chapters of the present volume indicate, that situation is no longer true today, and this is a change that all concerned with the well-being and optimal functioning of children will welcome. This collection demonstrates, moreover, that it is possible to investigate the behavior–environment interface without the all too one-sided reliance on such elaborate verbal techniques as the semantic differential and the personal construct that dominated this field in its earlier days.

At the same time, it is gratifying to find that the perspectives and approaches characterizing the chapters in this volume, however diverse, transcend a simplistic, deterministic conception of the relationship between children's behavior and the environment. We find, first of all, a concern for environmental images and meanings, extending the emphasis on these problems—well researched at the adult level—to that of the child. This material should prove of direct interest and benefit to the developmental psychologist, as much as to those on the environmental side. But equally welcome is the conception of children as more than passive pawns in the design of the environments in which they play, learn, and live, whose preferences and needs are thought to be known by the adults responsible for them or are simply ignored. Thus we find here a concern for the impact of both home and institutional environments on the child's long-term development and, at a different level, an interest in involving the child as an active participant in the design process.

For these reasons, I hope that this volume will reach an audience well beyond that of people in environmental design, whether academicians or practitioners, although it clearly deserves to become known and be consulted by them. I hope that my fellow developmental psychologists will want to familiarize themselves with its contents and to follow the further advances in this area that it should inspire. For it raises major issues of the place of the physical environment in development that developmentalists have been prone to neglect to their peril. Questions arise that are of concern at a conceptual level (What is the place of ecological variables in child behavior? Should these be defined in institutional or physical terms? How should we treat the interactive aspect of the relationship between environments and children's development?) and at a practical level (How important is the physical environment in devising conditions for the optimal functioning and growth of the child?).

These considerations lead me to voice a perhaps slightly discordant thought. How *much* design do we really want to provide for children? Or, to put it somewhat differently, should we provide them with more opportunities to create their own environments, or to seek out those that were perhaps created for a very different purpose (e.g., the play of urban children in places not designed or intended for them), or that were not created at all, at least by man (e.g., woods and fields)? Designers of environments for children have of course been aware of this issue; the "adventure-playground" movement is one concrete manifestation of that awareness. And, beyond that answer, it seems safe to rely on children's bent for exploration and discovery and for expanding their home range beyond the immediate environments provided for them, so that there may be little real danger of overdesigning the functional environment, at least for older children. For the younger child, however, who is less able to self-select its environment both in and outside the home, this is a question deserving of attention by both child psychologists and designers, as well as by those in between.

Admittedly, this may not be the most burning issue facing us, for environments—in the form of homes, schools at all levels from preschool to high school, and other institutions, as well as playgrounds and similar spaces for children—are being and will continue to be built. It is important that those who will be building them, or who will have a voice in how they will be designed, operate from an adequate base of relevant information about children and their development. This volume represents a landmark in providing such a basis and perhaps even more in stimulating further thinking and research on these issues that will result in a yet more adequate corpus of such information in the future.

I congratulate the editors on their good judgment in planning this volume and in assembling such a diverse group of contributors to it. The devoted labors of all who have been involved in it have made this a most valuable addition to the library of everyone with an interest in children and a stake in their optimal development.

JOACHIM F. WOHLWILL

Preface

Several years ago, the American Educational Research Association held its annual meeting in San Francisco. Among the hundreds of sessions was one entitled "The Physical Design of the Classroom: A Neglected Dimension." It had been organized by Carol Weinstein. In the audience was Tom David, who five years earlier had edited a special issue of *School Review* on classroom settings. At the close of the session, the two of us met for the first time. Our conversation was exciting. We shared the conviction that physical dimensions of the classroom have important effects on students' behavior and attitudes and agreed that design factors are typically overlooked in discussions of learning environments. Within five minutes of speaking, our cross-country collaboration on this volume had begun.

Our goal herein is to focus attention on the relationship between the built environment and children's development. Specifically, we hope to encourage researchers to examine interactions between children and physical settings. We also hope to persuade those who design and manage environments for children to give more consideration to their developmental needs.

Public spaces in the United States are rarely designed with children in mind. Airports are a particularly grim example, as any parent who has attempted air travel with young children can confirm. Housing developments, too, seldom give priority to children's needs. This is in stark contrast to the situation in Sweden, where space for children's play is an integral part of every housing project. Unfortunately, children's needs are often not a high priority *even in spaces specifically intended for them.* Architects frequently design children's settings without much thought to the developmental characteristics of the users and generally without their input. Child care professionals interact with children in centers and classrooms arranged more in response to custodial concerns than according to their understanding of children's behavior and development. We do not call for radical designs centering exclusively on children. Rather, we hope to encourage design efforts that reflect sensitivity to children's special needs in the same way that the physically disabled are increasingly accommodated with barrier-free design. We see such designs as affirming not only the child but also the family.

We have brought together work by designers and architects, child advocates, and researchers from a variety of backgrounds (developmental psychology, environmental psychology, education, sociology). Not surprisingly, our contributors operate from different knowledge bases, are guided by different sets of values, and study different settings. Such a diverse group of authors necessarily produces a diverse collection of chapters. We have in this book the reports of empirical research, experience-derived design heuristics or rules of thumb, and value positions regarding appropriate societal responses to children.

Our hope is that such diversity will inform rather than confuse. We have not attempted to "level" the differences or to reshape presentations in order to create a picture of an integrated field. Such a picture would be inaccurate. At the present time, only a limited number of researchers and practitioners scattered across the country are focusing on issues related to the built environment and children's development. Frequently working in different disciplines, they are often unaware of one another's work. Individuals publish in scholarly and professional journals with which others are totally unfamiliar. This leads to a situation in which research efforts are fragmented and practical knowledge is not shared. Only a few major centers of study exist. (One of the most active is at the City University of New York's Graduate Center, as reflected by the number of authors from CUNY who have contributed to this book.)

This work is intended as a resource for these researchers and practitioners. It is our hope that the book will stimulate further inquiry and interdisciplinary dialogue among people from early childhood education, applied child development, environmental psychology, architecture, and design. It is through debate, questioning, and attempts at synthesis that the field will progress. But one must first know what is available.

This volume focuses on immediate, small-scale, built environments. Since knowledge of effective practices and principles in one setting can enrich design efforts in other settings, we have included chapters dealing with child care centers, homes, schools, playgrounds, and residential institutions. Existing research is preponderantly on settings for young children—child care and schools—and that emphasis is preserved here. Other settings such as hospitals, libraries, and recreational settings (zoos, museums, theme parks, commercial spaces) have rarely been systematically examined from the viewpoint of child users.

The design process will always retain a subjective, judgmental element. When the process works well, the result is a space with an intangible, delightful presence, what Lee Shaw later in this volume calls "sense of place." Bringing research to bear on that process and on children's spatial experiences is not a simple matter. But our experiences with children have convinced us of the importance of pursuing that goal. The objective is not to create a set of foolproof prescriptions that will dictate design solutions but rather to enable designers to make decisions informed by a better understanding of children.

The book is the outgrowth of our meeting in 1979, but in a very real sense it is the product of interests spurred long ago by mentors with whom we were fortunate to work. We wish to express our gratitude to Jack Wohlwill and to Liz Prescott who first taught us to think about the significance of physical settings and who shared their wisdom with generosity and good will. We also want to acknowledge the encouragement, and particularly the patience, of our editor at Plenum Press, Eliot Werner. The Bush Foundation and the Rutgers Research Council provided financial support that made possible our involvement in the project; we gratefully acknowledge their assistance. To Rita Sannwaldt, who typed and retyped the many versions of each chapter, we owe a debt that even chocolate bars and gum drops will never repay. Our thanks, of course, must also go to our children—Rachel, Laura, and Owen—whose tent-building activities kept us mindful of children's desire for special places. Finally, our deepest gratitude to Neil and to Jane for putting up with our cross-country travels, our preoccupied demeanors, and our insistent moaning; for providing words of encouragement; and for sharing the word processor.

CAROL SIMON WEINSTEIN
THOMAS G. DAVID

Contents

PART III. DESIGNING SPACES FOR CHILDREN

PART IV. INVOLVING USERS IN THE DESIGN PROCESS

Part I

Introduction

Chapter 1

The Built Environment and Children's Development

THOMAS G. DAVID AND CAROL SIMON WEINSTEIN

INTRODUCTION

Children's interactions with physical settings tend to be direct and easy to observe. For the infant who delights in exploration and movement and the preschooler who strives to master physical skills, the immediate environment is the primary medium for learning. Moreover, attachments to beloved objects and places are central to the emotional life of the young child. As time goes on, exposure to a variety of group and institutional settings leads to new understandings about social roles and norms in the world beyond the home. The arrangement of classroom space, for example, communicates expectations for behavior that are reinforced by institutional policies.

Although learning becomes increasingly abstract with age and settings seem to grow less important, the environmental experiences of childhood continue to be influential. As Elizabeth Prescott notes in Chapter 4 of this volume, one way to assess that influence is by asking adults to recall favorite places from their childhood. The vividness of the images they conjure up and the accompanying depth of feeling transcend mere nostalgia. They testify to the significance of an aspect of individual development that we are only beginning to understand.

THOMAS G. DAVID • Bush Program in Child and Family Policy, University of California, Los Angeles, Los Angeles, CA 90024. CAROL SIMON WEINSTEIN • Graduate School of Education, Rutgers–The State University of New Jersey, New Brunswick, NJ 08903.

In recent years, there has been growing recognition of the importance of contextual variables in research on children's development. Missing from most considerations of context, however, has been an acknowledgment of the potential impact of the *physical* context—particularly the build environment—on children. Beyond appeals for "enriched" and "stimulating" settings, there has been a neglect of physical variables in mainstream child development research that reveals a tacit view of the physical setting as an unimportant backdrop.

This volume challenges that view. Although we would certainly not contend that the built environment is the major influence on the developing child, *we do believe that the developmental process can be influenced by characteristics of the physical setting.* This is particularly true for very young children, who have limited control over their surroundings and who spend much of their time engaged in interaction with the physical, rather than the social, environment (Parke, 1978; White, Kaban, Shapiro, & Attonucci, 1976).

We also believe that systematic knowledge about children and their interaction with the built environment can be used to improve the design of children's settings. From the perspective of children's developmental needs, schools, day-care centers, hospitals, psychiatric residences, and playgrounds are often poorly designed. Homes tend to be adult-oriented, to contain large spaces that are off limits to children, and to restrict opportunities for varied, stimulating experiences (Johnson, Shack, & Oster, 1980; Johnson, Chapter 7). Schools and institutions are often stark, uninviting, and designed for easy supervision and maintenance (Wolfe & Rivlin, Chapter 5); playgrounds consist of isolated pieces of single-purpose equipment and fenced-in blacktops.

The present volume reflects both of these beliefs. It focuses on two questions: first, what do we know about the nature of children's interactions with the built environment; and second, how can we apply our knowledge of children and the developmental process to the design of spaces for children?

THE STATE OF THE FIELD: CONCEPTUAL AND METHODOLOGICAL CONSIDERATIONS

In Chapter 13, Theodore Wachs notes that developmental psychology has moved far beyond a simple "main effects" conception of environmental influence on development to sophisticated, multivariate models capable of teasing out interactions between specific environmental factors, individual characteristics, and particular developmental outcomes. When it comes to the built environment, however, we are still at a fairly rudimentary level of inquiry. Few child-environment investigators are looking simultaneously at the interplay among these three sets of variables. For the most part, research has focused on the identification and description of molar patterns of child-environment interaction. Measures of settings have tended to be fairly simple (e.g., open–closed, soft–hard), and generally little attention has been paid to individual differences in the use of space.

What accounts for this state of the field? Three explanations come to mind: the lack of communication among child-environment researchers; the difficulty of measuring many important environmental attributes; and finally, the pragmatic function of the design process itself.

The study of children's environments has tended to be fragmented. Although particular types of environments (e.g., schools) or particular questions of interest (e.g., crowding) have received attention, there has been little bridge building among groups of investigators. In part, this lack of synthesis arises from the fact that the researchers have come from a variety of academic disciplines. For example, educators studying classroom physical settings have had little contact with the environmental psychologists who conduct parallel investigations. Similarly, researchers based in schools of architecture, who are primarily interested in the improvement of design, may never encounter child development scholars investigating spatial cognition in the laboratory. There are also a substantial number of practitioners, such as designers and therapists, who have developed experientially based notions of the role of space in children's lives but who may have never interacted with any of the above groups.

A consequence of this diversity of approach has been the development of widely divergent conceptualizations of the child's environment. Traditional experimental studies in child development research, for example, might define environment in terms of the type of toys provided in an otherwise barren observation room. Environmental psychologists have focused their attention on variables such as density or privacy or the "degree of openness" of design. In contrast, designers may define the critical dimensions of settings in terms of physical properties such as scale, texture, and light or more abstract attributes like mood and "sense of place."

These conceptualizations have been shaped by substantially different methodologies and perspectives. Academic researchers have relied on systematic observations and planned interventions. Designers' concepts often arise out of their direct experience and from informal observations and interviews. Furthermore, whereas some child-development investigators strive to maintain an impartial, "value-free" point of view, others operate from an explicit set of values about what is good for children. These different ways of understanding physical settings are not mutually exclusive; some of the authors in this volume derive their conclusions from a combination of controlled research, direct experience, and personal values. Nonetheless, different methodologies, perspectives, and conceptualizations of the built environment present obstacles to the synthesis necessary for the field to move forward.

A second problem facing child–environment researchers is the difficulty of defining and measuring many potentially important environmental attributes. The *perceived* environment, for example, may well be as important as the *objective* environment. But how do we measure a young child's perception of a physical setting? How do we begin to assess the emotional resonance of a place and its impact? How do we measure an environment's ability to provide privacy? In their concluding chapter to this volume, Zimring and Barnes reflect upon the difficulty that arises even at the level of setting definition: "Is a home where three unrelated children are cared for during the day a home or a day-care center?" They conclude that "the ambiguity of category definitions partly may account for conflicting findings so common in research on children's environments."

Third, we must recognize the societal function of physical design. Although it is possible to investigate individual differences in response to the built environment, most settings are designed to accommodate the needs of the group rather than the individual. A design can provide the opportunity to choose among a variety of spaces, but it is not possible (particularly within an institutional setting) to design "microspaces" for each individual user. Moreover, since the user population of those settings is constantly changing, individual requirements do not stay constant. The result of this group focus is that there is less impetus to investigate the relationship between individual characteristics and features of the built environment.

GUIDING PROPOSITIONS

Drawing on the work of the contributors to this volume, as well as other literature, we identify seven general propositions to guide inquiry on interactions between children and built environments:

1. *Built environments have both direct and symbolic impacts on children.* Elements of the physical setting may influence behavior directly by facilitating certain activities and obstructing others. Prescott (Chapter 4) has observed, for example, that the juxtaposition of several playground elements into a "super unit" will support sustained play by more children than the same pieces would individually. She also notes that the absence of a clear pathway to an activity area could result in underutilization by children, a pattern that could be reversed by a rearrangement of space.

In addition, physical settings communicate symbolic messages about the intentions and values of the adults who control the setting (Proshansky & Wolfe, 1974). Ittelson, Proshansky, Rivlin, and Winkel (1974) provide an example of the dual nature of environmental influence. They suggest that the construction of elaborate open-space schools in ghetto areas was intended not only to bring about quality education, a direct effect, but also to foster the development of a more positive self-image and to demonstrate to the students that others cared about their future, a symbolic effect. Similarly, the barrenness of the typical institution for mentally retarded children may have a direct, adverse impact on their cognitive and emotional development; it may also convey the message that the children are not worthy of more comfortable, more pleasing surroundings. According to Bettelheim (1974), the symbolic meaning of the environment is particularly salient to an emotionally disturbed child; moreover, since every physical detail is viewed as an indication of institutional policy, it is crucial that symbols and policies be consistent. Bettelheim warns: "A symbolic message which lies—to which the reality does not conform—is worse than no message at all" (p. 128).

2. *Study of the built environment and children's development will benefit from a multisetting perspective.* The design of institutional settings is dominated by programmatic considerations that are in turn shaped by a guiding image of the institution's function. Yet there are certain common needs of building users that cut across setting types. Young children, for example, have a need to play, whether they are in a home, school, hospital, or psychiatric setting. A sensitive design scheme can create niches for play within the overall scheme of the institution. A prime example is the work of Anita Olds (Chapter 6), who has "transplanted" the characteristics of preschool classrooms to pediatric hospital waiting rooms and play rooms. In her designs, the sterile, anxiety-producing waiting rooms so typical of hospitals and other institutions are transformed into inviting, comfortable play spaces that clearly meet the needs of children. Similarly, train stations and airports in Denmark have skillfully incorporated children's play spaces into the designs, a sensible idea that is yet to catch on in the United States. Adopting a multisetting perspective may help us to keep in mind the continuity of children's needs across environments.

A multisetting perspective is also useful in examining the *inappropriate* transplanting of design ideas from one setting to another. The image of the infirmary, for example, has shaped the design of many psychiatric facilities, even though the program of such institutions is markedly different from that of an acute care hospital. The powerful image of the classroom, with its desks and worksheets, has sometimes guided the design of child-care centers for preschoolers, even though the developmental expectations for those populations are quite different. The results of such inappropriate transfer of design features is an unfortunate mismatch between children's needs and the built environment.

Another argument for looking at more than one setting is the need to examine *links between environments* inhabited by children. This is a major theme of the chapter by Proshansky and Fabian (Chapter 2). They write: "The world is not simply an array of separate and isolated sociophysical settings." Children move from setting to setting, and it is likely that their experiences in one environment will influence their behavior in another.

For example, do children from crowded homes respond to the lack of privacy in classrooms differently than do children from less crowded homes? Does the provision of desks at which to do homework—often absent from low-income housing (Moore, 1969)—have an impact on school performance? Although there is some research on the relationship between home and school environments (Wilner, Walkley, Pinkerton, & Tayback, 1962; Murray, 1974), this is certainly an area in need of more attention.

3. *All built environments for children should serve certain common functions with respect to children's development: to foster personal identity; to encourage the development of competence; to provide opportunities for growth; to promote a sense of security and trust; and to allow both social interaction and privacy.* Each of these functions is described briefly.

a. *To foster personal identity.* Proshansky and Fabian (Chapter 2) refer to this function of the environment when they discuss "place identity," the notion that the sense of self includes a sense of place. We do not see ourselves as individuals in a vacuum, but as individuals who live in certain places and own certain objects. The parents of any two-year-old who has learned the word *mine* can attest to the fact that possessions and places are crucial elements in the development of personal identity. Cziskzentmihalyi and Rochberg-Halton (1981) have noted the persistence of attachment to personal objects across the life-span.

For young children, the home environment is normally the context in which a sense of self first develops. Ittelson *et al.* (1974) write:

> The stable setting that permits the child to associate specific physical attributes of the world with specific sets of expectations of behaviors very likely facilitates role learning. It also facilitates the development of a sense of place, so crucial in the acquisition of a sense of place identity. (p. 175)

With its personalized furnishings and individual territories, the home stands in marked contrast to institutions—homogeneous, impersonal environments in which people are generally not allowed physically to proclaim their individuality. Sommer (1969, 1974) has persuasively argued the adverse impact of such settings and has stressed the importance of allowing institutional clients to have their own things nearby, to personalize their living spaces, and to participate in decision making about the arrangement of space. Some empirical data are available to support these ideas. Berenson (1967), for example, examined the effects of the physical setting on the self-identity of emotionally disturbed girls. He found that there was a significant, positive change in their appearance and behavior when each girl was provided with a mirror near her bed. Apparently, the mirror served to define personal space, thereby enhancing a sense of self.

b. *To foster the development of competence.* In his classic work on motivation, White (1959) argues that the desire for competence is one of the basic motivators of human behavior. In childhood, this drive for competence is even more intense, since the child is constantly faced with new tasks and challenges. We propose that a crucial function of the designed environment is to enhance this drive for competence by allowing children opportunities to develop mastery and control over their physical surroundings. Olds (1979) stresses how important this is for children entering a hospital, who already feel anxious and out of control. She suggests that coat racks, clocks, water fountains, lights, and other fixtures be convenient for young children so that they can fulfill their basic personal needs without assistance. These ideas are echoed by Johnson in her chapter on home settings (Chapter 7); she provides guidelines on how houses can be adapted to meet the needs of children by placing fixtures at an appropriate height, by scaling down the size of tables and counters, and providing accessible storage areas.

The layout of the built environment can also facilitate competence if it is "comprehensible" (Little & Ryan, 1978). Environmental cues such as landmarks and boundaries help children represent the spatial environment and make it easier for them to plan and carry out goal-directed activity (Golbeck, 1985). This is illustrated in the research reported by Moore (Chapter 3), who found that spatially well-defined areas in child care centers supported a higher level of task engagement and exploratory behavior. Finally, the scale of the setting as a whole is also important. A more compact physical plan (at least within service units) makes it easier for children to understand and influence what goes on (Bettelheim, 1974).

c. *To provide opportunities for growth.* In addition to facilitating the development of competence, the opportunity to explore rich, varied environments appears related to cognitive, social, and motor development. Pines (1973), for example, found that children who were allowed to roam, explore, play with interesting materials, climb, and move were more competent in the intellectual and social skills required in the classroom and school yard than children who had been restricted with playpens and gates.

Yarrow, Rubinstein, and Pedersen (1975) have shown that three dimensions of inanimate stimulation—responsiveness, complexity, and variety—are highly related to infants' cognitive and motor development. Variety of play objects was related to the largest number of infant outcome variables: general mental and psychomotor development, cognitive motivational indices (reaching and grasping, goal directedness, secondary circular reactions), exploratory behavior, object permanence, and preference for novelty. Moreover, the impact of appropriate play materials is not limited to infancy; Bradley and Caldwell (1976) found that the provision of such materials was strongly correlated with IQ at 4½ years of age.

The need to explore, to move, and to play with responsive, interesting objects is a theme expressed by many of our authors (e.g., Prescott, Olds, Weinstein, Shaw). Indeed, Olds (Chapter 6) maintains that "restricting movement cuts off development at its source and may contribute to behavioral and learning difficulties later in life." She urges designers to create stimulating yet safe environments in which children can experience the risk taking, "doing, failing, redoing, and succeeding" that are necessary for growth.

d. *To foster a sense of security and trust.* It is reasonable to assume that predictable, comfortable surroundings foster the feelings of security and trust that are so critical to the development of the child. Unless children feel secure they will not explore their environments (Little & Ryan, 1978), and such exploration is crucial to cognitive, emotional, and motor development. In hospital and psychiatric residences, where children are already anxious, the need for comforting surroundings is even more extreme. Bettelheim (1974) suggests that tactile sensations are very important in conveying security: "The more architectural features invite touch, and give an impression of security, the more readily the building can be accepted as a safe home" (p. 118). Olds (Chapter 6) maintains that children feel frightened and disoriented by dramatic fluctuations of stimulation; she suggests that moderate variations in floor level, ceiling height, lighting, color, and other physical elements will enhance the feeling of a comfortable, interesting, safe place.

e. *To provide opportunities for both social contact and privacy.* The need to engage in social interaction has been frequently mentioned as a basic human drive. More recently, the need to *limit* social interaction has also been recognized (Altman, 1975; Wolfe, 1978). Physical space must be designed to meet both needs—to facilitate contact when desired while preserving the possibility of privacy. Several authors in this collection support this proposition. Olds's recommendations for infant and toddler centers include an open space for group activities with private spaces around the periphery. Leland G. Shaw (Chapter 9) advocates an open court in the center of a play structure, complemented by "defensible" spaces. Wolfe and Rivlin (Chapter 5) contend that a lack of privacy is one of the defining characteristics of contemporary institutions.

Although the distinction between sociopetal space (encouraging contact) and sociofugal space (inhibiting contact) is well known, the design features characterizing each type of space are not always obvious. For example, in a study of psychiatric ward bedrooms, Ittelson, Proshansky, and Rivlin (1970) found that social activity was more frequent in small bedrooms compared with larger bedrooms; isolated passive behavior was more often observed in large bedrooms than in small bedrooms. Presumably, patients in larger rooms used withdrawal as a way of excaping from unwanted social interaction. Examples like this underscore the need to address the question of how design can meet the dual needs of affiliation and privacy.

In addition to design features, objects within the environment can also influence social interaction. Quilitch and Risley (1973), for example, have demonstrated that toys such as pickup sticks and checkers facilitate cooperative activity, whereas clay and gyroscopes promote isolated play.

4. *There are substantial individual and cultural variations in the use and interpretation of settings.* Although there has been relatively little research on individual differences in response to the built environment (for reasons mentioned above), a few studies have addressed this issue. Weinstein (1982), for example, investigated individual differences in elementary students' desire for privacy. Four privacy booths were placed in a fourth-grade classroom, and booth use served as the measure of privacy seeking. For boys, booth use was positively related to teachers' ratings of aggressiveness and distractibility and negatively related to ratings of sociability; for girls, a significant positive relationship was found between privacy seeking at home and in school. There have also been a number of studies that have looked at the interaction between classroom seating arrangement and such variables as achievement level (Rosenfield, Lambert, & Black, 1985), self-esteem (Dykman & Reis, 1979; Morrison & Thomas, 1975), social desirability (Stires, 1980), and inclination to interact (Koneya, 1976).

Gender differences in children's responses to the environment have also been noted. Roger Hart (Chapter 10), for example, describes differences between the kinds of spaces that boys and girls create for themselves. Boys tend to build structures (e.g., forts), whereas girls concentrate on the furnishing and arrangement of elaborate interior spaces. Hart rejects a psychodynamic explanation for these differences as too simplistic and argues that they reflect sex-related social roles that boys and girls are encouraged to adopt. This socialization process is well illustrated in a study of children's bedrooms (Rheingold & Cook, 1975). These investigators found that boys are provided with objects that direct them away from the home toward sports, cars, and the military whereas girls are surrounded with objects that encourage home-oriented activities, such as keeping house and caring for children.

Gender also appears to be related to home range and indirectly to the amount of privacy a child may have. Several studies (Anderson & Tindall, 1972; Hart, 1978; Landy, 1965; Munroe & Munroe, 1971; Newson & Newson, 1968) have found that girls are likely to be kept under closer "surveillance" than boys. Wolfe (1978), reflecting upon these studies, has concluded that "the net result . . . is that girls are likely to be home more often, with fewer possibilities for achieving privacy as physical aloneness" (p. 284). Other studies have shown that parental restrictiveness is also related to social class and educational level (Gans, 1962; Newsom & Newson, 1968; Roy, 1950), with more highly educated parents in professional and managerial positions less restrictive than working-class parents.

5. *Wherever possible, children should be active participants in the planning and arrangement of the physical settings in which they live.* Even relatively young children are capable of articulating preferences and participating in decisions regarding interior design. At the simplest level, this can involve "personalization" of a child's room or cubby or desk at school.

Baldassari, Lehman, and Wolfe (Chapter 11) demonstrated that older children have a natural interest in helping to determine their own future and that they can tackle complicated neighborhood-scale planning issues. Hart observes in Chapter 10 that genuine participation by children in environmental decision making does not just result in more responsive physical arrangements. It also prepares young people for their roles as active, involved citizens in a democratic society.

Unfortunately, as Wolfe and Rivlin point out (Chapter 5), most institutional settings for children do not value participation and offer very limited opportunities for choice. Real participation, they and other authors observe, is dependent on the willingness of authority figures to share power. Without that, there are no real choices. We do not harbor romantic (and misguided) notions of child-controlled settings. However, we do see multiple benefits of child participation in the planning of spatial arrangements.

6. *The impact of the built environment must be examined in the context of the social, cultural system.* We recognize that it is fruitless to study physical elements of a building without considering how these elements are perceived, responded to, and used by the inhabitants. For example, Bakos, Bozic, and Chapin (Chapter 12) describe how the organizational culture of an institution for mentally retarded children affected the use of space in that setting and how the authors were able to mobilize staff support for their redesign proposals through participatory planning. Shaw (Chapter 9) points out the important role of the adult play leader in determining the ultimate success or failure of even the most innovative playground design.

Research on open-space schools provides another good example of the futility of investigating the impact of physical variables in isolation. Innumerable investigations have sought to establish the effects of open space by comparing the academic achievement of students in such schools with those in traditionally designed schools (for reviews, see George, 1975; Weinstein, 1979). Rarely have such studies taken into account how the open space was used, the type of instructional program that was being implemented, or the philosophies and selection of staff. The results of this research, not surprisingly, have been both inconclusive and contradictory. Despite the claim that "learning in the open space environment will lead the student to be more innovative, self-assured, intelligent, and understanding" (American Association of School Administrators, 1971), it is clear that open space, in and of itself, does not have a universal effect. Traditional modes of insruction can be carried on in open space, movable partitions can be erected, and teachers may team-teach or not. All of these are mediating variables that must be included in the equation.

7. *Children are not the only users of homes, schools, and special-care environments.* Since parents, teachers, nurses, and other adults share these settings with children, it is essential that their needs also be recognized. If not, adults will often implement regulations that create even more re-

strictive conditions for children (Golan, Makintosh, Rothenberg, Rivlin, & Wolfe, 1976). Johnson (Chapter 7) notes that homes must accommodate the conflicting needs of parents for quiet and order with children's needs for active, messy play. If adequately designed play spaces on the main floor are unavailable, children may be relegated to the basement or the bedrooms. Early childhood classrooms that are completely carpeted are aesthetically appealing, but teachers may decide to eliminate water play or painting because such activities are too messy. Provision of linoleum in one corner would help to alleviate their fears of ruining the appearance of the classroom. Olds (Chapter 6) emphasizes that adult needs such as these are legitimate and must not be overlooked in the design process. Moreover, the power of adults to control the environment makes it imperative that designers of facilities for children ask, "What will the impact on the adult users be?"

THE ORGANIZATION OF THE BOOK

The volume is divided into four sections, each with an organizing theme. The first section includes four quite different approaches to the general question, What is the impact of the built environment on children's behavior and development? Proshansky and Fabian (Chapter 2) are concerned with environmental influences on the development of the self. They identify a theoretical construct they call "place identity," comprised of cognitions about the physical environment that also serve to define the self. These cognitions relate both to specific settings or setting types and to relationships among settings. They include positive attachments to environments ("place belongingness") and more negatively charged spatial associations. The authors trace the development and successive differentiation of place identity in children as they move from the home out into the neighborhood and into school settings.

Moore (Chapter 3) examines available research evidence on the impact of child-care settings on children's cognitive development. Noting that the design of child-care centers is largely based on assumptions that have not been empirically verified, he identifies two design features for systematic study, degree of openness of interior plan and definition of activity settings. New measures were constructed for each of those design dimensions and systematic observations were conducted of "cognitive developmentally oriented" behaviors in centers that varied in design. His work has implications not only for the spatial arrangement of child-care environments but for future investigations of environmental impact in other settings.

Child-care environments are also the subject of Chapter 4. Prescott traces the evolution of her conceptualization of center environments over her 20 years of research on this topic. She describes a number of increasingly complex observational measures of environmental quality and discusses the implications of particular spatial features for program content and for child behavior. She also contrasts the observed environmental properties of family day-care homes with the (in her view) more restrictive and less natural settings of day-care centers.

Rivlin and Wolfe (Chapter 5) conclude the first section with an overview of the historical forces that shape institutional settings and the subsequent impact of such places on the children they serve. They draw on a substantive body of research by themselves and others to articulate four fundamental characteristics of institutional environments: routinization, control and authority, the public nature of life, and the paradox of independence as the stated goal but conformity as the reality. The authors cite examples of these practices in psychiatric facilities and schools and describe their efforts to counter such norms through the redesign of physical space.

The second section presents guidelines for the design of children's environments derived both from research knowledge about education and development and from cumulative design experience. Four types of environments are addressed: facilities for infants and toddlers, homes, preschool classrooms, and playgrounds.

Olds (Chapter 6) draws on research and on her experience as a designer of child-care centers, hospital playrooms, and specialized facilities for handicapped and high-risk children to prescribe a detailed set of design recommendations for settings serving infants and toddlers. Her designs for this age group appropriately focus on encouraging movement and stimulating the senses, as well as providing design features that assist caregivers in working with the children. She also proposes five attributes of well-defined activity areas: location, boundaries, work and sitting surfaces, materials storage and display, and a "mood" or personality.

Johnson (Chapter 7) takes a somewhat unexpected stance regarding home environments. Her research on family day-care homes in Canada left her with the conclusion that in many ways the typical home environment is not supportive of children's activities. Too often, she notes, children are restricted out of concern for possible damage to furnishings or potential hazards to themselves. Six design guidelines are suggested for the better arrangement of homes for children's needs, including play areas in the main living areas of the house, using the kitchen as a family room, and providing child-scale access to storage and fixtures.

Preschool classrooms are the subject of Chapter 8. Weinstein states that school spaces for young children should be designed to support the child's active engagement with the environment. She also notes the important role that institutional policies play in regulating the use of the environment. Drawing on a review of the child development and early childhood education literature, she lists 10 developmental goals for preschoolers and derives design implications for each. As an example, teachers can assist children's efforts to establish self-control by providing well-designed storage and physical cues for classroom organization, avoiding large open spaces in design, and providing appropriate places for retreat and materials for solitary play.

Chapter 9 is by Leland G. Shaw, an experienced designer of play environments. Although he has created settings for disabled children, he notes that the shared needs of all children transcend the able–disabled distinction. He articulates nine design guidelines for play spaces, including "sense of place" (organization of parts within an ordered theme or image), "unified environment" (connecting all parts physically and spatially allows play to flow from place to place), and "key places" (dominated by one major element, surrounded by a complex juxtaposition of spaces and pathways). He augments his guidelines with a series of accumulated informal observations of children at play that effectively illustrate the impact of a well-designed and managed play area.

The third section brings together papers on the topic of participation by children (and significant adult users of spaces) in the planning of built environments. Hart (Chapter 10) presents a rationale for child participation, describing the natural building activities children engage in and the benefits they derive from such activities. He also gives an overview of more formalized models for design participation including the criteria for genuine participation versus official strategies for cooptation or manipulation of input by children. Also described are a number of vehicles for children's participation in environmental decision making (many of them developed in Europe) such as city farms, community gardens, and urban studies centers.

In Chapter 11, Baldassari, Lehman, and Wolfe report on the development of a learning–teaching process through which they helped children to understand the nature of local environmental changes and to become active participants in designing their own future. Their work is an example of an action research model applied to the empowerment of young people through urban "environmental education." They describe not only their process but also an evaluation of its impact on the children, their families and neighbors, and the New York City schools in which they worked.

Chapter 12 ends this section with a reflection by Bakos, Bozic, and Chapin on the collaborative design process employed by their architecture firm (The ARC Group) in two design projects for children. In the first instance they substantially redesigned a playroom within a state institution for mentally retarded children. The second project was a play structure for a mixed-user group, including mentally and physically disabled children. They abstract four process principles for collaborative design with building users and offer some interesting insights into how physical settings designed in this way can transform institutional practices.

The concluding chapters by Wachs (Chapter 13) and Zimring and

Barnes (Chapter 14) comment on themes raised in the preceding chapters and propose new directions for research and design. Wachs begins by asking whether researchers investigating the built environment and children's development are focusing on "the right questions." He argues that it is time to ask, What specific aspects of the environment are relevant for what specific aspects of development, at what specific ages, for what specific individuals? Furthermore, Wachs contends, researchers adopting a developmental perspective must choose developmental outcomes, recognizing that changes in behavior may not signify true developmental growth. Finally, Wachs presents a model illustrating four potential relationships that can exist between the physical and social environments in terms of their relevance to development. He points out that the relevance of the physical setting will depend upon the type of environmental action pattern operating.

Zimring and Barnes urge future researchers to examine a much broader range of settings, children, and developmental needs; to clarify the definitions of environmental properties, attributes, and settings; and to employ multivariate research methods. They also suggest that, in order to increase the impact of research on design, recommendations should be published in popular trade magazines and environmental researchers should become involved with all levels of the "environmental delivery" process.

Almost a decade ago, Altman and Wohlwill (1978) observed that children may be especially vulnerable to the adverse effects of environmental problems. "Indeed," they wrote, "if we compare the evidence on effects of environmental stressors, such as noise and crowding, on children with those found in adults, it appears that the most deleterious effects may be reserved for the young, perhaps because they have not had an opportunity to adapt" (p. 2). At the same time, Altman and Wohlwill struck a more optimistic note, contending that the opportunity to affect children in a positive way through "suitable design of the environment" may also be greater.

With opportunity comes obligation. The chapters in this volume represent the work of environmental and developmental psychologists, architects, early childhood educators, and sociologists. Their sources of knowledge about the environment differ; they employ different methodologies and espouse different perspectives. But they share a firm commitment to the "suitable design of the environment," a commitment to creating the best possible spaces for children.

REFERENCES

Altman, I. *The environment and social behavior.* Monterey, CA: Brooks/Cole, 1975.

Altman, I., & Wohlwill, J. F. (Eds.) *Children and the environment.* New York: Plenum Press, 1978.

American Association of School Administrators. *Open space schools.* Washington, DC: Author, 1971.

Anderson, J., & Tindall, M. The concept of home range: New data for the study of territorial behavior. In W. Mitchell (Ed.), *Environmental design: Research and practice.* Los Angeles: University of California, 1972.

Berenson, B. Considerations for behavioral research in architecture. In C. W. Taylor, R. Bailey, and C. H. H. Branch (Eds.), *Second national conference on architectural psychology.* Salt Lake City: University of Utah, 1967.

Bettelheim, B. *A home for the heart.* New York: Knopf, 1974.

Bradley, R. H., & Caldwell, B. M. The relation of infant's home environments to mental test performance at 54 months: A follow-up study. *Child Development,* 1976, *47,* 1172–1174.

Cziskzentmihalyi, M., & Rochberg-Halton, E. *The meaning of things: Domestic symbols and the self.* Cambridge: Cambridge University Press, 1981.

Dykman, B. M., & Reis, H. T. Personality correlates of classroom seating position. *Journal of Educational Psychology,* 1979, *71*(3), 346–354.

Gans, H. J. *The urban villagers.* New York: Free Press, 1962.

George, P. S. *Ten years of open space schools: A review of the research.* Gainesville, FL: Florida Educational Research and Development Council, 1975.

Golan, M. B., Mackintosh, E., Rothenberg, M., Rivlin, L. G., & Wolfe, M. Children's environments evaluation research: Built environments. Paper presented at the Environmental Design Research Association Meeting, Vancouver, BC, May, 1976.

Golbeck, S. L. Spatial cognition as a function of environmental characteristics. In R. Cohen (Ed.), *The development of spatial cognition.* Hillsdale, NJ: Lawrence Erlbaum, 1985.

Hart, R. *Children's sense of place.* New York: Halstead Press, 1978.

Ittelson, W. H., Proshansky, H. M., & Rivlin, L. G. The environmental psychology of the psychiatric ward. In H. M. Proshansky, W. H. Ittelson, & L. G. Rivlin (Eds.), *Environmental psychology: Man and his physical setting.* New York: Holt, Rinehart and Winston, 1970.

Ittelson, W. H., Proshansky, H. M., Rivlin, L. G., & Winkel, G. H. *An introduction to environmental psychology.* New York: Holt, Rinehart and Winston, 1974.

Johnson, L. C., Shack, J., & Oster, K. *Out of the cellar and into the parlour.* Toronto, Ontario: Canada Mortgage and Housing Corporation, 1980.

Koneya, M. Location and interaction in row and column seating arrangements. *Environment and Behavior,* 1976, *8*(2), 265–282.

Landy, D. *Tropical childhood.* New York: Harper & Row, 1965.

Little, B. R., & Ryan, T. J. *Children in context: The social ecology of human development.* Ottawa, Ontario: Department of National Health and Welfare, 1978.

Moore, W. *The vertical ghetto: Everyday life in an urban project.* New York: Random House, 1969.

Morrison, T. L. & Thomas, M. D. Self-esteem and classroom participation. *Journal of Educational Research,* 1975, *68,* 374–377.

Munroe, R. L., & Munroe, R. H. Effects of environmental experience on spatial ability in an East African society. *Journal of Social Psychology,* 1971, *83,* 15–22.

Murray, R. The influence of crowding on children's behavior. In E. Canter & T. Lee (Eds.), *Psychology and the built environment.* London: Architectural Press, 1974.

Newson, J., & Newson, E. *Four years old in an urban community.* London: Pelican Books, 1968.

Olds, A. R. Designing developmentally optimal classrooms for children with special needs. In S. J. Meisels (Ed.), *Special education and development: Perspectives on young children with special needs.* Baltimore, MD: University Park Press, 1979.

Parke, R. D. Children's home environments. In I. Altman & J. F. Wohlwill (Eds.), *Children and the environment.* New York: Plenum Press, 1978.

Pines, M. A child's mind is shaped before age two. *Annual Editions Readings in Psychology, 1973–74.* Guildford, CT: Dushkin Publishing Group, 1973.

Proshansky, E., & Wolfe, M. The physical setting and open education. *School Review,* 1974, *82*(4), 557–574.

Quilitch, H. R., & Risley, T. R. The effects of play materials on social play. *Journal of Applied Behavior Analysis,* 1973, *6,* 573–578.

Rheingold, H. L., & Cook, K. V. The contents of boys' and girls' rooms as an index of parents' behavior. *Child Development,* 1975, *46,* 459–464.

Rosenfield, P., Lambert, N. M., & Black, A. Desk arrangement effects on pupil classroom behavior. *Journal of Educational Psychology,* 1985, *77*(1), 101–108.

Roy, K. Parents' attitudes toward their children. *Journal of Home Economics,* 1950, *42,* 652–653.

Sommer, R. *Personal space: The behavioral basis of design.* Englewood Cliffs, NJ: Prentice-Hall, 1969.

Sommer, R. *Tight spaces: Hard architecture and how to humanize it.* Englewood Cliffs, NJ: Prentice-Hall, 1974.

Stires, L. Classroom seating location, student grades, and attitudes: Environment or self-selection? *Environment and Behavior,* 1980, *12*(2), 241–254.

Weinstein, C. S. The physical environment of the school: A review of the research. *Review of Educational Research,* 1979, *49*(4), 577–610.

Weinstein, C. S. Privacy-seeking behavior in an elementary classroom. *Journal of Environmental Psychology,* 1982, *2,* 23–35.

White, R. W. Motivation reconsidered: The concept of competence. *Psychological Review,* 1959, *66,* 297–333.

White, B. L., Kaban, B., Shapiro, B., & Attonucci, J. Competence and experience. In I. C. Uzgiris & F. Weizmann (Eds.), *The structuring of experience.* New York: Plenum Press, 1976.

Wilner, D. M., Walkley, R. P., Pinkerton, T. C., & Taybeck, M. *The housing environment and family life.* Baltimore, MD: Johns Hopkins Press, 1962.

Wolfe, M. Childhood and privacy. In I. Altman & J. F. Wohlwill (Eds.), *Children and the environment.* New York: Plenum Press, 1978.

Yarrow, L. J., Rubinstein, J. L., & Pedersen, F. A. *Infant and environment: Early cognitive and motivational development.* New York: Wiley, 1975.

Part II

The Impact of the Built Environment on Children's Development

Research, Theory, and Recollection

Chapter 2

The Development of Place Identity in the Child

HAROLD M. PROSHANSKY AND ABBE K. FABIAN

INTRODUCTION

Developmental psychology and, to a lesser extent, social psychology have taught us that individuals, groups, and still larger aggregates of people change in the patterning of their physical, biological, social, and cultural characteristics over time. This "life-cycle" approach can be applied with equal success to the physical settings that define people's day-to-day lives. Conceptualizing the changing character of physical settings over extended periods of time requires that the environmental psychologist be very sensitive to and fully informed about the processes of human development.

Given such sensitivity and knowledge, environmental psychologists can readily begin to consider two very important questions that have been almost completely overlooked by developmental psychologists themselves. First is the question of the ways in which physical-setting properties are significant in the growth and development of the child. In other words, in what ways does the child derive meaning, purpose, form, and structure from the kinds of physical settings that he or she grows up in? And inextricably tied to this question is the no less important one of how physical settings are themselves shaped and influenced in unintended ways by the continuing growth and development of the child. Indeed, there are a number of interest-

HAROLD M. PROSHANSKY AND ABBE K. FABIAN • Graduate Center, City University of New York, New York, NY 10036.

ing questions raised when one incorporates developmental concepts into environmental psychology theory and research.

The concern in this chapter is with *place identity,* or what can be referred to as the physical-world socialization of the child. Simply stated, place identity is conceived of as a substructure of the person's self-identity that is comprised of cognitions about the physical environment that also serve to define who the person is. Our theory of place identity (Proshansky, Fabian, & Kaminoff, 1983) is derived from the existing body of literature about the formation and evolution of self-identity, but at the same time it provides a consideration of a long ignored set of factors in the formation of this identity.

The process of socialization and self-identity formation is incremental and has been broken down into stages by a number of developmental theorists (Piaget, 1954; Erikson, 1968). Individuation begins with the infant and evolves largely through sensory and perceptual experiences—vision, audition, tactile sense, and so on. It is later in this process that language begins to play a prominent role. The child not only learns the appropriate labels for objects and for people but also learns through social interaction and object use what its given relationship is to each such object and person. These relationships between the child and other people and objects indirectly serve to define who the child is to itself and therefore to others as well.

It is our contention, however, that a critical consideration is missing from the developmental literature of self-identity formation. There has been an almost complete neglect of the role of the physical environment in such identity formation. If a child acquires the knowledge and understanding of who it is by virtue of its dependent and continuing relationships to significant other people, then we must assume that such identity determinations are also rooted in the child's experience with rooms, clothes, playthings, and an entire range of objects and spaces that also support its existence. Certainly this inanimate world is ever present and inherent in the child's interactions and relationships with significant other people. In effect, children learn to view themselves as distinct from the physical environment as well as from other people and do so by learning their relationships to various objects, spaces, and places including ownership, exclusion, limited access, and so on. Certain spaces and places, because they are "owned," familiar, and useful and can be controlled, satisfy and maintain the integrity of the child's sense of self, including the *definition* of that self.

One must come to terms with the fact that socialization does take place in real-life physical contexts. Traditionally, however, developmental psychology has examined the developmental process apart from any particular physical setting or even types of settings in order to derive more general or universal principles of child socialization and development. Although this approach does shed light on some aspects of human development, this knowledge in the end becomes of doubtful validity when applied outside of the laboratory in the various physical settings in which socialization occurs. If, as is generally believed, there is no physical setting that is not also a social setting, the obverse is no less true.

The developmental psychologist is committed to trying to understand the complexity of a range of human phenomena that fall under the rubric of psychological growth and development. But, as we have already noted, there is no social environment that is not also a physical environment (Ittelson, Proshansky, Rivlin, & Winkel, 1974). This means that whether the concern is human development generally or, more specifically, self-identity formation, spaces and places must necessarily be fundamental considerations in this search for understanding the development of human behavior and experience. The question, What are the effects of the built environment on personal development? seems particularly important in this era of accelerated urbanization and rapid technological development in which the computer in concert with sophisticated electronic systems has had major effects on the mass media, telecommunications and social interaction, human mobility, and life in the family setting. Some may assess this new "high-tech" world as alienating to human growth and development, whereas others will see great potential and opportunity; in either case, it is clear that our physical and social environments are characterized by *change.* Similarly, our theories of human development must be dynamic and able to capture the flexibility as well as the stability that characterizes self-identity.

Historically, theories of self-identity have emphasized the stable and unchanging aspects of the individual. There are only a small number of theorists who have paid equal attention to the more flexible substructures of the self (Cumming & Cumming, 1962; Marris, 1974; Smith, 1968). We would particularly emphasize the fact that self-identity necessarily undergoes changes throughout the life cycle, particularly as the individual interacts with an ever changing physical environment.

Place identity, as a substructure of self-identity, should not be thought of as a stable and integrated cognitive structure. Certainly it has enduring aspects, but many of its other components are given to change over time. As we have already noted, place identity consists of accumulated cognitions about the physical world in which the person lives. The cognitions are represented as thoughts, memories, beliefs, values, ideas, preferences, and meanings relating to all the important settings of the person's daily life, past as well as present. The substantive nature of these cognitions for any one individual influences what he or she perceives, feels, and thinks about the day-to-day physical world. Indeed, place-identity cognitions monitor the person's behavior and experience in the physical world.

Place-identity cognitions can be conceived of as being organized into one of two types of "clusters." One type consists of the memories, thoughts, values, and preferences that relate to a particular setting which the person experienced or, more generally, to the type of setting it represents (e.g., school, household). The second type of cluster has to do with the relationship among settings, that is, the home, school, neighborhood, and so on. The world is not simply an array of separate and isolated sociophysical settings. Children play, eat, rest, socialize, and learn in a number of places in relation to which they have particular needs, expectations, and fears. Thus, the place-identity cognitions that connect one setting to another emerge or develop because of the successive and repeated pattern of their use and because of the overlapping activities and social roles across settings.

An individual's place-identity cognitions relate to the past, the present, and the future. It is the person's "environmental past"—that is, the early physical space and place cognitions of childhood—that has the most profound influence on the person's subsequent place identity. The environmental experience of children consists of objects, places, and spaces that satisfy their biological, social, physical, and cultural needs and still other objects, places, and spaces that do not. In this sense, then, some of the person's place-identity cognitions are positive and others are negative, but both kinds of cognitions serve to define who the person is. In others words, places, spaces, and objects that in effect tell the child, "This is not good for you" are as important in contributing to his or her self-identity as those that are useful and satisfying and therefore are the necessary reinforcers of this identity.

In addition to actual experiences with the physical environment, place identity is very much influenced by the *social* meanings that are attached to spaces and places by other people. The process of physical-world socialization is rooted in human learning growing out of individual experience and the ministrations of those adults who are influential in the child's life. The perspective and orientation of the parents as to the nature of the home and neightborhood, how those spaces are to be used, to what extent they are to be manipulated, and what dangers and taboos are to be recognized in them play a central role in the development of early place-identity cognitions. As children venture away from the residential area, go to school, and meet children from other kinds of neighborhoods and homes, they become aware of "outsiders'" evaluations of their neighborhood and home settings. The beliefs and attitudes of acquaintances as well as those expressed by the agents of socialization all contribute to children's definitions of who they are.

In terms of a child's physical world socialization, the home is undoubtedly an environment of primary importance. However, as the child grows and extends its range beyond the home, other settings such as the school and outdoor play areas in the neighborhood take on their own considerable importance in the socialization process. These three overlapping physical and social realms are probably the most influential settings in the life of the child and are the three we will discuss in greater detail later in this chapter.

Although we will talk about each setting individually, we want to make clear that it is the *pattern* and the interrelationships between and among the important settings of a child's life in which we are interested. The child develops particular preferences, skills, and behaviors within each setting; however, it is the interface between the settings that constitutes daily life and best captures what we mean by *place identity.*

It must be understood that place-identity cognitions do not evolve and change merely in response to properties of the physical environment. They are also a product of the social roles played by the person and the nature of his or her own physical makeup. The physical and social adjustments that accompany the adoption of an occupational role or parenthood, for example, have implications for the self-identity and therefore also for the place identity of the individual. These kinds of changes are more difficult to see when the discussion is limited to early childhood because so many of the basic social categories and social roles learned during this period (e.g., sex, race, religion) tend, at least in their broader definition, to remain stable throughout the person's life. However, for changes occurring late in the life cycle, for example, marriage, having children, beginning a professional career, one can more clearly see not only the social status shifts but also the important alterations in a person's physical environment since each new status carries with it a correspondingly altered or new physical setting. Such changes may not necessarily mean a significant or even a gross change in the physical setting but rather may represent only a change in the way one perceives the environment. A clear example is elderly people whose slow but inexorable decline in physical capacities very much limit their ability to travel around the city which for so many years before presented no difficulty at all. Certainly this new relationship for the elderly to their urban environment has implications for concurrent changes in self-identity. Further, at any time in the life cycle there are social forces that go beyond individual development and cause changes in self-identity and therefore in place identity as well. These forces include sudden and rapid technological changes, short-term changes in the attitudes and values of a society, and demographic and ecological changes in a community or city. In the turbulent 1960s, not only high-school and college youth were influenced by the values changes that occurred. Homes, workplaces, schools, and other institutional settings showed physical-setting changes reflecting normative changes in their purposes, how they were to be run, and by whom. Such normative changes in person–environment relationships however, become so deeply ingrained that they are integrated into the person's self-definition and are thus important components of place-identity cognitions. They are manifest not only in individual conceptions regarding the use of objects and spaces but in the norms, behaviors, rules, and regulations that are socially defined in any given physical context.

THE DEVELOPMENT OF PLACE IDENTITY

Although we have established that place-identity changes occur throughout a person's lifetime, in this chapter we will focus on the period of early childhood. Our purpose is to understand the relationship between the child's increasing knowledge and mastery of its physical environment and the emergence of its place identity. It is at this age that the more stable aspects of place identity are developed.

Together with other types of cognitions, those related to the physical world are woven into that fabric of self-knowledge that establishes self-identity. Children look at the environment, physical as well as social, for ways in which to understand their surroundings, to satisfy needs, and in doing so to behave appropriately. All of this in turn contributes to a place identity in which competence in and control of the physical world is an emergent aspect of self-identity.

A toddler learning to walk is confronted by a variety of surfaces and changing ground levels on which to practice and perfect its skills. There are stairs of different widths, moving stairways, pebbled paths, grass, and asphalt driveways for which slight adjustments must be made. The child's broadening experience with physical-setting features that directly relate to walking lead to mastery and confidence which in turn tell the child something about the success of its own development. Contributing to that self-knowledge are the praises (or admonitions) the child receives from parents, grandparents, brothers, and sisters who are pleased (or displeased) to see that the child is (or is not) acquiring the physical-world skills that are expected.

This physical-world socialization occurs primarily in the home, the neighborhood, and the school, the three physical settings that dominate the child's day-to-day existence. It is in these contexts that many of the important social roles and environmental skills and relationships are learned. All of these are aspects of place identity that persist and form the "lenses" through which the child will later recognize, evaluate, create, and manipulate physical spaces and places.

Let us note here that although almost all infants spend some time in the home setting, increasing numbers are spending a good portion of their waking hours in child-care settings. The range of physical environment experiences in the "home surrogate" setting may indeed differ from those available at home, but they serve the same function of providing the stimuli to which the child reacts in developing place-identity cognitions.

Place Identity and the Home Setting

Few studies have been conducted on the significance of the home as a critical physical setting in child development. Given the general neglect of physical settings in most, if not all, fields of psychology, this comes as no surprise. Yet, from the earliest moments of life, the infant's discovery of the world and growing self-awareness begin within the context of this setting. What is so often stressed in discussions of the development of self is the child's learning to distinguish the self from the "not-self." But inevitably the not-self implies distinguishing oneself from others, particularly those directly involved with socialization. To do this, however, children must also distinguish what is social in their environment and what is physical. It may be that to distinguish themselves from others children must first learn to distinguish themselves and those others from physical objects, spaces, and places.

Once children can distinguish themselves and others from the physical setting, the home indeed becomes their world. Therefore, the first place-identity cognitions reflect the home setting. Out of an undifferentiated mass of sound, light, texture, and movement come the recognition and identification of meaningful spaces and places and the steady comprehension of how to use them. As this process continues, children develop qualitative associations to objects, places, and spaces—some positive, some negative, some neutral, and some a combination of such reactions. As the child becomes mobile, its pattern of movement through the home will reveal intentions and motives that clearly imply the emerging development of a place identity. The child not only knows what objects are its own, but determines at some level where they should be kept, how they are to be used, and when they can be used by others. This identity is revealed by a whole set of physical-setting expectations which are expressed directly when they are not met.

The child learns in time that it is related not only to other people in the home but also to the physical objects and places within the home. The increasing independence of the child can be accomplished and demonstrated only through the manipulation of these physical objects and places. Both the child and those responsible for the child will use such accomplishments as indications of emerging *individuality.* This point may seem quite obvious, but it is critical for an understanding of the interplay between the social world and the physical world.

The child learns visual tracking by following the animals on a mobile hanging over head, learns to eat with a spoon, learns to dress by opening drawers and closet doors to get out the clothes, learns bowel control by using a potty seat. All of these developmental tasks are not simply a matter of acquiring perceptual-motor skills. They in effect define the child's self. The slow metamorphosis of a totally dependent infant into a separate and distinct individual is aided and continually reaffirmed by the acquisition of these skills, particularly when they involve objects, places, and spaces that "belong" to him or her. As we have stated elsewhere (Proshansky, Fabian, & Kaminoff, 1983), a child learns the distinction between "me" and "my mommy," but the distinction between "me" and "my room" equally serves to define who that child is. It can be said that a child's room, replete with all its belongings and its ability to provide sanctuary from the control of parents, is a place of disproportionate significance in the child's development of place identity and therefore in self-identity.

In addition to creating a personal world within the home, children also learn that spaces and places are shared. They learn that physical settings are not static but are continually changing because the presence of other people changes them. Thus, there is a tension between the normative and the personal uses of objects, spaces, and places. Autonomy and self-identity are defined by the knowledge that one has some control over one's physical environment, but it is equally true that self-identity involves dependence on and cooperation with other individuals. From the start, children are continually subject to a socialization process that defines their behavior with respect to other people, the activities they will engage in, the goals and tasks to be accomplished, and so on. Social class and ethnic and sex differences set the stage on which these expectations are played out, but from these basic social roles many other differences begin to emerge that affect the child's resources and capacity to cope.

What we wish to stress here is the very close relationship between the social roles the child must learn and the normative aspects of space and place utilization. The status of being a child carries with it many spatial restrictions which are slowly withdrawn as the child demonstrates competence and responsibility in the physical world. Very young children discover over time who controls the various spaces within the home and learn to respect the spatial autonomy and privileges of older household members. For example, they may first learn that access to the bathroom is not possible when it is occupied or that they may not go into Mommy's and Daddy's bedroom when the door is closed. But with increasing age accompanied by role changes and greater environmental skills, children achieve their own control and autonomy over particular spaces and places.

The issue of spatial autonomy is an important one and in a very real way marks the development of independence. Laufer, Proshansky, and Wolfe (1973), Laufer and Wolfe (1777), and Wolfe (1978) all observe that privacy as achieved through some degree of control over the physical environment is absolutely essential to healthy psychological development. In some ways, however, spatial autonomy for children is viewed more as a privilege than as a right in our culture and is granted only when children show evidence of internalizing the social roles and environmental skills that are expected of them.

Wolfe (1978) points out that the child has few if any opportunities for limiting other people's control or access to those things and spaces. However, the child's need for some degree of control is still present. This is clearly manifested in what the child says and does not say, that is, through the withholding of information, usually in the form of making up stories or telling lies. Wolfe describes this "information management" as the child's first opportunity to achieve personal privacy by creating and controlling boundaries between himself or herself and others. Over time children learn the spatial needs of other people in the household and as a result gain opportunities for achieving their own degree of spatial privacy. These person–environment relationships are very much a part of place-identity development and thereby influence the child's future needs for and methods of achieving, for example, privacy, territoriality, or personal space.

The development of place identity requires not only that children learn to recognize objects, places, and spaces and to share them with other people but also that they know how to use them. Physical-world socialization requires learning the particular behaviors and responses that are part of space utilization. When thinking of the home setting one thinks of rooms, hallways, furniture, and all kinds of utilitarian and decorative features, but in addition there are switches, electronic devices, radiators, refrigerators, lights, sharp edges, high places, low places, and door knobs. Although the home is a relatively small physical setting, it is filled with complexities that must be mastered. The environmental skills at first are quite limited and specific (e.g., walking a few steps, getting over a threshold). In time, as they become integrated and more goal-oriented, the child's intentions become clear, such as going from the living room to the bedroom or getting a toy down from a shelf. These skills in turn become more complex so that children know how to react and behave in a variety of situations. In time, they come to understand that the household is part of a larger context, whether it be a neighborhood of single- or multiple-family homes where strangers share sidewalks and public spaces or an apartment building where strangers share hallways and elevators.

In summary, the home is a critical sociophysical setting in the life of the child because it is the arena in which most early learning occurs. Self-knowledge, knowledge of others, and knowledge of the environment all begin there. Many of these early self-perceptions and place-identity cognitions will persist and determine the kind of experiences the child is likely to have in later settings.

Place Identity and the Neighborhood

There comes a point in early life when the physical world outside of the home becomes a known quantity. With biological and social growth comes the challenge of learning to be competent not just in the home but ouside it as well. This, of course, is an incremental process beginning with the parents' or other caretakers' having complete supervision and ending with the child's independent use of the neighborhood and finally of other neighborhoods as well.

As adults, we tend to lose sight of the drama involved in the move from the home to the neighborhood, but this "outside world" presents a far greater complexity. There are streets to be crossed, routes to be learned, stores to be recognized, and sounds, smells, lights, and shadows to be experienced. Furthermore, neighborhoods are full of people, including all the individuals whose recurring presence marks them as familiar and enduring features, the local butcher, the neighbors next door, the postman, and many others. In addition, there are relative strangers whom the child in time not only recognizes (as someone who lives down the street) but sees as another stable feature of the neighborhood. Children must learn their social role relationships to all of these individuals, and in every instance the relationships involve how they are to act in this neighborhood setting. Thus, one does not walk too close to strangers; the neighbor's lawn is not a public space; one says good morning to the person but not to an unidentified person who is visiting a neighbor down the block.

The child is faced with many situations in the neighborhood that require behavioral responses unnecessary in the home. Simply crossing a street involves a great many sensory discrimination skills to be learned. From a very early age, long before most children are permitted to venture out on their own, parents begin instructing them in the do's and don'ts of crossing streets: how to look both ways, how to cross at a crosswalk, and how to understand traffic lights. In addition, there are restrictions regarding which streets the child is allowed to cross; some are too heavily trafficked or are simply outside the defined bounds of the neighborhood.

Once exposed to the neighborhood setting, children become aware of a larger and more clearly differentiated world. Their cognitive task outside the home is a difficult one; they must assimilate the tremendous complexity of the neighborhood setting and at the same time learn to discriminate, make choices, selectively attend to stimuli, and clarify ambiguities (Rapoport, 1977).

The cognitive function that is clearly a prerequisite to the acquisition of environmental understanding, environmental control, and environmental competence in the neighborhood setting is large-scale environmental perception and cognitive mapping. Although there has been a good deal of discussion over the precise nature and developmental characteristics of a cognitive map, for our purposes we need only define it as an internal schematic representation of a given locale showing particular places and the connections among them. For a more complete review of the literature on the development of cognitive maps, the reader can refer to Siegal, Kirasic, and Kail (1978) or Downs and Stea (1973).

Clearly, the child's perceptions and conceptualizations of the physical environment build up slowly, becoming progressively more complete and sophisticated. Much of the relevant literature describes cognitive mapping only in large-scale settings vis-à-vis way-finding and locomotion, but it seems reasonable to assume that the young child first develops a cognitive map of the home. Moreover, our conception of cognitive maps is not simply that they consist of landmarks, paths and routes but that they also include all the social information collected by the child about that setting, including norms about what takes place in given spaces, behavior in response to others in these spaces, and how these spaces are controlled and by whom.

We would also extend the breadth of most cognitive mapping theory by suggesting some functions that this information may serve in the child's life. Cognitive representations of space are not only important for orientation purposes; they also help to establish that aspect of the child's sense of self that is influenced by the specific places and spaces in the life of that child and in the connections between them. Large-scale environmental perception is not a process by which the child simply registers and is shaped by such an environment. It is an active process whereby the child responds to certain features of the immediate outside world; these features are internalized in the form of cognitions that express not only their contents but also the child's feelings, attitudes, and behavior toward them. It is no exaggeration to say that place identity is in part a cognitive map of physical settings, past, present, and future.

There is no doubt that cognitive mapping in the large-scale environment, such as the neighborhood, is a more difficult task than cognitive mapping at home. Children not only experience a greater number and variety of physical spaces but also larger numbers of people moving through those spaces, many if not most of whom may be strangers. Thus, they must develop nonverbal strategic interaction skills in their use of and movement through the large-scale environment. By this we mean the body messages and gestures that people use to convey their spatial intentions, including the head and eyes, particularly in dense urban areas. For example, children walking to school may persistently keep their eyes focused so that they do not look at any strange adults as they pass. They may have been taught not to stare at strangers and instructed not to talk to them, and thus the focused look away communicates this intention. Of course, adults too have learned not to frighten young children they do not know by paying too much attention to them or staring at them.

Cognitive mapping and nonverbal strategic interaction skills are both important in that they enable children to act competently and confidently in the neighborhood setting. In the acquisition of these skills as a means of mastering this setting, further development of place identity is, of course, an important consequence. In some ways the neighborhood setting is even more critical than the home in its implications for place-identity development. It is by definition a public setting filled with other children and other adults who are there not only as objects and actors but also as observers and judges of the behavior of others. It is here that the child learns its public persona, which necessarily includes those environmental skills critical for relating to and using a physical setting. There is frequently a special status assigned to a child who can play stickball very well, run very fast, overcome barriers, and in other ways demonstrate environmental understanding, competence, and control. Additionally, the neighborhood setting is also of considerable importance in the child's social development. It provides the setting in which children can be away from the watchful eye of adults and as a consequence can explore the social role of "friend" rather than of "sister" or "daughter." By going outside alone, playing in a nearby schoolyard, or going beyond the neighborhood, the child learns to use a new and different setting outside the home with new and different people. In effect, the child's testing of its autonomy is slowly transferred into a conception of self as independent and relatively free.

The neighborhood is a setting that facilitates what Moore and Young (1978) have referred to as "volitional learning" (p. 88). There are opportunities for the child to manipulate elements of the outdoor neighborhood setting in ways that are not possible or permissible in the home, such as construction with found objects, playing in dirt and puddles, or using outside settings for other purposes (e.g., the stoop of the house becomes an entrance to the fortress). There has been research emphasizing that such environmental play contributes in an important way to social and cognitive development (Hart, 1978; Saegert & Hart, 1978). We would emphasize just as strongly that these experiences and the particular places and spaces they involve also become an essential part of place-identity cognitions.

We do not mean to imply that the child's involvement in the neighborhood setting is always synonymous with outdoor experience. The urban child's experience of the neighborhood may be extremely limited in these respects because of its threatening features—the dangers of street traffic, criminal elements, and even existing tensions between contiguous neighborhoods. These threats go far beyond what is encountered in the home or neighborhood of suburban children. On the other hand, one could speculate that the city child's exposure to local merchants, different racial and ethnic types, diverse street life, and a wider variety of spaces and places to explore provides greater diversity and environmental richness. The implication here is that the skills of household living that the child has acquired must be deepened and extended to deal with public spaces, and these skills must involve not only the richness and diversity of a complex physical setting but also those aspects of it that threaten and/or are an actual danger. In this respect, the environmental skills of understanding a setting, competence in using it, and control of it are critical.

Perhaps the most difficult aspect of a child's move from home to large-scale settings, in spatial terms, is the required redefinition of essential person–environment relationships such as privacy, territoriality, and personal space. The strategies the child develops for achieving privacy in the home are not easily transferable nor even relevant to the neighborhood. Merely the addition of large numbers of people to the child's experience who are essentially strangers makes new demands on the ability to achieve privacy or establish personal space when it is needed.

The strategies the child must develop in order to be alone or to withdraw in a public setting have to be and indeed turn out to be more sophisticated, creative, and complex than those required at home. The display of nonverbal messages, the reliance on fantasy, and the sensory ability to screen out unwanted stimulation all serve an adaptive function. Behavioral and cognitive coping mechanisms continue to develop as the child is exposed to an increasing number of public settings (e.g., theaters, parks, libraries, museums). Such strategies have become the hallmark of the urbanite who develops a complete repertoire of adjustments to meet the requirements of constantly changing daily experience.

Place Identity and the School Setting

Once the child is of school age, its waking life changes considerably. Much of the day is spent in the school setting, indeed much more than in the neighborhood setting while school is in session. With the increasing number of single-parent households and working mothers and a growing emphasis on early socialization experience, school age is beginning much earlier. By the age of two years many children are spending time in school-like settings (day-care centers, preschools). If for no other reason than the considerable time involved, the school is a sociophysical setting of considerable importance in the development of self-identity. Of course, there is much more to be considered besides the long periods of time involved.

By definition the school is a designed and premeditated agent of socialization. In comparison with the home and neighborhood settings, the school is in general the most predictable and most rigidly structured sociophysical setting in the child's early experience. Whatever physical space conceptions, needs, and expectations the child has developed in the home and neighborhood settings, these must be fitted into the requirements, activities, and normative demands of the classroom and social learning environment.

There has been some variability over time in the physical characteristics of the school, but it is also true that there has been remarkably little change in both popular and professional conceptions of what constitutes a proper classroom learning environment. Apart from the open education philosophy of the 1960s and early 1970s which specifically promoted the idea of individualized learning in a flexible, multipurpose space, the concept of rows of desks and chairs facing the teacher's desk in the front and center of the room has prevailed. In a review of the open classroom concept, Proshansky and Proshansky (1978) concluded that although open education attempted to address the unique learning and social needs of children, it ultimately returned to a focus on basic skills and traditional forms of teaching. The authors concluded that a changed physical environment, in this case a flexible classroom design, cannot improve the quality of education without corresponding changes in curriculum, teaching strategies, and methods of evaluation. The latter in turn requires a shift in educational philosophy and goals.

One can make a conceptual distinction between the school and the other settings we have discussed in this chapter by thinking of the school as an *institutional* setting. This has been a useful concept in the formulations of environmental psychologists to describe a sociophysical setting characterized by a high degree of organizational control, routinization of behavior, and limited opportunities for personal choice (Rivlin, Bogert, & Cirillo, 1981). A closer examination of the school setting from such a perspective makes possible the prediction of any one child's, or every child's, spatial experience and in this respect helps to reveal some important implications about place-identity development.

Physically, the school is larger than the home but is less well differentiated than the neighborhood. Frequently the child's experience of the school building is dominated by his or her own classroom. Travel through any other part of the building is generally monitored and controlled, at least insofar as primary education is concerned. Thus, describing the complexity of the whole school building may be a moot point in regard to the spatial experience of any particular child. Socially, the child's experience is a cohort experience, usually limited to children of the same age. The child is placed in a specific relationship to the teacher—a supervising and controlling adult who is not the child's parent, but who has legitimized power over the child's experiences and activities in the school.

It is the school's emphasis on control of the behavior and experience of the child that establishes the institutional nature of its physical setting. Unrelated to educational goals is the reality of 20 to 30 children in one classroom, a "box" with rows of seats in which the teacher is not only the educator but the agent of control. The most widely adopted strategy for teaching such a large group is to match the uniformity of the physical setting with uniformity in behavior so that the children can be dealt with as a manageable unit rather than as a collection of 20 very different individuals. Kindergarten children, for example, all nap at the same time, have snacks at the same time, and participate in learning activities at the same time. Although such a regimented group-oriented schedule may be justifiable in terms of insuring that all children will be treated equitably in their socialization experiences, one has to wonder what the consequences are of denying the children personal space and privacy and the inherent freedom of choice involved in both.

Rivlin and Wolfe (1970), in a discussion of another institutional setting for children (the hospital), cite research that provides evidence of increasing aggression and destructive behavior among children as the number of children in a room increases (Hutt & Vaizey, 1966; Hutt & Hutt, 1970). Although there are many differences between a child's experience of a psychiatric hospital and a school setting, one can look for some generalizations with regard to the phenomenon of crowding. If children do indeed have some need to separate themselves physically from the group at times, how do they compensate for the spatial restrictiveness of the classroom? One could make a convincing case that a child's psychological withdrawal, use of fantasy, and behavioral "acting out" are strategies for attaining a degree of privacy and isolation not permitted by the physical features of the classroom.

In terms of place-identity development there can be no question that the school setting plays an important role. The child's repeated and successive exposure to the school setting during the formative years necessarily implies that many of the impressions, attitudes, skills, and ideas regarding the physical conditions necessary for intellectual learning are developed in this context. The child must also learn an increased repertoire of behavioral strategies for achieving the kind of person–physical-environment relationships that it needs and wants. It may well be that some children learn better in private or standing up than in a group in which each child occupies a seat, but the teacher's control and supervisory function, not to mention the need for an appropriate classroom setting, make the "individual differences" approach to teaching difficult, if not virtually impossible. Nevertheless schools are social as well as educational settings, and despite their institutional nature children develop techniques for social interaction, social withdrawal, and even freedom of movement in the face of strictures against all of these. In addition to the prevailing spatial norms defined by the teacher and in turn by other children, there exists another more informal set of rules developed by children to circumvent the controls and restrictions. If we accept that children have different requirements for privacy and that opportunities therefore are critical to healthful psychological development, then undoubtedly one must look for latent as well as manifest norms in the use of physical space in the school setting.

The complexity and richness of the school setting is in a sense much diminished by the rule structure imposed upon the students. Certainly the spatial freedom that children have in the school setting varies according to the school and its educational philosophy, but in few if any cases does the school provide the opportunities for exploration, manipulation, and innovation in the physical environment that are readily available in the neighborhood or home. It is specifically in this regard that one can appreciate the virtues of open-classroom education when there is a relevant educational philosophy to support and complement it.

On the other hand, it is important not to overstate the case of the institutional nature of the school as a physical as well as social setting. The child does have space that "belongs" to him or her, free movement about the classroom does occur at specific times, and children are given the opportunity to decorate and personalize classroom spaces and places. Nor can we ignore the fact that learning to learn, work, and play in groups is an important aspect of the child's social education. What is needed is more attention to learning and experiencing in unique ways; to this end there has been a growing emphasis, at least in New York City, on alternative schools wherein classes are smaller, are theme-oriented, and above all are ready to consider individual need within the already established group setting (E. Proshansky, 1981).

PLACE IDENTITY AND PLACE BELONGINGNESS

The cognitions that form the basis of place identity include affective responses to settings that range from attachment to aversion. Consequently, self-identity is informed by cognitions of the physical world that are not only self-enhancing and supporting but also threatening and potentially damaging as well.

This notion stands in contrast to most research and theory regarding a person's feelings toward a given physical setting, other investigators having emphasized positive affective responses. For example, the term *place identity,* originally defined in Proshansky, Ittelson, and Rivlin (1970), is often responded to by others as if it meant strong emotional attachment to places and spaces developed during childhood which to some degree persisted throughout the person's life. It is easy enough to understand why, considering that such strong emotional attachments are by no means uncommon.

We have probably all experienced feelings of nostalgia and the recollection of significant and vivid childhood experiences when visiting the old neighborhood—the house one grew up in but then left, or one's elementary school, and so on. This occurs as a positive affective response if these places were satisfying and became associated with a constellation of positive memories. And when this is the case the attachment that the person feels is often deep, not easily explainable, and certainly not consciously connected with such things as social role learning or environmental skill acquisition. This kind of deep emotional attachment to place and space has been referred to as *place belongingness* by a number of "humanistic geographers" including Tuan (1980), Relph (1976), and Buttimer (1980). Our only argument with their point of view is that it is limited and focuses primarily on only one aspect of a larger system of psychological conceptions and feelings having to do with the world of physical settings. These phenomenological theorists talk only of the home setting in relation to place belongingness and explore only the positive affective connections to place and space.

The concept of place identity as we have defined it here not only is broader than place belongingness and similar "emotional attachment" theories but also describes how all the separate physical-setting cognitions are ordered into a larger substructure. Furthermore, although the home setting is indisputably instrumental in the development of the child's self-identity and place identity, it does not constitute the only significant physical-world experience. We have described above the influence of the neighborhood and school settings in the development of place identity, and even all three of these significant settings taken together represent only a part, albeit an important part, of the child's physical-world socialization. As the child gets older, more and more settings become part of its experience, resulting in a more fully elaborated cognitions relating to the physical environment. At each stage of growth, a step forward in the child's social development is accompanied by some new experience in the physical world.

The child's place identity reflects the *integration* of these physical-world settings including all their variety, diversity, and complexity as well as their interrelatedness. The child repeatedly leaves one setting to behave in another; and this movement from one setting to the next, in which there are differences both in the structure and content of the spaces and places, means that the child learns not only to differentiate these distinctive environmental properties and requirements but also to recognize their similarities. The child also learns how to adapt and modify its own behavior as movement from one setting to another occurs. Place identity conceived in this sense is not a simple cognitive structure, for in fact the day-to-day physical existence of the child is characterized by a growing number of settings, the presence of other people, and special skills needed to use these settings.

It should be evident when we talk about the development of place identity and the integration of a variety of settings that we refer to a complex social as well as cognitive process. The child necessarily develops a sense of who he or she is—defined not only by an array of specific physical settings but no less significantly by the social definitions of those settings as expressed by the other people, the activities, and the roles the child must exhibit in them. In effect, a child is subject to different sets of normative requirements, social roles and expectations in each of the three sociophysical settings we have identified. These very real inconsistencies in the child's relationships to the physical environment can lead to some degree of tension and frustration.

These tensions and frustrations are rooted in the lack of continuity in the social rules governing behavior in the important places and spaces in day-to-day existence. For example, a 14-year-old boy who is still subject to the restrictions of his parents may have far greater freedom and authority in the neighborhood setting than he does in the home. On the other hand, it appears that there are very few places in the community that support the social role of the teenager in his transition from child to responsible and independent adult. For example, teenage boys occupying a park bench late at night are less likely to be endorsed in this behavior by the neighbors or the local police than their own parents would be if they sat around engaged in the identical activity of loud, friendly talking. The control necessary to use, change, and adapt physical settings lies not in the child's hands but far more so in the hands of those already in charge of his socialization. How does the child narrow the gap between his physical setting desires and adult control?

No child can escape these inconsistencies, and furthermore the physical-setting issues become even more complex as the child establishes a wider range of relationships to the physical as well as the social world. Each new setting provides challenges and opportunities to develop environmental skills that broaden capabilities.

But it is not enough to point to the learning of environmental skills, that is, to learn to walk, open doors, use an elevator, cross a street. What all of this must lead to and indeed does—if it proceeds properly and is successful—is a sense of competence, independence, and self-assurance about the physical world. This not only insures the development of a place identity relevant to the variety, diversity, and complexity of the real world but also hastens the development of one's self-identity, which depends on a growing separation from the places and people upon whom one first relied.

URBAN IMAGE AND IDENTITY

If, as we have contended, the place identity of a person is a complex and integrated defining "image" of the physical world as he or she has experienced it, we must recognize that this image is becoming increasingly urban. All societies in this century, both eastern and western, are moving or have moved toward an *urban existence.* Within and between different nations, regions, or societies of the modern world, the degree of urban existence varies, and so too the extent to which place identity represents an urban identity. For those whose existence begins and ends in large metropolitan centers, the emergent urban identity will differ to some degree from that of those whose life is confined to a small town. On the other hand, because of increasing connections between big and small communities there will also be important common elements. Television sets, radios, automobiles, and now the computer have transformed and continue to transform small-town and suburban life to render it progressively more urban.

Increasing urbanism changes the frequency, variety, and intensity of human relationships. It also, of course, changes the form of the physical environment. For example, what our children will come to know as a bank—most likely a nonhuman, computerized, video display terminal setting—will be quite different from the image held by an earlier generation. And the changes are occurring with unprecedented speed. Because of this, the home, the neighborhood, and the school all constitute places of greater complexity for the individual. There are a great many new learning demands made on the child today, requiring language as well as motor skills. And superceding all of the specific skills required is an intellectual flexibility necessary to cope with the rapid technological and accompanying social changes we are now experiencing.

An important question to be answered is how to describe urban identity. At this stage in the conceptualization of place identity this is clearly an empirical question. To begin with, it would be important to "map" the place identities of a number of large-city residents—to describe the memories, attitudes, meanings, expectations, behavioral skills, and strategies that have emerged from their urban existence. What unifying and significant dimensions of place identity would emerge from such research one can of course only hypothesize about at this point. Such dimensions could be highly descriptive (defined in terms of crowding, noise, mobility patterns, and so on) or on a more abstract level (e.g., complexity, diversity, level of integration, affective nature). Still more abstract would be patterns of personal–physical setting relations involving privacy, personal space, territoriality, environmental cognition, and environmental control.

A complete definition of urban identity must wait until such empirical research has been conducted. For the moment, we must understand that urban identity, as we have formulated it here, is a type of place identity that characterizes all individuals brought up in and socialized over an extended period of time in an urban setting. Ways of seeing, using, and drawing satisfaction from the physical world of the city have been assimilated and integrated in the place identity of the person to the point that his or her thinking, experiencing, and behaving in the world are at times predetermined. Urbanites can no more escape the influence of their place identity than that of their social identity. We look forward to further study of these complex and fundamentally related conceptions.

REFERENCES

Buttimer, A. Home, reach, and the sense of place. In A. Buttimer & D. Seamon (Eds.), *The human experience of space and place.* London: Croom Helm, 1980, 166–187.

Cumming, J., & Cumming, E. *Ego and milieu.* New York: Atherton Press, 1962.

Downs, R. M., & Stea, D. (Eds.), *Image and environment: Cognitive mapping and spatial behavior.* Chicago: Aldine, 1973.

Erikson, E. H. *Identity: Youth and crisis.* New York: Norton, 1968.

Gesell, A., Ilg, F. L., & Bullis, G. E. *Vision: Its development in infant and child.* New York: Paul B. Hoeber, 1950.

Hart, R. *Children's experience of place.* New York: Irvington Press, 1978.

Hutt, S. J., & Hutt, C. *Direct observation and measurement of behavior.* Springfield, IL: Charles C Thomas, 1970.

Hutt, C., & Vaizey, M. J. Differential effects of group density on social behavior. *Nature,* 1966, *209,* 1371–1372.

Ittelson, W. H., Proshansky, H. M., Rivlin, L. G., & Winkel, G. H. *An introduction to environmental psychology.* New York: Holt, Rinehart, and Winston, 1974.

Laufer, R. S., Proshansky, H. M., & Wolfe, M. Some analytic dimensions of privacy. In R. Kuller (Ed.), *Architectural psychology.* Stroudsberg, PA: Dowden, Hutchinson and Ross, 1973.

Laufer, R. S., & Wolfe, M. Privacy as a concept and a social issue. *Journal of Social Issues,* 1977, *33,* 22–42.

Mahler, M. *On human symbiosis and the vicissitudes of individuation.* New York: International Universities Press, 1968.

Marris, P. *Loss and change.* New York: Pantheon Books, 1974.

Moore, R., & Young, D. Childhood outdoors: Towards a social ecology of the landscape. In I. Altman & J. F. Wohlwill (Eds.), *Children and the environment.* New York: Plenum Press, 1978, 83–130.

Piaget, J. *The construction of reality in the child.* New York: Basic Books, 1954.

Proshansky, E. W., & Proshansky, H. M. The open classroom: Another look. *Social Policy,* November–December, 1978, *9,* 52–55.

Proshansky, E. Choice not change in New York City. *Social Policy,* September–October, 1981, 24–26.

Proshansky, H. M., Fabian, A. K., & Kaminoff, R. Place-identity: Physical world socialization of the self. *Journal of Environmental Psychology,* 1983, *3,* 57–83.

Proshansky, H. M., Ittelson, W. H., & Rivlin, L. G. Freedom of choice and behavior in a physical setting. In H. M. Proshansky, W. H. Ittelson, & L. G. Rivlin (Eds.), *Environmental psychology: Man and his physical setting.* New York: Holt, 1970.

Rapoport, A. *Human aspects of human form: Towards a man–environment approach to urban form and design.* New York: Pergamon Press, 1977.

Relph, E. *Place and placelessness.* London: Pion, 1976.

Rivlin, L. G., Bogert, V., Cirillo, R. *Uncoupling institutional indicators.* New York: Center for Human Environments, City University of New York, 1981.

Rivlin, L. G., & Wolfe, M. The early history of a psychiatric hospital for children: Expectations and reality. In H. M. Proshansky, W. H. Ittelson, & L. G. Rivlin (Eds.), *Environmental psychology: People and their physical settings,* Vol. II, 1970, 459–479.

Saegert, S., & Hart, R. The development of sex differences in the environmental competence of girls and boys. In P. Stevens, Jr. (Ed.), *Studies in the anthropology of play.* Cornwall, NY: Leisure Press, 1978.

Siegel, A. W., Kirasic, K. C., & Kail, R. V. Stalking the elusive cognitive map: The development of children's representations of geographic space. In I. Altman & J. F. Wohlwill (Eds.), *Children and the environment.* New York: Plenum Press, 1978, 223–258.

Smith, M. B. The self and cognitive consistency. In R. P. Abelson, E. Aronson, W. J. McGuire, J. M. Newcomb, M. J. Rosenberg, & P. H. Tannenbaum (Eds.), *Theories of cognitive consistency.* Chicago: Rand McNally, 1968.

Tuan, Yi-Fu. Rootedness versus sense of place. *Landscape,* 1980, *24,* 3–8.

Wolfe, M. Childhood and privacy. In I. Altman & J. F. Wohlwill (Eds.), *Children and the environment.* New York: Plenum Press, 1978, 175–222.

Chapter 3

The Physical Environment and Cognitive Development in Child-Care Centers

GARY T. MOORE

According to projections given in the *Federal Register,* 9 out of 10 households in the United States with children under 4 years of age will use some form of day care in the 1980s. The figure of 1.2 million children in day care in 1976 may rise to more than 11½ million children by 1990. At the beginning of the decade, about 35% of children in day care were in in-home care, over 45% in family day care, and less than 20% in center-based day care (these figures are based on 1978 HEW statistics). If these trends continue, we might expect over 4 million children in in-home care, over 5 million in family day care, and around 2½ million in more formal child-care centers by the end of the decade.

For developmental psychologists, environmental psychologists, and others interested in the effects of the environment on human development, this trend presents a major challenge. For environmental professionals, it presents an unprecedented demand for services and facilities. Furthermore, as Clarke-Stewart and Gruber (1984) have recently pointed out, "The question of day care 'effects' is one of the most complex environmental issues developmental psychologists have yet faced" (p. 61). Although studies have been conducted on various aspects of day care (Belsky & Steinberg, 1978; Belsky, Steinberg, & Walker, 1982), and guidelines for the organization of day care

GARY T. MOORE • School of Architecture and Urban Planning, University of Wisconsin–Milwaukee, Milwaukee, WI 53201. Preparation of this chapter was aided by a Design Explorations Research grant from the National Endowment for the Arts.

have been promulgated (American Academy of Pediatrics, 1973), there has been little empirical research on the links between the quality of the physical setting and human development.

The purpose of this chapter is to examine these links and to evaluate the potential contribution of the physical environment of child care settings to child development. The focus will be cognitive development. Recent evidence will be reviewed about the effects of the child-care physical environment on behavioral indicators of cognitive development. The beginning of an interactional theory of child–environment relations will be proposed, a number of unresolved issues will be discussed, and lines of research will be suggested for continued exploration of theoretical, empirical, and applied issues.

CHILD CARE AND COGNITIVE DEVELOPMENT

Day care can refer to any kind of supplementary, nonparental care of young children. As used in this chapter, in most of the literature, and among parents, the term refers to out-of-the-home care, either in someone else's home or in an organized child-care center. There are three types of organized child-care centers: (1) centralized day-care centers specially designed for child-care needs in a centralized location (e.g., at a "Y" or near the place of work); (2) neighborhood day-care centers near family residences in a community context (e.g., in religious buildings or storefront locations); and (3) family day-care homes, organized home settings in the neighborhood caring for 6 to 12 children. In some locales, these three types have been combined into a network of child-care alternatives. (For a fuller description see, Moore, Lane, Hill, Cohen, & McGinty, 1979).

Once it was realized in the mid-1970s that organized out-of-the-home child care was here to stay, concerns were raised about adequate provision for cognitive development in those settings, and even as to whether day care was an appropriate alternative (or supplementary) setting to the family for insuring cognitive development (e.g., Fraiberg, 1977). The popular psychology classic that jacked every parent's paranoia into high gear was Burton White's *The First Three Years of Life* (1975) and his many lectures around the country during the middle and late 1970s. In his book, White maintained that during the first three years of life attending day care full time was "unlikely to be as beneficial to the child's early educational development as his own home" (p. 254). White called these his "considered opinions"; no scientific evidence was cited.

A number of studies published up to the mid-1970s (summarized in Kagan, Kearsley, & Zelazo, 1977) all appeared to indicate, however, that group care for young children did not seem to have much of an effect, either facilitating or debilitating, on cognitive or other aspects of development, with the exception of children from poorly educated and economically disadvantaged families, for whom it had an advantage. Kagan and his colleagues did acknowledge, nevertheless, the possibility of Type II errors in these early studies, that the criteria measures may have been too crude to detect real differences or that the wrong variables may have been assessed. To put those propositions to the test, Kagan and his colleagues studied two matched groups of children, one in organized child care and one remaining in parental care at home, over a period of two and a half years. The central question was answered with some assurance, supporting the view that day care, when responsibly and conscientiously implemented, did not appear to have hidden psychological dangers. In fact, the only significant cognitive developmental difference between day-care and home-reared children occurred in favor of day-care children (on the nonlanguage cognitive items of the Bayley Scales of Infant Development; Kagan *et al.*, 1977).

More recent studies of day care have continued to explore the question of whether day care may enhance cognitive development during the preschool years. The concern expressed by popular psychology writers (e.g., Fraiberg, 1977; White, 1975) that day care is not conducive to cognitive development has not received empirical support. Indeed, the overall conclusion drawn from extensive reviews (Belsky & Steinberg, 1978; Belsky *et al.*, 1982; Hoffman, 1984) is that there are no adverse effects but rather, to the contrary, cognitive gains in some cases. For example, day-care infants from impoverished backgrounds show improvements in cognitive development when compared with home-reared children (Doyle, 1975), though no differences in comparison with family day-care children (Doyle & Somers, 1978). Low-income children in publicly funded centers in New York City, many far from ideal, have higher IQ scores than a comparable group of children reared only at home (Golden *et al.*, 1978), and children from a broad spectrum of day-care centers in Chicago are more cognitively mature and competent on five intellectual measures than children without day-care experience (Clarke-Stewart & Gruber, 1984).

A series of reports by Ramey and his colleagues emanating from a longitudinal study has recently examined the effects of day-care intervention with high-risk infants and preschoolers. During the period from 6 to 18 months, performance on the Mental Development Index of the Bayley Scales of Infant Development declined for high-risk home-reared infants (from 104 to 86) but remained stable (near 104) for the high-risk children in day care (Ramey & Smith, 1976). The high-risk home-reared children's Stanford-Binet IQ score dropped to 83 at 2 years of age and to 81 at 3 years of age, whereas the matched day-care children remained just below 100 but rose slightly during the same time period (Ramey & Campbell, 1979). Further testing at age 4 indicated that these earlier differences remain stable (day care = 93; home care = 81; Ramey & Campbell, 1979). As pointed out in Belsky's and his colleagues' two reviews of the day care literature (Belsky &

⁄78; Belsky *et al.*, 1982), these findings do not indicate that IQ . children enrolled in day care increase as a function of their day-care …iences or that day care necessarily enhances cognitive functioning. …ather, they demonstrate that an enriching day-care experience attentuates some of the adverse effects typically associated with high-risk environments and prevents the decline in intellectual performance so frequently observed in high-risk children after age 2. Other studies summarized in Belsky *et al.* (1982) provide additional evidence for this conclusion.

Taken together, then, we are left with three general conclusions: that enrollment in formal child care does not adversely affect cognitive development for preschool children; that it leads to salutory effects for economically disadvantaged children; and that it leads to greater intellectual competence and cognitive maturity for a broad range of middle-class children.

Limitations and Unexplored Domains

There are four limitations to the research on the effects of day care to date, or, said differently, there are four domains where additional scientific work could be developed.

First, the findings to date apply only to day care in formal, organized day-care centers. Yet, over 80% of children in day care are in family day-care and in-home day care (Belsky *et al.*, 1982). We know most about the 20% in child-care centers and least about the types of care that are most often used and most in demand.

Second, with few exceptions, the research to date has focused on university-connected day-care centers and others with high staff–child ratios and well-designed programs intended to foster intellectual development. This is not representative of most of the day-care settings in this country. Some work to be reported later in this chapter begins to get around this limitation, as did the New York (Golden *et al.*, 1978) and Chicago (Clarke-Stewart & Gruber, 1984) studies.

A third limitation of much day-care research is its restriction to immediate effects. Although there is some support for the notion that early day care can have long-term effects (Kagan & Moss, 1962; Lazar, Hubbell, Murray, Rosche, & Royce, 1977; Ramey & Campbell, 1979), other evaluations of early intervention projects have documented a "wash-out" of early IQ gains (Bronfenbrenner, 1974, cited in Belsky *et al.*, 1982). As Belsky *et al.* (1982) have pointed out, only additional carefully controlled, longitudinal studies will be able to provide evidence for selecting between these two alternative conclusions.

Finally, we know more about the global effects of day care than we do about their causes and almost nothing about the causes that may or may not be attributable to the designed physical environment. Research in this area is only now beginning to isolate the characteristics of child-care settings that have particular effects and what the processes or mechanisms of influence are rather than seeking global judgments (Belsky *et al.*, 1982; Clarke-Stewart & Gruber, 1984; Hoffman, 1984). Bronfenbrenner (1977a) put the point well:

> Even when two or more environmental settings are included in a single research design, prevailing research models permit and encourage a primary if not exclusive focus on consequences for the child to the neglect of the characteristics of the environment that induced these consequences. Thus, over the past several decades, we have had studies beyond number on the behavior and development of children from different social classes, societies, and subcultures. More recently the interest has shifted to more concrete settings: the effects of father absence, the influence of family versus school on educational performance, or currently, the impact of day care versus home care on the child's development. In all these cases, however, the main emphasis is on analyzing the differential characteristics of the children, not of the settings in which they are found. (p. 120)

This neglect of setting variables is especially pronounced with respect to the physical environment. Yet, some data on children in diverse settings have emerged in recent years that are difficult to interpret in developmental terms without invoking physical environmental constructs. For example, why do children under 5 years of age who live in high-rise housing use outdoor play areas considerably less than children living closer to the ground (Jephcott, 1971; Stevenson, Martin, & O'Neil, 1967)? Or why is program quality in child-care centers inversely related to center size, that is, the larger the center, the lower the quality of the program, all other things held constant (Prescott, Jones, & Kritchevsky, 1972)? And why is there less cross-age interaction in large child centers (those with more than 60 children) than in small centers (Prescott *et al.*, 1973)? A reasonable interpretation is that in large centers the concerns for order and for controlling potential noise and rowdiness take precedence over more developmentally related concerns like working directly with children, encouraging age mixing, and allowing other less structured, more spontaneous activities. But this interpretation has not yet been put to the test. Furthermore, until recently, interactions between physical environmental variables (e.g., size, height off the ground, noise, complexity of setting) and social environmental variables (e.g., staff attitudes, type of curriculum, teaching styles) have not been explored for any possible joint role in affecting behavior.

In response to findings implicating the physical environment in child development, increasing numbers of developmental and environmental psychologists have begun to give attention to the interface between the sociophysical environment and child development. As a result, there is now a growing interdisciplinary literature on child–environment relations including systematic reviews (e.g., Weinstein, 1979; Wohlwill & Heft, in press), edited volumes (e.g., Altman & Wohlwill, 1978; Baird & Lutkus, 1982; Cohen, 1982; Liben, Patterson, & Newcombe, 1981), and a new journal (*Children's Environments Quarterly*). Wohlwill (1980) drew attention to this convergence between environmental and developmental psychology, pointing out that such problems as privacy and crowding, effects of noise, and the development of environmental cognition can benefit from joint efforts by environmental and developmental researchers.

The physical environment is that part of the total environment that environmental professionals (architects, planners, and policy makers) are manipulating with little understanding of human developmental consequences and scant scientific evidence on which to base design decisions (e.g., Dattner, 1969; Essa, 1981; Friedberg & Berkeley, 1970; Mangurian, 1975; Osmon, 1971; Waligura, 1969). The need for scientific information on which to ground policy, planning, and design decisions argues additionally for a convergence between developmental and environmental points of view.

Despite this emerging interest, a review of 1,500 child–environment articles and reports up to the end of the 1970s indicated that less than 5% of them were empirically based and that no general theory had emerged that presents child–environment links in a sociophysical context (Moore, Lane, & Lindberg, 1979).

An ecological view of child development, taking into consideration the role of the total sociophysical environment of behavior, would lead us to expect that the character of the built environment of child-care centers has an impact on early cognitive development. But what is the evidence?

RESEARCH ON COGNITIVE DEVELOPMENT AND THE PHYSICAL ENVIRONMENT IN CHILD-CARE CENTERS

Major theories like those of Piaget (1951), Montessori (1965), and Werner (1949) stress that the interaction of the child with his or her environment is the basis of development. Children need to play in an environment rich in resources, to explore, or test, and to learn from feedback on their own actions. Unfortunately, existing child-care centers are in many cases totally inadequate, often shoe-horned into old buildings that do not accommodate the needs of children (Moore, Lane *et al.*, 1979; Perry, 1981).

Variables that have been considered important in the better design of child-care centers have been described by a variety of agencies (American Academy of Pediatrics, 1973; Child Welfare League, 1973; Cohen for HEW, 1974) and by designers (Osmon, 1971; Waligura, 1969). Such reports have led to national standards on certain design features thought to have impact on child care and develpoment—the FIDCR regulations (U.S. Department of Health, Education, and Welfare, 1968; cf. recommended changes by Prescott & David, 1976). Few of the variables included in national standards, however, have been subjected to empirical test.

Recent research on the impacts of the physical environment of child care settings on cognitive development has looked at five issues: (1) effects of the differences between child-care centers and family day-care homes; (2) effects of center and group size, child–caregiver ratios, and density; (3) effects of technical design features such as acoustics, climate control, and lighting; (4) effects of open-plan versus closed-plan facilities; and (5) effects of the spatial definition of activity settings. I will treat the first three in this section, leaving open versus closed plan and the effects of the definition of activity settings for the next section.

Effects of Child-Care Centers and Family Day-Care Homes

A well-known study by Prescott (1973, reported in Anonymous, 1973; see also Prescott & David, 1976) compared three types of child-care environments: formal day-care centers, family day-care homes, and in-home care. Prescott found that exploratory behavior was most frequent in the home settings, whereas numerical and art activities were most frequent in the formal child-care centers. The New York City Infant Day Care Study (Golden *et al.*, 1978) provided evidence that infants in both day-care centers and family day-care homes outperformed their home-reared counterparts. We are left unsure, in both studies, whether these differences were a function of the built environment or of caregiver philosophy and style, or even the self-selectivity of family and children choosing one or the other type of care setting. Physical spatial characteristics were not systematically related to measures of the children's cognitive development in either study. Even a study that did measure the quality of the "physical plant" (Winnet, Fuchs, & Moffatt, 1974, cited in Belsky & Steinberg, 1978; see Winnet, Battersby & Edwards, 1975) confounded those variables with measures of staff interaction and experience, leaving us again unsure about whether the physical environment—as an independent variable and/or in interaction with social variables—had any impact or not. Considered together, these rather inconclusive data suggest that we could more valuably study cognitive development in child-care centers in a physical × social environmental research design.

Effects of Center and Group Size, Child–Caregiver Ratios, and Density

Although at first glance these four variables might not seem to be physical environmental variable, the size of a building certainly is a spatial variables, and it has been shown that decisions about group size, child–caregiver ratios, and density have massive implications for the spatial organization of child-care facilities (Moore, Lane *et al.*, 1979).

One of the most important decisions to be made in planning and programming child-care centers is the number of children to be served in one facility. Currently child-care center capacities range from fewer than 25 to several with over 200 children (Cohen, Moore, & McGinty, 1978); at least one is currently in the planning stage for close to 600 children (for a location outside Washington, D.C.). Several studies have looked at this question.

In the first study of this type, Prescott *et al.* (1967/1972) found that center size was a reliable predictor of program quality. The variety and quality of children's developmental experiences was directly affected by the size of the facility. In centers that served over 60 children, major emphasis tended to be placed on rules and routine guidance; the play areas tended to be low on organization, variety, and amount of things to do per child; and children were seldom observed to be highly interested or enthusiastically involved.

More careful, empirical studies of this issue must be done, but for the meantime this finding has been corroborated by a number of interviews conducted around the country (Cohen *et al.*, 1978). We found general agreement with these findings, namely, that from the child's point of view, 60 to a maximum of 75 children is ideal; if centers exceed this limit, the younger children around 2 years of age are overwhelmed by the numbers of staff members, the older children, the size of the space, and the total number of children. The National Day Care Study (Travers & Ruopp, 1978) also found that although larger centers cost a little less per child for operating expenses, it is harder to provide quality care even when favorable staff–child ratios are maintained. The best judgment of both Elizabeth Prescott of Pacific Oaks College and Richard Ruopp of Abt Associates, each after more than 10 years of experience studying child-care centers around the country, is that centers of 60 (Prescott) and 75 (Ruopp) are best, both for the children and for the caregivers (Cohen *et al.*, 1978, pp. 410–412).

In many cases, however, child-care organizations or sponsors have to serve many more than 60 or 75 children, for example, large neighborhoods, military bases, and the many employer-sponsored child-care centers (Perry, 1981). Two large centers (200+ each), judged from case-study post-occupancy evaluations (Cohen *et al.*, 1978) to be successful and to offer individualized, sensitive, developmentally oriented programs for children—Ft. Bragg Nursery Village and Pacific Oaks College Children's School—are planned on what I have come to call a *village* or *campus plan concept.* Different programs for different groups of children are housed in different buildings, each with its own qualified staff and head teacher and autonomy over program direction and building amenities. This is an emergent idea which may deserve to be a trend. We therefore recommend:

> Any center needing to service significantly more than 60 children should be administratively, conceptually, and architecturally subdivided into programs and modules of 60 to 75 children each. These programs and modules can be combined in a campus plan or village concept, either in separate buildings or in well-defined separate wings of one building. In the latter case, separate entrances should be assured. Separate buildings or wings in a village or campus plan might include an infant program, scheduled part- or full-time day care, drop-in care, formal preschool, and an after-school program. (Moore, Lane *et al.*, 1979, Pattern 410-3-4)

The second issue regarding size is the size of the group in which children spend most of their time while in day care. The National Day Care Study looked at 57 centers around the country over a four-year period and determined that "small groups work best" (Travers & Ruopp, 1978, p. 38). The size of the group in which the preschool child spends the most time makes the most difference in influencing quality day care. In fact, group size was the single most important determinant of quality care on a number of dimensions. In smaller groups (i.e., those with under 14 or 16 children) as contrasted with larger ones (over 16 children), children show more verbal initiative including giving opinions and information, more reflective behavior including contemplating or adding a new idea to an ongoing activity, and more task-involved behavior. They also make greater developmental gains over the period of a year on two standard measures of development, the Preschool Inventory and the Peabody Picture Vocabulary Test (Travers & Ruopp, 1978).

These findings have led us to a set of three recommendations about how to obtain appropriate group sizes in child-care centers by articulating spaces for optimum small group size. These recommendations are presented in detail elsewhere for general activity spaces (entitled "Just the right size spaces"), particular activity spaces ("Resource-rich activity pockets for 2–5 children"), and food preparation and eating areas ("Eating clusters"; Moore, Lane *et al.*, 1979, Patterns 907-1 and 1027-3).

With regard to ratios, the National Day Care Study found that child–caregiver ratio had little effect on development for preschoolers, though it did influence infants' experiences (Travers & Ruopp, 1978). Earlier studies were contradictory with each other on this issue. O'Conner (1975) finding positive effects for the older preschool children with lower child–staff ratios but Biemiller, Avis, and Lindsay (1976, cited in Belsky *et al.*, 1982) reporting findings similar to those of Travers and Ruopp for infant day-care programs.

Lastly, Weinstein's (1979) review concluded that density—the number of children to a space in child-care centers—while having demonstrable effects on social behavior (including on aggressive and destructive behavior; Rohe & Patterson, 1974), has little effect on intellectual performance and achievement. Two of the limitations of this research to date are that density has been confounded with open versus closed educational programs and that most outcome tasks studied in laboratory settings have not had the levels of cognitive complexity normally found in actual day-care centers. No studies of the impact of density on cognitive development in child-care settings have been done since then.

Effects of Technical Design Features

Several years ago, Prescott and David (1976) wrote an excellent and comprehensive "concept paper" reviewing many aspects of the physical environment on day care. Much of that review dealt with technical design features like acoustics, climate control, lighting, floor surfaces, wall surfaces, and color. As of 1976, there was little scientific evidence on many of these; rather, there were sometimes conflicting opinions and experience-based guidelines and standards promulgated by various national agencies. Our somewhat later review (Moore, Lane, & Lindberg, 1979) did not turn up much new evidence on these features, and to date, there is no new hard evidence on the effects of any of these factors on cognitive development in child-care centers.

A few studies that have looked at the question of noise in the environment, both noise generated by activities themselves and exterior noise, are relevant to our discussion, although they were not conducted in child-care settings. Wachs and his colleagues, for example, found that a high level of noise from which the child cannot escape is negatively related to cognitive development (Wachs, 1976; Wachs, Uzgiris & Hunt, 1971). On the other hand the availability of a room in the home to which the child can escape from too intense stimulation—what Wachs called a "stimulus shelter"—is a strong predictor of later cognitive development (Wachs, 1976). Noisy environments are also related to less efficient information processing in children, as has been found from a series of studies reported by Wohlwill and Heft (1977), and to lower teacher ratings of creativity and lower language achievement (Michelson, 1968; cited in Parke, 1978), though again there is evidence that children who have a separate room for study have higher achievement and language scores (Michelson, 1968).

Although the research conducted on the effects of exterior noise on behavior and on stress is voluminous (Cohen & Weinstein, 1982), less research has been conducted on the impact of noise on children's cognitive development. One of the best known studies is that by Cohen, Glass, and Singer (1973), who studied children living in 32-floor apartment buildings located adjacent to heavily traveled freeways. For children living in these apartments for four years or more, the lower the floor of the apartment, the poorer was their auditory discrimination and reading test scores, suggesting that impairments in auditory skills may be mediating poorer reading scores. Subsequent research has, for the most part, supported this general conclusion about the impact of exterior noise (see the review by Ahrentzen, Jue, Skorpanich, & Evans, 1982). We know, for instance, that exterior noise leads to lower academic performance on a number of dimensions—moderate decreases in speed of performance (Weinstein & Weinstein, 1979), lower reading scores (Bronzaft & McCarthy, 1975), lower auditory discrimination (Bronzaft & McCarthy, 1975), distractability (Cohen, Evans, Krantz, & Stokols, 1980), and "learned helplessness" or a lack of persistence on cognitive tasks (Cohen *et al.*, 1980)—in toto a fairly ringing indictment for noise.

RECENT RESEARCH ON TWO DIMENSIONS OF THE PHYSICAL ENVIRONMENT

What seems to be necessary, in order to create a true environment–behavior perspective on early childhood development, is to articulate the relevant dimensions of the designed environment that may arguably be thought to have an impact on cognitive development, to control for other aspects of the social and organizational environment (e.g., teacher styles, beliefs, educational models, socioeconomic status, family backgrounds), and to explore the complex interactions between physical and social environmental variables as they may independently and jointly affect development.

In order to begin such an exploration, we will look at two areas of recent study: research on the effects of the overall organization of space and research on the effects of the definition of particular activity settings.

Modified Open-Plan Facilities

The Controversy about Open-Plan Versus Closed-Plan Facilities. The concept of open-plan school facilities was introduced by Educational Facilities Laboratories in 1965. Since that time, controversy has surrounded the question of the impact of open-plan versus closed-plan *buildings* (i.e., not open versus traditional educational philosophies) on behavior. Open-plan child-care centers have unpartitioned space with few or no internal walls; closed-plan facilities have self-contained classrooms usually arranged along corridors or as in a house with several small interconnecting rooms. Most of the data have been collected at the elementary-school level, not child-care centers (George, 1975), so we must be cautious about making generalizations. The findings are mixed, with some presumed advantages being ascribed to both open and closed plan schools. In comparison to closed-plan schools, open-plan schools have been found to have more noise distractions, especially for teachers (Brunetti, 1972; Walsh, 1975), more prevention of noise by teacher admonitions (Gump & Iliff, 1971; cited in Gump, 1975), less structured activity patterns (Durlak, Beardley, & Murray, 1972), and more time during which a child cannot be seen or observed by staff (Twardosz, Cataldo, & Risley, 1974). On the more positive side, open-plan schools have also been found to have a greater number of learning centers encountered during the day (Gump, 1974), more personal teaching styles (Durlak *et al.*, 1972), less adult pressure (Prescott, 1973), more spontaneous activity change (Prescott, 1973), and smaller group sizes (Durlak *et al.*, 1972). These findings leave open the question of which type of environment is better for development. It is even more confusing that directly contradictory findings have emerged concerning transition time—the time children spend between active engagements in developmental activities. Gump (1975; Gump

& Good, 1976) found that more of children's time was used in transitions or "non-substance" phases between activities in open-plan schools, whereas Prescott (1973) found less transition time in open-plan preschools in comparison to those with a closed plan.

A few studies have been conducted more recently that look specifically at preschools or child-care centers and at behavioral indicators of cognitive development. In one, Field (1980) studied the effects on a number of social and cognitive developmental variables of teacher–child ratios and physical layout of day-care classrooms, finding more verbal interaction and fantasy play in classrooms with both low teacher–child ratios and partitioned play areas. This study, however, suffered from two limitations (both admitted by the author)—an inability to partial out the effects of ratios from physical layout and unmeasured and thus unknown differences in teacher style or personality between the settings. A second study by Neill and colleagues (Neill, 1982; Neill & Denham, 1982) compared more versus less open preschool building designs on a number of social, physical, and educationally related activities, finding, in general, that preschool children spend less time in educationally valuable activities in the more open-plan preschools. This study was also flawed in two ways (both of which again realized by the author)—a correlational design that made causal inference impossible and lack of control over staff philosophies and involvement.

Three methodological problems have marred these studies. One difficulty is separating out teacher styles, philosophies, and levels of involvement from physical environmental variables or, more generally, the self-selectivity of teachers in open-plan versus closed-plan facilities and the possible confounding of the philosophy of the curriculum (open versus traditional *education*) with the character of the space (open-plan versus closed-plan *facilities*). Second, there remains the problem of inference—over half of the studies to date were done in elementary schools, not preschool child-care environments. Finally, these studies of open versus closed plans in child-care settings were correlational in design, suggestive but not conclusive of causal effects.

Analysis of the findings on spatial organization has led us to the working hypothesis that the middle ground might be the best overall solution, that is, that what I have termed *modified open-plan facilities* midway between open and closed plan might resolve the difficulties of open and closed plans while retaining their advantages (Moore, Lane *et al.*, 1979). Modified open space is the organization of space into a variety of large and small activity spaces open enough to allow children to see the play possibilities available to them while providing enough enclosure for the child to be protected from noise and visual distractions.

Preliminary support for this notion of modified open space and its positive effects comes from four recent experiments in which elementary and secondary schools were modified to provide greater self-containment by the use of low partition, or to make them more open by removing some walls. In a random sample of open-plan schools, Gump and Ross (1977) found that two-thirds of the schools modified their space by the use of bookcases, file cabinets, chart and map easels, portable dividers, and the like, with a resulting reduction in visual distractions and physical mobility, though not in noise. Burns (1972) modified a secondary school from a relatively self-contained plan to a partially open, flexible plan. The changes resulted in greater social interaction but also in greater distractions. Weinstein (1977) redesigned an open classroom by rearranging furniture such as storage compartments and introducing extensive shelving, raised platforms, and a small cardboard "house," all functioning as partial dividers or partitions. The children used the space more fully and exhibited a greater range of behaviors, less fidgeting, less large physical activity, less passive behavior, and more object manipulative behavior. Finally, Evans and Lovell (1979) evaluated the effects of newly installed variable-height partitions in an open-plan high school. Results showed a reduction in classroom interruptions and an increase in substantive content questions by the children.

Effects of Modified Open-Plan Facilities on Children's Cognitive Development. The above analysis of the advantages and disadvantages of both open- and closed-plan facilities and the working hypothesis that modified open-plan facilities might combine the best of both worlds enabled us to proceed with a test of this general hypothesis. The validity of this line of reasoning was tested in a quasi-experimental field study (Moore, 1983a).

A major issue in the studies reviewed above is how to conduct causally valid studies in ecologically valid field settings. Many studies have erred on the side of ecological validity while sacrificing causal inference and control over extraneous or interacting variables, thus preferring correlational designs to causal designs (see the critique in Weinstein, 1979). In our study, an attempt was made to balance ecological validity with causal inference by employing an untreated control group design with multiple levels of treatment and proxy pretest measures. This design combines the features of two causally valid designs presented by Cook and Campbell (1979, pp. 98–99, 112–115).

Six settings in Milwaukee County were selected to provide two sets of centers, each with an open-plan center, a modified open-plan center, and a closed-plan center (see Figures 1–3). Each set of centers was selected to be the same or similar in terms of the size of the center, socioeconomic background of the children, educational philosophy of the center, and teacher styles of interaction with children, all of which were subsequently measured to permit statistical verification of equivalence or nonequivalence. Thus, for example, three church-sponsored centers were identified within eight blocks of each other in a lower-middle-income mixed ethnic area that

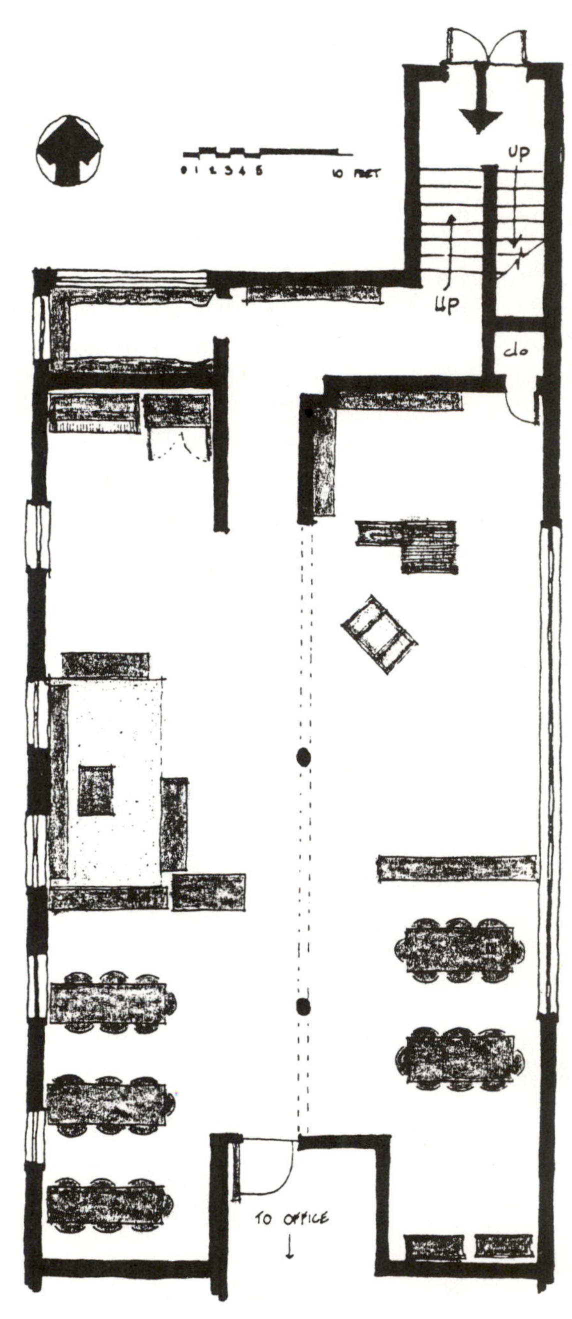

FIGURE 1. Plan of a typical open-plan child-care center used to evaluate the effects of spatial organization of children's behavior. Note there are no walls or partitions, only a few 3-foot-high bookcases and a curtain that can be drawn down the center of the building.

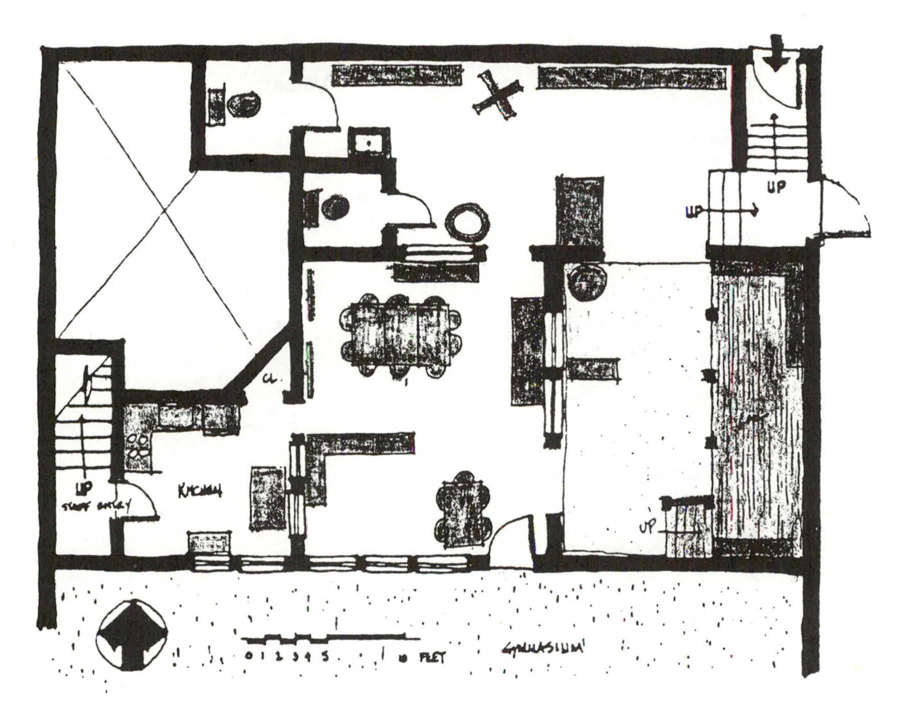

FIGURE 2. Plan of a typical modified open-plan child-care center. Note the archways, windows, and openings without doors connecting spaces, the loft, and the immediate connection (yet acoustic separation) between the large-motor gymnasium and the rest of the building.

had, respectively, a totally open-plan arrangement, a modified open plan, and a closed plan. Another set of centers were all members of the same chain of proprietary child-care centers; all followed the same philosophy and curriculum and were in comparable middle- to upper-middle-income, predominantly white suburbs. Within each of the centers, subjects were selected on a random space- and time-sampling basis. They ranged in age from 2 years 6 months to 6 years of age (N=1,030).

Three types of variables were measured: (1) independent physical environmental variables; (2) independent subject group variables (proxy and covariate measures for children, teachers, and centers); and (3) dependent behavioral variables including cognitive developmental variables (only the cognitive developmental variables and findings will be discussed in this chapter; cf. Moore, 1983a).

To insure construct validity of the environmental settings, a detailed rating scale was developed, fashioned after the Early Childhood Environment Rating Scale of Harms and Clifford (1980) and our own Facility Inventories used in an earlier study of child-care centers around the country

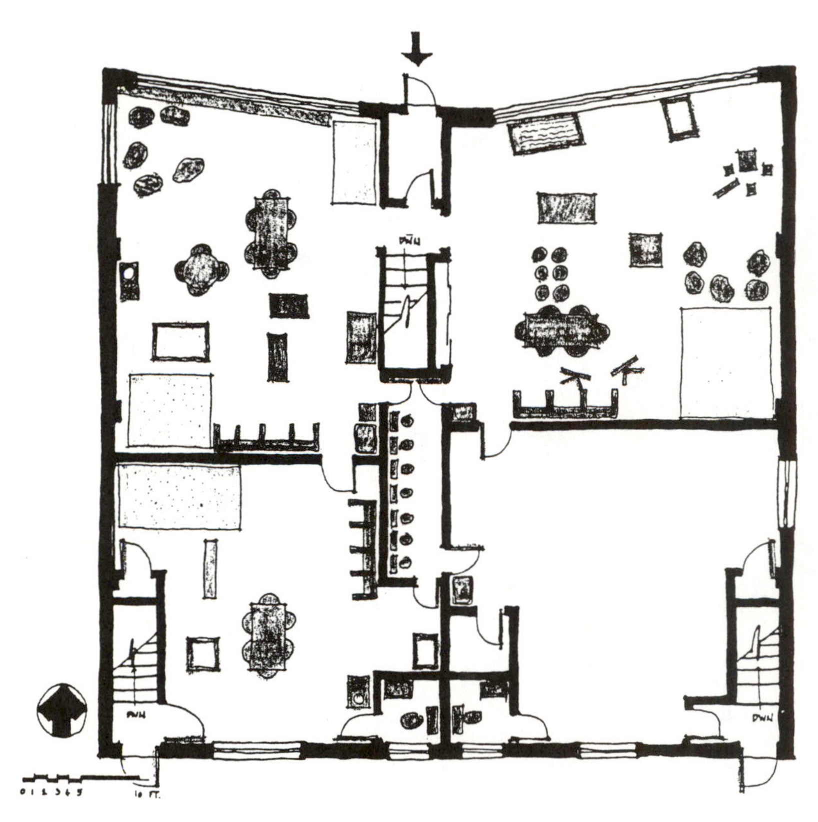

FIGURE 3. Plan of a typical closed-plan child care center. Note the self-contained classrooms, two of which have their own private lavatories.

(Cohen *et al.*, 1978). The scale is available as part of the Early Childhood Physical Environment Scales.*

The scale was based on ten critical dimensions of the organization of space in child-care centers (and other educational facilities) as a whole:

1. Degree of visual connection between spaces
2. Degree of closure of spaces
3. Degree of spatial separation of one space from another
4. Degree of mixture of large open areas and smaller enclosed spaces
5. Degree of separation of staff areas from children's activity areas
6. Degree of separation of functional areas from activity areas
7. Degree of separation of different age groups
8. Degree of separation of circulation from activity spaces

*These instruments are available from the Center for Architecture and Urban Planning Research, University of Wisconsin—Milwaukee, Milwaukee, WI 53201.

9. Degree of visibility of all major activity spaces from the entry
10. Degree of connection between indoor and outdoor activity spaces

Using these dimensions, the validity of the selection of settings was verified by a panel of three judges not familiar with the study.

An Environment/Behavior Observation Schedule (Figure 4) was also devised to measure group size, the number of learning activity centers encountered by the children, and the dependent behavioral variables of (a) general type of task behavior (engagement, transitional, functional, random, or withdrawn behavior), (b) initiation of behavior (spontaneous free, individual directed, or group directed behavior), (c) quality of exploratory behavior (immersed, somewhat involved, or not involved–not applicable), and other variables not pertinent to the present chapter. These variables were selected on the basis of earlier research showing that task-oriented, self-initiated, and exploratory behaviors are related to cognitive development (Gump, 1975; Neill, 1982; Neill & Denham, 1982) and on past research indicating that group size is important to development (Travers & Ruopp, 1978). The hypothesis under investigation was that modified open-plan centers would lead to a greater number of developmental activities encountered by the children, to smaller group sizes, and to more child-initiated, spontaneous, and exploratory behavior.

A series of distinct findings emerged from the analysis of the environment–behavior observational data when controlling for the subject group differences of center size, open versus traditional philosophy, and socioeconomic level (Moore, 1983a). It was very clear that the children in modified open-plan centers used significantly more activity settings and were in smaller group sizes than in either open-plan or closed-plan facilities.

Furthermore, engagement in cognitively oriented behaviors (engagement in activities involving persons, objects, or educational materials) is most pronounced in modified open-plan centers. Random behavior (no sustained activity) is most prevalent in open-plan centers, and transitional behavior (moving between activities or settings) and withdrawn behavior (staring into space) are more prevalent in closed plan centers. The child's degree of immersion in developmentally supportive behaviors is also significantly greater in modified open-plan centers. Controlling for the socioeconomic level of the children and the philosophy of the teacher indicated that these differences were more pronounced for children of higher socioeconomic levels and in centers where the teachers followed an open educational philosophy.

Critical also to an assessment of the developmental impacts of spatial organization is the analysis of self-directed versus teacher-oriented behaviors. The results of the study indicate that children initiate behaviors themselves significantly more often in modified open-plan centers than in centers of either of the two other types of spatial organization. Teacher style

Observer ________ Date ________ Time ________ Seq # ________

ENVIRONMENTAL SETTING
The Location of the Observed Behavior

Center	[ ]	☐
Room/Area	[ ]	☐
Observational Cell		☐

INDIVIDUALS INVOLVED
The Number and Characteristics of Children and Adults Involved

Group Size ☐	Children	☐
	Adults	☐
Genders	Girls	☐
	Boys	☐
Ages	2 to 3	☐
	3 to 4	☐
	4 to 5	☐
	5 to 6	☐
	6 and over	☐
Ethnicity	White	☐
	Black	☐
	Hispanic	☐
	Other	☐

OBSERVED BEHAVIORS
Observable Behaviors Charact
as a Whole or for Most of the Observation Segment

SECTION 1: GENERAL TYPE OF BEHAVIOR

Engagement	☐	Immersed	☐
		Attending	☐
		Distracted	☐
Transitional	☐	Only Transitional	☐
		Partially Transitional	☐
		Primarily Engaged	☐
Functional	☐	Only Functional	☐
		Partially Functional	☐
		Primarily Engaged	☐
Random	☐	No Sustained Activity	☐
		Directed Interest	☐
		Spontaneous Interest	☐
Withdrawn	☐	Vacant Staring	☐
		Intermittant Focusing	☐
		Passive Observation	☐
Empty Cell	☐	Unclear	☐

OBSERVED BEHAVIORS (continued)

SECTION 2: CHILD-INITIATED VS STAFF-DIRECTED BEHAVIOR

Initiated	☐	Spontaneous Free	☐
		Individual Directed	☐
		Group Directed	☐
		Unclear	☐

SECTION 3: EXPLORATION

Exploration	☐	Immersed	☐
		Somewhat Involved	☐
Not Applicable	☐	Unclear	☐

SECTION 4: SOCIAL INTERACTION

Interaction	☐	Reciprocated	☐
		Acknowledged	☐
		Not Acknowledged	☐
Not Applicable	☐	Unclear	☐

SECTION 5: COOPERATION, COMPETETION, AGGRESSION, AFFECTION

Cooperation	☐	Cooperative Activity	☐
		Associative Activity	☐
		Parallel Activity	☐
Competition	☐	Absolute Gains	☐
		Relative Gains	☐
		Rivalry	☐
Aggression	☐	Physical Attack	☐
		Threatened Attack	☐
		Verbal Abuse	☐
Affection	☐	Intimate Physical	☐
		Friendly Physical	☐
		Verbal	☐
Not Applicable	☐	Unclear	☐

SECTION 6: TYPE OF TEACHER INVOLVEMENT

Involvement	☐	Co-Action	☐
		Encouragement	☐
		Control	☐
		Information	☐
		Observation	☐
		No Involvement	☐
Not Applicable	☐	Unclear	☐

SECTION 7: TYPE OF STAFF-STAFF INTERACTION

Interaction	☐	Group	☐
		Colleague	☐
		Peer Observation	☐
		No Interaction	☐
Not Applicable	☐	Unclear	☐

FIGURE 4. The Environment/Behavior Observation Schedule for Early Childhood Environments. Complete instructions for its use are available from the author.

and socioeconomic level of the children are also significantly related to children's self-direction of behavior, with more self-initiated behavior in open education centers and for higher socioeconomic levels.

Similarly, the findings of this study indicated that exploratory behavior is significantly more pronounced in modified open-plan centers than in either closed- or open-plan centers. Center size and philosophy also affect exploratory behavior (children exploring more in smaller centers and in those with more open philosophies).

Taken together, these findings support the hypothesis that child-care centers organized in terms of modified open space lead to significant effects on a number of cognitive developmental variables (more behavior settings used; smaller group size, more task-related behavior and less transitional, functional, random, and withdrawn behavior; more spontaneous child-initiated behavior; and more exploratory behavior).

The findings also support the group × setting interactional model in that there are interactions between the socioeconomic level of the child, the philosophy of the center, the educational style of the teacher, and the physical environment in affecting task versus nontask behavior, child versus teacher-directed behavior, and exploratory behavior.

What appears to be happening is that the open-plan centers lead to more caretaking, random nondevelopmentally relevant behaviors, and a greater degree of attempted teacher control, whereas closed-plan centers contribute to more transitional and withdrawn behaviors, leading to lower levels of exploratory behavior. However, modified open-plan centers, being midway between the two extremes, apparently contribute significantly to greater degrees of a range of behavioral indicators of cognitive development (task engagement, child initiation of behaviors, exploratory behavior). However, the other clear phenomenon is that teachers with an open educational philosophy and children from higher socioeconomic backgrounds are able to make better use of the opportunities provided by the modified open plan, thus leading to still higher levels of cognitive development behavior and lower levels of "down time."

Spatially Well-Defined Behavior Settings

The Notion of Spatially Defined Behavior Settings. In most child-care centers, much of a child's time is spent in informal, unstructured learning situations—what Barker (1968) would call *behavior settings*—with several children working on different projects at once, some with a teacher, some on their own or in small groups. Discussions of behavior settings generally focus more on the sociobehavioral and temporal characteristics of settings than on their physical (geographical or architectural) features. In contrast, the following discussion of behavior settings will include behavior, program, temporal, and spatial characteristics, though we will concentrate on the spatial characteristics. How do the character and configuration of activity areas influence these activities, if at all?

A few studies have looked at behavior settings in child-care environments. Rosenthal (1974) studied the behavior of a heterogeneous population of preschoolers, balanced in terms of gender, race, and age, during 37 child-care sessions. Settings differed significantly in their attractive power as measured by the percentage of children involved in them, as well as their holding power as measured by the length of involvement. Settings for art, block play, and novel ventures were the most attractive settings, while role playing settings had the greatest holding power. Somewhat similar findings are reported by Shure (1963), who found that the most popular areas were block play and art, with the block play area having the greatest holding power, although there were significant gender differences. No conceptual explanation or theoretical discussion was offered in either study relating the characteristics of the settings to these activities. We do not know, for instance, whether the behavior has anything to do with the characteristics of the molar physical environment, of the materials provided, or of staff characteristics and involvement.

If we look at the size of naturally occurring play groups, it is known that children playing outdoors tend to congregate in groups of fewer than five children with a mean of just under two children per setting (Aiello, Gordon, & Farrell, 1974). Similarly, experts recommend that the best size for an indoor preschool play group is two to four children (Millar, 1968). The National Day Care Study indicated that the quality of child-care programs as measured by the Preschool Inventory and the Peabody Picture Vocabulary Test is related to small group sizes (Travers & Ruopp, 1978; Ruopp, 1979).

Effects of the Definition of Behavior Settings on Children's Cognitive Development. *Well-defined behavior settings* have been described as areas limited to one activity, with clear boundaries from circulation space and from other behavior settings, and with at least partial acoustic and visual separation (Moore, Lane *et al.*, 1979). Typically they are sized to accommodate two to five children and one teacher and include storage, surface area, electrical connections for equipment, and display for the activity. Poorly defined activity areas, on the other hand, are areas in which the spatial definition is low, the area is too large or too small for the group size, or the resources and work surfaces are not readily available or not suitable for the particular activity.

Extrapolation from the modified open-space findings suggested to us that architecturally defined behavior settings might decrease classroom interruptions and contribute to longer attention span and greater involvement with cognitive develpomental activities. This hypothesis was tested in a second study which compared the effects of centers with varying degrees of behavior setting definition on a number of cognitive development behaviors (reported in Moore, 1983b, 1986). To balance ecological validity (Brunswik,

1943) with internal and external validity (Cook & Campbell, 1979), this study again used a quasi-experimental design with multiple levels of treatment and proxy pretest measures.

The settings were a different set of 14 child-care centers in Milwaukee County selected to represent three levels of the spatial definition of behavior settings: well-defined, transitional, and poorly defined. The degree of spatial definition was measured in terms of ten dimensions, each rated on a five-point, Likert-type scale:

1. Degree of spatial definition and enclosure of the behavior settings in each room or area
2. Degree of visual connections to other behavior settings
3. Degree of appropriateness of the size of behavior settings for one to four children and one adult
4. Degree of appropriateness of the amount of storage, work surfaces, and display space
5. Degree of concentration of all resources in the settings that pertain to one activity
6. Degree of softness
7. Degree of flexibility
8. Variety of seating and working positions possible in the activity centers
9. Amount of resources
10. Degree of separation of behavior settings from circulation paths

This scale is part of the Early Childhood Physical Environment Scales.

The centers selected were similar in terms of size, socioeconomic status of the children, educational philosophy, and teacher styles. The only differences (center size, open versus traditional philosophy, and socioeconomic level) were used as proxy control variables in subsequent analyses.

The subjects were selected on a random space- and time-sampling basis and ranged in age from 2½ years to 6 years (N=1,061). The Environment/Behavior Observation Schedule was used to measure several dependent social and cognitive behavioral variables (see Figure 4). Although some of the dependent variables were the same as in the study summarized in the previous section, the molar physical environment variable was different and the centers and settings where the data were collected were entirely different from those involved in the earlier study.

Contrary to expectation, the amount of engaged versus random and withdrawn behavior does not differ between different types of behavior settings, although for centers with strongly open philosophies there is a significant interaction between the spatial definition of the behavior setting and the philosophy of education (with more engaged behavior occurring in open-education centers with well-defined settings). On the other hand, the *degree* or *level* of engagement in activities is directly affected by the spatial definition of the behavior settings and by the overall size of the center, with the degree of engagement higher in smaller centers with well-defined settings.

The definition of behavior setting does not appear to influence whether children or staff initiate behavioral episodes, although this is affected by philosophy of education. Furthermore, there were significant interactions between environment and teacher style affecting the initiation of behavior: spatially well-defined behavior settings and open education jointly increase self-directed behavior.

With regard to exploratory behavior, the results indicate that it is directly affected by the spatial definition of behavior settings. The highest degree of exploratory behavior occurs in spatially well-defined behavior settings in contrast to transitional and poorly defined settings.

Overall, the results provide support for the notion that the spatial definition of behavior settings is related to cognitive development and that there are complex group × setting interactions. Several analyses indicated quite clearly that the spatial definition of behavior settings is significantly related to degree of engagement in developmental activities and to exploratory behavior. But for several of these dependent variables, other main effects were found for subject-group variables (e.g., teaching style and socioeconomic level of the children). More importantly for the current conceptualization, several significant interaction effects were found for group × setting interactions. For example, the incidence of developmentally relevant or engaged behavior in contrast to functional and transitional behavior, as well as self-directed behavior, is related both to the spatial definition of the setting and to the teaching style of the staff members. We might speculate that well-defined behavior settings staffed by teachers leaning toward an open educational philosophy might lead to the highest levels of cognitive development, but such a hypothesis remains to be tested in a future study.

TOWARD AN INTERACTIONAL THEORY OF CHILD–ENVIRONMENT RELATIONS

Traditionally, theories of child–environment relations (Barker 1968; Gump, 1975, 1978) and theories of the ecology of human behavior (Bronfenbrenner 1977a, 1977b, 1979) have not focused on the physical aspects of the environment and have provided a rather incomplete basis for understanding the environment–behavior relationships of children. For example, Barker's concept of behavior setting focused on the measurement of social and behavioral phenomena (e.g., adaptive reactions to conditions of understaffing and overstaffing). Gump's (1978) review of preschool and elementary school environments devoted less than one page to the role of the physical environment, instead focusing on student motivation, teaching methods, classroom activities, and so on.

A more comprehensive perspective has been developed by Stokols (1981; Stokols & Shumaker, 1981). This interactional view highlights the active role of individuals and groups in creating and modifying their environments and joins the analysis of persons, social units, and the physical milieu. In contrast to other approaches, Stokols's analysis focuses on the concept of place (the geographical and architectural context of behavior), on bilateral interactions between people and places, and on social units and group-unit links.

The results of the two studies summarized here reinforce the idea that children's cognitive development in everyday environments can usefully be seen in ecological, interactional, and transactional terms. According to the findings to date, cognitive development is a function of the total ecological environment surrounding the individual child or group. It is important to understand the ecological context of these everyday behaviors—structured settings characterized by the interdependence of their physical, social, and personal components.

In distinction to earlier approaches in developmental psychology, it is now clear that the environment involves physical components that have measurable impacts on cognitive development. In contrast to many approaches in the professions concerned with the built environment, the current data also make it clear that it is important to see the environment as involving social components.

The conceptualization put forth here, therefore, intentionally crosses social and physical factors in developing explanations for observed trends in cognitive development. The data appear to indicate quite clearly that it is necessary to understand the effects of both social and physical factors as independent main effects and the interaction between the two.

Cognitive development may also be seen in transactional terms. Children have been seen to develop through a series of transactions with the sociophysical environment. The child is not a passive organism to be bombarded with stimuli; on the contrary, the child is an agent in his or her own development—exploring, discovering, testing, initiating,—and using the physical environment as an important medium for these transactions. It is through this dynamic series of transactions within the total environment and from feedback about the child's actions that development appears to occur.

UNRESOLVED ISSUES

The above studies may begin to resolve two issues about the role of the sociophysical environment in cognitive development, especially in the context of preschool child-care environments, but many other issues remain unresolved. For example, the impact of a child-care center's location is not yet fully understood. Lee (1964) found that preschool children walking to child-care centers have a better understanding of their physical environment than those having to be driven in a car, therefore suggesting the possible appropriateness of child-care centers being within the child's immediate neighborhood. It has also been found that parents are willing to pay extra for neighborhood-based care (Rowe, 1972). However, the placement of child-care centers within a neighborhood does not coincide with our societal goals of integration. We need to know, therefore, what the trade-offs are that people are willing to tolerate, ethically, financially, and pragmatically, regarding the distance a child-care center can be from the home. A plausible hypothesis is that centers located within walking distance of the majority of users' homes and on a *seam* between neighborhoods will maximize community involvement, provide for integrated settings, engage children more in their immediate physical environment, and contribute to the development of environmental cognition (Rahaim & Moore, 1982).

We also must know more about the effects of different spatial organizations of child-care centers in interaction with different educational philosophies and child characteristics on a wider range of cognitive developmental variables. Although there are arguments for the impacts of different principles of "zoning" on cross-age interaction (Cohen, McGinty, Armstrong, & Moore, 1982), this is as yet untested. Similarly, the argument has been made elsewhere (Osmon, 1971; Mangurian, 1975; Moore, Cohen *et al.*, 1979) that circulation paths should be separated from behavior settings yet should allow and encourage movement between settings in order to stimulate exploration and cognitive development, but again this working hypothesis is untested to date. Other related questions concern the variety of paths—do they lead to more on-task engaged behavior, and does "circulation that overlooks" lead to engagement in a wider variety of developmental activities and to greater cognitive exploration?

We know that over 80% of children in day care are in family day-care homes or in in-home care. What are the relative impacts of these three types of care on a range of cognitive developmental indicators? What specific physical features not only of formal day-care centers but also of day-care homes and in-home care lead to positive development? Are findings in everyday, far from ideal day-care centers comparable with findings from university-related day-care centers and others with high staff–child ratios and well-designed programs, and does the interaction between social and physical environmental variables differ in these different settings?

If, as has been shown, day care and the physical environment of day care have impacts on behavioral indicators of cognitive development, are these effects lasting? What are the long-range consequences of early day-care experience and the impacts in particular of the physical and socio-physical environment?

Also needed are more definitive studies on whether program quality in day care is inversely related to center size, and if so, why? That is, can it be corroborated that the larger the center, the lower the quality of the program and its potential impact on cognitive development? And if so, is it that concern for rules in larger centers inhibits more developmentally supportive interactions between staff and children and between children and children, or is it something about the quality of the physical environment of larger centers (e.g., noise), or is it some complex interaction between these factors? A related empirical question concerns the notion of campus-plan centers for very large installations. For organizations needing to provide care for large numbers of children, does breaking up the child-care facility into semi-autonomous modules or pods, each with its own architectural articulation, entrance, assistant director, and relative autonomy over program planning and materials lead to more cognitive developmentally supportive behavior, as has been predicted but not yet tested? And when not confounded by educational philosophy and teacher styles, do centers of differing density lead to differences in a range of behavioral indicators of cognitive development?

It is known that even in early childhood centers where the quality of indoor space and program is fairly high, outside areas have many problems. In one study (Prescott, Jones, & Kritchevsky, 1972), only 4% of 50 randomly selected centers had natural surfaces for play, and 70% were totally surfaced with asphalt. This has been confirmed more recently by some of our own data from 50 centers and play environments around the country (Cohen *et al.*, 1978). But the issue goes deeper. Considerable evidence has shown that the outdoor environment can be a rich source of stimulation for the cognitive development of the child and that the outdoor environment can be thought of as a classroom for primary development. Several studies have found that children imitate each other more frequently when they have clay and other outdoor materials available than when using typical indoor materials like wooden blocks, that minimally structured situations and settings produce a greater variety of fantasy themes than do highly structured settings, and that both of these types of settings are more prevalent in outdoor play areas (Cooper-Marcus, 1974; Pulaski, 1970; Updegraff & Herbst, 1933). But many questions remain, for example, about the mix of activities, about the character of space, about the effects of various degrees of indoor–outdoor connections, about zoning, about age groupings versus cross-age mixing, and about the impacts of different overall play configurations on cognitive development.

As a final example of needed empirical research, it is quite surprising that the role of space in the learning and development of physically and mentally handicapped children has not received more attention. Sensitive teachers all know how important the environment of childhood is, how it can facilitate or hinder the curriculum and activities planned for handicapped children, and how the children themselves are often frustrated by the environment around them. Yet empirical research on these topics is lacking. We do not know in what way, or even if, the space of special preschool centers for handicapped children has a direct stimulus or therapeutic value for handicapped children, though several lines of possible research have been presented elsewhere (Moore, 1980; see also Chapter 9 in this volume).

SUMMARY AND CONCLUSION

This chapter has focused on some of the ways in which the built environment and cognitive development interact. An attempt has been made to articulate some of the most salient physical environmental variables having an impact on cognitive development and behavior. Two molar variables have been examined in some detail: the spatial organization of child-care centers and the spatial definition of behavior settings. In the first case, evidence has been presented that appears to suggest that modified open space minimizes many of the problems of both closed and open space while capitalizing on many of the advantages of both, and in particular that modified open space contributes to smaller group sizes, encounters with more activity centers, greater engagement in developmentally oriented behavior, less functional, transitional, and withdrawn behavior, more self-directed behavior, and more exploratory behavior than either closed- or open-plan child-care centers. Regarding the definition of behavior settings, evidence has been summarized suggesting that spatially well-defined behavior settings contribute to a higher degree of engagement in activities and more exploratory behavior exhibited by preschool age children.

More importantly, it was seen from the data presented that many findings could not be accounted for strictly as a function of either physical or subject group variables. For example, contrary to initial expectations, the absolute amount of engaged behavior (i.e., differentiated from the degree of engagement) did not differ between well-defined and poorly defined settings, nor did it relate significantly to any social or subject group variables. Only when the data were more closely analyzed did it become evident that there were significant interactions between definition of the behavior setting and philosophy of education jointly affecting behavior. Similarly, analysis of the initiation of behavior indicated significant interactions between environment and style in affecting self-directed behavior. Furthermore, it was also found that differences between modified open plans and other types of spatial organization on other behavioral indicators of cognitive development were more pronounced for children of higher socioeconomic levels and for centers where the teachers follow an open educational philosophy. Taken together, these findings lend strong support to the notion that it is neither the physical environment nor the social environment working alone but rather all elements of the sociophysical environment working in interaction that affects cognitive development.

Finally, this chapter has put forth the outlines of an interactional theory of the effects of the sociophysical environment on cognitive development and has raised some unresolved issues and questions for continued scientific research.

Only by developing an adequate vocabulary for dealing with child–environment relations in their ecological context and through evolving methods appropriate for studying such contexts and drawing valid causal inferences will we better understand the complex links between the architecturally designed environment and the social system as they independently and in concert influence children's behavior and development.

ACKNOWLEDGMENTS

My thanks to Ina Uzgiris and Seymour Wapner for valuable advice; to Thomas Laurent, Naomi Leiseroff, Marleen Sobczak, John Rahaim, and Harry Van Oudenallen for assistance on the studies summarized in the chapter; to Ellen Bruce, Thomas David, David Stea, Daniel Stokols, and Carol Weinstein for comments on earlier versions of the chapter; and to Carol Weinstein also for her thorough editing.

REFERENCES

Ahrentzen, S. B., Jue, G. M., Skorpanich, M. A., & Evans, G. W. School environments and stress. In G. W. Evans (Ed.), *Environmental stress.* New York: Cambridge University Press, 1982.

Aiello, J. F., Gordon, B., & Farrell, T. J. Description of children's outdoor activities in a suburban residential area. In D. H. Carson (Ed.), *Man–environment interactions* (Part 6). Stroudsburg, PA.: Dowden, Hutchinson & Ross, 1974.

Altman, I. & Wohlwill, J. F. (Eds.). *Children and the environment.* New York: Plenum Press, 1978.

American Academy of Pediatrics. *Recommendations for Day Care Centers for Infants and Children.* Evanston, IL: Author, 1973.

Anonymous. General behavior of children is tip-off to preschools' practices. *Today's Child,* 1973, *21*(7), 6.

Baird, J. C., & Lutkus, A. D. (Eds.). *Mind child architecture.* Hanover, NH: University Press of New England, 1982.

Barker, R. G. *Ecological psychology.* Palo Alto, CA: Stanford University Press, 1968.

Belsky, J., & Steinberg, L. D. The effects of day care. A critical review. *Child Development,* 1978, *49,* 929–949.

Belsky, J., Steinberg, L. D., & Walker, A. The ecology of day care. In M. E. Lamb (Ed.), *Nontraditional families: Parenting and child development.* Hillsdale, NJ: Lawrence Erlbaum, 1982.

Biemiller, A., Avis, C., & Lindsay, A. Competence supporting aspects of day care environments: A preliminary study. Paper presented at the meeting of the Canadian Psychological Association, Toronto, June 1976.

Bronfenbrenner, U. *Is early intervention effective?* Washington, DC: U.S. Department of Health, Education, and Welfare, Publication No. (OHD)76-30025, 1974.

Bronfenbrenner, U. The ecology of human development in retrospect and prospect. In H. McGurk (Ed.), *Ecological factors in human development.* Amsterdam: North-Holland, 1977. (a)

Bronfenbrenner, U. Toward an experimental ecology of human development. *American Psychologist,* 1977, *32,* 513–531. (b)

Bronfenbrenner, U. *The ecology of human development: Experiments by nature and design.* Cambridge, MA: Harvard University Press, 1979.

Bronzaft, A. L., & McCarthy, D. P. The effect of elevated train noise on reading ability. *Environment and Behavior,* 1975, *7,* 517–527.

Brunetti, F. A. Noise, distraction, and privacy in conventional and open school environments. In W. J. Mitchell (Ed.), *Environmental design: Research and practice* (Vol. 1). Los Angeles: University of California, School of Archiecture and Urban Planning, 1972.

Brunswik, E. Organismic achievement and environmental probability. *Psychological Review,* 1943, *50,* 255–272.

Burns, J. Development and implementation of an environmental evaluation and redesign process for a high school science department. In W. J. Mitchell (Ed.), *Environmental design: Research and practice* (Vol. 1). Los Angeles: University of California, School of Architecture and Urban Planning, 1972.

Child Welfare League of America. *Child Welfare League of America Standards For Day Care* (rev. ed.). New York: Author, 1973.

Children's Environments Quarterly. New York: City University of New York, Center for Human Environments, 1984–present.

Clarke-Stewart, A. & Gruber, C. Day care: A new context for research and development. In M. Perlmutter (Ed.), *Parent–child interaction and parent–child relations in child development: The Minnesota Symposia on Child Psychology* (Vol. 17). Hillsdale, NJ: Lawrence Erlbaum, 1984.

Cohen, D. *Day care: 3. Serving preschool children.* Washington, DC: U.S. Department of Health, Education, and Welfare, 1974.

Cohen, R. (Ed.) *Children's conceptions of spatial relationships.* San Francisco: Jossey-Bass, 1982.

Cohen, S., Evans, G. W., Krantz, D. S., & Stokols, D. Physiological, motivational, and cognitive effects of aircraft noise on children: Moving from the laboratory to the field. *American Psychologist,* 1980, *35,* 231–243.

Cohen, S., Glass, D. C., & Singer, J. E. Apartment noise, auditory discrimination, and reading ability in children. *Journal of Experimental Social Psychology,* 1973, *9,* 407–422.

Cohen, S. & Weinstein, N. Noise and stress. In G. W. Evans (Ed.), *Environmental stress.* New York: Cambridge University Press, 1982.

Cohen, U., McGinty, T., Armstrong, B. T., & Moore, G. T. The spatial organization of an early childhood development center: Modified open space, zoning, and circulation. *Day Care Journal,* 1982, *1*(2), 35–38.

Cohen, U., Moore, G. T., & McGinty, T. *Case studies of child play areas and child support facilities.* Milwaukee: University of Wisconsin—Milwaukee, Center for Architecture and Urban Planning Research, 1978.

Cook, T. D., & Campbell, D. T. *Quasi-experimentations: Design and analysis issues in field settings.* Chicago: Rand McNally, 1979.

Cooper-Marcus, C. Children's play behavior in a low-rise inner-city housing development. In

D. H. Carson (Ed.), *Man–environment interactions,* Part 12. Stroudsburg, PA: Dowden, Hutchinson & Ross, 1974.

Dattner, R. *Design for play.* Cambridge, MA: MIT Press, 1969.

Doyle, A. B. Infant development and day care. *Developmental Psychology,* 1975, *11,* 655–656.

Doyle, A. B., & Somers, K. The effects of group and family day care on infant attachment behaviors. *Canadian Journal of Behavioral Science,* 1978, *10,* 38–45.

Durlak, J. T., Beardley, B. E., & Murray, J. S. Observation of user activity patterns in open and traditional plan school environments. In W. J. Mitchell (Ed.), *Environmental design: Research and practice* (Vol. 1). Los Angeles: University of California, School of Archiecture and Urban Planning, 1972.

Essa, E. L. An outdoor play area designed for learning. *Day Care and Early Education,* 1981, *9*(2), 37–42.

Evans, G. W., & Lovell, B. Design modifications in an open-plan school. *Journal of Educational Psychology,* 1979, *71,* 41–49.

Field, T. M. Preschool play: Effects of teacher/child ratios and organization of classroom space. *Child Study Journal,* 1980, *10,* 191–205.

Fraiberg, S. *Every child's birthright: In defense of mothering.* New York: Basic Books, 1977.

Friedberg, M. P., & Berkeley, E. P. *Play and interplay: A manifesto for new design in the urban recreational environment.* New York: Macmillan, 1970.

George, P. S. Ten years of open space schools: A review of the research. Special issue of *Florida Educational Research and Development Council Research Bulletin,* 1975, *9*(Whole No. 3).

Golden, M., Rosenbluth, L., Grossi, M. T., Policare, H. J., Freeman, H., & Brownlee, E. M. *The New York City Infant Day Care Study.* New York: Medical and Health Research Association of New York City, 1978.

Gump, P. V. Operating environments in schools of open and traditional design. *School Review,* 1974, *82,* 575–593.

Gump, P. V. *Ecological psychology and children.* Chicago: University of Chicago Press, 1975.

Gump, P. V. School environments. In I. Altman & J. F. Wohlwill (Eds.), *Children and the environment.* New York: Plenum Press, 1978.

Gump, P. V., & Good, L. R. Environments operating in open space and traditionally designed schools. *Journal of Architectural Research,* 1976, *5,* 20–26.

Gump, P. V., & Iliff, D. Interviews of teachers at open-area schools. Unpublished manuscript, Department of Psychology, University of Kansas, 1971.

Gump, P. V., & Ross, R. The fit of milieu and programme in school environments. In H. McGurk (Ed.), *Ecological factors in human development.* New York: North-Holland, 1977.

Harms, T., & Clifford, R. M. *Early Childhood Environment Rating Scale.* New York: Teachers College Press, 1980.

Hoffman, L. W. Matrenal employment and the young child. In M. Perlmutter (Ed.) *Parent–child interaction and parent–child relations in child development: The Minnesota Symposia on Child Psychology* (Vol. 17). Hillsdale, NJ: Lawrence Erlbaum, 1984.

Jephcott, P. *Homes in high flats.* Edinburgh, Scotland: Oliver and Boyd, 1971.

Kagan, J., Kearsley, R. B., & Zelazo, P. R. The effects of infant day care on psychological development. *Evaluation Quarterly,* 1977, *1,* 109–142.

Kagan, J., & Moss, H. A. *Birth to maturity: A study in psychological development.* New York: Wiley, 1962 (2nd ed. with a new preface by J. Kagan). New Haven, CN: Yale University Press, 1983.

Lazar, I., Hubbell, V., Murray, H., Rosche, M., & Royce, J. Summary report: The persistance of preschool effects. Summary of final report to the Administration on Children, Youth, and Families. Washington, DC: U.S. Department of Health, Education, and Welfare, October 1977.

Lee, T. R. Psychology and living space. *Transactions of the Bartlett Society* (London), 1964, *2,* 9–36.

Liben, L. S., Patterson, A. H., & Newcombe, N. (Eds.). *Spatial representation and behavior across the life span.* New York: Academic Press, 1981.

Mangurian, R. A celebration of space. *Day Care and Early Education,* November–December 1975, *3,* 14–16.

Michelson, W. The physical environment as a mediating factor in school achievement. Paper presented at the meeting of the Canadian Sociology and Anthropology Association, Calgary, June 1968.

Millar, S. *The psychology of play.* Harmondsworth, England: Penguin, 1968.

Montessori, M. *Spontaneous activity in education.* New York: Schocken, 1965.

Moore, G. T. The application of research to the design of therapeutic play environments for exceptional children. In W. M. Cruickshank (Ed.), *Approaches to learning.* Syracuse, NY: Syracuse University Press, 1980.

Moore, G. T. Some effects of the organization of the socio-physical environment on cognitive behavior in child care settings. Paper presented at the meeting of the Society for Research in Child Development, Detroit, April 1983(a).

Moore, G. T. Effects of the definition of behavior settings on children's behavior. Paper presented at the meeting of the American Psychological Association, Anaheim, California, August 1983(b).

Moore, G. T. Effects of the spatial definition of behavior settings on children's behavior: A quasi-experimental field study. *Journal of Environmental Psychology,* 1986, *6,* 205–231.

Moore, G. T., Lane, C. G., Hill, A. H., Cohen, U., & McGinty, T. *Recommendations for child care centers.* Milwaukee: University of Wisconsin—Milwaukee, Center for Architecture and Urban Planning Research, 1979.

Moore, G. T., Lane, C. G., & Lindberg, L. A. *Bibliography on children and the physical environment: Child care centers, outdoor play environments, and other children's environments.* Milwaukee: University of Wisconsin—Milwaukee, Center for Architecture and Urban Planning Research, 1979.

Neill, S. R. St. J. Preschool design and child behaviour. *Journal of Child Psychology and Psychiatry,* 1982, *23,* 309–318.

Neill, S. R. St. J., & Denham, E. J. M. The effects of pre-school design. *Educational Research,* 1982, *24,* 107–111.

O'Conner, M. The nursery school environment. *Developmental Psychology,* 1975, *11,* 556–561.

Osmon, F. L. *Patterns for designing children's centers.* New York: Educational Facilities Laboratories, 1971.

Parke, R. D. Children's home environments: Social and cognitive effects. In I. Altman & J. F. Wohlwill (Eds.), *Children and the environment.* New York: Plenum Press, 1978.

Perry, K. S. *Employers and child care: Establishing services through the workplace* (rev. ed.). Washington, DC: U.S. Government Printing Office and Department of Labor Women's Bureau, 1981.

Piaget, J. *Plays, dreams, and imitation in childhood* (*La formation du symbole,* orig. French ed. 1946). New York: Norton, 1951.

Prescott, E. A comparison of three types of day care and nursery school–home care. Paper presented at the meeting of the Society for Research in Child Development, Philadelphia, March 1973.

Prescott, E., & David, T. G. Effects of physical environments in child care systems. Paper presented at the meeting of the American Educational Research Association, New York, April 1976.

Prescott, E., Jones, E., & Kritchevsky, S. *Day care as a child-rearing environment.* Washington, DC: National Association for the Education of Young Children, 1967. Reprinted 1972.

Pulaski, M. A. Play as a function of toy structure and fantasy disposition. *Child Development,* 1970, *41,* 531–538.

Rahaim, J. S., & Moore, G. T. Selecting a location for an early childhood development center. *Day Care Journal,* 1982, *1*(2), 31–34.

Ramey, C. T., & Campbell, F. A. Compensatory education for disadvantaged children. *School Review,* 1979, *87,* 171–189.

Ramey, C., & Smith, B. Assessing the intellectual consequences of early intervention with high-risk infants. *American Journal of Mental Deficiency,* 1976, *81,* 318–324.

Rohe, W., & Patterson, A. H. The effects of varied levels of resources and density on behavior in a day care center. In D. H. Carson (Ed.), *Man–environment interactions* (Part 12). Stroudsburg, PA: Dowden, Hutchinson & Ross, 1974.

Rosenthal, B. A. An ecological study of free play in the nursery school. *Dissertation Abstracts International,* 1974, *34*(7-A), 4004A–4005A.

Rowe, R. Child care in Massachusetts: The public responsibility. Final report to the Massachusetts Advisory Council on Education, Boston, 1972.

Ruopp, R. R., & others. *Children at the center: Final report of the National Day Care Study.* Cambridge, MA: Abt Associates, 1979.

Shure, M. B. Psychological ecology of a nursery school. *Child Development,* 1963, *34,* 979–992.

Stevenson, A., Martin, E., & O'Neill, J. *High living: A study of family life in flats.* Melbourne, Australia: Melbourne University Press, 1967.

Stokols, D. Group × place transactions: Some neglected issues in psychological research on settings. In D. Magnusson (Ed.), *Toward a psychology of situations: An interactional perspective.* Hillsdale, NJ: Lawrence Erlbaum, 1981.

Stokols, D., & Shumaker, S. A. People in places: A transactional view of settings. In J. H. Harvey (Ed.), *Cognition, social behavior, and the environment.* Hillsdale, NJ: Lawrence Erlbaum, 1981.

Travers, J., & Ruopp, R. R., with others. *National Day Care Study: Preliminary findings and their implications.* Cambridge, MA: Abt Associates, 1978.

Twardosz, S., Cataldo, M., & Risley, T. Open environment design for infant and toddler day care. *Journal of Applied Behavioral Analysis,* 1974, *7,* 529–546.

Updegraff, R., & Herbst, E. K. An experimental study of the social behavior stimulated in young children by certain play materials. *Journal of Genetic Psychology,* 1933, *42,* 372–391.

U.S. Department of Health, Education, and Welfare. *Federal interagency day care requirements.* Washington, DC: Author, 1968.

Wachs, T. D. Utilization of a Piagetean approach in the investigation of early experience effects: A research strategy and some illustrative data. *Merrill-Palmer Quarterly,* 1976, *22,* 11–30.

Wachs, T. D., Uzgiris, I. C., & Hunt, J. McV. Cognitive development in infants of different age levels and from different environmental backgrounds: An exploratory investigation. *Merrill-Palmer Quarterly,* 1971, *17,* 283–317.

Waligura, R. L. *Environmental criteria: MR—Preschool day care facilities.* College Station, Texas: Texas A & M University, College of Architecture and Environmental Design, 1969.

Walsh, D. P. Noise levels and annoyance in open plan educational facilities. *Journal of Architectural Research,* 1975, *4,* 5–16.

Weinstein, C. S. Modifying student behavior in an open classroom through changes in physical design. *American Education Research Journal,* 1977, *14,* 249–262.

Weinstein, C. S. The physical environment of the school: A review of the research. *Review of Educational Research,* 1979, *49,* 577–610.

Weinstein, C. S., & Weinstein, N. D. Noise and reading performance in an open space school. *Journal of Educational Research,* 1979, *72,* 210–213.

Werner, H. *The comparative psychology of mental development* (rev. ed.). New York: International Universities Press, 1949.

White, B. L. *The first three years of life.* Engelwood Cliffs, NJ: Prentice-Hall, 1975.

Winett, R. A., Fuchs, W. L., & Moffatt, S. *An evaluative study of day care and non-day care children and their families.* Unpublished manuscript. Department of Education, University of Kentucky, 1974.

Winett, R. A., Battersby, C. D., & Edwards, S. M. The effects of architectural change, individualized instruction, and group contingencies on the academic performance and social behavior of sixth graders. *Journal of School Psychology,* 1975, *13,* 28–40.

Wohlwill, J. F. The confluence of environmental and developmental psychology: Signpost for an ecology of development? *Human Development,* 1980, *23,* 354–358.

Wohlwill, J. F., & Heft, H. Environments fit for the developing child. In H. McGurk (Ed.), *Ecological factors in human development.* Amsterdam: North Holland, 1977.

Wohlwill, J. F., & Heft, H. The physical environment and the development of the child. In D. Stokols & I. Altman (Eds.), *Handbook of environmental psychology.* New York: Wiley, in press.

Chapter 4

The Environment as Organizer of Intent in Child-Care Settings

ELIZABETH PRESCOTT

THE EVOLUTION OF AN IDEA

Once upon a time, even before Head Start was invented, we set out to look at the kinds of day care used by working mothers. Since virtually nothing was known about child-care arrangements at the time—except that there was not enough of it and that more was needed—we began by looking at a wide variety of centers. Their names gave some indication of their origins, sponsorship, and hopes for children. The old-time nurseries were often named for saints and were typically in old buildings, whereas the centers located on elementary-school sites usually bore unobtrusive street names. The privately owned centers sometimes had dignified names such as Miss Baines' School (the word *school* was often featured prominently in the title). Others were more colorfully named: Fairyland; Cherubs' Chalet; Kiddie Park; Kiddie College; even Kiddie Koop. Although we did not see it originally, eventually we came to identify some spatial patterns that fit certain categories of names.

In the beginning we mostly asked questions—of parents and of the people who were caring for their children. We learned that most parents did

ELIZABETH PRESCOTT • Department of Human Development, Pacific Oaks College, Pasadena, CA 91103.

not know a great deal about what was happening to their children but that they liked the play equipment and felt, for the most part, that the care was good. From the staff we learned that we did not know how to ask questions about the center's program that would elicit anything beyond a recitation of the daily schedule or a list of activities set up for children.

We also began to get a sense of differences among centers. At first we called this difference *climate* and attempted to define it according to the attitudes of the staff toward dependency and authority (Prescott, 1965). This approach gave us some center types ranging along a dimension of warm–cold. In "warm" centers, children were supported and comforted if things went badly, and the reasons for procedures were explained and demonstrated. In "cold" centers, children who wanted comforting were ignored or scolded, and there was an arbitrary insistence that things be done "*my* way."

In the beginning we did not know how to see very much when we visited centers. We did realize that sometimes a center that did not seem to have much to offer felt like a good place and vice versa. We then decided that we needed to look more closely at teacher–child interactions and to work toward developing some rudimentary vocabulary for talking about the context in which moment-to-moment events occurred.

For this study we drew a random sample of 50 day-care centers and used every wile we could think of to convince the director of each center that it would be safe and worthwhile to permit us to visit (Prescott & Jones, 1967). These randomly drawn centers were very ordinary places, burdened with all the limitations that are the lot of those who lack the extra services and attention that go with being a demonstration project with a research component. Our purpose was to learn more about the child's daily experience and how to describe it. We thought hard about the slippery concept of daily program. A close reading of Barker and Gump (Barker & Wright, 1954, 1968; Gump, 1963) had helped us to organize the day into a series of behavior–activity settings, a concept that vastly increased our power to perceive patterns.

Our observation schedule was designed to examine teachers' behavior, on the basis of our perception of their key role in carrying out the program. About halfway through this study we began noticing that our sharing of experiences after observations often revolved around two themes. One was the growing awareness that what the teacher was doing and expecting was not necessarily what was happening for any given child. For example, at first, when the teacher was playing "Simon Says" or having the children work puzzles, we naively thought of that as the activity. Eventually, it became clear to all of us that for any given child the activity might more accurately be named, "emptying sand out of your shoe and making designs on the floor with it" or "playing zip your jacket with a friend" or "transforming various puzzle pieces into people, cars and guns." When this discovery became so obvious that we could no longer ignore it, we built it into the design for the next study (Prescott, 1973).

Our other discovery grew out of listening to ourselves say things like "That teacher seemed to be responsive, but she really gave those children a hard time on the playground" or "The morning went so smoothly even though the teachers didn't seem to do much of anything." We finally realized that the physical environment was the variable that appeared to be implicated. We then devised a scheme for evaluating the quality of the environment and proceeded to rate the indoor and outdoor space in all of the centers in our sample (Kritchevsky in Prescott & Jones, 1967). As soon as we started working with our new tool, we found that we could see all sorts of things that had gone unnoticed. Our data also revealed that there was an association between spatial quality and behavior. In centers in which spatial quality was rated high, children were found to be more involved and teachers spent less time on management and enforcement of rules and more time in responding to children and fostering social interaction (Prescott & Jones, 1967).

Our environmental assessment looked at five aspects of the physical space: organization, variety, complexity, amount to do, and special problems. This initial identification of variables proved to be a turning point in our thinking and provided a framework for most of our further elaboration.

Organization

The criteria for good organization were clear and appropriate paths and adequate empty spaces:

> A path is the empty space on the floor or ground through which people move in getting from one place to another; it need be no different in composition from the rest of the surface. A clear path is broad, elongated and easily visible. Paths are very difficult to describe in words, but when they are well-defined they are easily seen. If an observer looking at a play area can't answer readily the question, "How do children get from one place to another?" probably the children can't either, and there is no clear path. (Kritchevsky & Prescott, 1969, p. 15)

The amount of empty space was also important. Difficulties could arise when there was either too much or too little. A surprise for us was the discovery that a space might easily have both problems; crowding, confusion, and resulting accidents in some areas combined with areas we called "dead space." Here the emptiness appeared to create a kind of trap which led to disorganized running and wrestling. "Potential space," the aspect of flexibility that permits new play spaces to be created, was also found to be important. Both indoor and outdoor spaces varied greatly in this degree of flexibility.

Variety

Variety referred to the number of different things to do in a setting, such as climbing, swinging, and building. Sometimes a space looked pleasing to adults and was perceived to have a great deal of variety, but in actuality it invited only a limited range of activities with a good deal of chasing and other roughhousing.

Complexity

Complexity was viewed as the potential that the setting and its props offered for manipulation and alteration. Our scheme identified three types of equipment. A *simple unit* is a play unit that has one obvious use and does not have subparts or attachments that would suggest multiple uses. Examples are swings, jungle gyms, rocking horses, slides, and tricycles. *Complex units* have subparts or a juxtaposition of two essentially different play materials that enable the child to manipulate or improvise, for example, a sand pile with digging equipment or a doll bed with dolls. Also included in this category are single play materials and objects which encourage substantial improvisation and/or have a considerable element of unpredictability, such as play dough or paints, a table with books to look at, or an area with animals. The most complex play units are *super units,* complex units with one or more additional play materials (i.e., three or more play materials juxtaposed). Examples include a sand pile with digging equipment and water; a jungle gym with moveable climbing boards and a blanket; and a dough table with tools.

Amount to Do

A particular space may contain a good supply of complex and super units and thus appear to provide a good deal for children to do. However, amount to do also depends on the number of children present. On the basis of observations we determined that complex units generally accommodate about four children at once and super units can accommodate eight. Though many simple units can be used by more than one child at a time, the fact that they are less continuously interesting than complex units led us to assign a value of one to simple units. Using these values, the total number of play places in a yard or room can be determined. This sum can then be divided by the number of children expected to use the space, and the ratio yields the approximate number of play places available to each child at any given time. We have found that when a play space has only 2–2.5 things to do per child, a free-choice period will not work very well. Really good space provides 4–5 choices per child.

In Figure 1, a play yard is analyzed as having a total of 30 play places. If

NUMBER OF PLAY UNITS	TYPE OF UNIT	NUMBER OF PLAY PLACES
12 Vehicles	Simple	12
1 Rocking boat	Simple	1
1 Tumble tub	Simple	1
1 Jungle gym with boxes and boards	Complex	4
1 Dirt area plus scoop trucks	Complex	4
1 Equipped sand table with water	Super unit	8
TOTAL PLAY PLACES		30

FIGURE 1. Calculating the amount to do (from Kritchevsky & Prescott, 1969).

the yard had 15 children, there would be 2.0 play places per child; if the yard had 25 children, there would be 1.2 play places per child.

Special Problems

We used this category to specify a variety of conditions that make space less pleasant or functional, such as too much sun or shade, noise, dust, or broken equipment. In addition, poor links between indoor and outdoor space or improperly located bathrooms can cause chronic problems. In some neighborhoods vandalism was found to discourage any attempt to develop good space.

DESIGNING THE ENVIRONMENT TO MAKE THINGS WORK BETTER

Our discoveries coincided with the burgeoning of early childhood programs. When we began to share with teachers our observations about the workings of physical space, we discovered that they were, for the most part, oblivious to the space in which they worked. They were fascinated by the possibilities it presented. Teachers wanted to make things work better and to feel more in control, and it became clear that our discoveries could help them.

Through our consultation work with teachers we developed four basic principles which we applied repeatedly, with specific advice tailored to the unique characteristics of each program:

1. *Pathways determine the flow of traffic.* Underused areas often have no path leading to them. We observed dramatic play areas standing empty because there were no paths there. We asked teachers to scrutinize pathways from the child's eye level, to ensure that they were visible. We also pointed out that pathways can sometimes create unintended interference and even danger. On a playground, for example, a path passing right under the overhead bars is a safety hazard.

2. *Subparts can be added and combined to create more complex play units.* The addition of a ramp, a ladder, and trucks can transform a packing crate into a center of activity. The possible play activities in a sandbox can be greatly enhanced by adding water and containers of various shapes and sizes. Combining large blocks, gas stations, and fireman's hats with tricycles creates an entirely different set of opportunities. These solutions also increase the amount to do.

3. *Children will invent super units.* If the adults in a setting do not want their children using Lego blocks for food, then they should not set them out near the housekeeping area. But we also asked teachers to appreciate the children's inventiveness in creating new combinations and to think carefully about their prohibitions.

4. *Problems that keep reoccurring often have spatial solutions.*We asked teachers to make notes on the things that were not working as they wished and to experiment with spatial changes. Time and again they reported successful resolutions similar to those described by Weinstein (1977).

When teachers set out to change their space, they began to think very specifically about what they wanted and why. Since these plans also often involved fellow workers, we began to get reports that staff members were communicating in ways that had not occurred before. It is much easier to talk about where the blocks should be and why you want the toy airplanes near them than to discuss differences in teaching style and personality. They were also rewarded by the remarkable changes in children's behavior. They could see that things were different after they had rearranged the environment. Since they were accustomed to viewing change as difficult to produce, they often viewed the changes as somewhat magical.

We began to see how the act of arranging the environment also helped to organize intent. Once a space had been carefully developed, children accepted the invitation to use it and the adults responded with much more clarity. Just as children use and manipulate objects in their play, the adults played by moving and manipulating. In both cases something was clarified.

BROADENING THE SENSE OF PLACES AND SPACES

In order to learn more about differences in environmental functioning, we next focused on the ways in which children used day-care settings. In our previous observations we had become aware of two strikingly different ways of organizing the day-care environment. In one, which we called *closed structure,* the day was organized much like that of the public school. Teacher-directed activities, in which everyone was expected to participate, alternated with recess, when teacher participation was usually limited to enforcement of playground rules. The other type, *open structure,* resembled the traditional morning nursery-school play groups in which cooperative and self-chosen play is encouraged and the teacher's role is to facilitate play.

We had already learned something about the ways in which scheduling, grouping, and use of physical space differed between these two program types, and we wished to know more about the differential impact of these environments on the children. We chose seven centers of each type, on the basis of our judgment and the directors' answers to our questions about the importance of choice of daily activities by the children versus by the teachers. Our study design included day-long observations in each center of individual children nominated by the staff as thrivers, average, or nonthrivers and an evaluation of the space and structure of activity settings (Prescott *et al.*, 1973).

Just as Barker's writings had suggested ways to think about the regulatory features of group day care as a behavior setting, Gump's refinement of the concept of activity setting helped us to plot a child's day (Gump & Sutton-Smith, 1955). Gump identified those subparts of a behavior setting that have a task–place focus dimension. This distinction is particularly useful in child-care settings to designate the variety of activities that occur in such a setting.

Our 15-second codings of the child's mode of behavior were placed in the context of the activity setting, such as story time, dramatic play in housekeeping area, or riding tricycles. We could then develop descriptors for these activities. These descriptors helped us broaden our sense of the uses of places and spaces. We could now broaden our original idea of play unit into a more versatile (for us) concept of an activity setting and keep track of its three aspects: (1) task or organizing theme, (2) place and props, and (3) social structure.

The Task or Organizing Theme

One of the interesting things that we discovered about activity settings was that the act of naming them helped us to see much more about the structure. For example, two children on the swings might turn out to be properly named as "Mary and friend trying to swing in unison while singing insults to each other" or "Tommy and friend swinging sideways and experimenting with how this works." In either case the setting was children on swings, but the motivation and, hence, the organizing theme were quite different.

Places and Props

The descriptors used under this heading varied depending on the particular interaction of the props with place. It makes a difference whether an activity occurs indoors or outdoors, in a place regularly designated for the activity or in a place that is unusual or ordinarily forbidden for the activity. For example, lunch eaten outside under the elm tree is different from the usual indoor lunch. Also, walking with painted feet on paper laid on tables permits for the moment a usually forbidden activity.

Simple–Complex. This descriptor was carried over from our previous work because of its usefulness in understanding how play themes developed and escalated. Nicholson's (1978) article, "The Theory of Loose Parts," describes this phenomenon. Because of our awareness that the availability of props necessary to increase complexity was highly dependent on storage, we added a rating for storage. (For a discussion of storage see Prescott & David, 1976, pp. 41–46).

Open–Closed. In the course of playing with groups of activities that we had coded on or simple–complex continuum we invented the category of *open–closed.* This dimension describes the coerciveness of the activity. Those that are rated open have no right answers and many ways of engagement. For example, painting, sand play, playdough, and clay are open activities, in the sense that there is no single correct proceeding. Other materials such as blocks, Snowflakes, and Tinker Toys are relatively open in the sense that a variety of constructions are possible but properties of the materials do limit possibilities. Materials such as puzzles, lotto games, and most Montessori equipment are considered to be closed because there is a single correct completion of the activity.

Common–Uncommon. Our realization of the importance of giving an accurate name to an activity setting enabled us to discover that some activity settings were seen routinely as we moved from one center to another whereas others stood out as unusual or creative. After completing our observations, we then went back over our collection of activity settings and classified them on a continuum from common to uncommon, indicating the frequency or rarity of occurrence. Some examples of common or typical servings were easel painting, tricycle riding, listening to a story, and playing in the sandpile with cups and handshovels. Some examples of uncommon, atypical settings were making lakes and rivers in the sand, melting ice in the corn popper, collecting worms and bugs and finding new homes for them, and arranging one's quilt and teddy bear to sleep under your cot at naptime.

High or Low Arousal. Though there were notable exceptions, common, routine activities were often more low key and generated less excitement than uncommon activities. Seeing this led us to categorize activities by the amount of excitement they generate. Sherman (1973) developed a similar category which he called "glee." For example, activities such as listening to a story, working with puzzles, or playing matching games are low in mobility and low in arousal. High-mobility activities typically generate more excitement, but degree of mobility does not necessarily predict excitement. Some examples of high-arousal activities are playing Batman with your friend in the park, pricking balloons covered with shaving foam, jumping around (at toileting time) with your pants down to your ankles pretending to be a kangaroo, playing the drums and cymbals without teacher direction, and seeing who can spit watermelon seeds the farthest. These kinds of activities that cause excitement and behavioral contagion are typically avoided in most day-care centers.

Risk and Daring. Another dividend from our attention to the true name of the activity was the realization that many activities with high interest and appeal appeared to have risk and daring as the purpose of the activity. Especially with children of four years and older, activities began to appear with these kinds of names: seeing how fast you can ride a trike, seeing how high you can pump a swing, climbing forbidden things (the tree, the swing structure, the wall), and jumping off a high place.

We also discovered that adults do not like these activities and quite routinely stop even the mildest attempt to experiment with risk. These activities were so rarely permitted that an observer once commented in surprise:

> Outdoors, there was some lively play on the swing—pumping, imitating each other, jumping off. The teacher was a bit concerned about the jumping off, told them to be careful no one was in the way, but didn't stop it! (Prescott *et al.* 1975, p. 50).

Social Structure

There can be great variations in the social structure of an activity. For example, play in the housekeeping corner might be solitary, with a best friend, a small group, or even a large group with the teacher providing the structure. As the configuration of children and adults varies, the play experience varies too, although the place and props remain the same. A change in the social structure was one of the predictors of a change in the name of the activity and, to our edification, turned out to be as important a marker of activity change as place and props.

THE USES OF SETTING

We made some other discoveries about the environment when we began to look closely at individual children as they moved from one activity setting to another. One discovery was that there were marked differences across activity settings in: (1) the amount of tactile sensory stimulation provided, (2) the amount of variation in social structure, and (3) opportunities to be uninterrupted and free from intrusion. Furthermore, we found that these three variables were interrelated in an unexpected way.

Soft–Hard

Some day-care centers provided a range of materials that we called *soft*, such as rugs, pillows, sand, mud, grass, clay, dough, shaving foam, finger paints, single-sling swings, and laps. The presence of these items seemed to generate opportunites for messy activities and feelings of body containment. Other centers did not include these materials as part of their environment and were at the *hard* end of the continuum.

Variations in Social Structure

In some centers we noted throughout the day that children played alone, with another child, in small groups of 3–5 children, and occasionally in larger groups. An adult might not be present during all of these activities, but there were also times when one or two children could and did have the adult's full attention. In other centers, the program was designed to keep the group together with the adult so that other kinds of social configurations seldom occurred. When they did, it was mostly during outdoor time. In such centers the opportunities to form friendships and to experiment with relationships and problem solving were severely curtailed.

Intrusion–Seclusion

Another outcome that was related to each of the two dimensions just described was a difference in opportunities to find secluded and protected places for private or intimate play, uninterrupted by intruders or constant demands to share. These kinds of places occurred most often in "soft" centers where rugs, corners of sandpiles, and grassy places under trees were found. Such places encouraged play with a best friend or solitary play.

A COMPARISON OF HOME VERSUS CENTER ENVIRONMENTS

As we ended our observations in centers, we moved into family day-care homes and into home settings of children who attended only morning nursery school. By this time we were very proficient in our coding and seldom encountered an incident that was puzzling. Our first days in the home settings, however, were a form of culture shock; we had repeated experiences of confusion and surprise.

Some Differences in Objects

Partly our perplexities stemmed from differences in objects, spaces, and their uses. Homes have adult-size furniture (including soft couches and easy chairs), books and magazines, objects that hold special meaning such as family photographs, and all the supplies and objects necessary to make a home run smoothly. Homes often have birds, cats, and dogs. Although these differences may seem obvious, they are in sharp contrast to centers that are typically furnished with items from a standardized list and ordered through the catalogue of a central purchasing agency. Such procedures result in a striking uniformity of child-size chairs and play objects.

The furniture in homes provides for a much greater variety of use and differentiation of experience—there are kitchen chairs, dining-room chairs, easy chairs, the special chair that is for company, and patio chairs of tubular aluminum that can be folded and carried. We also found unending combinations of objects. Books might be used to supplement a shortage of blocks. Empty paper-towel rolls and slot-car tracks borrowed from older children in the family might be incorporated into construction.

Differences in Space/Time Boundaries

The homes we visited had strikingly lower density than most centers. Even the smallest home afforded quiet places. There were also few time constraints. Children moved about freely within large blocks of time. If an activity captivated children's interest, it could often be left out or carried over to the next day for completion.

Some of the troubles we encountered in observing in homes were related to alterations of boundaries to which we had become accustomed. In centers our reliability in identifying the beginning and ending of activity segments was high, and in schedule-conscious "closed" centers it was almost perfect. Homes were more complicated. An activity might start with a clear focus and then slowly turn into something else. For example: "Two children are watching *Sesame Street;* one goes and gets a book. The two combine watching and looking at the book. They add playful punching and eventually are rolling and play wrestling on the floor." In most centers television watching is supervised, and this behavior would have been stopped or the children would have been required to leave the television area. In homes many activities overlapped and ran together in ways that were markedly different from centers.

In centers our presence as observers made little difference, and the day progressed much as usual. In no instance was an observer coded as part of a center observation. The program of a home setting is much more flexible and can be altered to incorporate any new input. This flexibility made it hard for us to extricate ourselves from direct involvement in the activities of adults and children in home settings.

Some Differences in Social Grouping

Homes have small numbers of people compared to institutional settings for children. Homes also have more kinds of people. It was common to visit homes in which there was an infant, some preschool children of varying ages, school-age children, and adolescents. In addition, relatives and neighbors would drop in.

These differences in environmental dimensions were associated with more frequent control by children in homes over the initiation and termination of activities, the more frequent creation of super units, and increased frequency of adult interaction with children (Prescott, 1973).

The Purpose of a Home

The differences in environmental dimensions just cited led us to think more about the purposes of a home and how these found expression. Hayward (1978) identified nine purposes of the home on the basis of interviews with young people in Manhattan: (1) relationship with others, (2) social networks, (3) statement of self-identity, (4) a place of privacy and refuge, (5) a place of stability and continuity, (6) a personalized place, (7) a locus of everyday behaviors and base of activity, (8) a childhood home and place of upbringing, and (9) shelter and physical structure.

These functions of a home appear unarguable and serve as the context that directs behavior in homes. Thinking in this way helped us to organize some of the perceptions about events that occur naturally in homes.

Play. We often saw rich play in homes. Typically it was supported by the absence of interruptions (such as group time, outside time, and snack time) that end play in centers. It was also free from intrusion, often occurring in the privacy of a space chosen only by one child or a space that could accommodate best friends with few demands or rules about sharing with a group. Thus, the provision of privacy, a personalized place of stability, and the continuity of a home setting appeared to support play that had a particularly intimate, wholehearted, self-expressive quality. The play also incorporated the diversity of objects that can be found in home settings. Chairs might be turned into ships with children taking delight in the unique qualities of "their" chair. If a key or a pirate's cape was need it could be found. The availability of props and adult help in procuring them appeared to enhance the expression of self-identity in this play.

Conversation. In homes we often heard long, involved conversations between adults and children. The photograph on the dresser led to a long conversation about the caregiver's son and all the complexities of the correct naming of the son's wife and other relatives. Dogs, cats, and babies produced much sharing about behavior. Subjects such as why the mail carrier was late or who had what plans for the weekend were common. Good conversation was not often observed by us in group care. Jerome Bruner (1980) also commented on the lack of extended conversation in his studies of child care in England. The purpose of home settings as places of relationships appears to support conversation and the opportunities for children to eavesdrop on adults who are modeling complex conversational forms in ways not observed in centers.

The Logic of Everyday Activities. Much of what we have described seemed to rest on the presence of everyday activities, those concrete acts that make the purpose of a home visible. In centers the logic for behavior was often unclear or abstract. Children were taught about "community helpers" but rarely encountered them. In homes, children greeted the mail carrier, watched repairmen, and accompanied the adult on errands. At home the tasks of sorting, identifying, or counting were built around table setting, loading the dishwasher, or trying to separate important mail from advertisements.

Time and again in homes we watched caregivers explaining and inquiring about the context of an act. For example, a child comes in with new shoes and the caregiver might ask questions such as, "Did you get them on the way home or after supper?" "What store did you go to—the one in the mall or the one downtown?" "How come you bought tennies when you wanted sandals?" In centers, new shoes might well be a conversational event, but after the first exclamation of admiration the comments more often turn to comparing the kinds of shoes each child is wearing, perhaps in terms of color or style. Conversation in centers appears to focus on naming and categorizing: "Is this a vegetable? What color is it? What shape is it?" "Is this a kitten or a cat?" "Is the red ball bigger or smaller?"

One of the disorienting aspects of observing in homes was our inexperience in coding the kinds of conversations that evolved from questions like "What shall we have for lunch?" or "How come you look so different in that picture on the dresser?" or "Why does the tea kettle make that noise?" The answers to these questions led children to understand how the world works, how needs are met, how things change over time, and how much there is to know.

Even the kinds of matching and comparing that occurred in homes took on a more personal quality. One day we observed two children looking at kitchen appliances in a Blue Chip stamp catalogue and matching each type to those found in the kitchens they knew well. Another time we watched children carefully documenting the differences between two almost identical kittens.

Kitchens and Bathrooms. Another aspect of everyday activities is their focus on care and maintenance. Homes do not have meals delivered in uniform tinfoil packets unseen by children until they arrive at the lunch table. Children typically have access to the kitchen, its smells, and its unique opportunities to lick bowls and sneak a taste. Bathrooms are cozier and a bath is often part of a relaxing transition to naptime. Bettelheim (1974) has pointed out the importance of settings in which bodily needs are met. Kitchens, bathrooms, and sleeping places in homes were all visible parts of the round of everyday activities and were accessible for much more personalized use and play than is ordinarily permitted in institutionalized settings.

It took us a long time to conceptualize some of the differences that have just been described. The thinking seemed to push us toward a view quite different from the early-schooling emphasis that was emerging with the establishment of Head Start.

WHAT IS QUALITY IN CHILDREN'S ENVIRONMENTS?

After all this time, what have we learned about quality environments for children? One thing is that child-care centers are often woefully simple compared to naturally occurring environments such as homes and neighborhoods and the range of outdoor places that they provide. One way we have successfully helped adults to appreciate this fact is to ask them to remember places they liked as very small children. They recall, often with great feeling, the water play in the creek, the mudpies in the backyard, being in the kitchen smelling cookies in the oven, the climbing, and indoor and outdoor secret places. They also realize that these activities were self-chosen and often occurred without adult direction, quite unlike the teacher-initiated activities that occupy children in many group-care settings.

Another thing we have learned is that planned environments do not ordinarily permit children to become attached to places, things, or adults. It has become possible for children to grow up with little sustained contact with adults who are doing the mundane things that are a part of the everyday world, such as deep-frying fish, sharpening a knife, negotiating a bank loan, or selecting a ripe melon. The complexities of the everyday world have ordinarily been mastered by children through tagging along, watching and asking questions, and then absorbing knowledge by imitation and experimentation. Studies of artificial intelligence have found that computers can be programmed to perform many impressive intellectual tasks such as the diagnosis of disease, but they cannot be programmed to handle the everyday decision making that we call "common sense." As Waldrop (1984) has written:

> Mastery of common sense seems to consist of massive expertise about the world in general. Quite aside from the questions about knowledge representation and reasoning ability, building a machine with common sense means building a knowledge base containing millions of rules and facts—which is impractical in itself. (p. 1283)

It is the development of common sense that gives people a sense of belonging in the world and an ability to separate the important from the trivial. We must question whether the curriculum of child-care centers is adequate for developing such common sense.

A third lesson we have learned is the importance of imbuing physical settings for children with the sense of being in nature. Natural things have three qualities that are unique: their unending diversity, the fact that they are not created by people, and their feeling of timelessness—the mountain, river, or trees described in fairy tales and myths still exist today. These qualities would seem to show children a different reality from that of man-made articles. Pets or animals that children come to know often hold an important place in childhood memories. Learning to garden or to raise animals is the source for much metaphor about the growth process.

Despite the knowledge of children's affinity for the natural world and their delight in experiences with it, there is little interest in or commitment to providing these experiences. Kakar (1982), viewing American research on children from an Eastern perspective, has commented that "the natural aspects of the environment—the quality of air, the quantity of sunlight, the presence of birds and animals, the plants and the trees—are *a priori* viewed, when they are considered at all, as irrelevant to intellectual and emotional development" (p. 235). It is time to prove Kakar wrong by designing environments for children that incorporate natural things.

As yet, our attempts to design child-rearing spaces have, for the most part, been too narrow and timid. We think about climbing structures and child-size furniture, but we do not think about the total child-rearing environment and its ultimate purposes. We must keep in mind that it is not only a place of continuity and stability for children but also a place wherein adults can remember the enchantments of childhood.

REFERENCES

Barker, R. G. *Ecological psychology.* Stanford, CA: Stanford University Press, 1968.

Barker, R. G., & Wright, H. F. *Midwest and its children. The psychological ecology of an American town.* Evanston, IL: Row Peterson, 1954.

Bettelheim, B. *A home for the heart.* New York: Knopf, 1974.

Bruner, J. *Under five in Britain.* Ypsilanti, MI: High/Scope Educational Foundation, 1980.

Gump, P. The behavior of the same child in different milieus. In R. G. Barker (Ed.), *The stream of behavior* pp. 169–202. New York: Appleton-Century-Crofts, 1963.

Gump, P., & Sutton-Smith, B. Activity setting and social interaction. *American Journal of Orthopsychiatry,* 1955, *25,* 755–760.

Hayward, G. D. An overview of psychological concepts of home. In R. L. Bauer (Ed.), *Priorities for environmental design research* (part 2). Washington, DC: Workshop Summaries, EDRA 8, 1978.

Kakar, S. *Shamons, mystics and doctors: A psychological inquiry into India and its healing traditions.* Boston: Beacon Press, 1982.

Kritchevsky, S., & Prescott, E. *Physical space: Planning environments for young children.* Washington, DC: National Association for the Education of Young Children, 1969.

Nicholson, S. How not to cheat children: The theory of loose parts. *Landscape Architecture,* 1970, *62*(1), 30–34.

Prescott, R. *A pilot study of day care centers and their clientele.* Washington, DC: U.S. Department of Health, Education, and Welfare, Children's Bureau, 1965.

Prescott, E. *A comparison of three types of day care and nursey school home care.* Paper presented at the biennial meeting of the Society for Research in Child Development, Philadelphia, PA, 1973.

Prescott, E., & David, T. G. (1976). *The effects of the physical environment on day care.* Concept paper prepared for the U.S. Department of Health, Education, and Welfare, Office of Child Development, 1976.

Prescott, E., & Jones, E. *Group day care as a child-rearing environment.* Pasadena, CA: Pacific Oaks College, 1967.

Prescott, E., Jones, E., Kritchevsky, S., Milich, C., & Haselholf, E. *Who thrives in group day care.* Pasadena, CA: Pacific Oaks College, 1975.

Sherman, L. A. An ecological study of glee in small groups of preschool children. *Child Development,* 1973, *46,* 53–61.

Waldrop, M. The necessity of intelligence. *Science,* 1984, *223,* 1279–1282.

Weinstein, C. S. Modifying student behavior in the open classroom through changes in the physical design. *American Educational Research Journal,* 1977, *11,* 249–162.

Chapter 5

The Institutions in Children's Lives

MAXINE WOLFE AND LEANNE G. RIVLIN

INTRODUCTION

This chapter is a reflection on 15 years of work focused on children in institutional environments, including schools, psychiatric facilities, and day-care centers.* We have attempted to understand the relationships between the stated goals of a particular place; the administrative, educational, and therapeutic programs developed to attain these goals; the physical, social, economic, and political environments in which these programs were implemented; and the eventual impact on the lives of the children housed within them. On the basis of our work, we have tried to extract generalizations concerning the child–environment relationship. In doing so, it has been impossible to ignore the powerful developmental implications of such places, especially their socializing power for children.

Development and Socialization

Except in a metaphysical sense, one cannot be without being in some place. The physical environment, the social structure within which it is

*Many students and research staff members in the Environmental Psychology Program of the City University of New York have contributed to our work including Marian Golan, Marilyn Rothenberg, and Arza Churchman. For more detailed descriptions of the research see Golan, 1978; Laufer & Wolfe, 1977; Proshansky & Wolfe, 1974; Rivlin, Bogert & Cirillo, 1981; Rivlin & Rothenberg, 1976; Rivlin & Wolfe, 1972, 1979; Wolfe, 1975, 1977, Wolfe, 1978; Wolfe & Golan, 1976.

MAXINE WOLFE AND LEANNE G. RIVLIN • Environmental Psychology Program, Graduate Center, City University of New York, New York, NY 10036.

embedded and which it supports and reflects, as well as its symbolic meanings determine to a large extent the kinds of experiences children have and what they learn about the world. The *content* of development—children's lived experiences, both material and social—cannot be separated from the *structure* of development. In this sense, all of child development, including cognitive development, involves socialization (Ingelby, 1974).

Since children learn about themselves through learning about the world, within a society the physical environments in which they grow up communicate messages to them about who they are now and who they can and should be in the future. Where one grows up, for example, on a particular "side of the tracks," not only creates a difference in the material reality of the child's daily life, it has symbolic meaning as well. Places and their descriptions within a society connote a set of images, values, and meanings about people which influence their development and their sense of themselves.

Through the socialization process, children internalize the normative social order, both its physical and social aspects. We do not subscribe to a deterministic theory of socialization. That is, although the goal of the socialization is clear, the socialization process is far from complete, especially in a heterogeneous society. Alternative views and possibilities can provide sources of support for deviation from the expected or acceptable. However, adults control the material and social conditions of children's lives. Children's access to alternatives is severely constrained and often serendipitous. Thus, their understanding of the world, their sense of themselves, and their competence will largely reflect the relationship between the dominant values and the extent to which they can realize these values within the reality of their lives.

Institutions as Agents of Socialization

The most dramatic change in the lives of children in the United States over the last 150 years has been that larger portions of their days and lives are spent outside of their home environments and, often, outside of their communities. A series of *institutions* and the laws governing their use have become the main agents of socialization.

The term *institution* has many meanings. We use it to designate social/physical settings that perform certain tasks deemed necessary in our society to insure the integration of people into the dominant culture. The names of these places designate their function and the group of people who are housed there, for example, orphan asylum or training school for delinquents. The development of these types of societal institutions in this country began in earnest in the early nineteenth century. Since the mid-1800s they have focused increasingly on children. In this chapter we examine two contemporary institutions for children, schools and residential psychiatric facilities.

The functions performed by these settings, education and dealing with deviance, once were the responsibility of kinship groups and community. One consequence of the transfer of these functions to institutions was the division of the child's life into separate and specialized components. The settings dealing with each of these parts have specific goals, some explicit and some implicit. These originate from perceived or presumed political, economic, and social needs translated by laws and other governmental mandates (including standards) as well as by a cadre of professionals. We have found that what happens on a day-to-day basis often bears little relation to the stated goals and instead reflects various implicit goals. Furthermore, although most of these settings remain physically separate from one another, within the last 75 years an institutional system has developed, linking them in direct and indirect ways.

Some of the actors in the institutional system are aware of, accept, and shape these implicit and unstated goals. Others are aware of the goals, though they do not always accept them or shape them, and indeed may see their role as changing them by working within the institutional system. Still others, perhaps the vast majority, are aware neither of these implicit goals nor that what they do on a day-to-day basis heavily reflects them. It is not our purpose to indict the individual administrator, psychiatric nurse, aide, or teacher. Indeed, it has become clear that much of the behavior of specific persons within the institution, whether children or staff, is not individually based. In this chapter, we will focus on the institutional *system* and its implicit goals as they are reflected in the daily lives of the children.

We began by looking at the physical environment as one of the components of the institutional system. The physical environment is only one part of the institutional environment. The political, economic, and social environments within the institution as well as that of the society within which the institution is imbedded have a tremendous impact on what occurs day to day. "Wars on poverty," Sputnik, White House conferences on children, and professional licensing are among the factors that have shaped both the social and physical form of the institutional environment affecting children's daily experiences within them.

Furthermore, institutional environments have a history in the United States. The reasons why children were moved out of their homes and the ways in which institutions developed are complex. Changes in the economy, the political context, and the structure and role of the household and its members in our society are important aspects of the explanation. These changes shaped conceptions of appropriate child development as well as attitudes toward child care and responsibility toward children, and ultimately the types of institutions, their physical and social forms, that were developed as agents of socialization.

In order to understand the goals and structures of contemporary institutional environments, their role as agents of socialization, and contemporary efforts at institutional change, we begin by considering the history of their development and the values, attitudes, and physical forms they have inherited. Then we describe the qualities shared by contemporary institutional settings and the ways in which they attempt to socialize children to specific values and behavior. This analysis reveals the type of unstated goals shared by these settings and their continuity with their historical predecessors. Finally, by evaluating our own attempts at change we will integrate historical and empirical research in terms of the challenges posed to those concerned with institutional changes and child development.

HISTORY OF INSTITUTIONS

An examination of the history of settings for learning and deviance adds more than color and background to a picture of children's institutions. It is central to understanding the structure and intent of the institutions we are analyzing as well as their resistance to change.*

Settings for Learning

There are various explanations for the development of schools and for the major turning points in the United States public educational system—the Common School reforms beginning in 1880, the Progressive education movement beginning late in the nineteenth century and continuing through the first 30 years of the twentieth century, and the more recent focus on open education, open admissions, and compensatory education. Some explanations focus on the changing economy, from agricultural to industrial to corporate, and society's need to produce the type of work force needed for it (Bowles & Gintes, 1976). For example, the development of separate vocational and academic high schools during the Progressive era (and the use of intelligence testing to ensure that students would attend a school appropriate to them) was based on grounds that each race, class, and sex should be prepared for their eventual role in the work force and in society (Nasaw, 1979). Other explanations stress the social control function of education, citing its use by those in power to insure a stable policy in the face of political and social unrest (Takanishi, 1978). Common School reformers, for example, felt that their schools were a way to insure that those who had won the vote would learn to use it properly and that children from the poorer classes with weak minds and morals would benefit from contact with the more affluent, whereas the children of the affluent would learn about their advantages and responsibilities. Each would be schooled for their position within society and for working together for the common goal (Nasaw, 1979).

* Space limits for this paper preclude the breadth and depth of historical analysis we should like to provide here. For a detailed analysis of the history of the form and functioning of children's psychiatric facilities, schools, and day care centers see Rivlin & Wolfe, 1985.

Educational changes also have been explained as an attempt by some to realize American ideology, especially the ideal of equal opportunity (Cremin, 1961; Butts & Cremin, 1953). Horace Mann and other Common School reformers believed that education would help the poor gain access to America's economic prosperity (Nasaw, 1979). Progressives argued that if middle-class values were brought to the immigrant ghetto, poor children would be able to reach toward the economic benefits that the American middle class already had (Rothman, 1980). Yet, reformers were not the only shapers of the educational system.

In the early part of the nineteenth century, most of the urban poor did not send their children to the charity schools. To survive, these schools changed their names to "public schools" and attempted to attract middle-class families. Although Progressive reformers pushed for the development of a high-school system that would segregate students by economic class into vocational or academic schools, the lack of support and resistence by students, parents, and unions produced instead the "comprehensive high school" (Nasaw, 1979). In recent decades, such movements as school desegregation, community control of schools, and open admissions have largely been the result of grass roots initiation and support from the U.S. minority community.

Although efforts at change and resistance by those most impacted by the educational system have had some effect, they have not altered its basic structure. Irish immigrants attempted to resist reform efforts to place their children in common schools (Bowles & Gintes, 1976), but compulsory education laws backed up by threats to incarcerate children in newly developed "houses of refuge" eventually meant that they had to comply. The comprehensive high schools, the compromise solution that was demanded by communities, did not eliminate the "tracking" of students.

By the last quarter of the nineteenth century, the modern school system much as we know it now was the norm in the urban Northeast. Katz (1971) asserts that by 1890 American public education had most of the structure common today; it was free, universal, compulsory, and supported by taxes but was also bureaucratic, racist, class-based, and, we might add, sexist.

The changes occurring between 1865 and 1930 reflected and created differing concepts of children and by implication of their families and their role in American society. Social and economic factors, including massive immigration, growth of the urban population, the employment of immigrants as low-paid factory workers, and severe economic depressions led to massive strikes and militant movements demanding economic and social justice. The corporate and governmental response to these conditions and movements was the use of force and economic regulation. The Progressive "child-saving movement" developed as a social parallel (Platt, 1977; Rothman, 1980).

Progressive reformers worked closely with business interests to secure the passage of laws and to finance the development of institutional systems. Many reformers were genuinely concerned with the horrible conditions in which immigrants lived, yet their remedies as well as their perceptions of the problems were clearly biased by their condescension towards the immigrants and their belief in the American system as proven by their own success. They felt they had to prevent children from following in the footsteps of their "ignorant" parents, and although many reforms began as arguments for the rights of children and the obligations of society they ended as obligations of children and their caretakers (Rothman, 1980; Takanishi, 1978). Progressives fought for the extension of compulsory schooling statutes because they would ensure children a "fair chance in life." They linked the child's right to education to child-labor reform and compulsory education was considered to be the "best child-labor law" (Takanishi, 1978, p. 15). By 1918 every state had a compulsory education law; yet it was not until 1938 that child-labor legislation was passed.

Many reform efforts used the environmental conditions of schools as justification for their programs and advocated structural changes to match what they said were new goals. Lancasterian schools, introduced to serve poor urban children during the early 1800s, were based on scientific arrangements of classrooms. Schoolrooms were set up in a hierarchical fashion, the teacher seated above the students on a raised platform while students sat at desks arranged in long rows. These were perceived as inexpensive and efficient means for teaching large numbers of children and compelling them to internalize respect for authority, a characteristic deemed necessary for their future work in factories (Nasaw, 1979).

Horace Mann used the poor physical conditions of existing one-room school houses to advocate building common schools. Progressive-era reformers passed legislation removing control of the schools from local communities by arguing that physical conditions of existing schools, including overcrowding and poor sanitary conditions, were evidence of the ignorance of immigrants and local residents. It was during this time, 1865–1930, that most of today's schools were built. In keeping with the spirit of scientific management prevalent at the time (Haber, 1964), factory concepts were applied with a focus on efficiency, and designs using corridors and separate entrances for girls and boys emphasized orderly movement patterns and arrangements (Nasaw, 1979).

Liberal school reformers across historical periods claimed three functions of public education in the United States: (1) integrating youth into their various roles as required by a changing economy as a way of ensuring the social continuity of life, (2) equalizing extremes of wealth and poverty by allowing equal opportunity, and (3) promoting psychological and moral development and therefore personal fulfillment. According to Bowles and Gintes (1976), the results of such attempts have been equivocal. Education has not led to economic mobility nor has it eliminated differences in the income of groups based on class, race, or sex (Bowles & Gintes, 1976; U.S. Bureau of Census, 1981). Nor can we claim that schools have promoted psychological development or personal fulfillment for the majority of those attending (Glasscote, Fishman, & Sonis, 1972). It is the integrative function of our educational system that continues to predominate as our own work will demonstrate, and the physical environment supports and reflects that function.

This point is illustrated in changes occurring in the last 20 years. Public education in the 1960s and 1970s must be examined in light of a number of events: the Supreme Court desegregation decision of 1954, the self-criticism following the Russian initiation of outer-space flights, the middle-class prosperity of the 1960s, "white flight" to the newly developed suburbs, the promise of equal opportunity of the war on poverty and the great society, the emergence of "flower children," consumerism, revolts in black urban communities, and the catastrophic consequences and protests that accompanied the war in Vietnam.

In the case of education, the 1960s have been viewed, on the one hand, as a period of educational experimentation and openness. The post-World War II "baby boom" along with suburban expansion and the development of new areas of the country led to a tremendous increase in school construction and heavy local investment in buildings. The schools constructed reflected some degree of architectural and programmatic variety. Open-space schools and informal education were part of this experimentation. The formality of schools changed as codes for dress and behavior disappeared in the wake of the impact of the counter culture. On the other hand, this was only a temporary period of expansion and openness, a time of educational optimism following extensive pressure by United States minority groups for equal opportunity. In elementary schools, the primary experiment was compensatory education programs, and for a very short period of time in some urban areas there was community control of schools. Many of these programs have been discontinued or remain in very limited form.

Open-design schools that appeared during this period were less a philosophic commitment than a matter of cost and expediency. The educational model, as it had developed in England, stressed a child-centered approach to learning that emphasized flexible grouping of students, individualized instruction, open access to learning materials, and the use of all available spaces (rooms, corridors, and outdoor areas) to support interaction, group projects, and manipulation of materials. Although this philosophy has been applied to all kinds of old and new buildings, the open-plan school theoretically represented its translation into a physical form. However, in the United States open plans were adopted as architects and local school boards recognized their cost efficiency over buildings with partitions. They also became symbols of "modern" school design and were widely adopted. In most of these schools, the open architecture was not accompanied by informal or "open" teaching. In contrast, some attempts were made to institute informal or open education into school buildings that were traditionally designed (Silberman, 1970). Over the years there has been considerable disillusionment with both approaches and a return to more traditional forms and programs (Ross & Gump, 1978).

In the current conservative political atmosphere and in the wake of budget cuts for education and other social programs, the optimism and the spirit of new forms and ideas that characterized the 1960s and 1970s have receded. There has been a strong move back to "basics," an emphasis on reading, writing, and mathematics skills and a move to reduce costs by eliminating all but the bare essentials. In the United States this occurs in a context in which enrollment at private schools is increasing, tax credits for tuition are being suggested, and many public schools, especially but not exclusively in urban areas, are serving largely poor or minority populations. Despite the introduction of new physical forms and programs, the main values underlying the educational system have not changed.

Settings for Deviance

Over the last 150 years, health-care clinics, day-care centers, and programmed recreational facilities accommodated increasing numbers of children. As children have come progressively more in contact with these environments, another set of institutions has developed for those judged to be unable to peform well in these settings. The definitions of deviance in children have varied with the social, political, and economic context. As the definitions changed, so, too, did the methods and places of treatment (Wolfensberger, 1972; Magaro, Gripp, & McDowell, 1978), but the definers of acceptable and unacceptable were those with power—generally the white middle and upper classes.

The first inpatient psychiatric treatment facility for children did not open until 1923. Where were troubled children prior to 1923?

> Children affected with what we would describe today as neurotic and psychotic illness were (prior to this century) variously labeled through the ages as "possessed," "wicked," "guilty," "insubordinate," "incorrigible," "unstable," "maladjusted," and "problem children" roughly in this order. (Despert, 1970, p. 28)

Prior to the nineteenth century in this country, poverty was considered evidence of deviance. State and church authorities could remove children from their parents for "neglect" since "It was presumed . . . that those who had not the 'moral character' to raise themselves out of poverty similarly lacked the qualities needed to rear their children" (Nasaw, 1979, p. 10). Children were "placed out"—apprenticed to other households as unpaid labor. Children of debtors remained with their families in almshouses and workhouses (Bremner, 1970). Other deviations from religious morality were treated with ridicule and shunning and many persons, including children, were put to death for being "evil" and "possessed by the devil" (Bremmer, 1970). The predominant institutions for children, relatively few until the 1880s, were orphan asylums.

With rapid industrialization and immigration (especially of Irish) during the early 1800s, and as Common School reforms were being instituted, the expansion of orphan asylums and the development of houses of refuge took over the problem of poor white children who did not go to the schools or who were otherwise found to be "disobedient" or "neglected." By the early 1850s, as the first compulsory education legislation was passed, the largest proportion of inmates were "foreign born." Most were Irish and entered as truants (Rothman, 1971; Nasaw, 1979; Shultz, 1973). But it was believed that these children were malleable. If they could be taken away from their corrupting environments and taught respect for authority through order, they could be returned to mainstream society (Rothman, 1971).

Refuges were built outside the community in isolated places. Children lined up and marched everywhere and the day was totally regimented. Boys labored in shops; girls cooked, cleaned, and mended. Children slept in locked cells, approximately 5 feet × 7 feet, and rules of silence were imposed during work periods and during the night. The monotony of routine was mirrored in the architecture, bare-brick structures of unvarying design. As the refuge expanded, additional wings were built, enhancing the blandness and imposing qualities. There were grading systems and punishments, ranging from loss of food or recreation to whipping and solitary confinement. Despite these conditions, the rhetoric of "family training" was used to describe the programs. While white immigrants were being sent to houses of refuge for their deviance, Native American children were removed from their communities and placed in mission schools to educate them to a set of values different from those of their communities, which were considered "basically deviant."

Explanations and categories of deviance have changed from this time period to the present and new institutions have been developed to match the new definitions, but the basic structure of institutions has not altered. What has happened over time has been the creation of a *system* of institutions, one being used as a back up sanction for the others, reaching larger numbers of children for a longer part of their lifetimes.

This system also began during the Progressive era. The development of social sciences was a turning point. College-educated reformers focused on gathering "objective facts" to find the causes of problems, discover the solutions, and persuade legislators to change laws. Reformers proposed to deal with each offender as an individual, believing, as many do today, that the institution should exist along with other programs but as a last resort. As educational reformers were developing high schools as a solution to the problems of adolescent employment and unemployment, reformers concerned with deviance used G. Stanley Hall's ideas of development and adolescence, as well as the techniques of psychological testing. They created the juvenile court system which, through probation, was supposed to avoid institutionalization. Yet, the main impact of this system was to create a new institution, the state training school, which brought increasing numbers of adolescents into the institutional system (Rothman, 1980). By defining deviance to include activities such as drinking, being sexually active, going to dance-halls and movies, and staying out late, these so-called reforms blurred the distinction between "delinquent" and "dependent" children (Platt, 1977).

These Progressive reforms did not eliminate problems within low-income, immigrant communities, and after World War I psychological explanations of deviance gained ground. Success as well as failure, in the decade of the "self-made man," was an individual phenomenon (Levine & Levine, 1970). Freud's ideas as well as those of Watson and Gesell gained ground. "If mental conflict was the root of the problem then social conflict was not. It was sex, not capitalism, it was images, not reality" (Rothman, 1980, p. 57). The decade from 1918 to 1928 was very significant in creating the children's institutional system we have today.

Backed by government conferences on children (Rosen, 1968) as well as laws, the question of emotional disturbance was separated from both delinquency and retardation, at least in a conceptual sense. Outpatient clinics were developed and researchers focused on "healthy, normal development." Parents, schools, and social agencies were to bring to these clinics children who showed "disturbing or otherwise puzzling behavior" (Glasscote *et al.*, 1972) focusing on preschool children between the ages of two and five who employed "undesirable methods to cope with their problems" (Rosen, 1968, p. 299). Services increased dramatically; in 1919 there were 11 such clinics (Glasscote *et al.*, 1972); by 1930 there were 300 (Castel, Castel, & Lovell, 1982). During the early part of the Progressive era, most of the cases had been referred from juvenile courts and were working-class and lower-class children. However, during the 1920s, clinics became increasingly professionalized, with staffs, including social workers, trained in psychiatry, using verbal therapy, and often requiring participation of the parents. With the shift away from community to a focus on the individual child and its parents, the cases which were seen as suitable were self-referred middle- and upper-middle-class groups. The "hard-core" cases, children of the working and lower classes, were now perceived as needing a different kind of treatment, one that could not be provided on an outpatient basis.

Since the 1920s residential treatment for these children has developed in two major ways (Glasscote *et al.*, 1972). One was the "psychiatrization" of existing institutions (Castel *et al.*, 1982). The other was the development of new services, first at large hospitals such as New York City's Bellevue Hospital which opened a unit in 1923, followed by similar units in the pediatric departments of large medical schools such as Johns Hopkins and Stanford (Rosen, 1968).

Correctional institutions presumably adopted psychologically oriented philosophies and programs (Rothman, 1980). However, the reality was different from the ideology. There were no programs to fit the diagnostic results, and vocational training consisted of kitchen or farm work. Assignment by classification to cottages was impossible because of severe overcrowding (Rothman, 1980). Facilities of this type have continued to the present day. Children's incarceration in a correctional facility as opposed to a mental-health facility was based less on their perceived deviance and more on the availability of facilities in the geographic area, admission policies, stated philosophy of care, and financial ability (Ohlin, 1973). Yet, it is questionable whether inpatient psychiatric services for emotionally disturbed children, developed during this same time period, provided a better alternative.

The purpose of new inpatient facilities also was to treat children who could no longer live in the community (Glasscote *et al.*, 1972). Beginning with the 1930s, the term "emotionally disturbed" was used (Despert, 1970) and research was stressed as a way of obtaining basic knowledge about child mental health, especially comparative studies of "well-adjusted" and "maladjusted" children. The formation of the American Academy of Pediatrics in 1931 and funding, through the child-welfare provisions of the Social Security Act in 1935, enabled the implementation of these ideas as the Depression continued (Rosen, 1968). Between 1940 and 1950, spurred on by the numbers of soldiers found to be unacceptable for military service during World War II for "neuropsychiatric reasons" (Castel *et al.*, 1982), there was an increased development and application of mental-health concepts to research on home, family, and institutions. This research stressed the role of early experience in the infant's future emotional makeup and ways of acting and feeling (Rosen, 1968). Despite studies such as Spitz's (1945) documenting the detrimental effects of institutionalization, increasing numbers of children were sent to residential treatment (Beyer & Wilson, 1976). The focus became developing *proper* institutional environments rather than eliminating them.

During the late 1940s and continuing into the 1950s and 1960s, the migration of minorities into urban areas and the Civil Rights and Black Liberation movements pushed poverty into the forefront as a central social issue. However, "poverty came to mean not merely the lack of resources, but rather a condition of deprivation in which [among other things] psychic imbalance took a terrible toll on a large number of cases" (Castel *et al.*, 1982, p. 72). Environmental explanations led to official rhetoric and laws focused on replacing the institution with *community* mental-health centers. Yet, the number of inpatient children's psychiatric units and residential treatment centers grew dramatically. By 1976 there were 20 state mental hospitals devoted exclusively to children, and by 1972 three times as many young people were admitted for treatment than in 1955 (Castel *et al.*, 1972). The notion of community inherent in the ideal of community mental-health centers did not do away with residential treatment any more than did the Progressive era reforms. Rather, it helped to consolidate existing services and to add new ones, creating large conglomerates, often decentralized—a consortium of places under one administration (Glasscote *et al.*, 1972).

From the 1950s through the 1970s, the reasons for institutionalization varied but were no more clear than those for children placed in correctional institutions. Our own research indicates that although the rhetoric changed, the daily reality remains depressingly similar to early institutions. Now there are "quiet rooms" or "time-out" rooms rather than "seclusion" or "isolation" rooms. The institution is called a "school" or a "center." The use of drugs has become widespread both within and outside of the institution. Grading systems and punishment remain, though physical punishment is less often reported. Still retaining the legacy of the Progressive era, each service provides a backup for yet another service, although now the entire system is centrally coordinated through federal funding and regulations. The outreach begins at an early age with the psychological screening in some states of all children in school to detect predelinquent or adjustment problems (Castel *et al.*, 1982).

Despite the ideology of "normalization" and deinstitutionalization developed in the 1970s, there has been little impact on children's psychiatric facilities. Indeed, one children's psychiatric hospital we studied, which was far below its capacity in 1969–76, now has more resident patients than it ever did, despite the fact that it is now part of a comprehensive community health center.

The rhetoric still focuses on creating "homelike environments." Yet, Rothman's comments concerning the training schools during the Progressive era seem just as applicable today:

> Why was it that the cottages were anything but homelike? Because the inmates had to be kept under firm control, because the fear of disorder ane escape was the nightmare that dominated the institutions. The rules of silence, the dormitory with the light on, the general rigid tone of daily life, *were not just random preferences on the part of the staff, but a way of keeping guard, of insuring control,* [italics added], of fulfilling the ultimate requirement of the training schools, that is, to confine its charges securely. (Rothman, 1980, p. 283)

THE NATURE OF CONTEMPORARY INSTITUTIONAL ENVIRONMENTS

Contemporary institutions vary along a number of dimensions. Some are private, others public; some are large, housing from a few hundred to a few thousand, others small, housing as few as 10. Some are considered *partial,* whereas others are called *total,* their categorization depending on whether or not they encompass the child's entire day and the extent to which they act as the sole agent legally responsible for the child. This chapter focuses on public institutions. Although the stereotype of the public institution is that it is large and impersonal, public as well as private institutions vary along these dimensions. The distinction between a public and private institution is not sharp since public tax monies often are used to support private institutions. We did not select public institutions because they are the worst institutions we have studied. We have concentrated on public institutions because they represent the clearest picture of societal goals since their programs, curricula, physical forms, and staff positions are most clearly mandated by government policies, whether on the state, local, or federal level. We also chose public institutions because they deal with the largest number of persons, particularly those with the least choice.

The distinction between partial and total institutions is ambiguous. The lives of children who spend any part of their lives in total institutions, for example, residential psychiatric facilities or centers for the developmentally disabled or even community-based residential facilities, will be profoundly shaped by these agents of socialization. They will be largely cut off from their households and communities, and their daily lives will be controlled by others. They will have little exposure to an alternative way of life and little power to affect changes. Yet, most children spend large portions of their daily lives in settings that share certain commonalities with total institutions. These are partial institutions such as schools or day-care centers. Children do not freely choose to spend time in such places and their parents' choices are limited. Schooling is compulsory and in most school systems caretakers cannot influence policy or daily program. If children do not adhere to rules of behavior they can be suspended or expelled, referred for psychological treatment, or moved to special schools and institutions. If their caretakers are judged to be failing to follow rules, they can be identified as neglectful and subject to various forms of institutional control including having their children removed from their care. The institution to which the child is sent does not necessarily provide a better alternative. Thus, calling an institution partial obscures the less obvious power such institutions as schools and day-care centers can have over the lives of children and their families. For the same reason we do not distinguish between more restrictive and less restrictive settings. Here we stress the qualities shared by institutions and the common messages they are giving to children.

The Quality of Daily Life and Its Experiences

Every institution that we have studied is striking in the routinization of daily life and lack of variety and change in both the physical qualities and activities. Despite differences in type of children, neighborhoods, or purpose of the facility, daily life is an unvarying series of events taking place in an endless repetition of similar spaces, built into an unvarying time schedule, all defined by some outside power. All aspects of life are structured including the physical environment, the activities within the setting, and the time frame within which they occur. This is most apparent in residential institutions wherein children must wake up at a scheduled hour every day of the week, eat meals at set times, and go to sleep at the same hour whether they are tired or not. These routines are backed up by a series of sanctions and punishments, including the use of drugs and physical isolation. Yet, the quality of the environment and of the time children spend in public schools is very similar. Though sanctions and punishments may be milder, this is not always the case. For example, drugs have been used in public school situations, most notably for children considered to be hyperactive (Brown & Bing, 1976).

The overriding goals of these institutions take precedence over children as people. Within the psychiatric institution everything is couched in therapeutic terms. Play is considered "recreational therapy," painting is "art therapy." As activities the goal of which is more than being simply part of life, special spaces and specially trained personnel are required. In psychiatric institutions we have studied it was rare to find art materials, table games, or even reading material in children's living areas since these activities took place in special places in special circumstances. Within schools, education is the prevailing theme all day. The child is seen less as a developing person and more as a student. Cooking is a way of teaching measurement to the youngest children rather than an enjoyable or valuable activity in itself. Along with block building, it disappears from the physical space as well as the curriculum as education becomes the more serious business of schools, usually by the second grade.

Little time or space belongs to the child. In children's psychiatric facilities we studied the one or two hours of unprogrammed time were not actually free. Children had to remain in a specific space limited in resources and potential activities. Nor were single bedrooms private. There were limits on what children could do in the bedrooms, and they could not control the access of others. Furniture was identical and there was little room for personal belongings other than a wardrobe unit. Cinderblock walls made it difficult for children to put anything on them and wall decorations were large-scale graphic designs painted by strangers. Although children in schools spend a portion of their days outside the school context, which could be considered free, much of their time within the institution is also programmed and the space restricted. The only personal spaces were desks, cubbies, and coat closets. Yet, children did not have free access even to these, and restrictions were placed on what could be kept in them. The classroom belonged to the teacher, who arranged the furniture and equipment and set the rules for use. Whether in open or traditional schools, the furniture arrangements did not change. Informal arrangements were quite static over the course of several school years. Teachers determined which materials were available and what was to be displayed on the walls. The orderly arrangements of wall decorations and their placement at adult-level sight lines made it clear that this was not the children's space.

The structuring of the day, routinization of time and activities, and adherence to overriding goals provide children few opportunities for serendipity. Spontaneity is not valued; it is viewed as impulsivity, as disruptive to ongoing plans, and as expendable in light of more important educational goals, even at very young ages. Although we may want to believe we have progressed, the attitudes, goals, and socio-spatial organizations are remarkably similar to those that existed 100 years ago. When describing the recent implementation of all-day kindergartens in New York City public schools, one principal said:

> "We believe in structure. Even at the possibility of damaging a student's spontaneity, we think structure is important. We intend for the child to recognize school as serious business." He said this was particularly important in neighborhoods such as Bedford-Stuyvesant [an economically diverse black neighborhood]. "Many of our youngsters come from unstructured home backgrounds, so school is the only place for them to get any structure." (Purnick, 1983, p. B1)

Control and Authority

One of the clearest, yet most unquestioned, examples of an institutional routine designed to provide structure is "lining up." It is rationalized as a necessary component of the ongoing program, as a method of making nonfunctional transition time as efficient as possible. In psychiatric facilities, children line up before and after every activity. After they wake up, they line up for showering; then they line up to go to the dining room for breakfast. They line up in the dining room to obtain their food, and they line up after eating to go back to their living areas. After a short while, they line up to go to their first activities of the day. In schools, students line up in the yard or basement before going to their classes; they line up within their classrooms even when they are going a short distance down the hall. They line up before and after lunch to go to the cafeteria and to the school yard and to reenter the school. In most lining-up situations children are expected to behave in a totally self-controlled manner even when they are compacted into a small space within a group. Children are required to remain lined up behaving appropriately for as long as it takes for this to be done properly by all involved.

Given its frequency in the institutional setting and the focus placed on it by those in authority, lining up carries more significance than the activity it leads to or from. The primacy of order and obedience is clear. The ubiquitousness of corridors, the legacy from the efficiency movement, symbolizes the emphasis on orderly movement of bodies from one place to another. Once long corridors exist, the free movement of children is further curtailed. Going somewhere distant and out of view leads to the suspicion of problem behavior. In schools, passes are issued to verify the legitimacy of the child's freedom of movement and to confront children who are breaking the rules.

In our observations we have seen numerous instances of demands that children be obedient, even when the imposition seemed patently arbitrary. We have observed 15 children in a psychiatric facility expected to line up to leave a playground within three minutes of being asked to do so, when they had no access to a clock or watch. We have seen school children told to undertake a project as a group and being reprimanded for talking. In each of these instances children were punished for failing to adhere to an impossible standard in a physical environment which provided no support for the expected behavior. Children in school were told to sit or stand in corners facing the wall or were sent for counseling; children in psychiatric hospitals were placed in seclusion rooms or confined to their living quarters for the entire day wearing their pajamas. These were not isolated instances in harsh institutions, but methods for disciplining children that staff perceived to be reasonable.

The assumption seems to be that if authority is not exercised and if obedience is not required children will behave in ways that are totally out of control. Although this is most obvious in the psychiatric facilities, where the labeling of children reflects the expectation of an imminent "blowup," it also underlies much of the behavior in school where at earlier and earlier ages children are referred for counseling and categorized as behavior problems. The focus on delinquent children has expanded to include the notion of *predelinquent*. Predelinquents commit no criminal offense but they can be sent to specialized schools or for special services because they "evidence a premature assertion of personal autonomy and defiance of adult authority, control and directions" (Ohlin, 1973, p. 181). One of the ways of insuring obedience to authority and exercising control is through constant surveillance.

Public versus Private Experience

Life in an institution, whether it is partial or total, is public. The concepts of publicness and privacy taught in these settings serve the purpose of the institution rather than aiding the development of the child. In the psychiatric hospital, dressing, undressing, and showers were done in groups, also as a public experience, often with no doors or shower curtains to preserve privacy. Children's behavior was often called inappropriate, especially in regard to expression of sexuality and dealing with bodily functions. It is difficult to understand why the publicness of these activities was not perceived as possibly contributing to the perceived problems. From our work the explanation seems to be that surveillance becomes the overriding goal even when it is unstated, unnecessary in functional terms, and when the outcomes contradict the stated therapeutic goals.

In psychiatric hospitals there is another distorted view of privacy. Although children are expected to share their feelings with everyone and are granted no time or space in which to be alone, privacy can become connected to being out of control. When the staff feels that children have lost control, the usual procedure is to place them in the seclusion rooms or confine them to their bedrooms while other children are in activities. In schools, another contradictory message is transmitted. In the service of fostering of group socialization, children are required to share materials and are reprimanded for failing to demonstrate a group spirit of cooperation. On the other hand, real success in school is based on examinations and grading children's individual performance. Children are taught to hide their work, connecting privacy to the protection of intellectual productions. Often this is rationalized as a means of assessing children's progress, but the unwillingness of school systems to adopt other systems of evaluation implies that there must be another rationale for continuing current practice.

In every one of the settings we have studied, the schools, the day-care centers, and psychiatric hospitals, children have virtually no time or space that is not prescribed by adults or to which adults can be denied access. Often liability is cited as a reason for such surveillance. Such views are part of the problem we are discussing. The quality of children's experiences are determined by laws and issues of liability which themselves reflect institutional values and goals rather than children's capabilities and needs.

Children are expected to learn to respect the privacy of adults but are not given examples of adults respecting their privacy. Yet there is considerable evidence that without such modeling the social-physical environment of institutions supports what then is defined as inappropriate behavior (Knight, Zimring, Weitzer, & Wheeler, 1977). The lack of access to privacy reflects the surveillance ethic deemed necessary to ensure control, the often unstated goals of institutions.

The physical environment alone tells you little about whether or not children can actually achieve privacy or escape surveillance. Our research documented situations in which children were not allowed out of the eye range of teachers in open-education classrooms where spaces supposedly had been set up to support individual and small-group work. Specially built lofts or partitioned areas were described as appropriate for quiet work or as supporting privacy, but teachers decided when and by whom these could be used. One teacher, who proclaimed her commitment to open education, suggested using mirrors placed high on walls as a way of observing children while they were working in interest areas hidden from her view. The director of one psychiatric hospital worked hard for several years to find funds to add doors to bedrooms. Yet, once they were installed the rules required that they be open when bedrooms were in use. Children were discouraged from remaining in the rooms unless placed there as punishment. Oddly enough, when they were involuntarily confined to their bedrooms or left alone in the seclusion room which had hard concrete block walls, the safety and liability issues seemed to disappear.

Privacy is so antithetical to the institutional goal of order, control, and enforced sociability, and is so impossible to achieve by ordinary means in the normal course of events, that children's attempts to seek out privacy are defined as a problem. Children in schools who find privacy by daydreaming are called inattentive or disinterested. Children in the psychiatric facility who choose not to interact socially at a time selected by the staff are described as withdrawn.

Labels are not insignificant. Those who apply them have the power to determine the fate of the children as they become part of children's permanent records, stigmatizing them well into the future (Rist, 1970).

Independence and Conformity

Although most children's institutions cite as their goal the development of independence, albeit in the context of sociability, there is a fine line between independence and unruliness from the staff's view. Any granting of independence usually is a result of the child's overall conformity to the goals of the setting and is a privilege given to those who obey. Although administrators describe to outsiders the access to a variety of places and resources, suggesting freedom of choice, we have found severe limitations placed on children that reveal the relationship between conformity and independence. In the psychiatric hospital there were many outdoor recreation areas and a variety of indoor community spaces. However, children were never found in these spaces. In one place, an inner court, for which we had several thousands of observations recorded, the only use in six years was for parts of five days by a young girl who was placed there by staff. The indoor nonresidential spaces were only used during program times, and an observation tour would raise the question of "Where is everyone?" as we would pass an empty gymnasium, an empty olympic-sized pool, an empty game room, an empty music room, an empty library, an empty auditorium, and corridors devoid of people. Children were led in groups by staff people from program activity to program activity. Their freedom of movement, aside from program times, was based on a grading system, with a trip to the local shopping area the ultimate reward for complete obedience, a privilege obtained by few.

Our observations of open-education classrooms, with stated philosophies of independent movement and individualized programs, revealed a very limited use of available space despite complaints by teachers of crowding. Teachers wanted the students to be within view, a contradiction to children's freedom, especially since teachers were observed to be more or less stationary in their location. The children who were considered trustworthy were given the freedom to go outside the classroom as they performed errands. For others the pass to the bathroom provided the only relief from surveillance. The stereotypic image of the open classroom as one of independent action was not justified by our observations.

In each of these settings, independent behavior is freedom granted when there is a fair degree of certainty that the child will not deviate from the norm, and a series of back-up actions in the event that they do deviate. Such programmed independence hides conformity from view.

What Are Children Learning in Institutions?

As in the past, contemporary institutions for children are guided by the same set of dominant values that defines appropriate and inappropriate behavior. Despite the variety of class and racial and ethnic backgrounds of children, institutions are teaching children and judging them by a set of criteria reflecting the status quo and designed to maintain it.

Children learn that the overriding purpose of daily settings is functional—there are places to prepare for schooling, places to learn, and places to receive therapy—and these purposes prescribe the range of appropriate behavior in that place. Life is a series of planned and timed events defining human needs rather than responding to them. Children are rewarded for individualism rather than individuality, for conformity rather than community. Although children are not always consciously aware of the complicated nature of this thinking, the message they receive is that behaving properly is paramount. Those children whose families or community styles mesh with this value and the defined proper behavior will find it easier to comply and will be rewarded, although we would question the price paid for adherence to this limited set of goals. For children whose communities and families have values and ways of life that run counter to those of the institutional system, the message is that left to their own devices or to their families and communities, their behavior would be inappropriate and unacceptable (Silverstein & Krate, 1975). Experiences with learning, nurturance, and personal support in their communities are not valued and are often judged by the institution to be inadequate or inferior. Initially this may create confusion, but for most children it is quickly replaced by the internalization of the values of the institution to judge their families and communities.

In these institutions the children who are rewarded are those who do not challenge authority, those who are compliant. Children are learning that life is structured by others who, by virtue of their age and position, have the power to make decisions. In effect, children are taught to be passive rather than active creators of their own lives and experiences.

Earlier we acknowledged that attempts at inculcating children with dominant values do not produce uniform responses. Giroux (1983) has discussed the fact that children often make attempts to resist this imposition. Our research has indicated that there are some children who manage to maintain a sense of themselves and of the institution despite pressure to do otherwise. For example, when we asked one 15-year-old girl in a psychiatric institution how this place compared with her home, she described her life outside the institution:

> I can go outside and play instead of being locked up in a cage over here. I can go outside and take a walk, go wherever I want to go; I can just open doors with no problem. I can close it. But this place—you can't do nothing. There's no locked doors in my house—there's no quiet rooms in my house.

When she was asked how she would change the hospital she said:

> It would be run with some strictness to it but not that much, because I don't think it's right for them to say what time you gotta be in, what time you gotta be out like they're your trainers or something, where you have to do what they say. You have your own mind and you do what you want to.

Yet, most children do not have as clear an image of the institution or of themselves and are unquestioning, passive, and compliant in the face of the power of others. Those children, such as the girl quoted above, who do challenge authority often find themselves, as she did, punished for their awareness. Their punishment then sets an example for other children of the consequences of resisting the institutional system.

Our observations in many institutions over many years document the overriding imposition of institutional norms resulting in institutional patterns of behavior backed up by sanctions for deviation. Much like Barker's (1968) behavior settings, these patterns persist despite changes in population, showing the limited impact that any one individual or set of individuals can have on the institutional environment. The stability of these patterns despite changes in verbalized philosophy and physical design is a powerful indicator of overriding institutional goals and their impact on children's lives.

Changing the Institutional Environment

Though much of our work in children's institutions was focused on discovering the reality of daily life, we also tried to play a more active role in changing the quality of children's experiences in these places. We worked with teachers to clarify the relationship between their stated educational goals and their behavior in the classroom, including ways in which the physical environment impeded or aided what they said they were trying to accomplish. In the psychiatric hospital we undertook several projects aimed at changing conditions that supported institutional practices we believed to be detrimental to the children. One such experience concerned the redesign of a room in the children's psychiatric hospital.

Over the course of our observations in this institution we found that children had very little privacy of any kind. They were given few, if any, opportunities to be physically alone. Attempts to achieve physical privacy were devalued and seen as inappropriate and antisocial. In interviews children expressed the need for a place to be alone or with another person. When a room in the common social space of the apartment units became vacant we convinced the administration to allow us to work with the children to create a private space. We tried to use a participatory design and planning process wherein we were facilitators and the children were planners and constructors of the space, out of our conviction that changes should not be imposed on children and that they should be active participants in planning for their own needs. We also hoped to reveal to the hospital staff that the children were capable of participating, challenging the assumption that they were incompetent.

The planning process we were allowed to implement was much different from the one we had envisioned. We were required to have a staff member present at meetings and were limited to working with the older children. Residents could not be involved in the construction and furnishings had to be selected from a state-approved supplier.

Despite these constraints, the planning sessions addressed the needs of the residents in a realistic and participatory manner. Two teams of adolescent residents separately planned the conversion of a small room in each of their units into a space they saw as being suitable to their expressed needs. It was to be a place in which an individual or a few people could comfortably sit, read, or talk in private. The residents were able to work within the financial, spatial, and institutional constraints. They discussed their images for the room, its functions and rules for use and upkeep. These discussions made it clear that some were aware of the discrepancies between staff's and adolescents' aesthetics and definitions of space, attempts by the administration to have control over the process, and fears that the redesigned space would create difficulties because surveillance of residents would be problematic.

The rooms that were created were in dramatic contrast to the rest of the hospital, although they would not qualify for design awards and were modest by virtue of a limited budget. A red color scheme was selected independently by each of the groups, in sharp contrast to the subdued pastels throughout the rest of the building. Instead of the cold plastic and vinyl, easy-care, hard finishes in the rest of the building, the residents selected soft, upholstered furniture and thick carpeting. When a staff person suggested that a painted wall mural might be a good addition, there was a strong shout of disapproval and one boy summarized the feelings of the group as he called out, "No hospital art!" Wood panelling and small, soft throw pillows completed the decoration.

Research done several months after the renovation revealed that both staff and residents felt that the rooms worked very well. Over time they continued to be well maintained with reasonable adherence to the rules that the residents had established.

The rooms served as a reminder of the possibilities of an alternative way of imaging life in that place. The name that was given to one of the rooms by the children was the "Red Room," emphasizing its contrast to the rest of the institutional environment. In these ways this project was highly successful. Yet, despite the success of the planning process, the outcome, the continuing use and maintenance of the room, and our own observation data to the contrary, staff said that the children who used it were "more in control," thus leaving their categorization system intact, failing to acknowledge that children's behavior could be a function of the environment rather than internal pathology. Some years later when we returned to the hospital, we found that both rooms had been dismantled. When the state required an on-unit space for record-keeping, it was the Red Room that was considered expendable, perhaps because it had been viewed as a luxury all along.

THE PROSPECTS FOR POSITIVE INSTITUTIONAL CHANGE

Through our attempts at making changes in institutions, the continuity of past and present institutional environments became clear, both in terms of their qualities and their goals. Those concerned with altering institutional environments often are unaware of their history, of the efforts made by others to change institutions, why they have made these efforts, and the results. We accept a whole series of assumptions about the goals and outcomes of such change as well as about the institutions and the children they serve.

Yet, the act of change can either be a potent mechanism for revealing what is hidden or can obscure underlying issues and support a continuation of the status quo. Recognizing this is especially important for those engaged in environmental change. Administrators can point out evaluation efforts or physical changes as signs that the children's lives are being improved, whether or not this is true. Often, the rationale given for efforts at change or evaluation is the belief that whatever is done must be making things better and that what we are doing is in the best interests of the children. Yet, it is important to take a critical stance in order to avoid a technocratic role (Knight & Campbell, 1980).

It is very easy to recommend changes that paint over serious problems or temporarily hide them from view. A case in point is reflected in a quotation from Carrie Smith, who suggested that to support individuality children needed their own rooms and a place for their possessions, a position echoed in contemporary physical design suggestions as a solution to the institutional qualities of children's psychiatric facilities. Smith held a view that some would consider "radical" even today. She said that "without such provisions we give *humane* treatment, as we do with dogs and cats, the while they are yearning for *human* treatment. Eliminate the "e" from humane and you have helped to eliminate the reformatory" (cited in Rothman, 1980, p. 265). However, the attempts of Smith and other Progressive reformers to eliminate the reformatory by altering its physical environment led to the institutions we have today.

It is more difficult to make changes that address the values behind the institution and that would, at the very least, challenge those values if not change them. This approach requires questioning the assumptions that are made about children and their needs and the ways in which these are translated into institutional goals and physical forms. Our role in institutional evaluation and change requires that we understand that institutional environments themselves, whether they are schools, day-care centers, or hospitals, have a history within any culture that shapes their form and function.

Furthermore, every place has its own life history. For example, the children's psychiatric hospital in which we worked was originally designed without any place to isolate children. In fact, the philosophy of care inherent in the design emphasized the need to deal with the child directly at any moment of crisis rather than deflect the behavior or isolate the child. This aspect of the program and design was presented to us as a radical departure from traditional methods. Yet, within one and one-half years after opening, an office in each of the living units was converted into a seculsion room. The room was 6 feet by 10 feet, devoid of anything save a mat on the floor, and had a door, with a peephole for surveillance, which could be locked from the outside. Within a short time a bedroom in each apartment was made into a seclusion room, providing one seclusion room for every 10 children. A great deal of time, effort, and money went into the design and construction of these new rooms. Carpeting was placed on the walls and floors to prevent children from injuring themselves. Thus, although initially it was the absence of a seclusion room that indicated the progressive attitude within this institution, eventually it was the safety precautions within these spaces that were used as evidence of their concern for children. It is important to know that over the course of these years the incidence of aggressive behavior observed, during hundreds of hours of systematic observation, had not increased and could not be used as justification for the proliferation of these spaces. The power of the institution allows it to have an unquestioned rationale for its functioning.

In acknowledging the resistance of institutions to change, one possible conclusion that could be drawn is that it is pointless to continue making those attempts. Another approach that has been suggested is the concept of "radical reform" (Gartner & Riessman, 1974; Riessman & Gartner, 1970). It is based on the premise that if the changes we seek to institute challenge the core values of the system, they have an impact far beyond the usual reform efforts. For example, creating a planning and design process in which children participate and make decisions challenges the image of children as being incapable. It also has the possibility of empowering them, helping them see themselves in ways different from the institution's view. Working with those who will be most affected by change, rather than with those who control power in the institution, is another alternative (Forester, 1980).

Using our understanding of history to reflect critically on our experience in institutional settings, we have the possibility of creating alternatives that foster the healthy development of children. Without such reflection, we can only continue the status quo.

REFERENCES

Barker, R. G. *Ecological psychology: Concepts and methods for studying the environment of human behavior.* Stanford, CA: Stanford University Press, 1968.

Beyer, H. A., & Wilson, J. P. The reluctant volunteer: A child's right to resist commitment. In G. P. Koocher (Ed.), *Children's rights and the mental health professions* (pp. 133–148). New York: John Wiley, 1976.

Bowles, S., & Gintes, H. *Schooling in capitalist America: Educational reform and the contradictions of economic life.* New York: Basic Books, 1976.

Bremner, R. H. *Children and youth in America; A documentary history* (Vols. 1–3). Cambridge, MA: Harvard University Press, 1970–1974.

Brown, J. L., & Bing, S. E. Drugging children: Child abuse by professionals. In G. P. Koocher (Ed.), *Children's rights and the mental health professions.* New York: John Wiley, 1976.

Butts, F. R., & Cremin, L. A. *A history of education in American culture.* New York: Holt, Rinehart & Winston, 1953.

Castel, R., Castel, F., & Lovell, A. *The psychiatric society.* New York: Columbia University Press, 1982. (Translated by A. Goldhammer.)

Cremin, L. A. *The transformation of the school.* New York: Knopf, 1961.

Despert, J. L. *The emotionally disturbed child: An inquiry into family patterns.* New York: Anchor Books, 1970.

Forester, J. *What are planners up against? Planning in the face of power. Working papers in planning.* Ithaca, NY: Cornell University, 1980.

Gartner, A., & Riessman, F. *The service society and the consumer vanguard.* New York: Harper & Row, 1974.

Giroux, H. A. Theories of reproduction and resistance in the new sociology of education: A critical analysis. *Harvard Educational Review,* 1983, *53,* 257–293.

Glasscote, R. M., Fishman, M. E., & Sonis, M. *Children and mental health centers: Programs, problems, prospects.* Washington, DC: Joint Information Service of the American Psychiatric Association and the National Association for Mental Health, 1972.

Golan, M. B. *Children in institutional settings: Privacy, social interaction, and self-esteem.* Doctoral dissertation, City University of New York Graduate School, 1978.

Haber, S. *Efficiency and uplift: Scientific management in the Progressive era, 1890–1920.* Chicago, IL: University of Chicago Press, 1964.

Ingelby, D. The psychology of child psychology. In M. P. M. Richards (Ed.), *The integration of a child into a social world.* London: Cambridge University Press, 1974.

Katz, M. *Class, bureaucracy and schools.* New York: Praeger, 1971.

Knight, R. C., & Cambell, D. E. Environmental evaluation research: Evaluator roles and inherent social commitments. *Environment and Behavior,* 1980, *12,* 520–532.

Knight, R. C., Zimring, C. M., Weitzer, W. H., & Wheeler, H. Social development and normalized institutional settings: A preliminary research report. Amherst, MA: Environment and Behavior Research Center, Institute for Man and Environment, University of Massachusetts, 1977.

Laufer, R., & Wolfe, M. Privacy as a concept and a social issue: A multidimensional developmental theory. *Journal of Social Issues,* 1977, *33,* 22–42.

Levine, M., & Levine, A. The more things change: A case history of child guidance clinics. *Journal of Social Issues,* 1970, *26* (3), 19–34.

Magaro, P. A., Gripp, R., & McDowell, D. J. *The mental health industry: A cultural phenomenon.* New York: John Wiley, 1978.

Nasaw, D. *Schooled to order: A social history of public schooling in the United States.* New York: Oxford University Press, 1979.

Ohlin, L. E. Institutions for predelinquent or delinquent children. In D. M. Pappenfort, D. M. Kilpatrick, & R. W. Roberts (Eds.), *Child caring, social policy and the institution* (pp. 177–199). Chicago, IL: Aldine, 1973.

Platt, A. M. *The child savers: The invention of delinquency* (2nd ed.) Chicago, IL: University of Chicago Press, 1977.

Proshansky, E., & Wolfe, M. The physical setting and open education: Philosophy and practice. *School Review,* August 1974, *82* (4), 557–574.

Purnick, J. How to teach kindergarten: The debate is on. *New York Times,* July 5, 1983.

Riessman, F. & Gartner, A. Community control and radical social change. *Social Policy,* 1970, 53–60.

Rist, R. C. Student social class and teacher expectations: The self-fulfilling prophecy in ghetto education. *Harvard Educational Review,* 1970, *40* (3), 411–451.

Rivlin, L. G., & Rothenberg, M. The use of space in open classrooms. In H. M. Proshansky, W. H. Ittelson, & L. G. Rivlin (Eds.), *Environmental psychology: People and their physical settings.* New York: Holt, Rinehart & Winston, 1976.

Rivlin, L. G., & Wolfe, M. The early history of a psychiatric hospital for children: Expectations and reality. *Environment and Behavior,* 1972, *4,* 33–72.

Rivlin, L. G., & Wolfe, M. Understanding and evaluating therapeutic environments for children. In D. Canter & S. Canter (Eds.), *Designing for therapeutic environments: A review of research.* London: John Wiley, 1979.

Rivlin, L. G., & Wolfe, M. *Institutional settings in children's lives.* New York: John Wiley, 1985.

Rivlin, L. G., Bogert, V., & Cirillo, R. Uncoupling institutional indicators. In A. E. Osterberg, C. P. Tiernan, & R. A. Findlay (Eds.), *Design research interactions: Proceedings of the Twelfth International Conference of the Environmental Design Research Association.* Washington, DC: Environmental Design Research Association, 1981.

Rosen, G. *Madness in society: Chapters in the historical sociology of mental illness.* Chicago, IL: University of Chicago Press, 1968.

Ross, R., & Gump, P. V. Measurement of designed and modified openness in elementary schools. In S. Weidman & R. Anderson (Eds.), *Priorities for environmental design research* (pp. 243–253). Washington, DC: Environmental Design Research Association, 1978.

Rothman, D. J. *The discovery of the asylum: Social order and disorder in the New Republic.* Boston, MA: Little, Brown, 1971.

Rothman, D. J. *From conscience to convenience: The asylum and its alternatives in progressive America.* Boston, MA: Little, Brown, 1980.

Shultz, S. *The culture factory: Boston public schools 1789–1860.* New York: Oxford University Press, 1973.

Silberman, C. *Crisis in the classroom: The remaking of American education.* New York: Random House, 1970.

Silverstein, B., & Krate, R. *Children of the dark ghetto: A developmental psychology.* New York: Praeger, 1975.

Spitz, R. A. Hospitalism: An inquiry into the genesis of psychiatric conditions in early childhood. *Psychoanalytic Study of the Child.* (Vol. 1, pp. 53–74). New York: International Universities Press, 1945.

Takanishi, R. Childhood as a social issue: Historical roots of contemporary child advocacy movements. *Journal of Social Issues,* 1978, *34* (2), 8–28.

United States Bureau of the Census Current Population Reports, Series P-60, No. 127. *Money income and poverty status of families and persons in the United States: 1980 (Advance data from the March 1981 current population survey).* Washington, DC: U.S. Government Printing Office, 1981.

Wolfe, M. Behavioral effects of group size, room size and density in a children's psychiatric hospital. *Environment and Behavior,* 1975, *7,* 199–224.

Wolfe, M. Environmental stimulation and design: For the "different who are not so different." In M. J. Bednar (Ed.), *Barrier-free environments.* Stroudsberg, PA: Dowden, Hutchinson & Ross, 1977.

Wolfe, M. Childhood and privacy. In I. Altman & J. Wohlwill (Eds.), *Children and environment: Advances in theory and research.* New York: Plenum Press, 1978.

Wolfe, M., & Golan, M. B. Privacy and institutionalization. Paper presented at meetings of the Environmental Design Research Association, Vancouver, BC, 1976. New York: City University of New York, Center for Human Environments, Publication #76-4.

Wolfensberger, W. The origin and nature of our institutional models. In R. B. Kugel & W. Wolfensberger (Eds.), *Changing patterns in residential services for the mentally retarded.* Presidential Committee on Mental Retardation. Washington, DC: United States Department of Health, Education and Welfare, Social and Rehabilitative Services Administration, 1972.

Part III

Designing Spaces for Children

Chapter 6

Designing Settings for Infants and Toddlers

ANITA RUI OLDS

INTRODUCTION

No adult can fail to be moved by the remarkable receptivity to experience of infants or toddlers engrossed in play. Invitations from every element in the environment fill children with wonder, encouraging them to indulge their senses and to explore the limitless motoric capacities of their bodies. Young children live continuously in the here and now of experience, feasting upon nuances of color, light, sound, odor, and touch, unfettered by adult demands to pursue goals, use time well, or respond to someone else's expectations. Their responses to the environment are immediate and inseparable from the sources of stimulation around them.

It is, therefore, illusory and potentially harmful to assume that an environment for infants and toddlers can be neutral. Environments are potent purveyors of stimulation, information, and affect, and infants and toddlers, in particular, are sensitive to all the qualitative aspects of a setting: its movements, sounds, volumes, textures, visual and kinesthetic vibrations, forms, colors, and rhythms. As the Hindus claim, "Sarvam annam [everything is food]." Thus, in the same way that we intentionally design a "habitat" for a person going to the bottom of the sea or to outer space, so too must we consciously create the infant–toddler habitat, to honor the critical role that

ANITA RUI OLDS • Anita Olds and Associates, Consultants, Environmental Facilities for Children, 10 Saville Street, Cambridge, MA 02138, and Child Study Department, Tufts University, Medford, MA 02155.

physical facilities play in nourishing native awareness and evolving capacities for assimilation and response.

Adults must recognize that infants and toddlers are highly sensitive to the appearance and organization of their surroundings and can think in terms of physical landmarks and bodily cues. For example, Acredolo and Evans (1980) have shown that if infants pass a window on their left while going down a hall, they will look for it on their right on the return trip. As infants go from sitting to crawling to walking to running, they have to figure out how to get from one place to the next and back again. They use environmental cues for navigating (voices, landmarks, boundaries, shapes, and mass), for understanding what is socially appropriate in different spaces and for determining which places are safe and which insecure. Although infant responsiveness to events at a distance emerges gradually, cognitive development is optimized when children are assisted to make predictions about how events, objects, and people around them will behave. Some of this predictability is clearly related to the characteristics, organization, and design of space.

Traditionally, environments for infants and toddlers have been mapped onto settings designed for adults. But infant and toddler development is optimized when the *entire* physical space is "sculpted" as a landscape to support child and caregiver activities. The room's shape and volume, its floors, ceilings, walls, and all its horizontal and vertical surfaces can be seen as interactive surfaces to which children are responding and from which they receive information and, one hopes, comfort and stimulation.

This is particularly important when the infant–toddler environment is intended for handicapped children who have an even greater need for support and sustenance from their physical surroundings. Here, environmental design can be crucial. Indeed, experience has shown (Olds, 1979b) that a physician's pessimistic diagnosis can be changed when infants grow within varied and stimulating environments responsive to their attempts at mastery and control.

The families of handicapped children also require similar considerations, since the child's lack of responsiveness may inhibit parental efforts to initiate play and stimulate the children in normal ways. Ideally, settings for handicapped infants and toddlers should be inviting, nonclinical places in which parents are helped to establish reasonable expectations and goals for their children's development and can receive training in the types of stimulation required. In addition, an infant–toddler center can help families assuage their often negative and unproductive feelings by promoting familial interaction, joyful experiences, and mutual-support resource groups. The presence of an art room or workshop which encourages the self-expression of every family member will also help each to feel personally fulfilled and gratified and there will be more energy and enthusiasm to support the needs of the handicapped child.

In 1974, I was a member of a team of educators commissioned by the Massachusetts Department of Mental Health to design an Infant/Toddler Family Creative Play Center as a state demonstration facility (see Olds, 1979b). Many of the environmental supports described in this chapter are derived from this experience of designing a setting for families with high-risk children under three. However, the chapter addresses the needs of both handicapped and able youngsters. It begins by establishing criteria for facilities that support the needs of both children and caregivers, provides strategies for shaping the environment, and describes some custom-designed facilities to stimulate each reader's creativity and inventiveness.*

ENVIRONMENTS THAT ASSIST CHILDREN'S DEVELOPMENT

Piaget (1963) called the first period of intellectual development the *sensorimotor stage,* during which infants deal with experience primarily through their senses and the capacity to move their bodies in space. Sensations and movements, rather than thoughts and plans, fill infants' awareness and stimulate their capacities for feeling, receiving, and responding. The environment, therefore, should be designed not only to support function, but also to nourish the child's sensory and aesthetic sensibilities. Specifically, environments for children under 3 years must encourage complete movement and exercise of all limbs and all aspects of mobility and be sensorially rich and varied.

Environments That Encourage Movement

When an organism shows any sign of motion, it is considered alive. When it moves easily, in accordance with its own structure, it is healthy and functioning well. Motion permits an organism to locate itself freely in space, assume different body postures, create its own boundaries, have access to diverse territories, manifest power, and fulfill its potential. Thus, motion is a manifestation of the body's wellness and is essential for its growth and the maintenance of its integrity.

Research with normal and premature infants demonstrates the importance of movement. For example, premature infants raised on water mattresses—a surface akin to the womb environment, which amplifies and provides feedback for every motion—have been found to mature significantly faster than premature babies raised on standard static crib mattresses (Burns, Deddish, Burns, & Hatcher, 1983). Clark, Kreutzberg, and Chee (1977) report that preambulatory normal infants 3 to 13 months old, exposed

*Portions of this chapter have been adapted from Olds, 1979a and 1982, with the permission of the publishers.

to mild semicircular canal stimulation two days per week for four weeks, showed a significant improvement in gross motor skills related to the prone and supine positions, head control, sitting, creeping, standing, and walking. There is also some suggestion of improved hand-to-mouth coordination as a result of the interventions. The authors hypothesize that vestibular stimulation facilitated maturation of the vestibuloocular reflex which enables the eye to maintain a stable retinal image during head movements. The more stable the retinal image, the more rapidly motor involvement with the environment can develop.

The ideal environment affords infants and toddlers frequent opportunities to learn to move and to learn by moving and stimulates a full range of movements for body control, object control, and control of self in space: sitting, swaying, crawling, bouncing, running, climbing, jumping, grasping, bending, and turning. It conceives of all surfaces, and the entire ambience, as an invitation to move in ways that give motoric capacities their fullest reign within safe and tolerable limits. Since most disabilities restrict rather than increase children's capacity to interact with their environment, handicapped children should be given even greater encouragement than able children to move about and to exercise fully whatever minimal abilities they possess. Items particularly suitable for developing gross motor skills at this age include air mattresses; water mattresses; foam- and air-filled wedges, bolsters, and seats; mats for rolling and tumbling; low balance beams; ladders that can be adjusted to different angles; 3-inch to 12-inch-high risers to climb and crawl over; bean bag chairs; rocking chairs; horizontal nets; foam boxes, swamps, and cushions; soft net chairs and hammocks; swings; slides and ramps; and swivel seats or rotating platforms for vestibular stimulation.

Research by Held and Bossom (1961) and Held and Hein (1963) suggests that adequate development depends upon self-induced experiences that give learners feedback about the consequences of their actions upon materials and their own movements through space. Thus, it is important that all exercise be performed by the individual child, regardless of ability, on an active rather than passive basis. Growth requires taking risks, doing, failing, redoing, and succeeding, as well as protection and safety, even for infants and toddlers.

Environments That Move and Stimulate the Senses

One can conceive of bodily movement on a continuum from observable gross bodily activity to inner states of sensory awareness. Although the inner movement is difficult to discern, the senses must themselves move and must receive changing stimulation from the external environment in order to function. The eyes "see" by virtue of scanning a visual field but are reduced to "blindness" when forced to stare at a stationary image. The ears hear when sound waves strike and vibrate the ear drum. Changes in air currents under our noses reveal odors that go undetected in static, enclosed spaces.

As organs designed to detect *changes* in stimulation, rather than to monitor constant input, the senses function on the basis of environmental movement. If the movement involves dramatic fluctuations in stimulation level, however, this can be frightening and disorienting. Instead, the senses will maintain optimal levels of responsivity if confronted with rhythmic patterns of predictable sameness combined with moderate diversity, what Fiske and Maddi (1961) refer to as "difference-within-sameness." Such subtle changes in stimulation occur frequently in the natural world; wafting breezes, babbling brooks, glowing hearths, and the odor of a pine forest are sources of solace and rejuvenation for children and adults alike. These moderate variations in sensory stimulation help maintain optimal levels of mental and physical alertness and foster feelings of comfort and playful attitudes toward events and materials.

Biofeedback studies seeking to alleviate tension in adults (Benson, 1979; Samuels & Samuels, 1975) affirm that restful, natural settings envisioned by the mind's eye produce meditative states and reduce the physiological effects of stress. But to envision a healing setting as an adult means that one must have experienced such a place and felt its soothing influence. The earlier in life and the more often such environments are experienced, the more likely it is that the stress of modern life will not take its negative toll later on. Lack of a regular relationship with nature may, in fact, be a major reason why urban inhabitants, including young children, experience stress adversely. If something as seemingly minor as an increase in negative ions in the air can "cure" allergies, headaches, dizziness, depression, and asthmatic attacks (Pihlcrantz, 1984), then how much more powerful must be light and sound waves, minerals in water and a sea breeze, and the organic compounds in sand and earth for the harmonious functioning of human beings?

The difference within sameness exquisitely present in nature must be experienced directly by children, so when weather permits the outdoors should be the primary playscape. Ideally, every infant–toddler space should open directly onto a covered and uncovered play area. Since outdoor play is not always possible, the presence of natural elements within interiors should be given great attention. Windows to natural light, ideally a good deal of sunlight, are essential. If vistas to lawns, trees, and sky are impossible, window boxes filled with evergreens in winter and geraniums in spring would provide some relief. Moderately expensive structural changes such as balconies, porches, courtyards, window wells, lowered windowsills, windows which can be opened, greenhouses, and clerestories all assist in providing vital links between the indoors and outside.

An ideal play environment varies stimulation for all the senses. Colors, shapes, patterns, window views, and gradations of light attract the eye.

Music, voices, and laughter provide a congenial auditory backdrop, while aromas of cookies baking, fresh flowers, and powder help define the essence of a place. Opportunities to taste and touch should be present as well.

Of the five senses, touch is the most neglected in nonresidential settings for children. Yet Montagu (1971) suggests that touch is the most critical sense for children under 3 years and for children with special needs because the skin is the largest organ of the body and is therefore a vital source of stimulation. Ayres (1973) has evidence that increased tactile and somatosensory stimulation improves perception of form and space in children with learning disorders. Prescott and David (1976) argue that degree of softness (as defined by 11 components) was predictive of the quality of a day-care center program, reflecting the responsiveness of the environment to the child on a sensual-tactile level and the willingness of staff to give children freedom of choice. Thus, textured elements, such as pillows and cozy furniture, and malleable and messy play materials, so often deemed luxuries in child-care settings, may in fact be critical developmentally, therapeutically, and aesthetically.

The senses are also aroused by moderate variations in physical space: scale (small and large spaces, areas for privacy and groups, and furniture for adults and children); floor height (raised and lowered platforms, lofts, and pits); ceiling height (canopies, eaves, trellises, and skylights); and boundary height (walls, half-height dividers, and low shelves). Sensory variety is further enhanced when unique, separate places for engaging in particular activities are created. In fact, the success of many child-care settings is often proportional to the number and variety of types of spaces that can be created within the four walls of the room (Prescott & David, 1976). Thus, there should be places that are warm, cozy, and comforting, others that are hard, sterile, and isolated, places that are dark and light, large and small, noisy and quiet. Varied minispaces prevent boredom, disinterest, and discomfort by enabling children to seek out activities and levels of stimulation appropriate to their own moods, needs, and levels of arousal at different points in the day.

The power of light as a major source of stimulation for the senses merits special mention since, next to movement, it is the variable most sorely neglected by interior-design practices. Natural light changes continuously. Light enables us to experience the passage of time, to estimate the time of day, and to enjoy an implicit form of variety as our perception of objects and spaces changes under different conditions of illumination. It provides motion, difference within sameness, variety, information, and orientation. Moreover, according to Wurtman (1975, 1982), "it seems clear that light is the most important environmental input, after food, in controlling bodily function." Research (Gruson, 1982) has shown that lights of different colors affect blood pressure, pulse and respiration rates, brain activity, and biorhythms. In the past decade, baths of blue light have become standard treatment for the cure of neonatal jaundice, ultraviolet light is used to cure psoriasis, and fluorescent light in conjunction with photosensitizing drugs is widely used to heal herpes sores.

Research with adults (Ott, 1973) suggests that the tendency for people to spend increasing hours behind windows and windshields, in front of television and display terminals, and under the partial spectrum of fluorescent bulbs affects the incidence of a large number of diseases. What appears to be required is that full-spectrum light enter the eye and strike the retina, thereby influencing the pineal gland's synthesis of melatonin. This in turn helps determine the body's output of the neurotransmitter serotonin. Thus, time spent outdoors (if only for naps—as practiced by the Scandinavians, who bundle babes in snowsuits and blankets and set their carriages outside regardless of the weather), as well as the presence of daylight streaming through open windows, may be critical to a child's health and overall development. Ideally, no space without windows should be used for child care. Sadly, the younger or more disabled the individual in this society, the more likely he or she is to be placed in settings lacking access to natural light.

To help reduce disturbances caused by inadequate exposure to the near ultra-violet and infra-red ends of the spectrum, full-spectrum bulbs, which approximate the range of wavelengths provided by sunshine, should replace standard fluorescent and tungsten bulbs (Hughes, 1980, 1983; Spivak & Tamer, 1983). Artificial interior lighting should also be balanced to complement the natural light entering through windows by employing a variety of lighting forms: general-ambient, task-specific, floor, desk, ceiling, wall. Reflected-light fixtures mounted on walls, to wash light down a wall and up over a ceiling, are superior to overhead fluorescents as a means of simulating the experience in nature of being surrounded by light.

ENVIRONMENTS THAT ASSIST CAREGIVERS

Children must move in order to grow, but the constant and often unpredictable movement of infants and active toddlers can be annoying to adults, who try to restrict the movement by introducing rules, withdrawing materials, and reducing the territory available for action. Since motion is more apparent in small spaces and makes space feel more congested, it is frowned upon even more when square footage is limited, a frequent occurrence in the "found" spaces utilized for infant–toddler centers.

Caregivers have legitimate concerns for the safety of young children with limited coordination and no understanding of danger, especially if the child has a special need. But restricting movement cuts off development at its source and may contribute to behavioral and learning difficulties later in life (Ayres, 1973). Moreover, constraints, prohibitions, and inadequate environmental supports can do little to inhibit a child's intrinsic need to move and perform. Infants fidget when they cannot get out of highchairs. Toddlers crawl and climb incessantly, oblivious to the height and nature of the climbing surfaces. Infant–toddler centers must be designed to allow infants and toddlers sufficient freedom to move expansively and safely, while reducing stress on caregivers.

The Floor

In homes, when infants are not strapped in infant seats or cribs, they are placed on floors, on wide beds, or in playpens. Infants require broad horizontal surfaces which accommodate them and adults comfortably without the need for boundaries or with boundaries that are quite distant. Toddlers, on the other hand, need plenty of opportunity to roam freely, over moderate changes in level that offer some challenge to their balancing and walking skills. The ideal toddler environment, a "corralled open range," is an expansive, undulating horizontal surface, larger than that for infants, with clearly defined boundaries. Adults can best relate to infants and toddlers by being with them at floor level or by placing them on limited horizontal surfaces less than 36 inches high (i.e., adult counter height).

If the center of the space is the room's floor, while changes in level and more enclosed spaces are placed at the perimeter, visual and auditory communication from the room's center to the periphery is unobstructed. Adults can then move quickly to the periphery for any child needing attention, and children are able to "keep an eye out" for caregivers as they roam and explore space. Depending on height and transparency, boundaries to these areas on the perimeter should be designed as play and sitting surfaces.

The center space, if kept open and reasonably free of tables, chairs, and adult furniture, can function as a hub or changing stage set to encourage spontaneous, playful activities in which everyone participates. Here, younger babies might receive special attention from adults, and portable equipment, such as mats, swings, parachutes, and air mattresses (stored elsewhere), can feature different play experiences at different times.

Changes in Level

Because toddlers have an almost insatiable need to exercise their walking and balancing skills by climbing and crawling over surfaces of different heights, an environment designed as an "up-and-down scape" with subtle changes in level can support the safe, spontaneous, and continual repetition of this behavior. Each level should be three to six inches high (7.6 to 15 cm) and at least 12 inches (30.5 cm) deep. Platform and level changes can also be used for quiet resting and cuddling. Wavy floors, waterbeds, ramps, "swamps" of bean bag pellets and foam of varying density, horizontal net

FIGURE 1. A room designed as a series of levels incorporating a waterbed culminates in a see-through balcony (upper left) overlooking activities outside the room.

climbers, mats, and mattresses, built into the levels, will challenge balance, coordination, and traversing skills (see Figure 1). Changes in level must allow for an easy, connected flow from one activity to the next and must afford the child a perspective, an interaction, or access to something that would not be available if the child remained in one place. Although changes in level appear to be fixed, they can be part of a "kit" of modular components that are rearrangeable.

Raised surfaces two to five feet (0.6 to 1.64 m) above floor level should not be eliminated solely on the grounds of safety because they exercise limbs and provide the child with a bird's eye view (comparable to the adult's perspective) that is vital to cognitive mapping of the world (see Figure 2). Platforms at three feet high (.9 m) enable caregivers to handle children comfortably and relate to them at eye level, but do require secure boundaries.

Ideally, boundaries should be no higher or more solid than is required to prevent a child from falling. Determining the height and depth of boundaries is especially difficult for a combined group of infants and toddlers. The bounding risers of "play pits" make good crawling surfaces for toddlers and should be kept to a height of 12 inches (30.5 cm). As the floor level rises, boundaries, must, through either height or depth, prevent a toddler from being able to climb up and over the perimeter. Visibility across such boundaries is ensured if bars, cutouts, or plexiglass panels are added as "portholes." When levels are built into a room's corner, walls constrain the activity on two sides and therefore fewer built boundaries are needed.

Spaces in which a child can lie down or stretch out (floor, platform, or

FIGURE 2. The infant group side of a dividing wall which incorporates a slide, stairs to climb, semienclosed and fully enclosed upper levels, an underneath crawl space, a beam from which to suspend gross motor apparatus, a diaper-changing area, and lattice work permitting visibility to the toddler side.

waterbed) relieve muscle tension and encourage body relaxation. Slight changes in level challenge both orthopedically disabled and motorically passive blind children, especially if textural cues (wood, carpet, or rubber) at level changes are used for orientation. Most blind children are fearful of moving through space, put little weight on their feet, and are tense in their upper bodies. Blindness exacerbates the difficulty with "grounding" and balancing skills that all toddlers are trying to master. Comfortable, soft furnishings encourage muscle relaxation, while gross motor equipment which holds children securely but encourages them to propel their bodies multidirectionally in space (swings, tumblers, rockers, trampolines) can be invaluable therapeutically. Because blind infants may also use echoes to identify features in the environment (Bower, 1977), not all surfaces in the room should absorb sound.

Changes in level also help the deaf child see what is going on elsewhere in the room and help others make contact with the child from different areas. Surfaces that transmit vibrations, especially wooden stairs, platforms, and lofts, increase the deaf child's awareness of ambient movements and sounds. Windows and doors with glass panels set low down near the floor enable children to see what they cannot hear coming toward them.

Sleeping

Where several children are cared for at one time, there must be options for some to sleep undisturbed while others play. A different room for napping physically separates the two functions, provided it is sufficiently nearby for an adult to hear or see into the room when a child awakens or is in difficulty. Intercom systems with or without video components can be helpful.

Since most licensing laws require that all children have their own sleep space and bedding, the amount of space usurped by cribs places a great constraint on the available square footage of a room. Portable cribs utilize less space, but they can be too small for toddlers and their height makes it difficult for adults to lift or lower a child. Cots and mats are sometimes permitted for toddlers, but they deprive children of a permanent, reliable place to rest at any time of the day.

Ideally, nap rooms should be like bedrooms in a house, with two to four cribs maximum, a rocking chair, rheostatic lighting, an operable window with shades to the outside, and plants, mobiles, and other decorative items to gently stimulate and reassure children as they awaken or drift off to sleep. Limiting the number of beds per room creates an initimate nondormitory atmosphere and reduces the amount of distraction a would-be sleeper will encounter from other children.

The napstacks shown in Figure 3, which cut required square footage in half, are an effective space-saving design. Experience has shown that infants and toddlers love the intimate feeling of these spaces and will go to sleep faster and sleep longer because there is less distraction from others in the room. The stacks can be built with varying ceiling heights and numbers of cutouts in the sides and to accommodate different size mattresses. To ease lifting the child in and out, the second level should never exceed 36 inches high; heavier toddlers can be placed on the lower tier.

FIGURE 3. Stacked sleep spaces, or "napstacks," which cut required square footage in half, are an effective space-saving design.

Feeding

Decisions about feeding should be based on the child's self-feeding ability, caregiver ease, and the amount of space available for the activity. Rocking chairs with wide seats and arms work well for nursing infants and those being fed with bottles. Seats that clip onto table rims securely hold infants six months and older and enable caregivers to sit at an adult-height table. When not in use, the seats store easily to free the table for other uses. Feeding-tray tables give the child a lot of surface area on which to play, but take up a great deal of room and do not store well. High chairs allow one-to-one interaction between an adult and child, are comfortable at adult height, and are quite safe if sturdily built and outfitted with a restraining strap. Collapsible models can free floor space at special times, although most caregivers find this inconvenient on a daily basis. Some high chairs come with removable car seats, reducing the amount of storage space required for two bulky items. Counter-height surfaces can also be built to accommodate car seats at meal times. In Figure 4, a low counter (12 inches or 30.5 cm high) reduces problems of safety and climbing and accommodates four infants or toddlers side by side under the supervision of one caregiver. Although the adult must sit on the floor, the low height and reduced size of the unit conserve floor space, create a child-height play surface, and furnish a support for standers and toddlers during non-meal times.

Toddlers who eat finger foods can be seated in groups of two to four children at small 6- to 10-inch-high tables. Children will focus more on eating if seated in sturdy, somewhat confining chairs, such as play cubes without legs, perhaps with a strap.

FIGURE 4. A 12-inch-high feeding table for four infants.

Diapering and Toilet Training

Diapering areas must minimize adult chores and maximize opportunities for adult and child to have a pleasant communicative time together. To assist the adult, the diapering surface should be about 36 inches high, easily washable, and close to a sink and should have shelves out of infant reach for storing needed supplies. A strap is necessary for holding an infant securely; alternatively, the surface can be placed in a trough about six inches deep, off of which the child cannot roll or climb. The under-portion of any changing table should contain space for a covered hamper and trash basket. Individual bins for a child's personal supply of diapers and clothing located within arm's reach of the changing area will reduce the risk of leaving the baby unattended.

Strategies for increasing communication during this important time are numerous. For example, tables or troughs can be oriented to enable an adult to stand at a child's feet; mobiles, reflective surfaces, and graphics overhead provide distraction and entertainment; mirrors along one side of the table enable infants to gaze at their whole bodies. Two troughs or tables on either side of a sink make maximum use of one water source and can facilitate interaction between two caregivers and two children at one time.

It is easiest to toilet train toddlers with potty seats. These can be placed in regular bathrooms or, for ease of supervision and to help the toddler feel connected to the play space, lined up in an area near water and a toilet. If not in bathrooms, the potties should be located some distance from the play space, in an area with good ventilation.

TYPES OF PLAY AREAS

Similar to the rooms of a home which support different functions, moods, body postures, numbers of occupants, and levels of interaction, infant–toddler environments must provide unique, separate places. Qualitatively different areas for active versus passive, noisy versus quiet, and messy versus clean activities make a space more manageable for caregivers and more interesting and interpretable for children.

The design of any infant–toddler space must be based upon the functions and activities of the room's occupants. One should begin, therefore, by listing all the activities, materials, and events that must be accommodated. Typical functions would include diapering, toileting, napping, feeding, and storage. Moreover, areas for at least five types of play experience are necessary in any infant–toddler setting: gross motor play; structured play (manipulatives, puzzles and toys, constructing); quiet play (reading, hiding, resting, listening); discovery play (water, sand, paint, clay); and dramatic play (kitchen and house props, dress-up, dolls). Supports for discovery and dramatic play merit special consideration.

Discovery Play

Malleable materials such as water, sand, paint, or clay, the properties of which children must discover and on which they impose a structure, are essential tools of experience at this age. Ideally, the space provided for messy play should be washable and should allow children the freedom to act on the materials in any way they choose. An abundance of materials, in easy-to-clean-up spaces, is the secret to success for these activities. Particularly convenient are tiled, glass-enclosed mud or wet rooms, with sloping drains and nonskid floors, that allow children to apply water, soapsuds, and paint to walls, floors, and even their own bodies! A built-in hand-held spray permits easy rinsing off of children and the room.

If a separate space cannot be provided, waterplay troughs mounted or free-standing under an existing faucet and over a drain save clean up. These can be designed with temperature control valves, lockable faucets, and removable covers that convert the troughs to platforms for quiet play. If children must stand with their backs to the room during water play activities, a mirror on the wall is essential for orientation and security.

For crayons and clay, the best work surface is a table that is 6 to 10 inches (15 to 25.4 cm) high at which children can squat, sit, or kneel on the floor without chairs. Such tables give children the freedom to move and to put the full force of their bodies into their work. A good easel for this age group is a wall-mounted or supported sheet of homasote fiber board extending 4 feet (1.2 m) up from the floor and 5 to 8 feet (1.6 to 2.4 m) across. This allows children to paint from as far down to as high up as they can reach and to cover a wide expanse of horizontal space. When sealed with semigloss paint and two coats of polyurethane, the homasote is fully washable.

Dramatic Play

Toddlers greatly enjoy playing house as much for the opening and closing of doors and the climbing in and out of enclosures as for the dramatic play value of the equipment, which is rarely sturdy enough to withstand such behavior. Equipment selected for this age group must therefore distinguish between spaces that have operable doors but are intentionally too small or high to climb into and spaces that are definitely large enough for a child to climb into or through safely without weakening the structure or hardware.

The best dramatic play areas are bounded spaces that provide four walls like the walls of a room; a "roof" adds greatly to the mood of being in a house. A limited stock of dress-up clothes and manipulable items such as real pots, pans, dishes, brooms, and recycled containers (e.g., cereal boxes, juice cans, and milk cartons) encourages fantasy and imitation.

STRATEGIES FOR DESIGNING AN AREA

Well-designed activity areas have five defining attributes: (1) a physical *location;* (2) visible *boundaries,* indicating where the area begins and ends; (3) *work* and *sitting surfaces;* (4) materials *storage* and *display;* and (5) a *mood* or personality. Designing appropriate boundaries and work and sitting surfaces are the two greatest challenges.

Location

To locate areas, empty the room—psychologically at least—of all movable elements, so that only its fixed features remain (e.g., doors, windows, lights, outlets, heaters, and sinks). Fixed features have great orientational power since they determine the two prime factors in locating areas: the position of major transit zones and the location of protected areas outside those zones. They must not be ignored; instead, they guide the room's design. A single path from entry to exit should be created to maximize the territory available for activity and minimize the amount of unprotected, exposed space. Activities requiring tables or the motion of people on their feet can be contiguous with pathways and are appropriate in open and busy spaces, whereas activities that use the floor or low platforms require the protection and seclusion characteristic of corners. Use of the floor as a play surface reduces the amount of required furniture, makes the space more flexible, and enables children to see and reach materials and other areas of the room more easily.

Additional factors to consider in locating areas include the need to separate conflicting activities (quiet and noisy), to locate messy areas near a sink, and to introduce platforms near windows so that children can view the outdoors. If the room contains unique architectural features, such as fireplaces, niches, or changes in ceiling height, these should be capitalized on and incorporated into appropriately matched activity areas as functional and salient aspects of the room.

Many small and architecturally poor spaces can only be laid out in one way to accommodate a broad range of functional requirements. However, the design and development of the other four attributes of an area can and should change as time and program progress.

Boundaries

Once activity areas have been placed in a room, they must be defined by permanent or fluid boundaries that signal where each activity physically begins and ends. Solid boundaries, appropriate for activities using the floor, are created by encircling a space with bookcases, storage units, furniture, or walls. Alternatives are needed for areas demanding greater fluidity. This can be achieved by raising the floor level onto a platform four or more inches high or by enclosing the space with an L, U, or rectangular arrangement of low, carpeted risers. Boundaries can also be obtained by changing the level of the ceiling with eaves, canopies, trellises, streamers, and mobiles or by changing the lighting so that the space under a spotlight or subdued lamp appears and feels distinct from surrounding zones.

In addition, an important way to create boundaries is through the use of color, our most powerful visual organizer. Variously hued door and window frames are colorful but draw the eye to inconsequential features of the room. Instead, colors placed at child level on work surfaces, display units, and dividers to areas signal that areas begin and end with particular hues.

In designing boundaries, height, mass, permeability, transparency, and rigidity must be considered so that children can be safe yet watch caregivers and others at play and so that adults can observe all activities without necessarily participating directly in each one. Boundaries such as risers and play panels can be designed to stimulate gross and fine motor actions and to function as seats and work and play surfaces.

Prior to 18 months of age, children resist entering fully enclosed spaces. Even an adult is most comfortable in settings that are only partially embracing, especially if they provide security at the person's back. Womblike enclosures induce arousal and uncertainty by creating too much environmental protection that can be as distracting and unsettling as too much immediate physical or visual input. Environmental predictability, upon which feelings of security and safety are based, depends upon access to information. Predictability is enhanced by boundaries designed with interior windows, by walls and doors of glass that give clues to the limits of a room or building, by bold graphics and informative lighting. Similarly, an overall layout that places the unpredictable life of the setting in the center of the room and the protected zones at the periphery offers a common visible locus toward which all the spaces orient.

Area Size and Private Places

By varying the size of areas, options are provided for solitude, small groups, whole-group meetings, and one-to-one interactions between an adult and a child. Areas scaled to accommodate about four persons minimize stress on staff and encourage individual participation. Private spaces, provided they are not womblike, allow toddlers to explore feelings without being watched and provide time-out spots from the fast pace of a group program. Small window seats, platforms, cubbyholes, soft enclosed seating, and spacious stair landings, are important for rest, observational learning, and preparing children for new situations. The provision of retreat areas is crucial to the development of self-concept, personal identity, and the need of children to come to terms with themselves. Such options tend to be built into the child-rearing environments of homes but are sorely neglected in group-care settings.

Children also require private settings or activities that allow them to express and release emotional anxieties, such as anger, tension, or frustration with themselves, others, or the environment. Thus, there should be things for them to build, knock down, throw, kick, or punch away violent and angry feelings; there should be places to run, fall, jump, and let off steam as well as soft areas for retreat. Color schemes can be used to reinforce the active or passive use of these spaces; warm tones are conducive to high activity, whereas cool tones are quieting and soothing (Birren, 1961).

Play and Sitting Surfaces

Normally, the topic of play and sitting surfaces conjures up images of tables and chairs, items that, at child's eye level, can make an environment appear more populated with legs than any other feature. To conserve floor space, introduce variety, and increase safety, the number of tables in an infant–toddler setting should be minimized and those retained kept small in scale. Different types and heights of tables are right for different kinds of play. Dual-purpose surfaces such as counters, tables that stack or flip up or down, or platforms and risers that double as work, sitting, and eating surfaces can be invented. Covers placed over water and sand troughs transform them into tables for adult use.

Beanbag chairs make excellent resting and holding devices for infants. Armchairs, couches, risers, pillows and cushions, low mattresses, and hammocks encourage cuddling and allow children really to settle in with books and toys. Modular foam furniture that opens to form a bed is especially useful for physically handicapped children. Rocking chairs, both adult- and child-scaled, encourage physical contact, calming rhythms, and constructive opportunities for movement.

The most powerful strategy, however, is to conceive of the whole room—the floors, walls, ceilings, and horizontal and vertical supports—as potential play and sitting surfaces. Anything can be a table, a seat, a wall, a divider, a support for toys, or a place to lie down. The trick is to stop thinking in terms of standard tables, chairs, and play pens and to start thinking in terms of the movements infants and toddlers must make in order to develop sensory-motor skills. For infants, these might include reaching vertically and laterally with hands and feet from a variety of positions; lying, sitting, and crawling on surfaces of different textures and degrees of responsivity, density, angles of inclination, and with varying degrees of enclosure; using head, neck, and trunk muscles in the pursuit of sounds, objects, events; bringing objects to the mouth; gathering, filling, dumping, stacking, and knocking down loose parts.

The toddler's repertoire expands to include a great deal of climbing up, over, and inside things, including up and down stairs, and needing supports to pull to standing and to hold onto while learning to walk and balance. Swinging, rocking, and spinning are required at both stages.

Ways to stimulate each of these motions are infinite. For example, walls can support play panels, vertically mounted toys, grab bars, textures, mirrors, and reflective surfaces at many heights. Play panels can themselves function as walls and as low dividers. Building off a wall horizontally creates seats, tables, counters, high and low platforms, and sloping work surfaces, depending on the element's height and depth. Floors and horizontal surfaces can be lowered or raised; hard or soft; textured or smooth; solid or slatted; flat, inclined, or wavy; and made of natural or manmade materials. These include water mattresses, air mattresses, sacks of beanbag pellets, trampolines, nets, suspension bridges, and other resilient materials. Carpeted risers can serve as boundaries, play and sitting surfaces for adults and children, objects to climb and crawl over, supports for pulling to stand, and for toddling.

Wherever there is a platform higher than 2 feet, the surface underneath can be designed with varying degrees of enclosure as a crawling and hiding place. The underneath surface of the platform (that is, the ceiling of the space below) can be decorated with mirrors, mylar paper, mobiles, graphics, and textures. If the platform is built into a corner or L-shaped, several distinct zones, both above and below, can expand orientational experiences.

Ceilings are woefully underutilized and invaluable for suspending movement apparatus and interactives, provided they are sturdy, within adult reach, and low enough to reduce the torque of swinging objects. Nonambulatory infants enjoy playing with objects within or slightly out of their lateral and vertical reach, but standard plaster walls and ceilings make the suspension of manipulables difficult. The ideal ceiling would support adjustable-height grids to make it easy to display mobiles, wind chimes, trapezes, and other devices or would consist of wooden slats, seven to nine feet off the ground, spanning the entire room at 6-inch intervals. Suspension could then happen anywhere. At least a portion of any room's ceiling should be so treated, over a floor space where the suspended items are most likely to be used. If these options are impossible, a single beam should span the room's narrowest dimension, at seven to nine feet high, to support equipment like an infant–toddler swing, a suspension bridge, or jolly jumper (see Figures 2 and 5).

Some examples of play surfaces are illustrated in Figures 6 and 7. In Figure 6, a series of boxes 3 to 18 inches high can be arranged in any configuration of highs and lows to create an infinite number of landscapes for children to crawl, walk, sit, or lie upon. Tops for the boxes, embellished with different materials to stimulate the senses can, like the bases, be rearranged to vary the horizontal playscape.

FIGURE 5. A low suspension bridge challenges balancing skills and promotes physical coordination while children are seated or walking.

Materials Storage and Display

Since the invitation to the child to play is communicated primarily by the visual presence of play materials, good storage is absolutely essential. It makes materials immediately accessible and allows children to know what is available, where it is to be used, and where it belongs. Infants and toddlers, however, have the tendency to use materials for gathering, filling, dumping, stacking, and knocking down as much as for the play value inherent in the toys themselves. This often results in all the toys being pulled off

FIGURE 6. Boxes of varied heights and box tops of varied textures can be rearranged to create many different playscapes.

FIGURE 7. Twelve-inch-high U-shaped carpeted risers for sitting, crawling, pulling to stand, and playing, form a "play pit."

shelves or simply transferred as "piles" from one place to another. Although these activities are to be encouraged, they can clutter floor space with objects over which others must step or crawl. Hence, it is easy to see the value of providing bounded areas and platforms that contain the toys in zones that are traffic-free. Like traditional play pens, these hold babies safely but are also large enough to hold adults; give infants supports by which to pull to a standing position; provide different levels for movement; and protect, store, and display the construction toys and manipulables that infants and toddlers so love to pull off shelves.

Equally important are varied storage containers and bins, as well as shelves with a restricted supply of materials, so that these behaviors occur within manageable limits. Toy boxes and milk crates (sometimes with wheels) ease the task of picking up loose items, but if they are too large they can overwhelm a child or lead to broken materials and lost pieces. In addition, lumping the items confuses young children who require more structure and organization for orientation and the setting of limits. It is advisable to have a combination of storage at child height and storage above four feet for adult access to bulk supplies for replenishing and varying the items placed at child level.

Mood

An effective way to meet the varying energy levels of infants, toddlers, and caregivers over the course of a long day is to give each area in the room its own mood. The appropriate mood for a particular function matches the

level of activity and physical energy children expend in performing it. Tranquil activities occur best in warm, soft, textured spaces; expansive activities require spaces that are cooler, harder, and more vibrant in tone.

Mood results from decorative techniques that make a space sensorially rich and varied—plants, pillows, colors, textures, fabric, knick-knacks, rugs, curtains, and wall hangings. Anything that moves, grows, or changes shape (mobiles, wind chimes, interactives, fish, animals) or that reflects movement (mirrors) will also add visual interest and excitement to the environment. Tablecloths, flowers, subdued lighting, and candles in jars at meal times create delightful "atmospheres" that are part of the good life children are entitled to share.

Mood setting also involves beauty. Although beautification of dwellings preoccupies many a homemaker, comparable consideration is rarely given to child-care spaces. These settings, by virtue of their anonymous ownership and limited financial resources, become an aesthetic no-man's-land designed more to assist the custodians who maintain them than the users who must grow within them. Aesthetic considerations invariably rank last or are totally ignored because of the presumed monetary costs involved.

However, "beauty is as beauty does," in the built as well as the social world. Far from their being a luxury, one must question whether the exquisite sensory sensitivities of young children can afford *not* to be exposed to the positive effects of aesthetically pleasing living and learning spaces. Furthermore, the need for beauty is particularly important in centers for handicapped children and their families. If parents associate only ugly places and experiences with their children, soon the child, too, is seen as ugly. I recall two mothers' comments about the Infant/Toddler Family Creative Play Center mentioned earlier. One mother noted, "For the first time, our handicapped child has been the family's ticket to pleasure!" The other observed, "One usually associates a dingy kind of place with these kinds of problems. The cheerfulness and beauty of the center is so surprising."

Perhaps the entrance to every child space should be graced by a *torre*, a Japanese arch signalling the transition from profane to sacred territory, from a realm of the spontaneous and ordinary to one of spiritual and aesthetic integrity. Passage beyong the *torre* would then surround all children with beauty, wholeness, and care, proclaiming that they, too, are graced with inner and outer loveliness.

Acknowledgments

Photographs by Anita Rui Olds. The environments in Figures 1, 2, 3, and 5 are part of an Infant/Toddler Family Creative Play Center designed in 1974 by Other Ways For Educational and Environmental Development (Anita Rui Olds, Henry F. Olds, and Walter Drew) for the Massachusetts Department of Mental Health and described in Olds, 1979b. The box tops in

Figure 6 were created by Lilli Ann Rosenberg. All other environments were designed by Anita Olds and Associates, Consultants, Environmental Facilities for Children, 10 Saville Street, Cambridge, MA 02138. Figure 1 is reprinted from Olds, 1982, with permission of Pro-Ed Publications.

REFERENCES

Acredolo, L., & Evans, D. Developmental changes in the effects of landmarks on infant spatial behavior. *Developmental Psychology*, 1980, 312–318.

Ayres, A. J. *Sensory integration and learning disorders.* Los Angeles: Western Psychological Services, 1973.

Benson, H. *The mind body effect.* New York: Simon & Schuster, 1979.

Birren, F. *Color psychology and color therapy.* Secaucus, NJ: Citadel Press, 1961.

Bower, T. G. R. *A primer of infant development.* San Francisco: W. H. Freeman, 1977.

Burns, K., Deddish, R., Burns, W., & Hatcher, R. Use of oscillating waterbeds and rhythmic sounds for premature infant stimulation. *Developmental Psychology*, 1983, *19*, 746–751.

Clark, D. L., Kreutzberg, J. R., & Chee, F. K. W. Vestibular stimulation influence on motor development in infants. *Science*, 1977, *196*, 1228–1229.

Fiske, D. W., & Maddi, S. R. *Functions of varied experience.* Homewood, IL: Dorsey, 1961.

Gruson, L. Color has powerful effect on behavior, researchers assert. *The New York Times*, October 19, 1982.

Held, R., & Bossom, J. Neonatal deprivation and adult rearrangement: Complementary techniques for analyzing plastic sensory-motor coordinations. *Journal of Comparative and Physiological Psychology*, 1961, *54*, 33–37.

Held, R., & Hein, A. Movement produced stimulation in the development of visually guided behavior. *Journal of Comparative and Physiological Psychology*, 1963, *56*, 872–876.

Hughes, P. C. The use of light and color in health. In Hasings, A. C., Fadiman, J., & Gordon, J. S. (Eds.), *Health for the whole person: The complete guide to holistic medicine.* Boulder, CO.: Westview Press, 1980.

Hughes, P. C. An examination of the beneficial action of natural light on the psychobiological system of man. Proceedings, Photobiology and photochemistry, *CIE 20th session*, D603/1-4, 1983.

Montagu, A. *Touching: The human significance of the skin.* New York: Harper & Row, 1971.

Olds, A. R. Designing developmentally optimal classrooms for children with special needs. In S. Meisels (Ed.), *Special education and development: Perspectives on young children with special needs.* Baltimore, MD.: University Park Press, 1979. (a)

Olds, A. R. A play center for handicapped infants and toddlers. In T. M. Field (Ed.), *Infants born at risk: Behavior and development.* New York: SP Medical and Scientific Books, 1979. (b)

Olds, A. R. Designing play environments for children under 3. *Topics in Early Childhood Special Education*, 1982, *2*(3), 87–95.

Ott, J. *Health and light.* New York: Simon & Schuster, 1973.

Piaget, J. *The origins of intelligence in children.* New York: Norton, 1963.

Pihlcrantz, D. W. Creating a healthier worksite. *Industry*, January, 1984.

Prescott, E., & David, T. G. *Concept paper on the effects of the physical environment on day care.* Pasadena, CA: Pacific Oaks College, 1976.

Samuels, M., & Samuels, N. *Seeing with the mind's eye.* New York: Random House, 1975.

Spivak, M., & Tamer, J. *Light and color: A designer's guide.* Washington, DC: AIA Press, 1983.

Wurtman, R. J. The effects of light on the human body. *Scientific American*, 1975, *233*(1), 68–77.

Wurtman, R. J., as quoted in Gruson, L., Color has powerful effect on behavior, researchers assert, *The New York Times*, October 19, 1982.

Chapter 7

The Developmental Implications of Home Environments

LAURA C. JOHNSON

INTRODUCTION

Recent changes in patterns of female labor-force participation combined with dramatic increases in the number of families headed by single parents have had profound influence on the nature of child rearing and family life in North America. At a time when such major alterations are occurring in family life, what is the reason to focus on the home, such a traditional child-care setting? The answer is that homes continue to be the main setting in which the great majority of young children are reared. Despite drastic demographic changes in the character of North American family life, with increased maternal labor-force participation and the resulting increase in parents' use of extrafamilial child-care arrangements, the home environment continues to provide the setting in which most children spend most of their time during their early years. Whether in the child's own home or that of a family day-care provider, a neighbor, or a relative, the indoor and outdoor environments of a home provide the primary settings for child development.

Additionally, it may be noted that continued technological changes in the workplace may mean that increased numbers of people will "go to work"

LAURA C. JOHNSON • Social Planning Council of Metropolitan Toronto, 950 Yonge Street, Toronto, Ontario, Canada M4W 2J4.

without leaving home. What futurist Alvin Toffler (1980) has termed the "electronic cottage"—the computerized work station located in a home—is already being introduced selectively on a pilot basis (Olson, 1981). Such work-at-home programs are frequently geared toward mothers of young children, with the expectation that the home-based work station will somehow alleviate the need for extrafamilial child care. To date, the electronic cottage is not a widespread work option. Should it become one, the home of the future may take on added functions as a child-care environment.

Some surprising findings emerged from a recent study of two groups of middle-class 18-month-olds (Rubenstein & Howes, 1979). One group consisted of children in a day-care center and their staff; another consisted of children reared at home and their mothers. The researchers observed and compared adult–child interactions and children's interactions with their peers in these two settings. They found that the day-care center children had many more positive exchanges with adults and more play with age peers. In contrast, the children at home had more negative exchanges with the adults caring for them (their mothers). The children in the home setting cried more and received more reprimands from their adult caretakers.

Why should mothers and their own children appear to get along less well together than do day-care workers and the children in their care? What might account for the higher level of reprimands from mothers of young children than from day-care workers? Why should children at home cry more than their counterparts in a day-care center? Is this, perhaps, some sort of evidence of a decline in the quality of family life?

Rubenstein and Howes (1979) suggest that the explanation of their results may lie in several key differences between these two child-care environments, the day-care center and the home. First, with regard to the physical space, they observe that the day-care setting is designed specifically around the needs of young children. A typical day-care center environment enables children to engage in a variety of activities without risk to their own safety or risk of damage to the physical settings. In such a context, they note, the adult caretakers have relatively little need to restrict children's play. In contrast, a typical home setting contains many more potential risks for youngsters and at the same time holds numerous objects and furnishings that may be damaged in the course of children's play. In the words of these researchers, "Mothers may need to exercise more control than do day care center caregivers because more objects are present that are not suitable for infant play" (p. 20).

The second key difference between the two environments, note Rubenstein and Howes, is that the day-care center tends to be structured around having several adult caregivers, whereas the typical parent at home is alone with the children much of the day. The supportive presence of other adults, these researchers argue, is important in helping caregivers to address the needs of young children. These two factors, the lack of a child-oriented home environment and the absence of adult companionship for caregivers, the researchers suggest, may account for the higher level of negative affect and make the home environment a less "playful" place than is the day-care center. This is an important finding for what it indicates about the limitations of the home as a child-rearing environment. The implication of this finding is not that we should seek alternatives to the home as a setting for child care but rather that we should investigate ways of improving the capacity of the home to accommodate the needs of developing children.

The two child-care settings studied by Rubenstein and Howes represent polar opposites. At the one extreme, there is the institutional setting in which caregivers, generally professionally trained, care for groups of children in programs that are usually subject to established standards and regulations. The parent and child in the home setting represent the opposite extreme of an informal and private situation. In between lies a wide range of home-based child-care situations varying in degree of formality, of government regulation, of caregiver training, and of "hominess." It is important to consider these various dimensions and to discover how they may affect the behavior of children and their caretakers.

The present chapter will begin with a review of the research literature dealing with the problems as well as the potential of the home as a place for caring for children. It will review the existing research that has been done to describe the home as a child-rearing environment and will further examine studies that investigate the relationship between characteristics of the home environment and child behavior. My own survey research on home environments of Canadian children will be reviewed. A variety of guidelines for creating child-oriented home environments will be discussed. Additionally, the chapter will explore some of the social-policy considerations involved with children in the home environment.

REVIEW OF THE LITERATURE

In a Swedish study undertaken by that country's National Institute for Building Research, researcher Louise Gaunt investigated the nature of preschool children's play inside the home (1980). The research involved interviews with a sample of 120 families with children aged 2 to 7 years, living in a variety of housing types. Each interview recorded the types of indoor play activities engaged in by children, as well as the location and duration of each activity.

Gaunt's study found that, for the sample as a whole, children tended to spend the greatest amount of their time engaged in those activities that placed the fewest demands on the household environment. Play routines involving quiet, passive behavior were considerably more frequent than were noisy, active, or potentially messy types of play. Although there was a tendency for those households located in larger living quarters to report a greater amount and frequency of active children's play, the overall pattern suggested that children's indoor activities involved quiet rather than noisy games, fine motor rather than gross motor activities, and passive rather than active and creative play.

Gaunt argues that such restriction of children's activity is not conducive to children's healthy development. It is through play that children acquire social, cognitive, and physical skills. Restrictions on their play behavior, Gaunt avers, may disrupt or hamper the developmental process. In a country such as Sweden, with a particularly cold climate, she notes, efforts should be made to ensure that the indoor home environment offers children a full range of play opportunities.

My own research in Canada has investigated informal, family day-care arrangements for young children (Johnson & Dineen, 1981). A survey interviewed a sample of almost 300 caregivers who provided day care in their own homes to children of working parents. Interviews probed the nature and location of children's activities in the caregivers' homes, with regard to children's inside activities. Results of this study were similar to those reported by Gaunt. It was found that the children spent relatively little time in active, creative, exploratory activities. Instead, the day-care children tended to watch television, look at books, and play with structured games and toys. In fact, when children's time spent in front of the television set was calculated as a proportion of their total time in cars, it was found that these Canadian children spent, on average, fully one-quarter of their day-care time viewing television.

In addition to asking caregivers to describe the activities of the children in their care, the Canadian survey also asked caregivers about any activities they prohibited. These answers also reflected a strong concern on the part of the caregivers with protecting the home from the children and with protecting the children from potential hazards in the home. Reading over the caregivers' answers, such as no drawing on the walls, no water play in the house, no jumping on chairs or beds, no climbing on the living room furniture, no touching breakable things, no touching the radiators, gives one an idea of the problems involved with having a home do double duty as a family residence and a children's day-care setting.

In addition to the practical problems involved with using a family residence as a day-care setting, there appear also to be difficulties associated with the symbolic value of the home as a private enclave, protected from the outside world. Particular parts of the home, notably bedroom spaces, may be considered most private and therefore may be off limits to day-care children. The combined result of the factors of home hazards and privacy of home spaces may be that the play activities of day-care children are severely restricted.

A lack of freedom to explore their own environment may be detrimental to the children in such a family day-care arrangement. Such is the conclusion to be drawn from Clarke-Stewart's extensive review (1977) of child development research. She writes:

> As well as suggesting criteria for the human environment in day care, the research on children and families supports the notion that children benefit from freedom to move and explore in a safe and stimulating physical environment. (p. 110)

Such restriction of exploratory behavior by young children may be a cultural pattern specific to North America, possibly associated with a notion of the home as a private territory. A study by Cochran compared developmental effects of group day care, family day care, and care in a child's own home on Swedish children of 12 months through 18 months (Cochran, 1977). Among the findings of that study was an observation that exploratory activities by children were observed significantly more often in both the own-home and the family day-care home than in the day-care-center setting. These results suggest that the degree of exploratory behavior permitted to young children may have more to do with prevailing attitudes toward children in the home than the issue of whether the children actually live in the home or are receiving care in a family day-care setting.

Returning to the North American context, there is one study that, although relatively short-term, utilized a longitudinal design to assess the developmental impacts of family day-care versus group day-care environments. This ambitious research project, the New York City Infant Day Care Study (Golden, Rosenblath, Grossi, Policare, Freeman, & Brownlee, 1978), utilized a sample of some 300 children up to 36 months of age from economically disadvantaged homes. Repeated assessments of the children's intellectual performance revealed that, although all children entering the programs made initial gains in intellectual performance, the group day-care children maintained the higher level, while the performance of the family day-care children declined after 18 months. The authors interpret the results to mean that the home environment in the family day-care arrangements provides less support for children's intellectual development than does the institutional group day-care environment.

The New York study observed significant differences in the social and physical environments of the two day-care situations. The group-care settings were found to offer more play materials, more equipment, and a greater amount of space per child than the family day-care settings. The family day-care homes, in turn, were judged to offer a higher ratio of caregivers to children.

It is clear that, at least in North America, the home can be a restrictive, inappropriate environment for young children. What of its potential advantages? Are there aspects of the home environment that can support children's social, cognitive, and physical development?

Prescott conducted a study (1973) comparing the environments in day-care centers, family day-care homes, and children's own homes. She examined the effects of these various settings on children's behavior and found that, in comparison to the group day-care center, adults in both of the home settings directed more attention to the children and generally spent more time engaged in activities with the children. The home settings also provided children with more opportunities to initiate and terminate their own activities at will. In contrast, Prescott concludes, the group day-care setting appears to dictate a more regimented and structured program, with less room for individual choices by the children.

Looking at other research on home-based, family day-care arrangements, it appears to be an open question as to whether home caregivers are, as Prescott believes, allowing the children to pursue activities of their own choosing or whether the caregivers are simply ignoring the children, leaving them to amuse themselves while the caregivers attend to their own housekeeping responsibilities. The degree of direct caregiver involvement in children's activities is one of the factors investigated in a recent United States National Day Care Home Study, a 4-year study of family day care in three American cities, sponsored by the Administration for Children, Youth, and Families (U.S. Department of Health and Human Services, 1981). This study examined care provided in three types of settings, (1) unregulated family day-care homes; (2) regulated family day-care homes, which, although they operate independently, maintain formal ties with regulatory agencies; and (3) sponsored family day-care homes, which are integrated parts of day-care systems administered by a sponsoring agency. In the United States, unregulated family day-care homes are a widely used form of day care, regulated homes are considerably fewer in number, and sponsored family day-care homes represent only a small proportion of the total arrangements in use.

The study reported a tendency for the unregulated caregiver to be "somewhat less child-focused than the regulated caregiver and much less so than the sponsored caregiver. She spends more time than either attending both to her own needs and to her household's while the day-care children are present." With regard to the sponsored caregiver, the study notes that her "added involvement with the children is apparent in several ways: there is more teaching, more play/participation, more supervision and preparation and less housekeeping and solitary recreation." (pp. 81–82). The authors of the report attribute these observed differences in caregivers' approaches to the job to differences in training. Alternatively, these differences in child–caregiver interaction might be explained by differences in the organization of physical space among the unregulated and the regulated caregivers. Further, although this factor is not explored systematically in the National Day Care Home Study, it may be the case that social class differences between groups of caregivers would be associated with different attitudes toward the use of the home environment.

Taken together, the studies described above suggest that features of the child's home environment can influence the behavior of children and their social interaction with their adult caregivers. At this point it is useful to direct attention to one study of home environments that were planned and designed with special attention to the needs of children.

SURVEY OF HOME ENVIRONMENTS

Following completion of the Canadian family day-care survey discussed earlier, my colleagues and I conducted another, smaller-scale survey designed to examine both private family homes and family day-care home environments that had been designed expressly as child-oriented spaces (Johnson, Shack, & Oster, 1980). Supported by the Canada Mortgage and Housing Corporation, the study began by identifying 25 homes reputed to provide excellent physical environments for young children. Approximately one-half of the sample consisted of homes of families with their own preschool children; the other half were family day-care homes. These survey homes were identified through a variety of referral channels, including day-care and other social and community agencies, preschool and parent education programs, and a variety of local neighborhood services.

The households in this study represented a relatively middle-class group. All but one of the survey respondents lived in houses, with 15 living in single detached dwellings, five more in semidetached homes, and another four in row or town housing. Only one respondent lived in an apartment, which was in a low-rise dwelling.

Data collection for the study consisted of a personal interview in the home with the parent or day-care provider, including questions about the physical plan of the home and about the frequency and location of children's activities in the indoor and outdoor environment of the home. A floor plan was drawn for each residence in the survey, and a diary was produced to record children's activities in and around the home during the previous week. The interview also tapped the adults' ideas about children's play in the home settings. Finally, respondents were asked about any alterations or renovations which they had made or intended to make in order to tailor the home for children's use.

Not surprisingly, these homes had an appearance and pattern of usage that was very different from the situations reported in the earlier random sample of family day-care homes. Selected because of their conspicuousness in the community as child-oriented settings, these households had been designed and planned around the needs of children. The great majority—some 80%—had made renovations to make the homes' interiors more suitable for children. These homes allowed children considerably more freedom to travel throughout and to use the various parts of the home. Furthermore, almost all of the homes reported the children regularly used household furnishings and equipment in their play.

The interiors of these homes had several distinctive features, involving the allocation of rooms by function, the placement of windows, lighting, flooring and wall surfaces, storage, and furnishings and equipment. Although all of these features were important, it was the way in which these households allocated rooms and generally used household space that most notably set them off from others. In these homes, children were generally allowed free access to most major living areas of the home. The caregivers in these households—parents and family day-care providers alike—understood the principle that has been cited in the literature by Pollowy (1977), that young children want to play within visual and acoustic contact of the adults caring for them. Children's access to the main living area was achieved in one of two ways, either by adapting one centrally located room into a playroom (the dining room was a good candidate for this transformation) or by locating a number of smaller activity areas through the major living area of the home. Although even this select group of households tended to limit children's use of the living room, there was a high level of use of kitchens, bedrooms, and main-floor playrooms.

The results of this Canadian survey show that it is possible to design a home environment in such a way as to support a variety of play activities by young children. They show, further, that such an approach to housing design tends to be associated with nontraditional notions about the importance of children's play activities and with a particular set of attitudes about the home itself.

These homes certainly represent a departure from the prototypical ideal home in North America. The main living area of the home is not reserved as a showplace to be used only on special occasions; children's play is not relegated to basement recreation rooms; and kitchens are not used exclusively as food-preparation areas. Furthermore, throughout these homes there is evidence of the presence of children. From display of children's artwork at heights that can be easily viewed by children, to provision of low shelving for easy storage of and access to play equipment and materials in various areas throughout the home, to placement of light switches at levels that can be reached by children, it is clear to the observer that these homes are occupied by children. The homes conveyed the symbolic message that children and their activities are valued.

Nevertheless, the surveyed homes are far from looking like nursery schools! There were only isolated examples wherein provision for children's needs interfered with the use of the home for other functions. The fact that a kitchen could be used for children's arts and crafts activities did not interfere with subsequent use of the same space for cooking. In fact, there was only one situation in which the location of children's play equipment in a major living area of the home precluded the use of that room for other purposes. In that case, a living room had been transformed into an indoor playground, complete with a large climbing frame which occupied most of the available space. That was an exceptional case; the rest of the homes were as well-suited to meeting the needs of adult members of the household as they were suited to children's needs. In fact, the results of this small-scale survey suggest that through the structuring of the home environment to accommodate the needs of young children, the task of the child's caregiver is made considerably easier. Both supervision of youngsters and the work involved in cleaning up after their play activities are eased considerably in these child-oriented environments.

One policy issue emerging from these results concerns the possibility of influencing the opportunities available to young children by restructuring the built environment. Granted that the households surveyed were exceptional in tailoring the built environment to accommodate a wide range of indoor play activities by children. In theory, however, it is possible to develop residential housing to accommodate either family day-care providers or families with young children and to design such housing units to support the activities of children as well as of adults. Particularly with regard to home-based family day care, such a program might greatly enhance the quality of care.

DESIGN GUIDELINES

There have been a number of planners and researchers concerned with developing guidelines for the design of child-oriented home environments. Some have directed their attention to family day-care homes; others have focused on private family homes. In most cases, this distinction is irrelevant. Both sets of circumstances have the same functional requirements. The following section reviews a variety of such design guidelines, derived in part from Johnson *et al.* (1980) and in part from other published literature.

Play Areas in the Main Living Areas of the Home

Most young children want to play within visual and acoustic range of adults. Their adult caretakers generally must supervise the children at play. Locating opportunities for children's play activities in the home's central living areas meets both of these needs. Kitchens, hallways, dining and living room areas can provide rich and varied settings for children's activities close to the parts of the home generally occupied by adults. This represents a radical departure from traditional North American family housing designs, which generally relegate children's play areas to basement playrooms or upstairs bedrooms.

Our survey of successful, child-oriented housing plans identified a number that managed to adapt main living areas to accommodate the needs of both children and adults. Specially designed play facilities were located in kitchens, dining rooms, and other centrally located areas. Some of the homes had one large, centrally located playroom; others used a number of smaller play areas distributed through the main living space of the home (see Figure 1). Living rooms tended to remain the preserve of adults, although some permitted passive activities such as listening to music, reading, or games and puzzles within the living room (Johnson *et al.*, 1980).

A rich source of information on the design of child-oriented environments is the work produced by Cohen and Moore and their associates at the University of Wisconsin's Children's Environments Project. This work involved the application of child development theory and empirical research to the production of design guidelines for children's play areas (Cohen, Hill, Lane, McGinty, & Moore, 1979) and for child-care centers (Moore, Lane, Hill, Cohen, & McGinty, 1979). Most of their recommendations pertain to formal day-care centers and outdoor playgrounds, but there are a number of ideas that are applicable to the home child-care environment.

Their concept of creating a series of small activity pockets (Moore *et al.*, 1979, Recommendation #908) is an effective way to encourage varied play activities within a home setting. Rather than designating entire rooms as the locus of particular activities, smaller units of space can be arranged in such a way as to support specific activities, by one or a small group of children with the possible inclusion of an adult. Such activity pockets may be designated through display and storage of resource materials and equipment appropriate to the activity and through use of lighting, seating arrangement, and furnishings (see Figure 2). This approach to arrangement of household space has the advantage of flexibility, encouraging provision of a range and variety of activities over time. Playing or listening to music, reading, looking at picture books or listening to stories, using puppets for dramatic play, water play, and arts or crafts are all examples of activities that can be structured in such a manner.

One set of recommendations from that study specifically concerns the modification of homes for use as family day-care facilities (Moore *et al.*, 1979, Recommendation #921). The recommendations include simple suggestions for ways to transform a home into a developmentally appropriate child-care setting. For example, it is suggested that ample table surfaces of varying heights be made accessible to children. When covered with appropriate materials (cork board, blackboard paint, clear adhesive vinyl wall covering), wall surfaces can be used by children for tacking up drawings, for chalk drawing, and as drawing surfaces.

Another useful source of information on structuring the home to support children's activities is a Canadian "how-to" book intended to involve parents and their children in planning the child-care environment (Urban Design Centre, 1974). That book advocates thinking about the essential

FIGURE 1. Plan for children's play area integrated throughout the main living areas.

FIGURE 2. "Activity pockets" within a room can be created through lighting, seating, and storage of materials accessible to children.

parts of the home—the walls, floors, and windows—as resources for planning and design. For example, it recommends treating interior walls as parts of the activity centers they surround. Walls are to be seen as edges of activities rather than as barriers. Suggested uses for such so-called thick walls are built-in storage of play materials and equipment, tack-up surfaces for display of children's work, built-in seating, and built-in alcoves or nooks. Floors, it suggests, should be thought of as furniture. As a place for children to sit, floor area is often more comfortable than child-size tables and chairs. Windows, it observes, can be designed as three-dimensional "window places," rather than simply as flat windows or flat walls. By building bay windows with window seats, one creates a window place that forms a comfortable transition space between indoor and outdoor environments.

The Kitchen as a Family Room

In many homes the kitchen serves as a center of family activity. It can be a convenient setting for a number of supervised children's play activities, including arts and crafts, cooking, and water play (see Figure 3). Successful use of the kitchen as a play space requires a physical plan that allows for storage of materials and equipment and easy access for children to equipment and counters.

Since all kitchens contain potential hazards and risks for children, considerations of safety also apply when locating a children's play area in a

FIGURE 3. Cooking together.

kitchen. In general, young children should be kept out of the work area of the kitchen while having access to sink and counter tops. Range top, oven, and other potentially dangerous appliances should be located farthest away from circulation routes through and within the kitchen.

Access

One aspect of sharing the main living areas of a home with children involves providing children with easy access to the household environment. The scale and positioning of various fixtures in the home must be carefully considered. The height of light fixtures, shelves, coat hooks and racks, door knobs and light switches, mirrors, and towel racks should all be planned according to children's needs (see Figure 4). Such planning serves to encourage independence.

Privacy

Planners of institutional child-care environments have noted the importance of including quiet places or "places to pause" in the design of space

FIGURE 4. Positioning fixtures, shelves, coat hooks, and switches within children's reach promotes independence.

(Osmon, 1971; Urban Design Centre, 1979). Despite the finding by Prescott (1978) that home day-care environments are more likely than day-care centers to provide such opportunities for private space, it is still important to consider children's privacy needs when planning a home child-care environment. Both the interior as well as the exterior area of the home should include semienclosed spaces where children can rest and/or retreat from social activity (see Figure 5; Johnson *et al.*, 1980).

Active Play

A number of the sources cited in this chapter stress the importance of providing for children's gross motor activity within the home. Moore *et al.* (1979), for example, emphasize the need to clear enough open space inside the home to allow for movement and for construction activities. They suggest that at least one large room be furnished in such a way that furniture can be easily moved aside to allow active play.

In the Soviet Union, recent interest in preschool education has focused

FIGURE 5. Indoor and outdoor areas should include semienclosed spaces where children can rest or retreat from social activity.

on this very issue of supporting children's physical activity within the home environment. Boris and Lena Nikitin (1980) are popular Soviet child development experts and advocates of physical activity for children from very early infancy. On the basis of their experiences raising their own children, the Nikitins recommended outfitting the home with a variety of sports and play equipment designed to encourage children's gross and fine motor development. In numerous television appearances, several best-selling parenting handbooks, and frequent meetings with groups of young and expectant parents, the Nikitins' approach to child rearing has gained an enthusiastic following among the younger generation of Soviet parents.

Vladimir Skripalev is another popular Soviet proponent of a vigorous program of physical activity as a key part of children's preprimary education (1981). Skripalev has identified a variety of specific activities including climbing, sliding, jumping, and swinging that he considers to be essential for child development. In the context of a limited supply of family housing and therefore relatively small average dwelling size, Skripalev has designed indoor play equipment that will encourage young children to participate in a variety of physical activities. This "apartment-sized gymnasium" fastens to an interior wall and ceiling and has a variety of ladders, rings, slides, ropes, and pulleys. Although some of the equipment can be folded and stored away when not in use, the basic structure remains in view. The resulting effect is more like a school gym than a typical living room, but Skirpalev feels that the educational benefits are worth the cost (see Figure 6).

Outdoor Opportunities

Finally, although the design of the indoor home environment is critical in encouraging a range of play activity by children, it is also important to consider the organization of the environment out-of-doors. The design of outside play space, the ease of access to outdoor play areas, and the ease of adult supervision of the areas will influence the amount of outdoor activity.

Outdoor play spaces can accommodate a variety of children's play activities that may be either impossible or difficult to do indoors. Sand and water play, construction, gardening, arts and crafts, climbing, swinging, and riding wheeled toys are all activities that children can enjoy in well-planned

FIGURE 6. The apartment-sized gymnasium designed by Vladimir Skripalev.

outdoor play areas. Back or front yards, terraces, decks, or balconies can be adapted to provide safe and appealing play areas for children.

Pollowy (1977) notes the importance of establishing a transitional space between indoor and outdoor spaces in order to provide storage space for outerwear and equipment. Such a buffer zone should not be an area in which children can harm the furnishings. It should provide hooks and shelves that the children can reach easily.

Barry (1982) recently examined patterns of outdoor play by young children in inner-city areas of Washington, D.C., and found that the amount of outdoor play permitted young children was influenced by the observability of the area directly surrounding the house. Apartment complexes featuring courtyard designs enabled young children to play outside with passive supervision by adults who remained indoors. Especially in dangerous neighborhoods, such enclosed and observable play spaces make it possible for young children to play safely out-of-doors.

Cohen *et al.* (1979) also stress the importance of semiprivate play spaces in the immediate vicinity of a young child's home. Examples include yards, courtyards, alleys, driveways, and sidewalks. Such places afford opportunities for spontaneous social interaction with friends and neighbors while still permitting children to stay within sight of home. These semiprivate spaces tend to be the most heavily used of all play areas (Cooper Marcus, 1975).

It is possible to include the equivalent of a front porch in some forms of apartment housing. A different kind of semiprivate space, this could take the form of an expanded part of the corridor in front of an apartment entry. Such an area should have windows for bright, natural light and ventilation. This type of apartment "porch" is achievable in dwellings that have access galleries or are grouped around common stairs (see Figure 7; Johnson *et al.*, 1980).

CONCLUSION

This review of guidelines indicates that there is already a large body of empirically based information concerning the influence of the home environment on young children. However, it is the case that the homes in which most North American children spend their time—family day-care homes and private family homes—bear little resemblance to the environments described in these guidelines.

The prerequisite to changing this situation is a change in popular attitudes toward children's use of home facilities. There is currently much discussion about the importance of quality education for children. Education begins long before children enter the formal school system. Those early years are spent largely in the home setting. If those years are not to be spent

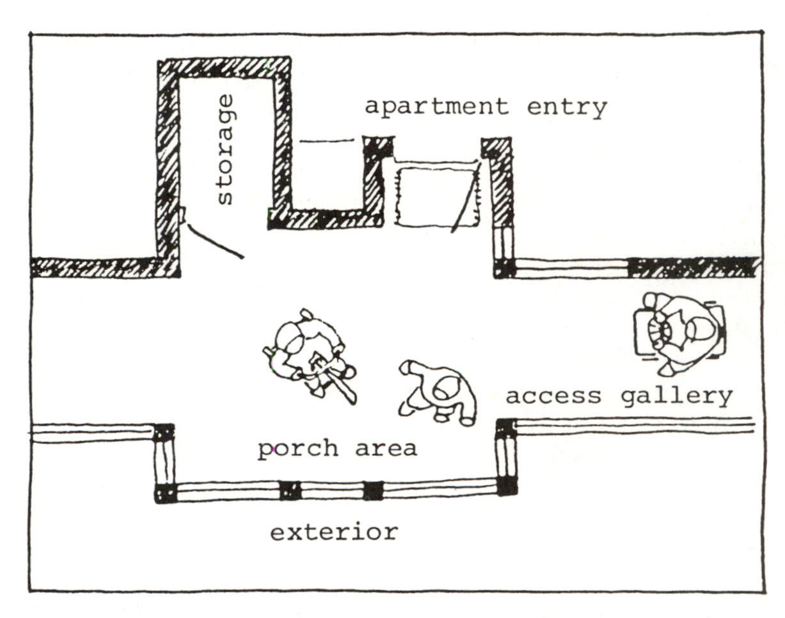

FIGURE 7. An apartment "porch."

tucked away in a basement recreation room watching television, then radical changes will have to be made in the way children utilize the home.

It is necessary to view the entire home as a potential resource for children. Yet most parents planning children's spaces in the home consider only small bedrooms and basement recreation or playrooms to be suited to children's activities. Bookstores and libraries offer numerous volumes on decorating ideas for children's rooms. There is little information available, however, on how to redesign the interior and exterior of the entire home to meet children's needs. Rethinking the home environment to accommodate family members of all ages—ranging from the very young to the elderly—will mean radical change in our traditional notions of family housing.

Acknowledgments

The author is grateful to the Canada Mortgage and Housing Corporation, Ottawa, for permission to reprint six drawings prepared by Joel Shack (Figures 1–5 and 7) which appeared originally in Johnson *et al.* (1980).

REFERENCES

Barry, V. T. R. Kidspace: Family life in the city. *Children Today,* 1982, 11–15.
Clarke-Stewart, A. *Child care in the family.* New York: Academic Press, 1977.

Cochran, M. A comparison of group and family child-rearing patterns in Sweden. *Child Development, 1977, 48,* 702–707.

Cohen, U., Hill, A., Lane, C. G., McGinty, T., & Moore, G. T. *Recommendations for child play areas.* Milwaukee, WI: University of Wisconsin School of Architecture and Urban Planning, 1979.

Cooper Marcus, C. *Easter Hill Village: Some social implications of design.* New York: Free Press, 1975.

Gaunt, L. Can children play at home? In P. F. Wilkinson (Ed.), *Innovation in play environments.* London: Croom Helm, 1980.

Golden, M., Rosenblath, L., Grossi, L., Policare, M., Freeman, Jr., H., & Brownlee, E. *The New York infant day care study.* New York: Medical and Health Research Association of New York City, 1978.

Johnson, L., & Dineen, J. *The kin trade.* Toronto: McGraw-Hill Ryerson, 1981.

Johnson, L., Shack, J., & Oster, K. *Out of the cellar and into the parlour.* Ottawa, Ontario: Canada Mortgage and Housing Corporation, 1980.

Moore, G. T., Lane, C. G., Hill, A. B., Cohen, U., & McGinty, T. *Recommendations for child care centers.* Milwaukee, WI: School of Architecture and Urban Planning, 1979.

Nikitin, B. & L. *My i nashi deti* [We and our children] (2nd ed.). Moscow: Molodaia gvardiia, 1980.

Olson, M. Remote office work: Implications for individuals and organizations. New York: New York University Center for Research on Information Systems, 1981.

Osmon, F. L. *Patterns for designing children's centers.* New York: Educational Facilities Laboratories, 1971.

Pollowy, A-M. *The urban nest.* Stroudsburg, PA: Dowden, Hutchinson and Ross, 1977.

Prescott, E. *A comparison of three types of day care and nursery school care.* Paper presented at the Society of Research in Child Development, Philadelphia, PA, 1973.

Prescott, E. Is day care as good as a good home? *Young Children,* 1978, *44,* 13–19.

Skripalev, V. *Stadion v kvartire* (A gym at home). Moscow: Fizkultura i sport, 1981.

Toffler, Alvin, *The third wave.* New York: Morrow, 1980.

Urban Design Centre. *Design for child care.* Vancouver, B.C., 1974.

Rubenstein, J. L. & Howes, C. Caregiving and infant behavior in day care and in homes. *Developmental Psychology,* 1979, *15,* 1–24.

U.S. Department of Health and Human Services. *Family day care in the United States* (Final report of the National Day Care Home Study). Vol. 1: Summary of findings. Washington, DC: Author, 1981.

Chapter 8

Designing Preschool Classrooms to Support Development

Research and Reflection

CAROL SIMON WEINSTEIN

INTRODUCTION

Many fields of study are concerned with children's development or with the built environment. Only early childhood education, however, has focused attention on both of these topics. The concern with development was recently impressed upon me when I searched for a preschool for my 3-year-old daughter, Laura. Each school I visited thrust into my hands a written statement of its philosophy and objectives. Consider a small sample:

- Our goal is to offer a well-balanced program for preschool-age children, which will enrich the social, emotional, physical, and intellectual development of each child. . . . We try to meet the individual needs of each child, while helping the child to develop self-confidence, self-esteem, a constructive approach toward learning, and a sense of curiosity and independence.
- Our objectives—joy in learning, concentration, self-confidence, respect for others and the equipment, self-control and courtesy, coordination, intellectual growth.

CAROL SIMON WEINSTEIN • Graduate School of Education, Rutgers–The State University of New Jersey, New Brunswick, NJ 08903.

- Why your child should attend our school—

  It helps him to mature emotionally: he is helped to overcome his shyness; he loses some of the fears and anxieties common to little people; he enjoys working and playing with other children; he acquires pleasure in his own accomplishments.

  It helps him to mature socially: he learns to show consideration and respect for others, to give and to accept help from others, to participate and to lead in group activities, to accept responsibility.

  It helps him to mature intellectually: he learns to express himself, to create in many ways, to use his initiative and imagination, to be alert to the world around him.

  It helps him to mature physically: he develops better control of his large muscles; he improves his posture; he develops good health habits.

Although there is often great disparity between written objectives and actual programs, statements such as these nevertheless reflect a new breadth. Nursery schools of the 1920s were primarily concerned with promoting habits for good physical health; the schools of the 1940s focused on social and emotional growth, and those of the 1960s emphasized cognitive achievement to an unprecedented degree (Kamii, 1971). In contrast, the preschools of the 1980s appear to strive for a balance among these alternatives. It appears that increasing numbers of early childhood educators have come to recognize that the child has "a body, a mind, and feelings" (Shapiro & Biber, 1972, p. 57) and are defining the goal of preschool education as effecting developmental changes in all three (Evans, 1975).

Early childhood education has also paid an unusual degree of attention to the physical setting. Indeed, the belief that the physical environment influences children's behavior has a long tradition in this field.* Seefeldt (1980) traces the beginning of this belief to Froebel, who compared his kindergarten to a garden wherein children could bloom as naturally as flowers. Montessori's entire curriculum emphasized the importance of an ordered environment to help children concentrate on learning, and Harriet Johnson, founder of the first nursery school in the United States, wrote: "Our environment must be one in which the processes for growth go on fully and at an adequate rate" (1928, p. 65).

Current books and articles on early childhood education continue this tradition by stressing the importance of careful spatial organization and by providing suggestions for creating learning centers, partitioning space, and arranging materials (e.g., Feeney, Christensen, & Moravcik, 1983; Cohen, 1974). There is a clear consensus that classroom space is important

> because it affects everything the children do. It affects the degree to which they can be active and to which they can talk about their work. It affects the choices

*For a comprehensive review of research in this area, see Phyfe-Perkins (1980).

> they can make and the ease with which they can carry out their plans. It affects their relationships with other people and the ways in which they use materials. (Hohmann, Banet, & Weikart, 1979, p. 35)

Yet, rarely do writers base prescriptions for the preschool environment on an analysis of children's development needs.* Although instructional strategies, curricula, and interpersonal communication are often described in terms of their developmental appropriateness, guidelines for the environment tend to be pragmatic (e.g., the art area should be near the sink for easy cleanup) or to reflect conventional practice (e.g., classroom space should be divided into five basic learning centers: blocks, art, housekeeping, library, and table games).

Moreover, actual preschool programs are all too frequently housed in facilities that are woefully inadequate when examined from a developmental perspective. This is not simply a matter of being housed in the "damp, dark, dungeonlike basements of public buildings and churches . . . converted storefronts, worn out houses, and abandoned and crumbling buildings" (Day, 1983, p. 165). More pertinent for the present discussion is the fact that the organization and contents of available classroom space, *wherever* it is found, rarely reflect the developmental goals so eloquently described in the brochures for parents.

The purpose of the present chapter is to delineate some of the major socioemotional, cognitive, and physical goals of preschool education and to consider their implications for the design of classrooms. I have drawn extensively upon work by Osmon (1971), Moore, Lane, Hill, Cohen, and McGinty (1979), Olds (1979), and others who provide excellent, detailed recommendations for classroom space. My intent is not to derive entirely new guidelines but rather to articulate the links between the preschool child's developmental needs and the physical setting. Wherever possible, I refer to the available research base in educational and developmental psychology to support these links. In the absence of empirical data, however, I have relied on the reasoning of early childhood practitioners and theoreticians and on my own reflections.

Two basic ideas underlie the discussion to follow. First is the belief in the importance of children's active engagement with the physical environment. In writing about development, this perspective has been given various names: "transactionism" (Day, 1983), the "developmental-interaction approach" (Shapiro & Biber, 1972), the "cognitive-developmental view" (Kohlberg, 1968). Regardless of terminology, this perspective reflects the belief expressed by Kohlberg (1968) that "the cognitive and affective structures which education should nourish are natural emergents from the interaction between the child and the environment under conditions where such interaction is allowed or fostered" (p. 1015).

*Notable exceptions are Olds (1979), Day (1983), and Moore, Lane, Hill, Cohen, & McGinty (1979).

Second, as Kohlberg's comment suggests, the effect of the environment is mediated by the policies governing its use. Day (1983) relates a compelling anecdote of a preschool classroom divided into several permanent activity centers—table games, blocks, science, and books—none of which the children were allowed to use. Instead, they spent their time receiving formal, direct instruction in language, art, and group circle games. This program-setting incongruity resulted in the need for continual vigilance on the part of teachers to prevent children from visiting the activity areas. One can only speculate on why such efforts were expended to create an environment that children were not free to explore. Clearly, a setting that is off limits to children cannot support their development.

DEVELOPMENTAL GOALS AND DESIGN IMPLICATIONS

The 10 developmental goals discussed in this section are not meant to be exhaustive, nor is the list intended to portray development as a series of independent strands of growth. Furthermore, design recommendations discussed under one developmental goal may also be relevant to other goals. A need for brevity, however, precludes discussion of design guidelines at every relevant point.

Socioemotional Development

Self-esteem. Between the ages of 2 and 5, children construct a personal identity through their encounters with other people and with the physical environment. Briggs (1975) suggests that positive self-esteem is based on two convictions: "I matter and have value" and "I can handle myself and my environment with competence." How can the physical setting support the development of these two convictions? First, let us consider the feeling "I matter."

The general approach for achieving this goal is to create a classroom environment that reflects the presence of children. Too often classrooms resemble motel rooms—anonymous, impersonal spaces designed to serve everyone and to belong to no one. Classrooms must be personalized in ways that communicate information about the identity, the uniqueness, and the importance of the children who use the space. For example, it is standard practice to provide children with a place to store their personal possessions—jackets, lunch boxes, treasures from home—but cubbies can be more than convenient storage. They can become a child's own special place if an attractively lettered name and a photograph are added (Osmon, 1971). Children can decorate their cubbies or paint them in their favorite color.

Similarly, the classroom walls and bulletin boards should reflect the existence of the children who work and play there. In one preschool I recently visited, bulletin boards were carefully created by the teachers. It was obvious that a great deal of time and effort had gone into the displays, one of which illustrated nursery rhymes while the other had a seasonal theme. They provided evidence of hardworking teachers, but evidence of the children was noticeably lacking. Posting children's photographs, art work, and projects, stories they have dictated or written, and charts listing heights, weights, or birthdays can serve as a tangible statement to children that they do indeed matter.

The second component of self-esteem, the feeling of being competent, can be supported by ensuring that there is not too great a discrepancy between what children want to do and what they can do. If children are to feel effective and competent in regard to their personal needs, the environment must be "child-scaled" (Moore, Lane, Hill, Cohen, & McGinty, 1979). Fountains, sinks, toilets, doorknobs, and light switches must be accessible and convenient for children to use. Since most preschools are housed in leftover spaces, it is unlikely that such equipment will be designed for children's use. Stools must therefore be provided so children can step up to adult-sized tables or sinks.

A similar principle applies to the storage of materials, toys, and equipment. Shelving should be low, open, well organized, and labeled so that children can select items independently and return them to the proper places when finished. Work surfaces should be adjacent to storage so that children do not have to go searching for a place to work. This does not necessarily imply regulation nursery-school tables. Children enjoy working on very low tables (Olds, 1979, recommends 10 inches in height), wooden crates, and the floor. This was vividly illustrated in a study by Pfluger and Zola (1974) in which preschoolers removed all materials, equipment, and furniture from their classroom and were then allowed to bring back whatever they wanted. Eventually almost everything was returned—except the tables, which remained in the hall. The children much preferred to use the floor for creative projects and snacks.

The choice of materials and their care are particularly critical to the development of competence. Children cannot possibly feel effective if everything they try is too difficult. A glue bottle that is clogged, paint that is too thin, or a puzzle with a piece missing make the completion of a task frustrating, if not impossible. Berk (1971) compared a Montessori classroom with a traditional nursery school, focusing on instances of conflict between children's desires to do something and their own inability to accomplish the chosen task. She found that there were far more conflicts in the traditional school, where children frequently selected activities that were too difficult. In contrast, the Montessori school was designed for success. All preschools must learn from Montessori to provide "graded challenges." Puzzles can range from those with few pieces, where each piece is a complete picture of an object, to those with 10 to 15 pieces, each of which is a fragment of an object or scene. Large-muscle equipment should also offer graded challenges. Climbers, for example, should have several different ways to get up and down, some more difficult than others. Children can then decide what route to take and how high to go. The fact that children can make such decisions wisely is illustrated in a study by Karlsson and Ellis (1972). These investigators observed preschoolers playing with a variety of climbing equipment and found that children balance the need for challenge against the need for security. Children's preferred height was inversely related to the complexity of the equipment. They went highest on a climber made of flat boxes; least high on a rope net.

Finally, it is essential to plan classroom space so that it is comprehensible to children. Children need to be able to represent the spatial environment in order to plan and carry out goal-directed activity. Golbeck (1985) notes that both the presence of distinctive physical features and the organization of such features can enhance representation and memory of the classroom space. Since young children rely extensively on physical cues in the environment for remembering spatial location, constancy and stability in the physical environment are essential. Adults conceptualize location in terms of both proximal and distal landmarks; in contrast, young children often use only the closest objects to encode spatial position (see, for example, Acredolo, 1976). If a landmark object is moved, young children may have difficulty compensating for the change. Boundaries, such as walls, partitions, the edges of a rug, or markings on the floor, also support children's ability to remember location. As with landmarks, children can encode locations as "near" a boundary. Furthermore, children can also use boundaries and floor coverings to identity "inside-outside" or "on-off" relationships. For example, keeping blocks "on the rug" is a spatial relationship the young child can easily represent.

The logical organization of items in the classroom can also enhance children's understanding of space. Golbeck, Rand, and Soundy (1986) found that preschoolers were quite well able to identify the logical organization of their well-defined classroom (e.g., places for playing with blocks, for drawing and painting, and for playing house) and that reminding children about these functionally defined areas of the room actually increased their ability to arrange an accurate small-scale model of the space. It is reasonable to assume that children also make use of such representational knowledge as they carry out activities in the classroom.

The effects of such rational space planning are evident in this 4-year-old's description of his classroom (Nash, 1981):

> Over here we make lots of things, and here, we find things out. This is where we pretend, and build, and be as grown-up as anything. And this is a nice quiet place where the puzzles and books are—you can't ride a trike or play balls or bring sand in here. This is a good place to be. (p. 155)

Security and Comfort. For many children, going to preschool is the first major venture outside the home and away from their primary caregivers. It is not without threat. Here they are exposed to an unfamiliar world of strange adults, competing peers, and new regulations. Clearly, a major concern of preschool education must be to enhance children's sense of security and trust. There are several ways in which the physical environment can contribute to these feelings.

First, children's view of the classroom from the entrance should be inviting, familiar, and friendly (Moore, Lane, Hill, Cohen, & McGinty, 1979). Children should be able to see several appealing activity areas from that point, so they can be reassured that good things happen in this place. If clear glass is used at the entrance, children can see in before actually crossing the threshold. Although this is not always possible in found spaces, care can still be taken to use warm colors, bright accents, textures, plants, animals, and interesting materials in or near the entry way. All of these convey a feeling of hominess and help to entice the child into the classroom (Osmon, 1971). On Laura's first day at the preschool we eventually selected, she was feeling somewhat nervous, especially as we reached the entrance. Inside the front door, however, stood a large cage containing a long-haired guinea pig named Fluffy. Forgetting her anxiety, Laura rushed over to the cage and then proceeded eagerly into the classroom to tell the teacher all about Annie, the guinea pig we had at home. A fortuitous coincidence, but a striking example of how a friendly entrance can help to assuage children's insecurity. In addition to a friendly entrance, Osmon (1971) suggests that a transition area be created near the doorway so that parents and children can pause, look around, grab a quick hug, and say goodbye. Courtyards, porches, anterooms, and corridors can all serve as transition spaces.

A second way of enhancing children's sense of comfort is to provide variety in both sensory stimulation and types of spaces. Olds (1979; see also Chapter 6) recommends variations in floor, ceiling, and boundary heights and in types of lighting and textures. She also emphasizes the importance of having different kinds of spaces available for children—some that are small and cozy, others that are large and more open; some that are bright, some that are dim; some that are noisy; and some that are quiet. Since children differ in their need for stimulation, and since even individual children experience varying levels of arousal and need for stimulation during the school day, spatial options within the classroom increase the likelihood of finding a suitable environmental niche.

Third, Jones and Prescott (1978) suggest that environments are more comfortable and less stressful if they contain elements that are soft or responsive to touch: beanbag chairs, stuffed couches, carpeting, sand, dirt, furry animals, sling swings, clay, paint, laps, and water. These writers, as well as others (Hartley, Frank, & Goldenson, 1952; Osmon, 1971) emphasize the importance of water as a particularly effective vehicle for enhancing comfort. Not only does water play provide tactile pleasure, but it constitutes a soothing, absorbing, nonthreatening experience. Hartley and his colleagues (1952) provide numerous anecdotal descriptions of the relaxing effects of water. One episode concerns 4-year-old Jake, normally a difficult, aggressive, explosive child:

> Jake goes into the play kitchen, takes a basin, puts all the play dishes in it, carries it over to the teacher, and asks her if he may wash them. She says yes and he goes into the bathroom. He fills the basin with water and gets a rag to wash with. Engrossed in his work, he then fills each dish and cup with water and stands them all around the edge of the sink. He works slowly and carefully to prevent spilling, and pays no attention to the others around him. . . . Another child comes in to fill a pan. Jake stretches out his hand and says, "I'll get some water for you." The boy gives him the pan and Jake fills it. . . . He takes a damp mop and starts to mop the floor and says, "I'm helping to clean up." . . . He puts the mop away and takes a towel offered by the teacher to help dry the dishes. He is helping another little girl and says to her, "I'm doing a good job, aren't I?" They work together. He dries the dishes and puts them on the shelf. (pp. 168–169)

Self-control. One of the most striking changes of the preschool years is children's increasing ability to regulate their own behavior. Gradually, preschoolers become better able to follow directions, to refrain from tempting but forbidden or inappropriate behavior, to postpone gratification, and to act in accordance with external standards of behavior (Marion, 1981). By designing an environment that makes it easier to follow classroom rules and procedures, teachers can support children's efforts toward self-control.

Schickedanz (1976) has identified three common classroom rules and the design principles that follow from them. First, teachers who expect children to return materials to the proper place can facilitate this behavior by providing storage spaces that are uncluttered, categorized, labeled, and adjacent to work surfaces. Second, it is easier to sit attentively during group meetings if the teacher is at a different level from the children, if there is sufficient room to spread out, and if physical indicators such as tape or carpet squares are used to specify seating positions. Finally, the familiar admonition "Walk, don't run" is more likely to be obeyed when circulation paths are somewhat meandering rather than long and straight and when the space in the room is broken up by the use of furniture, partitions, and varying floor levels.

The importance of avoiding large open spaces has also been stressed by other writers (Day, 1983; Day & Sheehan, 1974; Kritchevsky & Prescott, 1969), and a recent study by Neill and Denham (1982) lends empirical support to their arguments. Neill compared the behavior of children in classrooms varying in terms of openness, density, and size of group. Openness had by far the largest number of significant effects. Children in the more open rooms were more aggressive, moved around more, did more watching, and engaged in fewer school-oriented activities and in more active play. (See also Moore, Chapter 3 in this volume.)

Another aspect of classroom design that may influence children's emerging self-control is the opportunity to be alone. Although children's need for privacy in the classroom has received little attention, there are some data suggesting that places to be alone are particularly important for children who are less popular and more aggressive—in short, children who may have difficulty dealing with the constant presence of others so typical of school situations (Weinstein, 1982). As Olds (1979) has noted:

> Rarely are so many people placed together for such long periods of time, in such confined space, with so few options for withdrawal, as are children in schools. While the developmental consequences of this practice are unknown, it does suggest that the sizes of areas in the room should be varied to provide options for privacy. (p. 111)

Osmon (1971) recommends the creation of "places to pause for a while," and Moore and his colleagues (1979) suggest "retreat spaces." The goal is the same: to allow an overstimulated, upset, or tired child to be alone, to escape from the continual presence of others, to enjoy a quiet moment, to think through a conflict. Advocates of behavior modification know the usefulness of social isolation or "time-out" as a strategy for dealing with inappropriate behavior. Although its effectiveness is usually explained in terms of removing opportunities for positive reinforcement, it may be that social isolation also provides a much-needed opportunity to be alone and quiet, to reflect, and to calm down (Elias, 1981).

Private spaces need not be entirely enclosed to seem private. Indeed, total enclosure may make them less desirable. Curtis and Smith (1974) describe how they created places for children "to crawl away into," only to find that children would not use them because they could not see what was going on (p. 679). The problem was solved by installing clear acrylic panels, which provided children with a sense of physical privacy yet allowed them visual access to the room.

A corollary to the principle of creating places to be alone is providing materials that allow children to play alone. It is well established that certain materials and activities encourage social play, whereas others—such as art activities, water play, and manipulative materials—foster solitary play (Green, 1933; Hendrickson, Strain, Tremblay, & Shores, 1981; Murphy, 1937; Quilitch & Risley, 1973; Rubin, 1977; Shure, 1963; Van Alstyne, 1932). Solitary play has traditionally been considered as socially less mature behavior (Parten, 1932). Viewed from a privacy perspective, however, it is apparent that opportunities to play alone can serve as calming interludes between more interactive play episodes. According to Hartley *et al.* (1952), for example, block play has an almost "magical power" to restore the equanimity of an upset child. They suggest that this is because blocks allow solitary play with nonthreatening, sturdy, clean, and controllable materials. Not only do blocks provide a good substitute object for hostility (they can be knocked down without fear of retribution), but they can also be used to build a cozy place of retreat.

Peer Interaction and Prosocial Behavior. The preschool years mark an increase in the amount of time children engage in associative or group play (Parten, 1932; Green, 1933; Rubin, Watson, & Jambor, 1976) and a concomitant decrease in solitary play. This developmental change is accompanied by increasing ability to show empathy, altruism, and cooperation. Such prosocial behavior appears to be clearly related to the child's growing capacity to assume the point of view of others; in other words, to engage in social role taking. Rubin (1976) found that performance on a social role-taking task was negatively correlated with parallel play and positively correlated to associative play. Although the correlational nature of the data preclude cause-and-effect statements, the data support Piaget's (1926) contention that social play often involves interpersonal disputes that force children to assume the other's point of view. Thus, designing classroom spaces to encourage peer interaction not only supports the natural developmental progression toward group play but also enhances opportunities for role-taking experiences and consequently for prosocial behavior. There are three basic design guidelines to consider: partitioning space, providing materials that support group play, and minimizing conflict by offering children a sufficient amount to do.

Since preschoolers generally play in small groups of two to four children, it is helpful to partition classroom space into small, well-defined areas, or "activity pockets" (Moore, Lane, Hill, Cohen, & McGinty, 1979). Work by Kounin and his students (e.g., Houseman, 1972) suggests that the "clarity of one's activity boundary . . . appears associated with minimum conflict" (Gump, 1978, p. 149). Similarly, studies by Field (1980), Rohe and Nuffer (1977), and Neill and Denham (1982) indicate that partitioned space increases cooperative play. Field has suggested that small, bounded spaces enhance feelings of closeness, intimacy, and safety. Well-defined areas also prevent ongoing play from being disrupted by intruders.

Cooperative interaction can also be supported by providing activity areas and materials that encourage group play. There is a good deal of empirical evidence that interactive behavior occurs most frequently in the housekeeping or dramatic play areas, in the block area, with vehicles (trucks, wagons, carriages), and on "multiple niche" large-muscle apparatus (Shure, 1963; Charlesworth & Hartup, 1967; Doyle, 1975; Hendrickson *et al.*, 1981; Rubin, Maioni, & Hornung, 1976). Such play occurs less frequently when children are involved with manipulative materials such as puzzles and shape-sorting toys, art projects, books, sand and water play, and single-person large-muscle equipment (tricycles, rocking horses).

Finally, children's interactions are partly dependent on the amount of material available. Houseman (1972), Smith and Green (1975), and Dawe (1934) have all noted that most aggressive behavior is a result of "property fights"—disputes about who owns or controls specific materials and space. Kritchevsky and Prescott (1969) have devised a simple method for calculating the amount to do per child or the number of play spaces that a room contains. They use the analogy of musical chairs to illustrate the consequences of an insufficient number of play spaces:

> We shall assume that the objective of the game is not to eliminate participants, but to provide each child with a chair each time the music stops. In a game with 20 chairs and 10 children (2.0 chairs per child), when the music stops children can easily find an empty chair without help. . . . But the closer the number of chairs is to the number of children, the more likely it will be that a teacher will need to help children find the empty chairs. If there are fewer chairs than children, either someone (or more) must stand every time the music stops, or children must double up on chairs. (p. 15)

Kritchevsky and Prescott's analogy is well substantiated by research. Busse, Ree, and Gutride (1970) found that there was significantly more cooperative play with toys (although for boys only) in "environmentally enriched" classrooms containing abundant learning materials than in control classes. Johnson (1935) found that a reduction of playground equipment led to more teasing, crying, quarreling, and hitting. Similar findings are reported by Smith and Connelly (1977) in a series of studies: a decrease in play equipment led consistently to an increase in aggressive behavior. Murphy, Murphy, and Newcomb (1937) report that even when a large supply of toys is available competition and quarreling occur if there are only one or two of a kind.

Property fights are particularly common in the sand play area (Green, 1933) and the block area (Houseman, 1972) where there is often ambiguity about who owns the material and where children frequently need the sand, the blocks, or the space being used by others (Gump, 1978). By ensuring that there is a sufficient number of blocks or an abundant amount of sand one can minimize conflict in these areas. Bender (1978) observed six 4-year-old boys playing first with 20 blocks and later with 70 blocks. With the fewer number, there was little cooperative conversation, a predominance of parallel play, and numerous disputes. Play with the larger number was characterized by more interaction, cooperative conversation, role playing, and an absence of arguing. Osmon (1971) also suggests that aggressive behavior in the block area can be minimized by using movable storage shelves to divide the area into separate spaces of different sizes. These can then be reunited when children wish to play together in a larger group.

Sex-role Identification. At age 3, Laura announced that she was going to be a doctor, a firefighter, a mommy, and a daddy when she grew up. When challenged by her infinitely wiser 7-year-old sister, Laura agreed that girls were mommies and boys were daddies. Nonetheless, she persisted in proclaiming her right to be both.

Despite Laura's confusion about her parenting future, she had clearly learned the correct gender labels for herself and for mommies and daddies. She knew she was a girl, and she had acquired information about the expected and appropriate behavior for each sex. Observations of her play behavior revealed her sex-typed activity preferences: in preschool she walked quickly past the blocks and trucks toward the housekeeping corner to cook, clean, and take care of the baby.

She is not alone. Empirical evidence documents clearly that by the time they are 3 or 4 years old, children demonstrate a relatively consistent preference to engage in sex-typed activity and to play with children of the same sex. By age 5, their knowledge of "boy toys" and "girl toys," is almost perfect (Nadelman, 1974) and preference for the same-sex toys is well engrained (Frasher, Nurss, & Brogan, 1980).

A number of writers have suggested that such rigid sex-role behavior is maladaptive and that an important goal of the preschool years is to encourage androgyny (Bem, 1974), a blend of male and female characteristics. For example, Frasher *et al.* (1980) comment that

> packaging and designating certain toys as appropriate for only girls or only boys and reinforcing or permitting their use by only girls or boys deprive both sexes of valuable cognitive and social experiences that have important implications for later development. . . . Androgynous play behavior provides both sexes with a wider range of potential alternatives and better equips them to confront the realities of contemporary life. (pp. 26–27)

If we accept androgyny as a valid goal for early childhood education, the issue of feasibility must be addressed. Given the strong preference for sex-typed behavior, is the development of androgyny even possible? Two relatively recent studies (Bianchi & Bakeman, 1978; DiLeo, Moely, & Sulzer, 1979) suggest that it is. Moreover, Eisenberg, Murray, and Hite (1982) found that children rarely justify their own toy preferences with sex-typed reasoning but instead refer to what the toys can *do.* One explanation for this finding is that preferences reflect previous exposure to the same-sex toys rather than a conscious attempt to adhere to sex-role standards. If this explanation is correct, the preschool environment can contribute to the development of androgyny by enticing children into opposite-sex activity areas containing materials and toys they would not normally encounter.

Several writers have suggested that the typical housekeeping corner with its sink, stove, and doll's high chair reinforces sex stereotypes. Hartley *et al.* (1952) asked a group of preschool teachers why boys did not play at being fathers in the housekeeping areas. The teachers' subsequent examination of these areas revealed that the materials were generally female-oriented. When items of men's clothing, masculine paraphernalia, and water-play materials were added, boys participated far more frequently. Osmon (1971) further recommends equipping the housekeeping area with a variety of "junk materials"—bottles, boxes, flower pots, gears, wheels—that can serve as a stimulus for all kinds of dramatic play, lessening dependence on traditional sex-typed props.

In an effort to encourage children to enter an opposite-sex setting, Kinsman and Berk (1979) joined the block and housekeeping areas in a preschool and a kindergarten. Although the results were not entirely consistent with the hypothesis, the intervention did lead to an increase in mixed-sex groups in both areas. Interestingly, the younger children seemed far more amenable to the changes than the kindergarteners, who tried to rebuild the wall between the areas using trucks, a mirror, an ironing board, and other equipment. Similarly, girls adapted more readily to the removal of the partitions than boys, for whom sex-related play activities are clearly more rigid.

Cognitive Development

Symbolic Expression. The major cognitive achievement of the first two years of life is the transition from sensorimotor to representational thought (Piaget, 1962). No longer tied to the actual, concrete presence of objects and people, 2-year-olds can use symbols to imagine, to anticipate, and to remember. The years from 2 to 5 are characterized by impressive growth in this capacity, particularly as children engage in pretend play and language. We will consider each of these in turn.

Symbolic or pretend play is an especially popular activity among young children. Educators, however, have not always agreed on whether such play belongs in preschools (e.g., Bereiter & Engelmann, 1966; Montessori, 1964). "To pretend or not to pretend"—the decision at least partly depends upon the values and functions attributed to symbolic play.

From a traditional psychodynamic perspective, symbolic play is seen as an outlet for the child's problems, tensions, and normally unacceptable urges (see Hartley *et al.*, 1952). From the perspective of social role learning, it is argued that symbolic play allows the child to practice appropriate role behavior and to imitate adults (Kohlberg, 1969). More recently, research has emphasized the cognitive value of symbolic play. Studies have indicated that dramatic play is positively correlated with classification skills (Rubin & Maioni, 1975), creativity (Dansky, 1980), the ability to assume the spatial viewpoints of others (Rosen, 1974; Rubin & Maioni, 1975), cooperative problem-solving behavior (Rosen, 1974), and conservation of quantity (Golomb & Cornelius, 1977).

Given the emotional, social, and cognitive value of symbolic play, it would seem to deserve inclusion in every preschool curriculum. This means allocating a special space for a dramatic play area. Although dramatic play may occur in many areas—blocks, water, and sand—it is most likely to occur in an area specifically designed to promote such behavior. Evans,

Shub, and Weinstein (1971) recommend that the dramatic play area contain a kitchen and a bedroom, because these are the two areas of the house that are most important to children.

The kinds of props that should appear in the dramatic play area depend on the age of the children who play there. Guidelines can be derived from research on the developmental changes in symbolic play with objects. McCune-Nicolich and Carroll (1981) enumerate four developmental stages between the ages of 2 and 5. First, realistic toys are used for their "real" purpose (e.g., brushing hair with a toy brush). Next, objects similar in function or appearance to the pretend object can be substituted (an appropriately shaped block can serve as a telephone). Later, ambiguous objects—pieces of wood, plastic, string—that have no functional meaning can be used; finally, completely dissimilar objects can serve as substitutes. I recall a 4-year-old who invited me to watch as she "fished in shark-infested waters." Perched on a chair, she dangled a piece of string onto the floor. Colored felt pens served as fish; a pair of sandals were the sharks.

Such use of dissimilar objects is especially difficult for younger children. Elder and Pederson (1978) asked 2½ and 3½-year-olds to do specific pretend actions with similar or dissimilar substitute objects (e.g., to use a car as a shovel). They describe the difficulties faced by the youngest children when presented with objects that were physically unlike the referents. The children often insisted that they could not do what was requested and used the object according to its own appropriate use (e.g., driving the car back and forth across the table).

Apparently, for very young children, the physical characteristics of an object determine what can be done with it. Thus, dramatic play areas for 2- and 3-year-olds should contain realistic props as a stimulus for pretend play, and the more the better. Olszewski and Fuson (1982) found that 3-year-olds engaged in more verbal fantasy play when supplemental objects such as toy furniture, a doll house, and a bus were provided in addition to a play family. For older children, however, such additional props were actually inhibiting. Research also indicates that less structured objects are preferable for older children. For example, Pulaski (1970) found that materials such as clay, simple dolls, blocks, boxes, and pipe cleaners elicited a greater variety of fantasy themes than more structured toys (Barbie dolls or a service station with cars).

In addition to an increased ability to pretend, the preschool years mark a shift from egocentric to socialized speech (Piaget, 1955). Very young children may repeat syllables, words, or phrases simply for the pleasure of vocalizing, may talk to themselves, or may engage in "collective monologue" (two or more children talking *at* each other rather than *with* each other). In contrast, older preschoolers generally speak to communite—to ask questions, to provide answers, to report, threaten, plead.

Although the role of peer talk in language development is not clear

(Fein & Clarke-Stewart, 1973), it would appear that children's emerging language ability can be supported by an environment that contains activities and materials that encourage peer interaction. Once again, the provision of a dramatic play area is of primary importance (Fox, 1976; Garvey, 1974, 1979). Here children gain valuable language practice from dramatic play with peers or sociodramatic play. There is evidence that dramatic play is particularly likely to produce mature language behavior (Cowe, 1967), and a study by Marshall (1961) has indicated that the most frequent use of language to communicate suggestions, agreement, and hostility occurs during dramatic play rather than during reality contacts with peers. Christie and Johnsen (1983) observe that sociodramatic play requires children to use two types of verbal exchange: pretend communications appropriate to their roles and "metacommunications" necessary to structure the play episode. These verbal exchanges are vividly described by McCune-Nicolich and Carroll (1980):

> [During sociodramatic play children face the] challenge of transmitting personal fantasies to a peer, securing the cooperation of a peer, and managing an interaction that is more complex than everyday life (which, for a child, is managed by others). Objects and substances can be transformed or invented as needed, but for play to proceed, agreement must be reached on the location of the imaginary bathtub, or the edible quality of the building blocks. A child who was previously happy to mime a maternal attitude by holding and rocking a doll must now negotiate and obtain agreement about who is the baby, and who is the mother. A new desire for realism in play requires that episodes have clear beginnings, central themes . . . , and endings or resolutions. In short, sociodramatic play requires a new level of communication and organization not required for solitary make-believe. (p. 9)

In addition to fostering children's oral language ability, a goal of the preschool period is the development of interest in printed language. Early childhood educators have written extensively about the importance of planned programs that provide children with the opportunity to have pleasurable experiences with literature (Arbuthnot & Sutherland, 1977; Cullinan, 1977; Huck, 1976; Stewig & Sebesta, 1978). These writers encourage teachers to read daily to children, to discuss the stories, and to integrate literature with other areas of the curriculum.

The classroom environment can support these activities by providing an appealing, well-organized library corner or reading area (Coody, 1973; Huck, 1976). Yet such areas are often neglected. Morrow (1982) surveyed literature use in nursery schools and kindergartens and found that library corners were either poorly designed or nonexistent. Moreover, children rarely, if ever, used library corners during free play. Similar results were found in two studies that observed children's behavior patterns in the preschool classroom. Both Rosenthal (1973) and Shure (1963) reported that the block and art areas were the most popular during free play, whereas the book area was among the least popular. These studies suggest that young children are unlikely to choose literature as a free-play activity without some inducement.

Studies that a colleague and I recently conducted (Morrow & Weinstein, 1982; Morrow & Weinstein, 1986) indicate that a well-designed, inviting library area can entice children to look at books during free play. We devised a simple set of guidelines for the design of such areas, specifying that library corners should be located in quiet areas of the room, partitioned off from the rest of the space, contain shelves for displaying books with the covers showing, have some element of softness, and be well-stocked with a wide variety of books and "literature props," such as felt board stories, cassettes, roll movies, and puppets. In classrooms where such corners were introduced, voluntary literature use during free play increased dramatically.

Logical Thought: Putting Things into Relation. The preschool years are the period of preoperational thought (Piaget, 1926). During this time, children's thinking about physical phenomena is dominated by what they see. For example, pouring a liquid from a short, wide container into a tall, narrow container causes a change in the observable appearance of the liquid. A typical preoperational child will assert that this has caused a change in the amount of liquid; the child has not yet achieved conservation, the understanding that irrelevant changes in shape or arrangement do not affect number or amount.

Conservation is one aspect of what Piaget calls "logico-mathematical knowledge," knowledge of relationships, classes, measuring, and counting (Kamii & DeVries, 1977). The development of logico-mathematical knowledge is one of the primary objectives of the preschool years and involves classification (matching, sorting, and labeling), seriation (comparing and coordinating differences), and number concepts (the process of establishing equivalence). In order to support these developing abilities the environment must contain interesting materials that invite these activities. According to Kamii and DeVries, the more children become involved, "the more new connections they will make and their logico-mathematical structure necessarily develops. The art of teaching, then, begins with how to provide a setting and materials that suggest interesting ideas to children" (p. 386).

To increase opportunities for classification, Hohmann *et al.* (1979) suggest that classrooms contain sets of materials that are similar but vary along one dimension (e.g., dump trucks that are the same make and shape but are different colors), as well as materials that vary along more than one dimension. Similarly, opportunities for seriation can be supported by equipping each area with similar materials in three or four sizes. For example, the housekeeping area might contain books, pots, measuring spoons, and food containers, each in graduated sizes. The art area can be stocked with different-sized paper, brushes, paper plates, and macaroni. In the woodworking area, nails, hammers, screwdrivers and pieces of sandpaper can all vary in size; sandpaper can also vary in texture, from very fine to very rough.

Hohman *et al.* recommend that teachers make a list of comparative terms (heavier–lighter, rougher–smoother, bigger–smaller) in order to think of materials that can be compared in different ways.

In addition to providing materials that invite investigation, comparison, sorting, and counting, it is important to arrange and store the materials in a way that also supports these activities. For example, similar objects should be stored together on shelves or in containers that are labeled with pictures or outlines. Seriated materials can be arranged in order (e.g., pans, hammers, and hats can all hang on a pegboard in size order). Labels can be varied to provide different kinds of classification experiences (e.g., using *not* labels—"red" and "not red"—or labeling in terms of two attributes—big wooden trucks and small wooden trucks). Hohmann *et al.* (1979) also suggest that not everything be labeled; in this way, children can be encouraged to sort according to their own categories (e.g., trucks can be arranged according to size on one day and according to color on another).

Although there are substantial data indicating that the organization of materials facilitates their use (e.g., Weinstein, 1977; Phyfe-Perkins, 1982), there is little evidence that such use actually enhances logical reasoning. A recent study by Nash (1981) is noteworthy in this regard. Nash compared the behavior and achievements of children in 19 "randomly arranged" preschool classrooms with those of children in 19 "spatially planned" rooms. In the randomly arranged rooms, equipment and materials were arranged in either a haphazard fashion or according to pragmatic criteria (the water table should be near a sink). In the spatially planned rooms, the same equipment and materials were thoughtfully and intentionally organized to promote specific learning outcomes. Scheduling, activity choices, and interaction patterns were similar in all rooms. Yet not only did children in the spatially planned rooms engage in more manipulative activities; they produced more complex shape, color, and number patterns using those materials (beads, pegboards, unit blocks). The most striking finding was that conservation was achieved earlier and by a greater number of children in the spatially planned rooms. Nash's investigation provides the first empirical evidence that logico-mathematical knowledge can be supported by classroom design.

A final design guideline focuses once again on allocating space for a dramatic play area. As suggested earlier, it appears that symbolic play experiences can have an impact on children's logical thinking ability. Rubin and Maioni (1975) found that children who engaged in dramatic play had superior classification skills compared with children who engaged in less mature play. One possible explanation for this finding is that during dramatic play children take the roles of others and thus learn to understand the reciprocal relations necessary for logical reasoning. Golomb and Cornelius (1977) explored this further and found that nonconserving 4-year-olds who engaged in symbolic play sessions showed significant improvement on conservation of quantity tasks. They concluded that during symbolic play children use a kind of reversibility; for example, they recognize the identity of a play object and its temporary transformation in make-believe. Thus, in both conservation tasks and symbolic play children perform reversible transformations of objects. Although a partial replication of this study failed to find similar results (Guthrie & Hudson, 1979), the data on the cognitive value of symbolic play are sufficiently suggestive to warrant the creation of a dramatic play area.

Creativity and Problem-solving Ability. Wallach and Kogan (1965) define creativity as "first, the production of association content that is abundant and that is unique; second the presence in the associator of a playful, permissive task attitude" (p. 289). In other words, creativity is characterized not only by the fluent generation of novel responses but also by a playful approach to the task at hand.

Recent research on stimulating creativity (see Christie & Johnsen, 1983, for a comprehensive review) indicates that play can have a significant impact on creativity. Dansky and Silverman (1975), for example, allowed one group of preschoolers to play with materials (such as paper clips, index cards, corks, and spools), while a second group imitated an experimenter's actions with the same objects, and a third group participated in a verbal guessing game with the experimenter about the objects. Subjects were subsequently asked to generate all of the uses they could for each of the objects in another set. Children in the play condition produced significantly more standard and nonstandard uses for the objects than the subjects in either of the two other groups.

In a subsequent study, Dansky (1980) hypothesized that the occurrence of *symbolic activity* during the free play was responsible for the subsequent increase in associative fluency. His hypothesis was based on the idea that both symbolic play and creativity involve novel, unusual transformations of objects and actions—the playful distortion of reality. Preexperimental observations of preschoolers during free play allowed the children to be identified as "players" or "nonplayers" depending on the degree of make-believe in their play. They were then assigned to one of the three treatments used in the earlier study and afterward were given the alternative uses test with different materials. As in the earlier study, only the free-play subjects exhibited enhanced associative fluency. However, a significant interaction effect indicated that it was the players in the free-play condition who were responsible for this finding. Thus, it appears that free-play experiences will only stimulate creativity if children engage in make-believe during the play.

A number of investigators have also looked at the links between play and problem-solving ability (e.g., Smith & Dutton, 1979). Of particular interest is a study by Pepler and Ross (1981) in which 3- and 4-year-olds played with five sets of play materials—animals, vehicles, regular shapes, random shapes, and squares. These could be used either as a puzzle by fitting the pieces into a form board (the "convergent play condition") or as freestanding blocks (the "divergent play condition"). The children were then given both divergent and convergent problems to solve. Both groups did equally well on the convergent tasks, but the children with the divergent play experiences did better on the divergent tasks.

An interesting aspect of this study is that although children in the convergent play sessions were *not told* to place the pieces in the form boards, they spent two-thirds of their time doing exactly that. The mere presence of the form boards seemed to direct the children's activities, a compelling demonstration of the influence of materials on play. The investigators compare the convergent play materials of this study with the cognitive materials designed by Montessori. Although these materials "elicit attention to properties and strategies which relate to the properties," they are also designed to "suppress fantasy and imaginative play" (p. 1209). Dansky's research suggests that "the learning derived from this type of material may be limited to the lesson inherent in the materials" (p. 1209).

What design guidelines can be derived from this research? First, it is essential that the environment support opportunities for pretend play by creating a dramatic play area well-stocked with age-appropriate materials. Second, materials that facilitate divergent play should be available throughout the classroom. Jones and Prescott (1978) distinguish between materials that are "open"—water, paint, dough, sand—and "closed"—puzzles, workbooks, tracing patterns. This open–closed dimension describes the extent to which restrictions inherent in a material impose a clear, correct use or solution. Analyzing play materials in these terms can help teachers structure a setting that encourages creativity and problem-solving ability.

Attention Span and Task Involvement. Young children have a notorious reputation for short attention spans. Early childhood teachers are taught to make activities brief and not to require young children to attend to a demonstration or story for any substantial length of time. Yet research evidence demonstrates that attention span varies greatly depending upon the activity in which the child is engaged, the complexity of the materials being used, and the spatial arrangement of the setting.

An early study by McDowell (1937), for example, looked at how long children played with a wide variety of materials generally available during free play, such as dolls, books, clay, paints, blocks, dishes, nesting toys, and vehicles. She found that children played longest with materials used in constructing other objects (e.g., blocks), with materials requiring small muscle manipulation, and those used in playing house. Least sustaining were books, pull toys, and vehicles. In a similar vein, Rosenthal (1973) demonstrated that activity areas vary greatly in their "holding power"—the ability to sustain children's participation and involvement. Art and role playing had the highest holding power (approximately eight to ten minutes), whereas dress-up, displays (pictures, objects, and animals to observe and discuss), and vehicles were extremely low (one to two minutes). Such marked variation prompted Rosenthal to conclude that "it is relatively naive to speak about a child's attention span without specifying its ecological anchorage . . . For any given child, span of interest appears to be greatly dependent upon the nature of the occupation with which the youngster is involved" (p. 188).

Similar conclusions were drawn by Moyer and Gilmer (1955), who investigated to what extent the attention spans of children ranging in age from 18 months to 7 years could be maximized. Using toys specially designed to sustain children's involvement, they obtained mean spans of 15 to 40 minutes, far longer than would normally be expected. Moreover, there was no regular increase in attention span from year to year. At each age, certain toys were more effective in sustaining children's interest than others. Moyer and Gilmer concluded that "the concept of attention span, used in the singular, is meaningless" (p. 200).

Although Moyer and Gilmer do not provide specific guidelines for the design of toys that support sustained involvement, holding power appears to be related to the *variety* of behaviors elicited by an activity or material (Kounin & Sherman, 1979). Jones and Prescott (1978) distinguish between *simple* materials with one obvious use and *complex* materials with subparts or separate, juxtaposed elements that allow children to manipulate and improvise. The more complex the material, the more effective it is in holding a child's attention. Greater complexity can also mitigate the effect of repeated exposure. Scholz and Ellis (1975), for example, found that although preference for play objects declined with familiarity, the rate of decline was inversely related to the complexity of the object.

Assessing complexity requires careful analysis. Kritchevsky and Prescott (1969) insightfully observed that adults can be deceived by equipment that may appear, at first glance, to be particularly interesting or complex. Slides disguised as brightly colored elephants or rocket ships may be delightful to look at, but they are still simple units that direct children to line up, climb up, and slide down.

Children's attention spans are also dependent on the spatial organization of the classroom. In the very first classroom I designed, I innocently located the book area and the block area next to one another on the only available rug, reasoning that children would want to sit on the floor for both activities. Although that was certainly true, I had not anticipated the detrimental effect of fort construction and tower toppling on sustained involvement with books. Altering the arrangement corrected the problem.

Anecdotal evidence like this is bolstered by recent experimental efforts to improve low-quality space in preschools and kindergartens. Using adaptations of an environmental inventory developed by Prescott, Jones, and Kritchevsky (1967), Hoffman (1976), Teets (1980), and Sutfin (1982) all report greater task involvement as a result of improved spatial arrangements. These investigators reiterate the need for clear traffic paths that do not intersect activity areas, abundant storage, the separation of incompatible activities (messy–neat, quiet–noisy), well-defined, partitioned areas, and a sufficient amount to do. Children's attention spans are clearly more variable than we tend to think. By providing complex materials and arranging classrooms to achieve high-quality space, we can greatly enhance the degree of involvement.

Motor Development

During the summer of her fourth birthday, Laura learned how to buckle her sandals. Her excitement and pride were almost palpable. Together we exulted in how she had accomplished with relative ease a task that had been beyond her abilities the previous summer. Such are the preschool years—the period of learning to tie shoes and to button shirts, to skip, hop, and balance. Achievements like these reflect the preschooler's increasing large- and small-muscle control. Yet, although preschool teachers often pay considerable attention to provisioning the environment to encourage small-muscle activities, they often neglect to provide opportunities for large movement.

Omwake (1971) suggests that one reason for this relative neglect is the attitude that large-motor ability is innate (i.e., some children are born clumsy and will remain so) or, conversely, that increasing movement control is simply a matter of time (i.e., all children will eventually become skillful). Halverson (1971) cautions against these attitudes, arguing that children will not achieve mature motor control unless provided with opportunities and guidance.

A second reason for the neglect is more pragmatic: large-movement centers require space. Most schools attempt to solve this problem by relegating large-movement activities to the outdoors. (See Moore, Cohen, Oertel, & van Ryzin, 1979, and Shaw's Chapter 9 in this volume for detailed, developmentally based guidelines for outdoor play areas.) Halverson, Roberton, and Harper (1973), however, contend that an indoor movement center is essential for preschoolers, especially in regions where the use of the outdoors is severely curtailed because of climate. Although a movement center might not be large enough to contain large climbing equipment, there might still be sufficient space to throw beanbags and to balance, jump, and tumble. The movement center could be set up as a free-play option like any other activity area or could be set up each day in a large open space for a specified time and then dismantled.

The provisioning of a movement center can be particularly problematic for teachers. According to Herkowitz (1978), the preschool years are marked by a substantial variability in motor skills; yet, commercially available equipment is often suited for use only by children with highly developed skills. Frequently, balls are too heavy, bats are too long, and hoop targets are too high. Since equipment will affect the way a child can move (Halverson, 1971), it is essential to provide for a wide range of skill. Herkowitz recommends three ways of accommodating this range. First, classrooms should contain multiple pieces of the same equipment—bats, balls, ladders, chinning bars—that vary in terms of the relevant dimension (height, weight, size, etc.). Second, it is helpful to have equipment that children can adjust to accommodate their own levels of skill (e.g., a sliding board that children can tilt to any inclination, a wand supported by vertical standards that can be raised or lowered before the child jumps). Finally, children can be given pieces of equipment which, by their very nature, accommodate a wide range of ability (e.g., a walking board that is very wide at one end, then narrows gradually). Herkowitz also suggests that evaluation devices be built into the movement center so that children can assess their skillfulness and progress. Each rung of a ladder, for example, can be painted a different color so that children can easily keep track of how high they are able to climb.

Young children's need for movement can be nervewracking for adults, who often find it difficult to tolerate "the incessant, unpredictable activity of so many little bodies, each moving to its own separate drummer" (Olds, 1979, p. 92). Teachers typically respond by issuing orders to slow down or stop completely or by removing equipment that encourages large movement. But such attempts may not only be detrimental to children's development; they are futile. An alternative is to provide an environment that inhibits inappropriate running, climbing, and rough-and-tumble play (see section on self-control), while providing legitimate, constructive opportunities for large-movement activities.

SOME FINAL THOUGHTS

Not too long ago, I heard a noted playground designer, William Weisz, decry the use of single swings and explain his preference for tire swings that can accommodate three children at one time. The single swing, he contended, encourages children to lose themselves in isolated, spaced-out reverie, while tire swings foster social interaction. Some time later, I found Kritchevsky and Prescott's dictum on children's need to be alone: "We can think of no unit which so effectively and naturally insulates a child from the rest of the group [as the single swing]" (p. 29). Both statements acknowledge the isolation that a single swing provides; yet Weisz abhors the isolation, whereas Kritchevsky and Prescott see value in it. Their respective playgrounds would differ because of a fundamental difference of opinion about the goal of a swing ride.

Despite their differences, Weisz, Kritchevsky, and Prescott all view the built environment as a *means for achieving an outcome.* They have articulated their values and their objectives and they intentionally manipulate the setting to achieve them. This way of thinking about the environment is perhaps the most important message of this chapter.

A 1979 study by Sheehan and Abbott looked at the physical settings of nine federally funded day-care centers. Their results were discouraging: 85% of the activity areas observed were not distinctly divided from one another; children's work was displayed in only 13% of the areas; 58% of the activity areas suffered distractions from adjacent activities; only 2.4% of the areas provided space for a child to work alone. Sheehan and Abbott concluded that although the centers were generally well-supplied with materials, they were noisy and distracting, provided no privacy, were impersonal, and were not conducive to individual, uninterrupted work.

Findings like these underline the need to acquaint early childhood practitioners with the empirical research on design–behavior relationships and to encourage them to think in terms of designing to achieve educational and developmental goals. We must promulgate the idea so well expressed by Olds (1979):

> The motivation to interact with the environment exists in all children as an intrinsic property of life, but the quality of the interactions is dependent upon the possibilities for engagement that the environment provides. Hence, in all its manifestations, the environment is the curriculum and the physical parameters of classrooms, as much as books, toys, and work sheets, must be manipulated by teachers as essential aspects of the educational process. (p. 91)

Only when teachers begin to view the environment as a tool for education and development will they be able to make thoughtful, well-informed decisions about their classroom settings.

REFERENCES

Acredolo, L. P. Frames of reference used by children for orientation in unfamiliar places. In G. Moore & R. Golledge (Eds.), *Environmental knowing.* Stroudsburg, PA: Dowden, Hutchinson, and Ross, 1976.

Arbuthnot, M. H., & Sutherland, Z. *Children and books* (5th ed.). Glenview, IL: Scott, Foresman, 1977.

Bem, S. L. The measurement of psychological androgyny. *Journal of Consulting & Clinical Psychology,* 1974, *42,* 155–162.

Bender, J. Large hollow blocks: Relationship of quantity to block building behaviors. *Young Children,* 1978, *33*(6), 17–23.

Bereiter, C., & Engelmann, S. *Teaching disadvantaged children in the preschool.* Englewood Cliffs, NJ: Prentice-Hall, 1966.

Berk, L. E. Effects of variations in the nursery school setting on environmental constraints and children's modes of adaptation. *Child Development,* 1971, *42,* 839–869.

Bianchi, B. D., & Bakeman, R. Sex-typed affiliation preferences observed in preschoolers: Traditional and open school differences. *Child Development,* 1978, *49*(3), 910–912.

Briggs, D. *Your child's self-esteem.* New York: Doubleday (Dolphin), 1975.

Busse, T. V., Ree, M., & Gutride, M. Environmentally enriched classrooms and the play behavior of Negro preschool children. *Urban Education,* 1970, *5*(2), 128–140.

Charlesworth, R., & Hartup, W. W. Positive social reinforcement in the nursery school peer group. *Child Development,* 1967, *38,* 973–1002.

Christie, J. F., & Johnsen, E. P. The role of play in social-intellectual development, *Review of Educational Research,* 1983, *53*(1), 93–115.

Cohen, D. J. *Serving Preschool Children #3.* Washington, DC: U.S. Department of Health, Education and Welfare, Office of Human Development, Publication #74-1057, 1974.

Coody, B. *Using literature with young children.* Dubuque, IA: Brown, 1973.

Cowe, E. G. A study of kindergarten activities for language development. Unpublished doctoral dissertation, Columbia University, 1967.

Cullinan, B. E. Books in the life of the young child. In B. E. Cullinan & C. Carmichael (Eds.), *Literature and young children.* Urbana, IL: National Council of Teachers of English, 1977.

Curtis, P., & Smith, R. A child's exploration of space. *School Review,* 1974, *82*(4), 671–680.

Dansky, J. L. Make-believe: A mediator of the relationship between play and associative fluency. *Child Development,* 1980, *51,* 576–579.

Dansky, J. L., & Silverman, I. W. Play: A general facilitator of associative fluency. *Developmental Psychology,* 1975, *11,* 104.

Dawe, H. C. An analysis of 200 quarrels of preschool children. *Child Development,* 1934, *5,* 139–157.

Day, D. E. *Early childhood education: A human ecological approach.* Glenview, IL: Scott, Foresman, 1983.

Day, D. E., & Sheehan, R. Elements of a better preschool. *Young Children,* 1974, *30*(1), 4–14.

DiLeo, J. C., Moely, B. E., & Sulzer, J. L. Frequency and modifiability of children's preferences for sex-typed toys, games, and occupations. *Child Study Journal,* 1979, *9*(2), 141–160.

Doyle, P. H. The efficacy of the ecological model: A study of the impact of activity setting on the social behavior of preschool children. Doctoral dissertation, Wayne State University (DAI, Vol. *36,* 2710-A), 1975.

Eisenberg, N., Murray, E., & Hite, T. Children's reasoning regarding sex-typed toy choices. *Child Development,* 1982, *53*(1), 81–86.

Elder, J. L., & Pederson, D. R. Preschool children's use of objects in symbolic play. *Child Development,* 1978, *49*(2), 500–504.

Elias, H. (1981). Personal communication. Rutgers—The State University of New Jersey, 1981.

Evans, E. D. *Contemporary influences in early childhood education.* New York: Holt, Rinehart and Winston, 1975.

Evans, E. B., Shub, B., & Weinstein, M. *Day care: How to plan, develop, and operate a day care center.* Boston: Beacon Press, 1971.

Feeney, S., Christensen, D., & Moravcik, E. *Who am I in the lives of children?* Columbus, Ohio: Charles E. Merrill, 1983.

Fein, G., & Clarke-Stewart, A. *Day care in context.* New York: John Wiley, 1973.

Field, T. M. Preschool play: Effects of teacher/child ratios and organization of classroom space. *Child Study Journal,* 1980, *10*(3), 191–205.

Fox, E. Assisting children's language development. *Reading Teacher,* 1976, *29*(7), 666–670.

Frasher, R. S., Nurss, J. R., & Brogan, D. R. Children's toy preferences revisisted: Implications for early childhood education. *Child Care Quarterly,* 1980, *9*(1), 26–31.

Garvey, C. Some properties of social play. *Merrill-Palmer Quarterly,* 1974, *20,* 163–180.

Garvey, C. Communicational controls in social play. In B. Sutton-Smith (Ed.), *Play and learning.* New York: Gardner Press, 1979.

Golbeck, S. L. Spatial cognition as a function of environmental characteristics. In R. Cohen (Ed.), *The development of spatial cognition.* Hillsdale, NJ: Lawrence Erlbaum, 1985.

Golbeck, S. L., Rand, M., & Soundy, C. Constructing a model of a large-scale space with the space in view: Effects of guidance and cognitive restructuring in preschoolers. *Merrill-Palmer Quarterly,* 1986, *32,* 187–203.

Golomb, C., & Cornelius, C. B. Symbolic play and its cognitive significance. *Developmental Psychology,* 1977, *13*(3), 246–252.

Green, E. H. Group play and quarreling among preschool children. *Child Development*, 1933, *4*, 302–307.

Gump, P. V. School environments. In I. Altman & J. F. Wohlwill (Eds.), *Children and the environment*. New York: Plenum Press, 1978.

Guthrie, K., & Hudson, L. M. Training conservation through symbolic play: A second look. *Child Development*, 1979, *50*, 1269–1271.

Halverson, L. E. The significance of motor development. In G. Engstrom (Ed.), *The significance of the young child's motor development*. Washington, DC: National Association for the Education of Young Children, 1971.

Halverson, L. E., Roberton, M. A., & Harper, C. J. Current research in motor development. *Journal of Research and Development in Education*, 1973, *6*(3), 56–69.

Hartley, R. E., Frank, L. K., & Goldenson, R. M. *Understanding children's play*. New York: Columbia University Press, 1952.

Hendrickson, J. M., Strain, P. S., Tremblay, A., & Shores, R. E. Relationship between toy and material use and the occurrence of social interaction behaviors by normally developing preschool children. *Psychology in the Schools*, 1981, *18*(4), 500–504.

Herkowitz, J. The design and evaluation of playspaces for children. In M. V. Ridenour (Ed.), *Motor development: Issues and applications* (pp. 115–37). Princeton, NJ: Princeton Book Company, 1978.

Hoffman, M. Nursery school rooms and their effect on children's involvement. *Graduate Research in Education and Related Disciplines*, 1976, *8*(2), 54–87.

Hohmann, M., Banet, B., Weikart, D. *Young children in action—A manual for preschool educators*. Ypsilanti, MI: High/Scope Press, 1979.

Houseman, J. *An ecological study of interpersonal conflict among preschool children*. Unpublished doctoral dissertation, Wayne State University (DAI, *33*, 6175-A), 1972.

Huck, C. S. Children's literature in the elementary school (3rd ed.). New York: Holt, Rinehart & Winston, 1976.

Johnson, H. *Children in the nursery school*. New York: John Day, 1928.

Johnson, M. W. The effect on behavior of variations in amount of play equipment. *Child Development*, 1935, *6*, 56–68.

Jones, E., & Prescott, E. *Dimensions of teaching learning environments. II: Focus on day care*. Pasadena, CA: Pacific Oaks College, 1978.

Kamii, C. Evaluation of pupil learning in preschool education: Socioemotional, perceptual motor, and cognitive development. In B. S. Bloom, J. T. Hastings, & G. Madaus (Eds.), *Handbook on formative and summative evaluation of student learning*. New York: McGraw-Hill, 1971.

Kamii, C., & DeVries, R. Piaget for early education. In M. C. Day & R. K. Parker (Eds.), *The preschool in action: Exploring early childhood programs*. Boston: Allyn and Bacon, 1977.

Karlsson, K. A., & Ellis, M. J. Height preferences of young children at play. *Journal of Leisure Research*, 1972, *4*(1), 33–42.

Kinsman, C. A., & Berk, L. E. Joining the block and housekeeping areas: Changes in play and social behavior. *Young Children*, 1979, *35*(1), 66–75.

Kohlberg, L. Early education: A cognitive development view. *Child Development*, 1968, *39*, 1013–1062.

Kohlberg, L. Stage and sequence: The cognitive development approach to socialization. In D. A. Goslin (Ed.), *Handbook of socialization theory and research* (pp. 347–480). Chicago: Rand McNally, 1969.

Kounin, J. S., & Sherman, L. W. School environments as behavior settings. *Theory into Practice*, 1979, *18*(3), 145–151.

Kritchevsky, S., & Prescott, E., with Walling, L. *Planning environments for young children: Physical space*. Washington, DC: National Association for the Education of Young Children, 1969.

Marion, M. *Guidance of young children*, St. Louis: C. V. Mosby, 1981.

Marshall, H. R. Relations between home experience and children's use of language in play interactions with peers. *Psychological Monographs*, 1961, *75*, #509.

McCune-Nicolich, L., & Carroll, S. Development of symbolic play: Implications for the language specialist. *Topics in Language Disorders,* 1981, *2*(1), 1–16.

McDowell, M. S. Frequency of choice of play materials by preschool children. *Child Development,* 1937, *8,* 305–310.

Montessori, M. *The Montessori method.* New York: Schocken, 1964.

Moore, G. T., Cohen, U., Oertel, J., & van Ryzin, L. Designing environments for handicapped children. New York: Educational Facilities Laboratories, 1979.

Moore, G. T., Lane, C. G., Hill, A. B., Cohen, U., & McGinty, T. *Recommendations for child care centers.* Milwaukee, WI: Center for Architecture and Urban Planning Research, University of Wisconsin, 1979.

Morrow, L. M. Relationship between literature programs, library corner designs, and children's use of literature. *Journal of Educational Research,* 1982, *83,* 339–344.

Morrow, L. M., & Weinstein, C. S. Increasing children's literature through program and physical design changes. *Elementary School Journal,* 1982, *83*(2), 131–137.

Morrow, L. M., & Weinstein, C. S. Encouraging voluntary reading: The impact of a literature program on children's use of library centers. *Reading Research Quarterly,* 1986, *21*(3), 330–346.

Moyer, K. E., & Gilmer, B. H. Attention span for experimentally designed toys. *Journal of Genetic Psychology,* 1955, *87,* 187–201.

Murphy, L. B. *Social behavior and child personality.* New York: Columbia University Press, 1937.

Murphy, G., Murphy, L. B., & Newcomb, T. M. *Experimental social psychology* (rev. ed.). New York: Harper, 1937.

Nadelman, L. Sex identity in American children: Memory, knowledge and preference tests. *Developmental Psychology,* 1974, *10,* 413–417.

Nash, B. C. The effects of classroom spatial organization on four- and five-year old children's learning. *British Journal of Educational Psychology,* 1981, *51*(2), 144–155.

Neill, S. R. St. J., & Denham, E. J. M. The effects of pre-school building design. *Educational Research,* 1982, *24*(2), 107–111.

Olds, A. R. Designing developmentally optimal classrooms for children with special needs. In. S. J. Meisels (Ed.), *Special education and development: Perspectives on young children with special needs.* Baltimore, MD: University Park Press, 1979.

Olszewski, P., & Fuson, K. C. Verbally expressed fantasy play of preschoolers as a function of toy structure. *Developmental Psychology,* 1982, *18*(1), 57–61.

Omwake, E. B. We know so much—we know so little. In G. Engstrom (Ed.), *The significance of the young child's motor development,* Washington, DC: National Association for the Education of Young Children, 1971.

Osmon, F. L. *Patterns for designing children's centers.* New York: Educational Facilities Laboratories, 1971.

Parten, M. B. Social participation among preschool children. *Journal of Abnormal and Social Psychology,* 1932, *27,* 243–269.

Pepler, D. J., & Ross, H. S. The effects of play on convergent and divergent problem solving. *Child Development,* 1981, *52*(4), 1202–1210.

Pfluger, L. W., & Zola, J. M. A room planned by children. In G. J. Coates (Ed.), *Alternative Learning Environments* (pp. 75–79). Stroudsburg, PA: Dowden, Hutchinson & Ross, 1974.

Phyfe-Perkins, E. Children's behavior in preschool settings: A review of research concerning the influence of the physical environment. In L. G. Katz (Ed.), Current topics in early childhood education, Vol. 3. Norwood, NJ: Ablex Publishing Company, 1980.

Phyfe-Perkins, E. The pre-school setting and children's behavior: An environmental intervention. *Journal of Man-Environment Relations,* 1982, *1*(3), 10–29.

Piaget, J. *The language and thought of the child.* London: Routledge & Kegan Paul, 1926.

Piaget, J. *Play, dreams, and imitation,* New York: W. W. Norton, 1962.

Prescott, E., Jones, E., & Kritchevsky, S. *Group day care as a child rearing environment: An observational study of day care programs.* Pasadena, CA: Pacific Oaks College, 1967.

Pulaski, M. A. S. Play as a function of toy structure and fantasy predisposition. *Child Development,* 1970, *41,* 531–537.

Quilitch, H. R., & Risley, T. R. The effects of play materials on social play. *Journal of Applied Behavior Analysis,* 1973, *6*(4), 573–578.

Rohe, W. M., & Nuffer, E. L. The effects of density and partitioning on children's behavior. Paper presented at the 85th meeting of the American Psychological Association, San Francisco, CA, 1977.

Rosen, C. E. The effects of socio-dramatic play on problem-solving behavior among culturally disadvantaged preschool children. *Child Development,* 1974, *45,* 920–927.

Rosenthal, B. A. L. An ecological study of free play in the nursery school. Doctoral dissertation, Wayne State University, 1973.

Rubin, K. H. The relationship of social play preference to role-taking skill in preschool children. *Psychological Reports,* 1976, *39,* 823–826.

Rubin, K. H. The social and cognitive value of preschool toys and activities. *Canadian Journal of Behavioral Science,* 1977, 9(4), 382–385.

Rubin, K. H., & Maioni, T. L. Play preference and its relationship to egocentrism, popularity, and classification skills in preschoolers. *Merrill-Palmer Quarterly,* 1975, *21,* 171–179.

Rubin, K. H., Maioni, T. L., & Hornung, M. Free play behaviors in middle- and lower-class preschoolers: Parten and Piaget revisited. *Child Development,* 1976, *47,* 414–419.

Rubin, K. H., Watson, K. S., & Jambor, T. W. Free play behaviors in preschool and kindergarten children. Unpublished manuscript, University of Waterloo, 1976.

Schickedanz, J. A. Structure and the learning limits in preschool classrooms. Paper presented at the National Conference of the National Association for the Education of Young Children (NAEYC), Anaheim, CA, 1976.

Scholtz, G. J., & Ellis, M. J. Repeated exposure to objects and peers in a play setting. *Journal of Experimental Child Psychology,* 1975, *19*(3), 448–455.

Seefeldt, C. *Teaching young children.* Englewood Cliffs, NJ: Prentice-Hall, 1980.

Shapiro, E., & Biber, B. The education of young children: A developmental interaction approach. *Teacher's College Record,* 1972, *74*(1), 55–79.

Sheehan, A., & Abbott, M. S. A descriptive study of day care characteristics. *Child Care Quarterly,* 1979, *8*(3), 206–219.

Shure, M. B. Psychological ecology of a nursery school. *Child Development,* 1963, *34,* 979–992.

Smith, P. K., & Connolly, K. J. Social and aggressive behaviour in preschool children as a factor of crowding. *Social Science Information,* 1977, *16*(5), 601–620.

Smith, P. K., & Dutton, S. Play and training on direct and innovative problem-solving. *Child Development,* 1979, *50,* 830–836.

Smith, P. K., & Green, M. Aggressive behavior in English nurseries and play groups: Sex differences and response of adults. *Child Development,* 1975, *46,* 211–214.

Stewig, J. W., & Sebesta, S. (Eds.). *Using literature in the elementary classroom.* Urbana, IL: National Council of Teachers of English, 1978.

Sutfin, H. D. The effect on children's behavior of a change in the physical design of a kindergarten classroom. *Journal of Man–Environment Relations,* 1982, *1*(3), 30–41.

Teets, S. S. *Play behaviors of preschool children in low- and high-quality space arrangements.* Doctoral dissertation, University of Texas at Austin (Dissertation Abstracts International, 1980, *40*(7-A), 3878).

Van Alstyne, D. *Play behavior and choice of play materials of preschool children.* Chicago: University of Chicago Press, 1932.

Wallach, M. A., & Kogan, N. *Modes of thinking in young children: A study of the creativity–intelligence distinction.* New York: Holt, Rinehart & Winston, 1965.

Weinstein, C. S. Modifying children's behavior in an open classroom through changes in the physical design. *American Educational Research Journal,* 1977, *14,* 242–262.

Weinstein, C. S. Privacy-seeking behavior in an elementary classroom. *Journal of Environmental Psychology,* 1982, *2,* 23–35.

Chapter 9

Designing Playgrounds for Able and Disabled Children

LELAND G. SHAW

INTRODUCTION

In *The Use of Lateral Thinking* (1967), Edward deBono discusses the difference between vertical and lateral thinking. According to deBono, vertical thinking is trying to solve a problem by fixating on the subject or the "hole," to use deBono's metaphor, and digging that hole deeper and bigger. If the hole is in the wrong place, however, no amoint of digging will put it right. What is needed is trying again elsewhere; deBono calls this approach lateral thinking.

In 1968 I was commissioned to design a playground for physically disabled children. Since I had not designed a playground before, I had no body of previous work or experience to draw on; no hole to try to dig deeper. Few guidelines were available in the research literature, and the existing playgrounds I studied consisted of collections of standard equipment modified to include safety devices to compensate for the presumed problems of disabled children.

Unfettered by preexisting assumptions about disabled children's play, I felt that designing playgrounds by fixating on equipment rather than environment was the wrong approach. Instead, I felt that we should be focusing on the children who would be the users of the proposed facility to learn how to shape a place that would support and maximize their potential for

LELAND G. SHAW • College of Architecture, University of Florida, Gainesville, FL 32611.

free play. That is what our design team did. Without realizing it, we applied the principle of lateral thinking.

The facility that resulted was the Environmental Therapy Complex (ETC) at Forrest Park, Orlando, Florida. The ETC was based upon untested ideas generated by observation. Our goal was to create a "place," unified physically and spatially, scaled to the user and complex enough to generate interest over time. The ETC proved to be popular with teachers, play leaders, therapists, and (most importantly) children.

Those initial "gut level" design concepts were subsequently tested in a series of research efforts and other playground designs for different populations of children—physically disabled, mentally retarded (profound and trainable), emotionally disturbed, and normal. The resulting set of design guidelines was first published in 1980 (Shaw, 1980). Since that time, additional research and playground commissions have given me the opportunity to expand and refine the guidelines. The present chapter is the product of this work.

Although it is difficult to generalize about the exact age of the children for whom the guidelines are intended, they are targeted for children who are functioning developmentally between the ages of 2 and 10 years. This clearly includes a wide range of physical and social abilities and identifies most of the potential users who could benefit developmentally from environments that encourage free play. It is true that both younger and older children may often enjoy such a playground, but their sustained high use is unpredictable. Babies and very young children receive much of their stimulation from the constant attention of adults, whereas older children involve themselves regularly in organized sports and games and need different kinds of diversified support environments, such as playing fields.

Before discussing the guidelines themselves, I want to address three issues with which playground designers must grapple. First is the notion that the use of design guidelines will limit a designer's creative potential. In fact, the opposite is intended. Design guidelines are developed to free a designer to be creative while still addressing the users' needs. Equally upsetting is the attitude held by some designers that their intuition and recollections of childhood are a better basis for design than guidelines generated from observational research. I want to caution designers that such romantic child-eye views are usually adult constructions of what being a child is all about and often have little or no relevance to actual childhood.

A second issue involves the tendency to think in terms of the able versus the disabled. Of course, there really is no *versus.* Disabled children are children first and disabled second. The common bond of childhood is far stronger and more important than are the separating aspects of a disability. Playgrounds for disabled children should first be considered as a place for child's play. My ideas about forming a playground come from this fundamental construct, not fom some notion that disabled children need gimmicks and trickery and magic to enjoy playgrounds. What makes the solution to a play environment for one group of children different from another does not lie in the design guidelines employed but rather in the execution of playground parts so that they respond to the particular social and physical needs of the users and the site's constraints.

A third issue involves the importance of the play leader. Arvid Bengtsson (1973), the famous Danish designer and playground expert, has written: "The playground is as much an element of town planning as streets and squares, and it should function at all times. . . . It is, however, only when personnel are present . . . that the playground assumes its true identity" (p. 98). Similarly, Lady Allen (1969) has asserted that "the key to a successful adventure playground lies largely in the quality of the leader. . . . The best of them are priceless" (p. 56). Observational research has shown that although children with mnior disabilities may need little direct interaction with play leaders, children with severe disabilities, either physical or mental, need increased assistance from leaders in order to benefit fully from the playground. In other words, as the potential for freely initiated interactions with the physical environment decreases, input by teachers, aides, and therapists must increase. For all children, however, the play leader is fundamental to the success of the playground.

DESIGN GUIDELINES

The guidelines discussed in this section can be used by a design team in both the preliminary planning phase of a playground and during the actual design stage. I want to stress from the outset that the term *design team* is meant to refer not to designers alone but also to teachers, parents, therapists, and indeed all individuals who take an active role in the project.

Each guideline will be introduced with a short definition. The subsequent discussion will summarize my past writings and elaborate on the new ideas and expanded concepts developed from more recent work. Although each guideline is discussed separately, it must be recognized that they are interrelated. They are meant to be used not as isolated ideas but in concert with one another.

Sense of Place

Every play environment must be given a unique spirit, a *genius loci.* The formation of the design concept is the organization of the parts within an ordered theme. This creates its sense of place. Sense of place impacts upon the mind of the users, affecting imageability and the cognitive mapping of the place.

This is the first guideline because it deals with an issue that must be considered initially in any design process but must also be kept in mind until the environment is built. It is also very intangible, keeps slipping through my fingers, and is the most difficult guideline to explain. It marks a rough beginning.

Sense of place involves the environment's overall image and the feeling its presence transmits to the user. It must be the goal of the design team to create a simple concept that orders the specific constraints of the problem in such a manner that when the environment is built a prevailing atmosphere is created. A "place" must be made. We speak of successful adult places (city squares, restaurants, and so on) as having atmosphere or ambience. Each play environment wants to have an ambience as well, and so that it may, one must order the various parts into a whole. While each part of the environment forms a specific place for play to occur—in, around, and through—it is the overall organization of these parts that creates the stage for play through time; that stage creates a sense of place.

Sense of place implies not only that the individual parts of an environment are created for their specific functional purpose also that they must be shaped together into a context that reflects an overall order. No single playground can be all places. It must be its own place—and that place wants to be unique, different from all other places its users experience in the rest of their daily lives. It wants to have a "there–there," to use Gertrude Stein's words. The unique aspects of a special physical design allow the users to feel special, in a special place. When a playground establishes a sense of place, its cognitive map will be unique. This is often apparent from the nicknames the users give to a well-designed playground. Catalogue-purchased playgrounds, like chain restaurants, are all the same and have no single spirit or identity.

Sense of place is influenced by spatial configuration. A plaza space which operates as the town center of the play environment has proved to be an effective organizing device. Observation has shown that it stimulates gathering, dispersing, and returning. A defined plaza contains major activities and encourages others to occur around its edges. More will be said about open centers throughout the discussion of the guidelines.

The context in which the environment will be placed can also contribute to sense of place. Context can be general and apply to the physical and social characteristics of a board region as well as the nonphysical administrative environment. But most important for sense of place are the specific site characteristics and the surrounding physical context—the relationship, spatial configurations, and character of existing buildings, the orientation of views, landscaping, slope of the site, where the users come from and return to, orientation to sun and breeze. These are all unique features of each setting. The design team must take advantage of the uniqueness of the context and use it in creating a sense of place.

When all is said and done, perhaps the Latin term *genius loci*–spirit of a place–is the best way to think about this guideline. The spirit of a place reflects understanding, keys the internalized reading of the overall play yard, and sets the tone for use.

Unified Environment

Unifying all parts of a playground, connecting them physically and spatially, allows play to flow from place to place. Unified, all parts of the environment have a role to play. Smooth transitions between places and natural variations in play occur.

This guideline reflects the notion that the whole, when it can be perceived (and hence used) as a whole, is much more stimulating (and more used) than isolated parts. It is clear that a unified perception of a whole also reinforces sense of place. Often we see play environments that are collections of isolated pieces of play apparatus. This fragments play, making it very difficult for activities to flow from one to the other. When the users of a playground are disabled, the effect of having isolated pieces of equipment is even more severe.

Unless play environments are unified, as shown in Figure 1, the majority of the activity will center around the most complex pieces, while the rest of the yard receives little or no use. We all recognize that no balanced environment can be made up of elements that are all key places. Every environment should have some elements that are stars and others that are supporting characters. If these supporting characters are linked to the stars, activities can be linked. Sliding, for example, can naturally flow into jumping, climbing, hiding, and swinging. When elements cannot be physically connected, careful spatial relationships between them should be created. The surrounding context of the playground may be able to help here. A design might "borrow" a nearby wall of an existing building or a large tree to unify the space.

Repeated observations with able and disabled children have shown that unifying the play yard unifies the play experience and increases significantly the time spent engaged with the physical structure of the place (Shaw, 1976). Research dealing with the cognitive mapping by children using models of unified and fragmented play environments appears to indicate that the ability to develop and sustain workable cognitive maps is also related to the configuration of the play yard (Shaw, 1978).

Design solutions can physically connect many of the elements of the environment in such a way that they create a central plaza. The linked elements then form the space-defining structure for the open center, with understandable insides and outsides. When such a physical and psychological barrier to the outside is created, play will tend to be contained within. In order to promote overall site use, it is essential to have clear release areas to

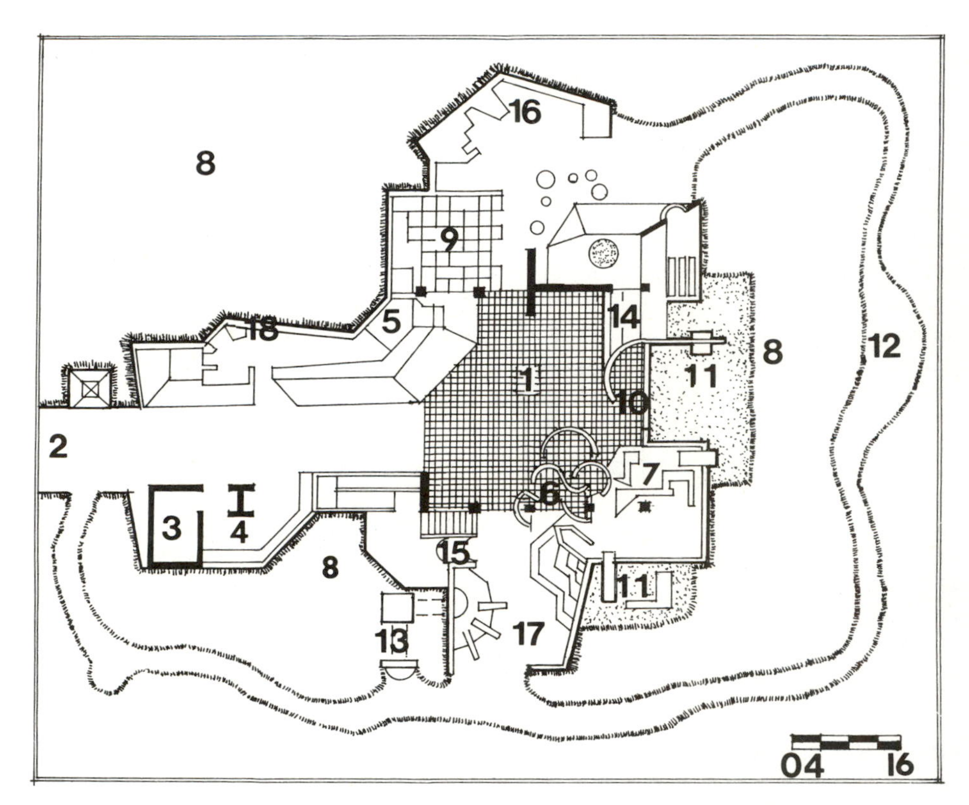

FIGURE 1. Plan of a unified play space: environmental therapy complex (ETC), Forrest Park School, Orlando, Florida. Legend: 1, open center; 2, playground entrance (covered) from school; 3, toy storage; 4, unbracing area; 5, falling pad; 6, curved maze; 7, rectangular maze; 8, rolling grass hill; 9, irregular steps; 10, drawing wall; 11, sand area; 12, loop path; 13, tunnel; 14, rolling hill; 15, slide; 16, cave area; 17, stage area; 18, walking board. (Drawing by Leland G. Shaw.)

the outside. Moore and Cohen (1976) have used the term "retreat and breakway points" to refer to places that allow the user to retreat from stressful situations. Paths that release from the open center work best if they are loop paths, leading to the outer areas of the yard but then looping back to the open center rather than dead-ending. For example, a loop path may lead to a group of swings that must, for safety's sake, be kept out of the active center. The path can pass by a rabbit cage on the way to the swings and then go over a water play area on the way back to the center plaza. The design team must take care, however, not to develop too extensively the events along loop paths or they will bleed too many activities away from the central plaza. One needs only to look at how this has happened in our downtowns since the arrival of suburban shopping malls to understand the ramifications.

Another way of contributing to an environment's unity is to have a

FIGURE 2. The exterior of the ETC, showing the large roof.

large roof covering the open center and its surrounding elements (see Figure 2). Of course, a roof also keeps a play environment dry, helps create a tolerant temperature range, and symbolically adds to a sense of place.

The plan of a play environment included in this chapter can be studied as an example of how to link and unify physically and spatially. Unifying the environment gives the design team the key to manipulating the next four design guidelines. As Robert Browning has written, "Image the whole; then execute the parts."

Variety of Spaces

A wide variety of juxtaposed spatial situations (i.e., big to little, open to closed, dark to light) are necessary to support a rich pattern of play behavior. Fantasy play needs a variety of spaces as stage sets.

The use of the word *space* here signifies degree of enclosure. The design team must think in terms of space. In designing environments for children's play, the total area (that is, the amount of land available for the project) can be divided into many spaces that vary in size and closure. This will create a range of spaces from small, well-enclosed places highly defined by walls and a ceiling to large open places that lack clear spatial definition. Conversely, there should be large, very well-defined spaces and small areas that lack specific spatial definition. *Variety* is the key word. It is the juxtaposition of many different kinds of spaces that creates a rich landscape that will tolerate and support a wide variety of child-generated activities. Every design should be carefully checked to see whether a variety of spatial situations has been created. Some spaces will be static places; others are active pathways. Some spaces will be both, used differently at different times. A play yard's spaces are not always used in predictable ways. Although it is true that small enclosed spaces may be used a great deal of the time by one or two children playing and interacting quietly, one will often see many children packed into a small space. Designers should think of several different ways a space might be used to avoid the problem of making design decisions that will limit the use of a space.

Bengtsson (1970) has described a playground as a series of outdoor rooms:

> Far too often we talk as though creating a playground was a matter of equipment alone. . . . One of the most common reasons for our failure with regards to playgrounds is that we overlook the need for some sort of enclosing wall or screen which will bring a room-like quality. It is essential to create room-like atmosphere in most areas of play. . . . Enclosures can be devised in many ways from ramparts, plantings, planks, bricks, etc. (p. 154)

This quotation stresses the fact that a sense of closure, a definition of space, is needed to achieve the concept of outdoor rooms (see Figure 3). Spatial definition can be literal (for instance, a wall) or implied. Implied spatial definition can be accomplished in many ways, by a change in level, a change in surface material, or even by something as subtle as a change in the level of light.

In my work, the largest defined outdoor room has been the open center plaza. It can functure as a multipurpose space suitable for both impromptu gatherings and planned games. At the ETC, the play leaders used this space for organized exercise and body awareness activities. Weatherproof exterior electrical outlets allowed the use of a portable record player to provide the rhythm and verbal commands while the children mimic the actions of a play leader. Such outlets are an essential component of a play environment.

Observation has shown that in a complex, varied playground one cannot predict from day to day where the majority of play activities might center. Given many spaces, the children tend to seek out the best place for a particular game. Fantasy games are often influenced by major events that are occurring in the lives of the children. For example, the advent of a new *Star Wars* movie will be reflected in the kind of fantasy games played on the playground. Climate changes from fall to winter, spring to summer, and important special events such as Christmas impart a seasonal quality to play. A variety of spaces allows the playground to meet these needs as they arise.

Observation has revealed that children particularly enjoy defensible

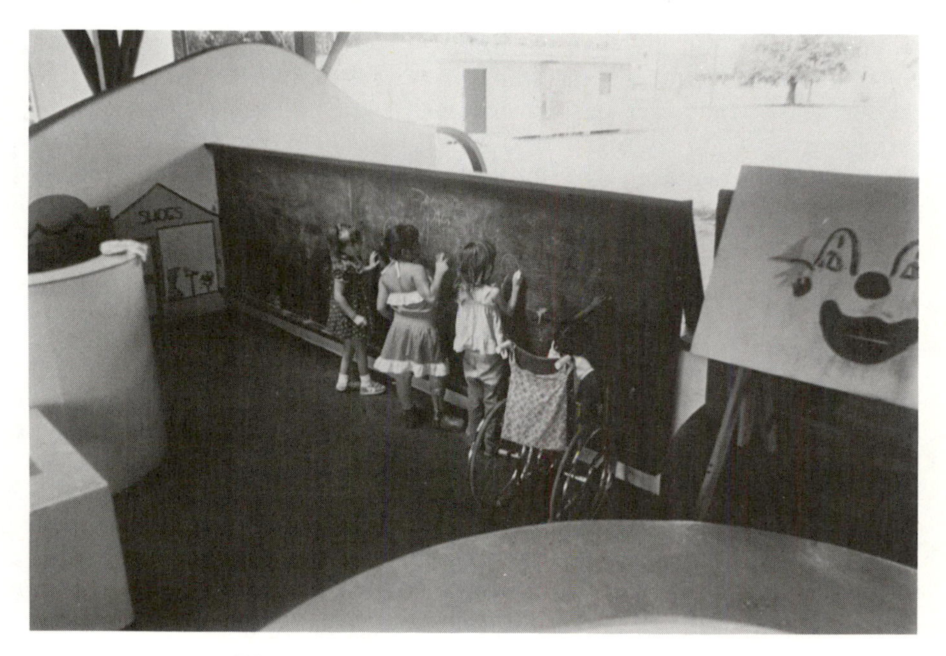

FIGURE 3. Children drawing on a chalkboard wall.

spaces. Defensible spaces are usually small and quite enclosed with only one entrance–exit. Such spaces appear to be most successful when they are located adjacent to major pathways and activity areas, because they can then be incorporated spontaneously into fantasy play. For the same reasons, these spaces will be good retreat places, somewhere from which to observe a group activity while deciding whether or not to join in. Such spaces are often named; "store," "rocket ship," "kitchen," and "jail" are common designations. On one playground, a small enclosed place that used a plastic skylight for a window became known as the "TV." Children would go inside the TV and perform for those in the central plaza. One last use of small defensible spaces should not be overlooked: they serve as excellent places in which to hide from the play leaders when it is time to go back to class.

When thinking about the kinds of spaces needed, it is important to realize that adults need places to use as a home base or as an observation point. The design team should also realize that children tend to gather around adults. Benches placed in the play yard do not feel like an integral part of the environment and usually are not used. It is far better to have play forms designed for adults to sit on located strategically throughout the environment. Some should be elevated and overlook a significant portion of the yard. Such places are quickly understood by adults to be good supervision places.

When discussing sense of place, I noted that the conceptual organization of a design must be kept simple. The reason for that statement may now be clearer, for as the designer begins to articulate a series of different spatial situations linked together, a strong, simple, overriding concept must exist to control the placement of these spaces. The design concept does not dictate the way in which an environment is to be used, but it does establish a perceivable order.

Key Places

A key place will be dominated by one major element such as a slide or a falling pad. Surrounding the major element will be a complex juxtaposition of spaces and pathways. A playground needs several complex key places to anchor the overall order of the environment.

Most standard pieces of manufactured play equipment have single functions and channel use into repetitive patterns. The standard slide, for example, has a ladder to climb, a platform to sit on big enough for one child, and a trough-like sliding surface. A child must climb up, sit, slide down, run around back to the ladder, and climb up again. If there are many children, they are expected to queue up and wait a turn. In addition, the slide is designed to sit by itself. No interaction is encouraged with other similarly designed isolated pieces of play equipment in the play yard.

In contrast, a key place in a unified play environment will be complex enough to embrace a variety of activities. For example, in a key slide piece several different pathways and platforms will be clustered around a large sliding surface, with a group-size gathering space at the top. The user is provided with choices. Slides like this, as well as climbing towers, falling pads, multiple tunnels, complex platform stages, and sand and water areas are potential key places that can anchor the play environment.

It is essential to consider the juxtaposition of the key places. For example, a big slide and a falling pad complement each other well. On the other hand, unrelated key activity areas may interfere with one another if juxtaposed too closely. Their individual spheres of activity should end at relatively neutral places or natural seams in the environment. As the geometry of the design is formed, the key areas should be located so that they will reinforce each other spatially and behaviorally. Research has clearly shown that by unifying the environment so that the key places connect to lesser support areas, the entire playground use is increased.

One can usually tell what the key places on a particular playground are by listening to the children. They are usually the places that are given specific names. Adult users of the playground also often name key areas but for administrative reasons—to set boundaries, rules, restrict use. By naming them, they tend to think of them as entities in themselves. If a design team does this while designing, they may end up designing pieces of equipment and not integrated environments. The guideline, unified environment, must be kept in mind at all times.

I want to focus on several key places that have proved to be effective on playgrounds for all children—falling pads, big slides, and sand and water areas. (Although each key place has been given the name of its major element, it should be understood that they are much more complex than the name implies.) This is by no means a comprehensive list; design teams can develop many others by focusing on combinations of major activities and developing complex support structures into key places. An activity not included in a list of key places, however, is swinging. I do not mean to suggest that swinging is not an important activity. Observation has disclosed that swing sets and tire swings do get a significant amount of use, particularly from older children, and a wide range of behaviors do occur on swings. All this suggests that they should be part of a play yard. Yet swings must, for safety's sake, be separated from the other areas of a playground; they cannot be comfortably integrated into a unified play space. A good place to locate swings is directly off a loop path. An alternate approach is to set up rope swings temporarily in the open center of the play environment, accepting the fact that they will affect the use of this area. In either case, what this means is that their placement is not important in the early design phase; and since they do not influence order or spatial configuration, swings do not qualify as a key activity area.

FIGURE 4. A slide and steps with gathering platform at top.

Falling or Jumping Pad. A vinyl-covered foam pad can be the heart of a key place that will generate a wide range of play activities. Those elements that define the pad's edges; platforms, steps, slides, tunnels, are all an integral part of the area. Falling pads obviously promote body movement, but they also are great places to rest and talk to friends. Observation has shown that at play children do not rest on benches; they collapse where convenient, and falling pads make great places to sprawl after strenuous play.

The surface of the falling pad should be large enough for several children to use at the same time and at least one foot thick. Sizes are usually not specified in this chapter, but this is an exception; a square pad ten feet on a side has proved to be large enough to support a wide range of different uses. Observation has shown that the larger the pad, the harder it is to steal. Unfortunately, that does not protect it from vandals, so the pad should be put in secure storage at night. For ease of handling, it can be made in four equal squares, the whole contained in a rigid frame of wood that can be cushioned with a carpet cover.

Falling pads, like most key places, should be extensions of paths. In other words, they should not be dead-end places but should be located so that they are at the crossroads of many marked and unmarked paths, the vital nodal points of the overall system. A big slide is an excellent example of a path extension.

Big Slide. In contrast to the traditional slide, this key place has several features that enhance its complexity and richness. First of all, underline the word *big.* This can mean high or wide, but preferably both. A wide slide allows numerous children to slide down simultaneously, an exciting activity, although one that sometimes causes play leaders to age quickly. Since it is as much fun to go up slides as down them, exterior carpets can be used on a section of the surface to increase traction. If a length of thick rope is attached to that section, the complexity of the slide increases even more.

Slides can be tunnels, half-round, flat, wavy, straight; only the imagination of the design team limits their shape. Every play environment should have several slides, each with its own character. It is one experience to go down a flat slide that ends on a falling pad and quite another to slide through a tunnel slide into the sand area.

The top of a big slide constitutes a gathering platform, a popular place for overlooking the playground, while the space underneath serves as an excellent enclosed gathering place. Intermediate platforms, ladders, and steps attached to the slide structure further increase complexity.

Sand. Sand piles seem such standard fare that designers often tend not to include them in contemporary environments—a mistake I once made myself. But large, deep sand areas (some standards recommend several feet of depth) are key activity areas that support a wide range of play behavior from solitary play to group interaction. Although small sand areas do not generate the kind of complex use large ones do, they can still be of value as support places in a complete play yard.

The interface of any sand pile and its defining elements always needs careful consideration. Creating several different kinds of connections in the same sand area will increase its complexity and use. The edge between sand and grass might be as simple as a two-by-eight piece of treated pine or as complex as an entire system of enclosed cubbies, while the edge of that same sand area against an active pathway or even a falling pad might be a wall or a two-foot apron.

Children in wheelchairs should have an accessible sand play area. Because wheelchairs and children come in such a variety of different heights and widths, it is difficult to design sand tables that will work well for all users. So-called "flexible height" tables have, for me, proved to be unworkable; they are expensive, clumsy, and never seem to be adjusted properly. In spite of the limitations, I would suggest incorporating a fixed-height sand area for wheelchairs into the edge of the key place sand area. The table height can be determined by measuring the arm height of the largest wheel chair that will be in common use on the playground. Small temporary platforms placed under smaller chairs can be used to raise them to the fixed table height. By joining the two sand areas, the isolation of the wheelchair is minimized.

Temporary solutions that allow sand play from wheelchairs should also be encouraged. For example, a play leader at the ETC discovered that she could place a child in a wheelchair close to a platform part of the playground that was conveniently the proper height, lay an old blanket over that surface, and add sand. When playtime was over, the blanket was folded up and the sand was returned to its home—a very creative *ad hoc* solution.

Water. Water has fascinating play potential. Unfortunately it is seldom incorporated into playground design, usually because of administrative rules, maintenance problems, and health concerns. Although these are real issues, I am convinced that with the proper outlook, reasonable adult supervision, care, and maintenance, they can be resolved.

In order to be truly effective, water should be flowing; therefore, stagnant water tables are not recommended. My favorite water play areas are at Chelsea and Lady Allen Playgrounds run by the Handicapped Adventure Playground Association in London (see Shaw, 1982). Unlike many water play extravaganzas found in America, they do not depend upon expensive mechanical devices and gimmicks. Their three major attributes are that they are large, they are pathway systems, and they interface with sand areas. Sand and water go well together, if a good water filter system is installed and the playleader can tolerate a certain amount of mess.

Water play areas are probably not for everyone. It is sad to see an expensive water play area not used because it cannot be maintained or for administrative reasons. Therefore, adults planning a playground should fully understand the challenge that will be encountered. If included and incorporated with a sand area, a water area can without doubt become one of the most popular and well-used key areas of the playground.

System of Pathways

A system of pathways is necessary to link key activity areas. Paths should be diverse in their size and shape and in the challenge they present. Such a system provides the children with choices and adds a significant amount of richness to a play environment.

Paths infer movement, and movement to some is synonymous with play. Therefore, creating a system of pathways that weave throughout the play yard is of primary concern to the design team. While some sections of the paths are integral parts of key places and must be included in the design of the key place, others link one key place to another. The linking of support pieces to the key areas will begin to solve this problem naturally.

One might ask whether certain elements of a playground, such as a set of irregular steps or a falling pad, are paths or key places. In fact, they can be both and fulfill both needs, depending upon the particular behaviors they are called upon to support at any given time. Irregular steps may look like a path, whereas a falling pad does not. Yet, in actuality, the falling pad may contain many invisible paths that are established and defined by the users.

Paths should intersect, so that playground users are confronted with decision points and are able to exercise choice. Small paths can converge into a large one, and major paths can branch out. Observation has disclosed that children prefer to move forward at all times. Although this may seem like a rather ridiculous statement, it has significant implications for playground design. Long dead-end paths ought to be avoided. Loop pathways, discussed earlier, should pass through one or more key places (such as through a falling pad) and return to the open center plaza. If one visualizes paths moving vertically as well as horizontally, a pathway can have the quality of a Mobius strip. The user can constantly move forward, looking for an opportunity to engage in a place-oriented activity should the opportunity arise. Looping, as a behavior, has been observed to range from great loops that encompass a major portion of the yard to small loops, such as those often seen in a slide area.

The use of tunnels (see Figure 5) should also be considered when designing the system of pathways. Tunnels should never dead-end. Access into tunnels should be located on major paths to promote their spontaneous use. Tunnels that are below ground should be relatively short. If a long tunnel is needed, segment its length with release places. These shorter lengths of tunnel allow for easier supervision and increase the choices in the pathway system.

FIGURE 5. Looking into a tunnel entrance.

Tunnels can also be created above the major play surface. Such "sky tunnels" are very popular because their visual release points are playground overlooks. Tunnels can be square or round, straight or crooked, and can come in many sizes. Tunnels with small diameters and narrow paths with high sides are good for physically disabled children because they provide many surfaces against which to brace. Any tunnel with a diameter of less than 18 inches, however, should be very short. Play leaders need access to all tunnels from one end or the other.

As adults, we must remember that children like to chase, and paths are natural places for chase games. Play leaders can use pathway systems for races or challenge courses. A few paths can be designed as "specialty paths" to develop specific body skills and strengths. For example, a walking board spanning two elements requires users to develop balance, and parallel bars mounted above a path can be used to develop upper body strength. A wooden ladder was used for this purpose at the ETC. It was hung about 15 inches above a part of a ramped surface. Children used it to pull themselves up to the falling pad. These specialty paths should be used sparingly, however, or the play environment will begin to seem like an obstacle course. Ideally, special elements can be added to a path and not adversely affect its use (for example, removable or adjustable overhead bars).

The issue of accessibility for physically disabled children is especially pertinent when discussing pathways. If children in wheelchairs are to be users of a playground, segments of the pathway system should be accessible. I do not design playgrounds so that the wheelchair can have complete accessibility. I believe that whenever possible children should be taken out of wheelchairs and allowed to experience the environment by crawling, scooting, or rolling. If all pathways accommodated wheelchairs, a great deal of variety would be lost. But it would be naive to assume that all wheelchair users can always leave their chairs outside the playground. Therefore, the design team must design sections of the pathway system so that a child in a wheelchair will have an opportunity to reach key activity areas, for example, the top of a big slide. Even if the child cannot use the slide, he or she enjoys the opportunity to share that perspective of the playground with others. Like all paths, those that can be used by wheelchairs (or bicycles and tricycles) should not all be the same but should have variety in shape, texture, size, and slope. The only distinction is that this variety must lie within the tolerance of the wheelchair.

Also related to the issue of accessibility is the use of handrails. Observation has shown that handrails are often not necessary and should be used only where considered absolutely essential. Children who need extra support get along fine using walls and ledges.

Three-dimensional Juxtaposition of Parts

Layer the parts of the playground during design so that spaces, places, platforms, and paths interact vertically. This stacking will maximize physical, verbal, and visual interactions between users.

Consider for a moment the game tic-tac-toe. Played on paper, it is very simple. Only a few variations on the opening move are possible. One soon gets bored with it. But envision the game played three-dimensionally. The board becomes three sheets of clear plastic, stacked one above the other, two inches apart. Different colored marbles are used instead of *X*'s and *O*'s. This game is complex and stimulating.

The typical fragmented, ground-oriented playground is similar to the two-dimensional tic-tac-toe game. Some individual pieces of play equipment may allow the child to get above the ground, but interconnected, multilevel, complex play with overall playground interaction cannot be achieved. A truly three-dimensional play environment is a matrix of defined spaces, platforms, and pathways juxtaposed to maximize the potential for user interaction—physical, verbal, and visual. It is very important to overlap spaces and paths. This will allow play to overlap. Stacking children at play stacks interactions.

The elements that can be used to change levels between overlapping planes offer the design team a rich opportunity to introduce variety. Ramps can be gentle or steep, smooth or rough, straight or crooked. Steps can be regular or irregular, large or small. Slides can be rolling or straight, wide or narrow, transparent or opaque, wet or dry. Ropes, cattle walks, tires, poles, tunnels, and ladders are just a few examples of elements that can be used to change levels. Size, shape, degree of difficulty, and texture can be combined in endless possibilities. Children can select the path that best suits their needs and their physical abilities. Since school children will be exposed to their play environment on a regular basis for many years, it is especially crucial to have variety. Gentle paths are necessary so that each child can master some vertical pathways in their early exposure to the environment; on the other hand, some paths must be complex and difficult enough to sustain interest over time and to present challenges to be conquered as the child develops.

Research that mapped children in unified environments (Shaw, 1976) has documented the fact that children play a great deal of the time above the ground plane and that much of that play is group play. We often tend to equate height above ground with danger: the higher the children, the more dangerous. There are ways, however, of insuring significant levels of safety on platforms quite high above ground. Intermediate levels that surround high places, for example, can form ledges. Large handrails, administrative rules, and the children's own natural sense of danger have proved to be quite effective in preventing accidents. One can also enclose steep vertical pathways and high platforms with rubber-coated chain-link fence, plexiglass, and plywood. This guarantees a very safe situation and allows the users to relate to the layers of play below while viewing the play yard and the surrounding area. I have designed situations that allow the children to be 10 feet above the ground plane. When you are used to viewing the world from a child's perspective on the ground, that can be a very special experience. Variety, again, is important in juxtaposing spaces. Many kinds of platform spaces are necessary to support a range of social interactions between users: high, low, big, small, open, and enclosed.

Several particularly interesting behaviors observed on three-dimensional playgrounds (Shaw & Williams, 1983) are worth mentioning here.

Hide and Reveal. Stacked arrangements of play spaces allow a child to hide and to "spy" on group activities, joining in when ready. Elevated open platforms increase visual exposure and make good places from which to play "look at me"; they become stages for impromptu performances. A three-dimensional juxtaposition of parts will effectively support rich games of hide-and-seek, always a popular play yard activity.

Looping. Searching for the action is more rewarding than passively waiting for something to happen. By unifying a play yard above the ground, children can loop through and above many group areas in search of activities. Chance interactions and group formations for fantasy games can occur more frequently. Play environments that physically isolate or "pocket" groups at play inhibit this behavior.

Overlooking. This is a very important behavior which is supported by having platform places located above the major surfaces of the play, particularly when such places overlook the open center and are accessible for wheelchairs. Such places make good spots for a child in a chair to overlook the action, participating verbally and, when possible, physically. Vicarious participants become, in effect, an audience, and this enriches the play for all. Children use such places in complex fantasy activities, and play leaders often station themselves at overlook places to overview the play yard and to monitor play behavior.

Groundhogging. Tunnels allow this activity, the reverse of overlooking, to occur. A child can pop out of a tunnel to see what is happening, to look for a friend, or to see if the playleader is aware of his of her questionably acceptable activity. . . .

Verbal Communication. Children playing together at different levels on a playground find that verbal communication is easier and more effective than physical communication. From this, one can assume that a playground rich in three-dimensional juxtaposition of parts will encourage the development of language skills. This has been shown to be particularly valuable for mentally retarded children.

Nonobjective Environment

The fixed elements of a play environment should be nonobjective in nature. Nonobjective spaces will support a wide range of activities and fantasy games. Realistic representations (for example, turtles and whales) stifle creative play.

Playgrounds around the world are littered with abandoned, rusting rocking ducks and lonely, chipped concrete turtles. A lesson can be learned from children's constructions. They seldom worry if an *ad hoc* collection of cardboard boxes and blankets resembles something specific. In fact, what is so nice about a box is that at one time it can be a jail, the next time a palace, and later a rocket ship or the inside of a whale. The design team should design nonobjective spaces—round, square, irregular, regular, bright, dark, big, little.

Highly literal backdrops, such as a store front or a bank, do have a place in play environments, but I recommend that they be portable frames that can be placed in group activity areas at specific times. This way they can be placed where needed, something difficult to anticipate during the design phase, and removed when not applicable to the use of the space. In effect, they then become a loose part, a guideline that will be discussed shortly.

Variety of Surface Finishes

Different textures allow the child to experience different tactile sensations. A variety of finishes on the horizontal, vertical, and inclined surfaces of the playground adds richness to the users' experences. Textured differences should reinforce major design decisions.

As children crawl, climb, roll, and jump, there is a great deal of direct body contact with the surfaces of the play environment. Exposed, hard, structural materials, such as wood or concrete, should have smooth finishes to avoid unnecessary abrasiveness. Exterior carpets, vinyl, or cloth should be used to soften many of the structural surfaces, but they must be kept dry or they will quickly rot. Fine artifical turf and exterior carpet provide traction on surfaces that are meant to be climbed. Do not avoid using rough textures, but use them cautiously in places where a child is unlikely to made a sudden or sharp contact with the surface.

Covering similar surfaces with the same material helps to reinforce the design concept and to organize a color–texture scheme. If this type of multiple coding is overused, however, the environment may become overly simplified. Certain elements of a play yard naturally code themselves. Sand, for example, has a texture, sound, smell, color range, and taste that signifies it as being sand. This is true for water and most natural materials. Their use will signify a kind of overall coding or organization. A playground is a place for discovering; redundantly coding all elements of the play environment may result in a rigid organization that is predictable, visually repetitive, and not desirable for use over long periods of time.

Loose Parts

> There is evidence that all children love to interact with variables, such as materials and shapes; physical phenomena such as electricity, magnetism, and gravity; media such as gases and fluids; sounds, music, and motion; chemical interactions, cooking and fire; and other people, animals, plants, words, concepts, and ideas. With all these things all children love to play, experiment, discover and invent, and have fun . . . in any environment. Both the degree of inventiveness and creativity, and the possibility of discovery, are directly proportional to the number and kind of variables in it. (Nicholson, 1971)

The term *loose parts* seems to have originated with Simon Nicholson in the 1971 article, "How Not to Cheat Children: The Theory of Loose Parts." As Moore (1980) has said, the article is "the most articulate statement of the need for manipulatable parts." Since its publication, play researchers and designers have been using the term to include anything that was not nailed, glued, or bolted in place. To this extent, the original meaning of the term has probably been bastardized. Nonetheless, I find the broader definition a useful one and will therefore use it in this discussion.

It is clear from observation that a play environment without loose parts cannot be nearly so successful as that same one with loose parts. Most of these are supplied by the users, the playground staff and the children, in a process that begins as soon as the playground is occupied and continues for the life of the facility. Other loose parts can be designed into the concept of the playground. These will be discussed shortly. Regardless of who designs or supplies the loose parts, however, the design team must have a comprehensive understanding of the subject to create an effective support system for this vital ingredient in children's play. It is the design team's responsibility, for example, to ensure that storage space for loose parts is an integral part of the playground design.

To begin with, let us look at those kinds of loose parts the design team can provide. Moving parts of the playground structure—pully systems, tramways, flexible tubes, swinging lifts—constitute one category. Here the design team can be quite creative, but some words of caution are in order. Such special elements are characterized by high-energy, intense use, but the use tends to be rather object-specific. Like teeter-totters or round-a-bouts, they are used only for short periods of time, and, since they need their own space, they often integrate poorly with the rest of the play environment. I have also observed that the moving elements of a playground are the first to break or to be vandalized. If a playground is designed to be dependent upon such elements and they cease to function, the playground will be maimed. Finally, movable parts are more expensive to build and much more expensive to maintain than fixed ones. No play environment is maintenance free (an assumption often erroneously made); but when yearly maintenance budgets are limited, the inclusion of moving parts as an integral part of the design is not recommended. If security, expense, and maintenance problems can be resolved, the inclusion of a movable part in a playground will be a welcome addition.

Specially designed elements that do not move but can be moved are probably more in the true spirit of loose parts. In this category, we have large, heavy units that take several staff members to move and smaller, lighter objects that can be moved by the children. The maze pieces designed for the ETC are an example of the former. In use for over 15 years, they proved to be flexible, integral parts of the playground. Because they are very heavy, they are stable enough for the children to climb on, in, and through. Two or three adults could move them around and within minutes give the play yard a fresh look. This kind of change is akin to reorganizing the furniture in your living room. The space is seen in a different light, and use patterns will change. Another important feature of these maze pieces is that they were nonobjective. Many "object" toys will be used on a playground, and designed loose parts such as these can provide a better environmental support.

In addition to the maze pieces (see Figure 6), and to provide a contrast, several large vinyl-covered foam pieces were designed for the ETC. These are three feet high and one foot thick, with modular dimensions so that they can interlock. These pieces are used singly and in groups for forts, houses, and places to rest. Even though they are quite large, most of the children can move them around. Movement of such objects is usually a group activity

FIGURE 6. Maze and foam pieces in an open center.

and often more fun than the result of the move. To be able to move a large lightweight object can give small, young, or physically disabled children a great sense of accomplishment.

Sand and water are important loose parts that demand additional loose parts to enrich their use. A sand area devoid of toys is usually an unused one. What makes sand so much fun is what you can do with it. It can take on thousands of shapes by molding it. Specific loose parts needed for sand and water play will be discussed shortly (see Figure 7).

One must recognize that anything movable is susceptible to theft. That is why playgrounds should never be built around movable elements. I have found that the kind of objects most commonly stolen from playgrounds are things that can be used in adult environments—tables, benches, balls, water beds, foam pads. Big nonobjective pieces, like Rolls Royce hubcaps, do not seem to be in great demand. This is why adequate, secure storage space for all but the largest of loose parts is so important. At the end of each day, loose parts will be scattered throughout the playground. They must be rounded up and put in a storage space. As previously suggested, the location of the storage unit should be determined during the design process so that it will

FIGURE 7. Sand in containers along a stepped path.

be an integral part of the environment. I have designed various methods of storage, ranging from one large central storeroom to several small storage units dispersed throughout the play yard. The concept behind the latter approach assumed that smaller loose parts—toys, for example—could then be available throughout the play yard at a moment's notice. Although the idea seemed a good one, it created problems for the play leaders. It proved very difficult to maintain several places that had to be stocked, opened, and locked up each day. The most viable solution appears to be a large central storeroom located near the play leader's home base. Such a storage unit should be compartmentalized so that loose parts can be stored in various categories. A separate entrance can be provided for ride-on wheel toys and other large loose parts.

A good method for the distribution of loose parts throughout the playground is to have the play leaders "seed" the playground each day prior to the children's arrival. In a seeded playground, a child may come upon a ball or truck in an unexpected place, setting the stage for a novel activity that capitalizes on the physical characteristics of the place and the manipulable qualities of the toy.

In addition to the loose parts that are part of the overall design, there are those supplied by the administrators responsible for the play environment. These "purchased loose parts" are, by necessity, consumable items. Toys get broken and lost, and the demand for certain ones will change over time. Although it is true that one can never have too many purchased loose parts, one can have too many on a play yard at one time. Too many loose parts will hamper natural patterns of movement and create a kind of "toy overkill." The following classification of purchased loose parts is offered so that we may better understand the wide range of items that can contribute to a play yard's enrichment.

The first category is nonobjective loose parts, such as boards, blankets, and cardboard boxes. These objects are not specific toys in themselves but can be used in concert with the fixed structure of the play environment to make temporary huts, cages, caves, and rocketships. This category could also be called "building materials." Tools, such as hammers, saws, and shovels, fall in this category as well. Their inclusion will depend upon the playground concept and the administrative environment. Such tools will always be found on an adventure playground. Strange as it may seem to some, fire is also a common loose part on adventure playgrounds in England, including those for disabled children.

The word *toy* can be used as a catchall term for an extremely wide variety of loose parts—model cars and trucks, balls, jump ropes, dolls, dress-up clothes; the list is endless. Because there are so many kinds of toys, and the use of specific ones is so sporadic and unpredictable, it is advisable to have a wide range kept in storage on a playground. Two of the most commonly used toys on playgrounds that are designed using these guidelines are balls (of all sorts of sizes and shapes) and push-pull toys. I suspect the reason this is so is that a rich support structure will create a lot of potential for child–object–environment interaction with these toys.

Another category of loose parts is containers—pots and pans, cups, muffin tins, bowls. Containers are fundamental to the success of sand and water play areas. Observation has verified that what a container looks like is not nearly so important to a child as such criteria as what it can hold, whether it is easily transportable when full, and whether it will mold. In other words, what a child can do with a container in sand and water is what is important, not what it is. For this reason, one will find many nontraditional containers in a sand area.

Game equipment represents another category—jump ropes, hula hoops, yo-yos, and so on. As discussed earlier, play is often affected by the season and by significant events. Football helmets become very popular around Superbowl time; movies like *Star Wars* present a demand for masks, space guns, and rockets.

Games such as checkers, jacks, and cards can also be used on playgrounds. Such games can complement a place usually used for passive activities. Beanbag toss is an example of the type of game that can use the structure of the playground as an integral part of the activity.

Although they are uncommon in the United States, most adventure play situations in Europe will have animal loose parts; chickens, goats, birds, turtles, cats, snakes, and dogs are frequently seen. These do present health and maintenance problems, but animals can be very exciting in a comprehensive play experience. I recommend that they have their own area, separated from the active play structure, perhaps at the apex of a loop path.

The final category of loose parts, ride-on toys or "wheels," includes bicycles, tricycles, wagons, and carts. Wheels provoke a great deal of debate over their appropriateness on creative playgrounds. They have several drawbacks: (1) They require a fairly hard surface and an extensive path system; (2) too many in use at once restrict the movement of other users; (3) they are expensive to purchase and to maintain; (4) they can be overused by disabled children who should be trying to develop their limited mobility; and (5) they need large storage spaces (Shaw, 1982). Extensive observation, however, has documented their popularity, and it is clear that a range of wheels should be available. It is the responsibility of the design team to minimize some of the potential problems by creating a suitable pathway system and providing adequate storage. A playground that has places accessible for wheelchairs (as discussed earlier) will also be acceptable for ride-on toys. It will be up to the play leaders to develop rules for their use that will minimize the other problems as they arise.

CONCLUSION

Observations

Before concluding this chapter, I would like to discuss a few additional musings. Some are observations of children's behavior gleaned from playground research. Others refer more to the organizational context of the play yard; some fit no neat category. Although these are informal and still exploratory, I think it is important to share them, since it is from watching the users that designers generate new ideas.

Mimicking. One child will observe another child engaged in a specific activity and want to mimic that activity. For example, one child bouncing a ball off a playground surface often results in one or more other children wishing to do so as well. This usually changes the activity from a solitary behavior to a group activity. A playground rich in three-dimensionaly stacked spaces reinforces this because it increases visual contact.

I Hurt Myself. Children often fall down but seldom get hurt. Children will be inclined to cry and seek adult comfort if they know they have been observed falling or if an adult rushes to their aid.

Significant Others. Children often perform for adults or other children on playgrounds. "Look at me do this" is a common request. The richer the play environment, the wider the range of "look at me" activities it will support.

Help. Children like to "help" the play leader. Good activities can begin by allowing children to help the play leader in various ways, such as finding a missing toy or helping to put up a rope swing.

Play Variety. A comprehensive play yard supports such a wide range of behaviors that one will seldom observe all the users engaged in one single group activity unless that activity is insisted upon by a play leader (e.g., group dancing). Additionally, when a playground has a good balance of key places, one cannot predict any specific pattern of use from day to day.

Sound. Certain materials make interesting sounds when walked on, pounded on, or yelled through. This should be kept in mind when choosing materials for construction.

Length of Play Period. A longer play period will allow a much wider range of play behavior than a short one, and this results in a richer experience for the children. Short play periods seem to encourage active, repetitive play patterns. The users never reach the point at which they can explore the yard in depth.

Size of Play Group. Observation has shown that a playground seems to be at its best when it is supporting play for a specific "critical mass" of users. Too few children do not get enough stimulation from one another, whereas too many will create chaos. The age, size, and mobility of the children in the group also affect the number that can best use a play environment. Through trial and error, an observant play leader can fit each group size to the playground.

Time of Play. The characteristics and, to some extent, the quality of the play experience are affected by the time of day the children play in the yard. A playtime after the afternoon nap is different than one before lunch. Each group's playtime should be changed during a school year to compensate for this.

Climate. Specific climatological conditions will alter play use. Users will seek the warmer sunny places in a playground on cool days and the shaded ones on warm days. Additionally, adults on a playground, because they are usually less active, seem to be more affected by extremes in temperature than are the children.

Adult Roles. A playground can be a very different place under different play leaders. Therefore, the administrative environment has significant ramifications for play. A potentially exciting playground design can be stifled with too many administrative rules. I have found that a play leader who is familiar with a complex play environment will usually have fewer restrictive rules for its use than one who is unfamiliar with it. In addition, play leaders who want to control and organize play do not feel comfortable in a sensory-rich environment that encourages independent play. Perhaps all play leaders should think about the following comment from Lady Allen (1969): "It is my opinion that the children ought to be free and by themselves to the greatest possible extent. . . . I am firmly convinced that one ought to be exceedingly careful when interfering in the lives and activities of children." Similarly, Lambert (1974) writes: "I feel it's dangerous to go around talking about the significance of children's play . . . our job is simply to allow them the space and scope they need to do it."

A Final Note

I have written this chapter in the first person to emphasize that it is a personal statement. In the introduction I explained how I began my work with children and playgrounds, and I set some constraints for the work. The body of the text dealt with the explanation of a series of phrases I have called design guidelines. The concluding observations returned to the children and described some behaviors and factors influencing behavior that lead to further questions rather than supplying answers.

In writing this text, I have been frustrated by the inadequacies of my own terms. After all, what does "three-dimensional juxtaposition of parts," taken as an isolated phrase, say to anyone? I realize that the terms are meaningless without the discussions that follow them; in reality the discussions are the design guidelines. If I have been successful, they will be what is of value.

I also have stated the guideline phrases in an architectural language rather than a behavioral one; therefore, to some, they may seem more like geometrical constructs than guidelines for user needs. This was intended so that designers, more at home with this vocabulary, would find the guidelines "user friendly."

In conclusion, I must add that these guidelines are intended to be just that: guides—helpful for the journey, but not predetermining the process and certainly not dictating the resulting forms. Each play setting is different; the children, the goals of educators and play leaders, the physical constaints of the site, the budget, and the climate are all factors that determine the uniqueness of each design. These factors give the design team the opportunity to be creative, to solve the problem, and to fulfill the needs of the children in a right and special way. The design guidelines are intended to enhance this process.

REFERENCES

Lady Allen of Hurtwood. *Planning for play.* Cambridge, MA: MIT Press, 1969.

deBono, E. *Use of lateral thinking.* Harmondsworth, Middlesex: Penguin, 1971.

Bengtsson, A. *Environmental planning for children's play,* New York: Praeger, 1970.

Bengtsson, A. *Adventure playgrounds.* New York: Praeger, 1973.

Lambert, J., Pearson, J. *Adventure playgrounds.* Penguin, 1974.

Moore, G. *The application of research to the design of therapeutic play environments for exceptional children.* 1980.

Moore, G. T., Cohen, U., Oertel, J., & van Ryzin, L. *Designing environments for handicapped children.* New York: Editorial Facilities Laboratory, 1979.

Nicholson, S. How not to cheat children: The theory of loose parts. *Landscape Architecture Magazine,* 1971, *62,* 30–33.

Shaw, L. G. "A child's creative learning space." Final report to the National Institute of Mental Health (unpublished), 1976.

Shaw, L. G. A test using scale models of playgrounds to understand cognitive mapping abilities of pre-school children. Unpublished paper, meeting of the Environmental Design Research Association, 1978.

Shaw, L. G. Design guidelines for handicapped children's play environments. In P. Wilkinson (Ed.), *In celebration of play.* London: Croom-Helm, 1980.

Shaw, L. G. *Adventure play environments for disabled children.* Gainesville, FL: Florida Architecture and Building Research Center, College of Architecture, University of Florida, 1982.

Shaw, L. G., & Katherine S. Williams. The use of toys and other loose parts on playgrounds for disabled children. *Children's Environment Quarterly,* 1984, *1*(2), 17–22.

Part IV

Involving Users in the Design Process

Chapter 10

Children's Participation in Planning and Design

Theory, Research, and Practice

ROGER A. HART

INTRODUCTION

Democratic responsibility can be acquired only through practice and involvement. It does not arise suddenly in adulthood through simple maturation; it must be fostered directly from an early age.I believe that the environments we occupy as children and the extent to which we feel involved in shaping them, or caring for them, is a particularly important domain for such learning. Motivating the following account is the general conviction that genuine participation, involving the responsible sharing of power, is critical to the achievement of democracy. What this means for children's participation is an important question for all of us who work with children, whether in research or in practice. This chapter is a beginning attempt to answer this question. It outlines the benefits of children's participation in environmental planning and design and summarizes what we know from psychology and other disciplines as a beginning guide to the practice of this all-too-rare activity.

It is clear from a comparison of western industrialized nations with nonindustrialized societies that *childhood* is an invention of culture. In rural countries, most children are working by 10 or 12 years of age and

---

ROGER A. HART • Sub-Program in Environmental Psychology, Graduate Center, City University of New York, New York, NY 10036.

frequently begin to work when 5 years old. In marked contrast, in the industrially developed countries, youths are denied direct participation in society until 16 years of age, at the earliest. Consequently, much of what is written herein applies not only to children but to young people throughout their teens.

CHILDREN'S SPONTANEOUS DESIGN

The Natural History of Children as Designers

Children create places for themselves from at least the age of 3 and probably earlier. The earliest forms of places are "found" rather than built; they are imaginal rather than physical transformations. Consequently, we cannot know just how early this kind of architecture begins. I have even observed children as young as 3 years of age create the familiar form of architecture in which materials are physically moved and juxtaposed to create new kinds of spaces. Although my observations have been primarily in the United States, particularly in a New England town (Hart, 1979), children's architecture appears to be a universal phenomenon. Perhaps the making of places to be in is one of a small set of archetypal human behaviors with important survival value for a culture and developmental advantages for the individual (Spivack, 1973). Before discussing the developmental importance of this kind of activity to children, a brief survey will be made of the natural history of children's architectural activity.

It is difficult to specify the normal ages at which the particular types of building occur. The type of building is strongly influenced by the available materials, and these vary dramatically according to an area's climate and vegetation and to different cultural and occupational practices around the world. Within North America, however, an approximate developmental sequence can be identified. It should be noted first that although girls thoroughly enjoy architectural activity, their form of it is different from that of boys. They are commonly discouraged from engaging in the business of building structures by parents because of the belief that such activity is inappropriate for girls. In addition, girls themselves commonly have a predilection to "play house" and to modify and decorate the interiors of houses rather than build them. As with much of children's play, part of what they are doing is preparing for adult roles and, although sex roles are changing, traditionally architects and builders are men and homemakers are women (Hart, 1979; Saegert & Hart, 1979).

The earliest architecture, as already described, consists of found places. Inside the home they are beneath chairs or tables and under sheets; out of doors, they are in bushes, boxes, or piles of dried leaves. It is a small jump from this imaginal architecture to the movement and combination of such elements as sheets and blankets, chairs, beds, turned couches, benches, mown grass, leaves, and discarded scrap materials. It is important to note that in almost all instances, even with these young children, this architecture is cooperative. Isaacs (1933) found the same to be true in her observations of children making "cozy places" in her school.

As children become older they are less well satisfied with such simple spaces where most of the parts and furnishings are imagined. Children of 8 years and older more often make serious attempts to build physical structures. It is then that the differences between boys' and girls' architecture become clear. Boys more often build structures with walls, and even roofs, such as tree forts, lean-tos, and tunnels. Girls emphasize the interiors, often adding great detail with shelves full of old bottles, cans, and plates, even when there are no walls. These differences, it will be argued in the following section, are reflections of the different sex-related social roles boys and girls are commonly encouraged to follow. Sometimes when the environment allows it, girls build "houses" or "dens" in bushes or among young sapling trees. These do not involve any banging of nails; adequate walls and ceilings are provided by simply bending back a few twigs, and interiors can then be swept and cleaned. Occasionally I have observed further attempts at improving these structures by hanging sheets from horizontal branches and even by weaving reeds together. But energies usually go into the making of seats, tables, telephones, television sets, and other furnishings, and to their continual reorganization.

The attitudes that parents and other child caretakers have toward the use of materials by their children are more important than the type of materials available in determining whether or not children build. The two often go hand in hand, however. Highly manicured outdoor settings with few loose parts are usually also highly controlled by adults, whereas gardens and yards with long grass, untrimmed bushes and trees, and many odds and ends lying around are often the kinds of homes in which adults allow their children a lot of freedom to use the environment as they wish. Many new suburban housing tracts are of the first category. All of the landscape elements most important to children are systematically removed from this kind of housing, and often a bizarre kind of competition between adults begins with every household's trying to make its yard the smoothest green carpet. Ideally, parents who do care about manicuring their property should think also of their children and leave some areas undefined, unless they have some kind of common wildland nearby. In this respect the children of impoverished inner cities often have a richer environment in abandoned lots containing piles of dirt, scrap wood, and other materials suitable for modifying the physical landscape. Rural children seem to have the best material opportunities for architecture.

Keeping this issue of adult ownership in mind, one can identify some of the qualities of the outdoor landscape most valued by children. Trees and

FIGURE 1. The use of trees in spontaneous architecture. Photo by Roger A. Hart.

bushes are clearly most important (see Figure 1). Deciduous trees are usually used instead of dense and dark coniferous woods. Ground-level tree buildings usually use young, straight trees for their structure; these young secondary-growth trees offer much opportunity for the children to make a plan that suits them (usually square) and to tie sheets or nail boards across these vertical posts. In contrast, "aerial" tree houses are almost always built in mature trees with many lateral branches, which will accept planks across the inner elbows of their main limbs. The most valued bushes for building are those with lush green canopies but with a relatively open network of thin branches beneath, where spaces may be found or made by the children.

The next most frequently used construction materials are discarded loose parts from around the home, such as tables, chairs, prams, old windows, and doors. Very large boxes, such as those used to carry refrigerators, are also highly valued, especially by young children, because they require so little modification. Whenever they become available, they are transported around dozens of locations before being destroyed by rain and heavy use.

I have observed other materials being used on numerous occasions. Tall grass is especially suitable for quickly making places. When associated with lush weeds, very young children find these "jungles" superb for making burrow-like forts that often have the luxury of a roof. Cut grass in the summer and the dried leaves of fall are also wonderful building materials for younger children.

Snow is another excellent resource with which children can exercise their skills as architects. It also commonly erases the constraints caused by adult domination of the landscape. My own observation of New England children revealed that with this medium even children under 8 years of age could create roofed structures by digging tunnels. Particularly valued are drifts created by walls and fences and high banks of snow created by plows.

Children spend a great deal of time modeling places in dirt and sand and constructing with blocks. Again, the play of girls and boys is different. Boys tend to build large structures such as racetracks, airports, railroads, and towns with highways and, more recently, space stations, whereas girls more commonly build houses and their interiors. In a famous study of children's block play, Erikson (1951) observed that boys tended to build structures, particularly tall ones, and girls built enclosures with interior space. He interpreted these differences as reflections of the different psychosexual concerns of girls and boys. I find the evidence for this unconvincing. I have observed enough chastisement by their own peers to keep girls building girl-type things such as house interiors and boys building boy-type things such as towers to suggest that sex-role socialization alone is a satisfactory explanation.

Experiments in Children's Spontaneous Architecture

A few studies have systematically investigated children's spontaneous architecture through drawings and models rather than the creation of a finished product (e.g. Muntanola-Thornberg, 1973, 1974; Zerner, 1972). In contrast is a remarkable series of experiments conducted in France by an architect and a social psychologist (Boris & Hirschler, 1971). The studies involved children aged 8 to 14 in both regular school classes and a slow class of children with character or retardation problems generally related to difficult sociofamilial situations. Four different-sized and different-shaped prismatic polyurethane foam forms were produced that could be used by children for constructing flat, octagonal, and curved surfaces. In each experiment, the building decisions were made by the children, assembled in a council. They voted whenever a choice had to be made or whenever there was a conflict. Not only was the children's building process observed, but discussions were held with the children during the construction, once the edifice was finished, and after a stay in the "domain" for a period of days.

From 10 experiments, the investigators made some tentative observations, warning that they might not generalize to other age groups, cultures, and environments. First of all, although the children were given full freedom to play with the materials in any way they chose, without any adult suggestion that they build with them, the children always chose to use them to create an environment after only a very short time of playing more "rough and tumble" games. The groups always started by making rectangular, parallelipedic shapes; several hours or days later, these were rejected, sometimes with great violence, and replaced with extremely rich, free forms. The children explained that they would like to live in complicated spaces with a variety of shapes and much character. They designed the spaces to fit closely the activities to be performed in them, but these activities did not reflect the traditional categories of the school curriculum such as painting or geography; instead, activities such as collective work, councils, individual work, small group, dance, and intimacy were used as the focus of the designs. In other words, the activities were clustered by the children according to the similarity of their social and psychological characteristics.

Boris and Hirschler (1971) suggest some of the learning children gained from the process. Most notable was an increased awareness of architectural surroundings which extended after their experience to other settings. (This emphasis upon the value of the process over the product is a point that occurs frequently in the writings of those who have experimented with children's involvement in design.) They also comment that the details the children reported "in their increasing awareness of the relations between inside and outside seemed to us to be a strong indication of the territorial qualities the children needed, to feel at ease and secure" (p. 16). This theme will be developed in the discussion of the psychological benefits of building.

In 1978, during the United Nations Habitat conference, I was given an opportunity to design an exciting project that involved children's spontaneous architecture. Asked to help organize a children's conference, I decided that it was important to let the children know from the beginning that this was a chance for them to express their housing and environmental concerns. The vehicle for this expression was the creation of an environment in which they would work for the duration of the conference. Within one day the 35 primary-school children, the majority of whom were strangers to one another, had converted a school gymnasium into a community of houses using cardboard, string, tape, and pens. Periodically the children were asked to come together, usually to solve problems that emerged between the groups: How do we divide up our gardens? Who decides where the roads go? How can we stop people from looking into our windows? and so on. In creating this settlement and solving its problems in this collective manner, the children faced a large number of the critical habitat issues being dealt with by the adult conference. They were able to draw ideas from, and generalize to, their more complex everyday home environment. What would normally have been abstract environmental issues to them—crowding, density, privacy, and limited resources—became clear and important problems for which they enthusiastically pursued solutions.

The Social and Psychological Benefits of Building

No one theory can explain the rich diversity of play and adequately describe its significance in human development (see, for example, reviews by Bruner, Jolly, & Sylva, 1976; Millar, 1968; Rubin, Fein, & Vandenburg, 1983; Schwartzman, 1978). One must look at them together to understand the psychological and social benefits that ensue from constructive play with materials: the learning of adult roles; the opportunity to deal with emotional conflict; the discovery of physical processes and principles of spatial relationship; the ordering of the world as a means of establishing one's place in it and sense of control over it; and, perhaps most important of all, the development of a sense of environmental competence. I will consider each of these in turn.

One of the better-known sets of play theories stresses its value for the learning of adult roles. This function has already been highlighted through the above discussion of the differences in the building activities of boys and girls. It is further revealed in the uses to which the houses and forts are put after they are built. Girls frequently play house and spend large amounts of time cleaning, whereas boys devote most of their time to building and rebuilding the structures themselves and spend very little time inside them. I have observed that although both younger boys and girls engage in highly imaginative dramatic house play, boys older than about 7 years of age rarely do so. Boys do, however, continue to act out imaginative dramas on their dirt-built model scenes. The reason for these differences undoubtedly lies again in the heavily socialized attitude that model interiors and model exteriors, like their real-world equivalents, are for girls and boys respectively. Dramatic play in these environments allows both girls and boys the opportunity to act out real-life situations, express personal needs, explore solutions, and even to experiment in the reversal of roles.

The micro-modelling of places and events is also important in enabling children better to understand places and physical events and how they work. Frequently in this kind of play there is an extreme fascination with how the environment functions, as in the detailed building of miniature tarmac roads with all of the various layers and processes. Children are building maps of environments, experienced or imagined. Such play offers the opportunity to reduce in scale environments too large to be experienced by children directly and thereby to understand them better.

It is most likely that the modelling of places also offers the opportunity for children to deal with emotional conflict by symbolizing phenomena and dealing with them through manipulation in a manner that is not possible in the everyday social world with adults (see, for example, Erikson, 1951). No doubt it is because this activity is so familiar to children and so valuable to them that psychoanalysts have formalized it into a diagnostic technique (Erikson, 1963; Klein, 1975; Murphy, 1956; Winnicott, 1971). In the "small worlds" method, a child is offered a wide variety of toys and building materials. The psychoanalyst can obtain valuable diagnostic insights by observing and interpreting the building of miniature landscapes and the acting out of dramas in these settings.

An additional reason that children build places for themselves must surely be related to their growing sense of identity. The establishment of spatial order in the world, the making of place from space, has become an important theme in recent years for humanistically and behaviorally oriented geographers (Buttimer, 1976; Cooper, 1971; Duncan, 1981; Relph, 1976; Seamon, 1979). Little has been written of this by the child-development and child-care professions, but the writers of children's stories are clearly aware of its importance (see Appendix A-3 of Hart, 1979). It has also been recognised by a small number of environmental planning and design professionals (Muntanola-Thornberg, 1982; Rudofsky, 1964). One of the special qualities of the physical environment is that it remains stable. Children come to know themselves through their transactions both with a physical and a social world. Because, unlike the world of people, the physical world does not itself change in response to a child's actions but simply reflects his or her manipulations, it offers a particularly valuable domain for developing one's sense of self. Demonstration that places are built by children more for the joy and the challenge of building than for their use as finished artifacts is that even self-built places may be freely used by other children, as long as there is overt recognition of the builders. Once built, houses are furnished, modified, destroyed, and rebuilt; they are rarely played in as finished artifacts. It appears that children need to see themselves as competent individuals and for this to be recognized by others. Consequently, arguments on the use of places appear to arise only when there is doubt about, or failure to recognize, who has built them.

In observing young children's love of "cozy places" (the children's own term), Isaacs (1933) offered a psychoanalytic interpretation. She explained that there is frequently a defensive element to children's play with objects such as upturned chairs and tables: "so that nobody can look in," "to keep us warm," "to keep the tigers out" or "to keep out the foxes." It was clear to her that the feeling of being warm and safe inside these places was central to their importance. "Enemies" are always outside; anyone coming inside, child or adult, was treated in a friendly, affectionate manner. By being inside, Isaacs argued, the children not only made themselves warm and safe, but friendly, loving and good as well. From here, Isaacs takes a massive psychoanalytical leap in her interpretation, however, by arguing that "the whole situation indeed represented a good mother with her good children inside her, all safe and all loving" (p. 363). According to Isaacs, all the bad feelings are projected onto the father who is kept outside. The child, she says, believes that "If I am inside my mommy, I don't have to do anything bad to her to make her give me what I want. I only have to be there and everything is given to me."

These kinds of direct links to deep, unconscious feelings possibly play a part, but as with Erikson's interpretation of towers built by boys, it is too simplistic and deterministic to explain the making of cozy places entirely in this way. Rooms are not just wombs. On the other hand, it is true that one of the achievements a child has to make in coming to deal with the complexity of the environment is to order it and give it meaning. The creation of safe or "sacred" places from which to explore the dangerous or "profane" world beyond (Eliade, 1965) seems intuitively to be a basic way of establishing order. It links directly to Spivack's (1973) idea of homemaking as an archetypal kind of human activity.

The most important outcome of children's opportunity to transform environments is the effect this undoubtedly has on their sense of *environmental competence.* Environmental competence might be defined as "the knowledge, skill and confidence to use the environment to carry out one's own goals and to enrich one's experience" (Saegert & Hart, 1978). If children do not feel competent in their engagement with the environment, we might reasonably assume that they are less likely to take part in changing or managing the environment when they become adults. Erikson (1951) wrote of the importance of the "microsphere," that "small, safe, manageable world of toys," to a child's development. He argued that this microsphere of physical objects allows preschool children to gain competence and confidence before venturing out into the complex social macrosphere. This makes good sense, but I should note that in my own research I have noticed little or no decrease in children's interest in constructional play until they approach 12 years of age.

CHILDREN'S PARTICIPATION IN PLANNING AND DESIGN

The Social and Psychological Benefits

All that has been said previously concerning the benefits to children of being free to design and build places for themselves is true of their participation with adults in the creation of settings. An important additional value of such "real" projects is that the child develops a sense of meaningful involvement and responsibility in society. For many years, enlightened social caseworkers have known that allowing children or youths who have been characterized as delinquent to participate in creating environments is a very effective means for helping to assimilate them into society (e.g., Benjamin, 1974; Ward, 1978; Ward & Fyson, 1976).

Allowing children and youth to participate in environmental projects not only helps them to realize their potential but can also assist in the building of group cohesion. The physical environment is particularly useful for this because it offers opportunities for a group to see the impact of its joint efforts in a direct and lasting way. Although designed for more directly practical reasons, "barn-raising" served this community-building function. More recently, the community garden movement in United States cities has done more than simply enhance attractiveness and provide some food resources (Francis, Cashdan, & Paxson, 1981). It has frequently served as the basis for community groups to form around a simple, easily understood, and politically neutral project. People can then go on to more ambitious projects that may have more importance to their lives, such as creating day-care facilities and rebuilding their own housing.

Implications for the Quality and Maintenance of the Finished Product

It is impossible for a designer or planner to take into account all of the important details of a project without some participation by the clients. Nowhere is this more obvious than in the design of play environments. Adventure playgrounds, when properly managed, can occupy hundreds of children at a time because they are entirely built by children and youth. At the opposite extreme, we see thousands of concrete turtles and other weird science fiction-like objects lying unnoticed and unused on American playgrounds because of no involvement in their design by the users, children. Unfortunately, there is little motivation for most environmental designers to be sensitive to the needs of users, since design critics focus on form. Designers with a conscience have to bear the extra time and expense often implied by participatory design, and so they cannot bid competitively for contracts. One must hope that some degree of participation will eventually be mandated for all public projects.

Participation can result in a better finished product not only because the ideas of individuals have been recognized but also because of the results of collective creativity. In truly participatory environmental projects, there is room for each individual to discover new, and otherwise unused, abilities which result in a collective creativity beyond what any individual might produce. Halprin (1975) provides an impassioned account of this perspective and suggests ways of achieving it.

Not only does children's involvement in participation lead to a better quality environment, but it also has implications for its maintenance. In the first *Childhood City Newsletter* (1981a) on participation, eight experts were interviewed by our collaborating teenagers. They all said that participation was valuable as a means of developing in young people a sense of responsibility toward environments. Joe Benjamin, for example, related his experiences on British playgrounds; he found that when the work had been done by children, there were no graffiti and no vandalism. It is unfortunate that this principle seems to be the major and often the only factor influencing public administrators' decisions to involve youth. They commonly fail to recognize the fundamental benefit of valid participation to a person's development. Nevertheless, it is a valuable point to make whenever one is trying to articulate the value of participation to more conservative thinkers who do not easily understand such concern with human development.

Tokenism in Child Participation

Participation has become a catchword with many, very different meanings. To be anything other than tokenism, participation must involve the sharing of power, although children cannot, of course, share equally with adults. How much power children *should* have, however, can be a thorny issue. Children are neither magical saviors who, if left alone, could transform society nor completely ignorant creatures who must be shaped and informed by adults until they reach their own adulthood and can participate in society.

Between these two extremes lies a model of children's socialization which is *interactive.* In such a model, children become competent persons with meaningful roles in society through their participation. Although the extent and nature of children's ability to participate change as they develop, adults have a continuing responsibility to try to maximize their children's participation in their everyday environment. In any society, the degree of opportunity children have to collaborate with adults in the everyday management of family and community institutions is directly and positively related to the competence and sense of responsibility held by adults in that society. Intervening to improve children's participation is therefore one means of fundamentally improving society. Boulding states this idea clearly (1979):

> Adult–child relationships offer a critical intervention point for breaking the vicious cycles of dominance behaviors that pervade public and international life. These patterns are laid down in the house with daily acts of inappropriate exercises of power, invisibly interwoven with the acts of human caring that sustain the institution of the family as a continuously viable setting for human growth. We may be unnecessarily sabotaging our present, and our children's future, by being blind to the inconsistencies and irrationalities of adult–child interaction in family and community in this century. (p. 9)

By comparing the assignment of responsibility in western industrial nations with that in nonindustrial societies, it becomes clear, as we have noted, that childhood is an invention of culture (Boulding, 1979; Rogoff, Sellers, Pirotta, Fox, & White, 1976). In many ways teenagers' role in society is even less acceptable than that of children. The period of childhood has been extended further and further until now North American and most European countries keep their children in school and away from meaningful participation until the age of 16 or later. Sometimes this large unused work force is employed on large-scale conservation projects, but this is rarely at an acceptable level of responsibility or with serious training or apprenticeship in mind. The remarkable thing is that even when teenagers are employed in a quasi-voluntary manner they are invariably treated as mindless labor rather than participants. If one wishes to have some real impact on young people's development and to invite more than fleeting involvement in a project, it is necessary to give them some genuine control or responsibility in the situation.

It is very common for adults to involve children in a subtly condescending way. Classic examples of this involve sitting young children on conference panels, with little or no preparation and no recognition by the adults that there might be alternate methods and media of communication more suited to children. The result, no matter what the children say, is a large amount of applause by the adults and a big press response. Children's participation makes a good story, but rarely is there any recognition that the children could have made any serious contribution to the issue. It is highly likely that the long-term effects of such performances are to alienate children further and to convince them that genuine participation is not possible.

Arnstein (1969) has developed a typology to describe the range of different kinds of involvement by people in the planning and operating of public programs. In her model, each rung of a ladder corresponds to a different degree of citizen power in determining the end products. It is useful to summarize these levels in order to obtain a more precise understanding of tokenism in children's involvement.*

In *manipulation*, people are placed on rubber-stamp advisory committees as a way of engineering their support. Examples of this with children can be found on those many occasions when children are asked to sit on panels at conferences, using an adult mode of participation but with none of the advantages of preparation for the occasion or familiarity with the style of communication. *Therapy*, the second rung of the ladder, represents the condition during which mental health experts, from social workers to psychiatrists, mistakenly assume powerlessness to be synonymous with mental illness. Arnstein gives the example of a public-housing tenant group's meeting being used as a forum for a "control-your-child" workshop rather

*For another typology designed to shatter the rhetoric of participation, the reader may turn to the only journal that consistently argues for child and youth environmental participation, *The Bulletin for Environmental Education*. In the November 1979 issue, Jim Johnson, an architect from Strathclyde, Scotland, describes "a trench eye view of participation" in his article, "A Plain Man's Guide to Participation."

than a discussion of such real issues as arbitrary evictions. A common example with children is the so-called pollution and conservation education program wherein children are made aware of these important issues by having to pick up garbage or clean streams; they are rarely informed about the root causes, which lie primarily within the domain of the adult world.

Instead of being a valuable first step in a genuine participation program, *informing*, the next rung on Arnstein's ladder, is commonly done too late in a process for people to have any impact on it. This is probably the most common approach used by adults with children. Similarly, in *consultation*, citizens' opinions are discovered through attitude surveys, neighborhood meetings, and public hearings. If this is not combined with other genuine modes of participation there is no way of guaranteeing that the citizens' concerns will actually be acted upon. Planners and researchers, for example, may ask children to draw their ideal city or play environment, take these drawings, and never return to tell them whether they used any of the information. Consultation then becomes a sham, like informing.

Placation is the term used by Arnstein to describe those instances in which true representation is allowed, but the power elite makes sure that there is never enough representation to challenge their traditional power. Many children have experienced this as class representatives sitting on school committees. *Partnership* is usually found where there is an organized power base in a community which has negotiated with the power holders to effect a redistribution of power. Although such partnership would seem an obvious way of running playgrounds and other recreational facilities with teenagers, Robin Moore and I found no such equal-sharing models in the collection of over 400 files of our Young People's Participation Project.

Citizen control is the ultimate level. An example in the adult world is the community control of schools. There are, of course, no institutional examples in which children have such complete autonomy. Fortunately they manage to practice it in their play when enlightened parents or institutional caretakers allow them to establish periodic autonomy in their bedrooms or in the block corner of their kindergarten rooms.

The Development of Children's Ability to Participate

If one takes the time to look at what children do spontaneously or if one listens to them, it is clear that they are able to participate in a multitude of ways. Goodman (1956) and Ward (1978) offer superb reflections on this issue. Nonetheless, adults must recognize that there are developmental limitations to this participation; children cannot function at the level expected of an adult.

One factor influencing the nature of children's ability to participate is their basic competence in perspective taking. The process begins in the second or third year with their first awareness of psychological processes in others and continues up through adolescence, with the development of a truly third-person or "generalized other" perspective. (For a complete account, see Selman, 1980). Youths who think at this level can "see the need to coordinate reciprocal perspectives, and believe social satisfaction, understanding or resolution must be mutual and coordinated to be genuine and effective" (Selman, 1980, p. 39).

Beyond this mutual perspective-taking ability, Selman hypothesizes an even higher level of "societal-symbolic perspective taking." A person can now imagine multiple mutual perspectives forming a generalized societal, legal, or moral perspective in which all individuals can share. A person believes others use this shared point of view in order to facilitate accurate communication and understanding.

This final phase, which Selman believes can emerge at any time from the age of 10, is obviously the one to be desired for the most fruitful participatory behavior. It is clear, however, that even during earlier phases children are very capable of working with older persons. What is essential is that these persons understand some of the limitations children have in being able to take the perspective of others.

Children's participation is also influenced by their language ability. Since facility with verbal language develops slowly, it may be necessary to use other media in order to engage children fully in the participation process. Our teenage interviewers in the survey for the Young People's Participation Project found that adults usually tend to monopolize discussions and that children are particularly reticent when adults are talking. For this reason it is useful at the beginning of a participation project to allow subgroups of people, such as children or teenagers, to meet alone in order to gain some strength (*Childhood City Quarterly*, 1982/1983).

If one is using verbal language, it is necessary to listen closely and to be careful not to extend beyond the children's vocabulary or speak too abstractly. Techniques and materials that make comprehension and communication visual and accessible to a wide age range, such as drawings, models, photographs, iconic maps, and plans, should be used whenever appropriate. Through these alternative media of communication one can demystify the process of decision making and design and allow children to explore, develop, and communicate ideas to others. Finally, one must always remember that we are not speaking of *the* child but of children. Like adults, they have different styles and competencies of communication and hence may prefer different media regardless of their age.

SOME GUIDING PRINCIPLES

Participation advocates are frequently criticized for naively assuming that all persons wish to participate when in fact very few do. Such criticisms, however, are themselves naive because they fail to distinguish between awareness and desire or between opportunity and desire to participate. Although it is true that not everyone wishes to participate in every project, it is important to be aware that a failure to come forward often does not reflect a lack of interest. Two alternative explanations are feelings of futility resulting from past experiences with the political powers and a sense of inadequacy ("I'm too shy, inarticulate," etc.). We should also remember that not all people can afford to volunteer to the same degree because of financial hardship. For these reasons, a truly participatory project with any group will probably have to engage in some liberating practices, such as convincing individuals that the process will not be monopolized by dominant or highly verbal persons and describing realistically the support available and the goals that can be achieved.

As a general principle, it is important to make sure that all those persons, children or adults, that are likely to be affected by a project have the opportunity and are even encouraged to participate. However, it is not always a simple matter to determine who will be the users of the environment that is to be created. Such issues are complicated and delicate. Consequently, it is important that the representativeness of the group be discussed at the first meeting and that invitations to others be extended if there is any doubt.

Not everyone, of course, desires to be involved in all stages of a project. People usually prefer one phase over another. Nevertheless, it is important that everyone, including children, understand the whole process. Good open discussion about this at the beginning of a project can enable a suitable schedule to be designed for all. One can also discover at this stage the great variety of skills and special resources available. It is important to recognize that adults can do some things children cannot—for example, during a gardening project, knowing how to prod the city system's resources, getting the sanitation department to come out with a truck (Fox, in *Childhood City Newsletter,* 1981a). On the other hand, children can better contribute ideas regarding the design and use of play space.

In all participatory projects with children, the role of the animator is critical. Although an animator may stimulate a group to begin a project, more often he or she joins a group after it has formed. In either case, the animator's goal is to enable the group to suspend disbelief through fantasy, to brainstorm, and to engage in street theater exercises or improvisations in order to awaken creative responses. Inter-action, a British nonprofit organization, is an example of a group that uses an animator to stimulate community involvement through creative activities. It emphasizes mutual help projects in neighborhoods, enabling more community participation, especially with children and teenagers. The animators use enviromental theater and games to invite children and adults to work with them on community problem identification and solution. (See Figure 2.)

FIGURE 2. In Britain, Inter-action stimulates community involvement in neighborhood projects (photo courtesy of Inter-action Trust, London, England).

It is often valuable to have participants exchange roles in a group. Francis (Childhood City Newsletter, 1981a) began working with a group of teenagers, 13 to 19 years, who attended a high school in Cambridge, Massachusetts, that was being redesigned. He relates:

> We thought we'd talk about what this new school should be and how it should be designed according to ideas the kids had. We all took different roles. Somebody was a principal, somebody was an architect, and somebody was the teacher. There were some kids representing kids. We had a whole evening discussion about how to design this new high school. A 15-year-old kid really got into the role as a principal. He said "You can't give kids a space because they're gonna destroy it, and they're gonna vandalize it and they're not gonna take care of it." He became their principal and he could understand how adults sometimes think. (p. 26)

Perhaps one of the most difficult skills for an animator is knowing when to stop animating, to retreat and to relinquish responsibility. Working hard from the beginning to make sure that the children and all other participants feel "ownership" of the project is the best way to guarantee that they will assume the responsibility. How people feel regarding their entry into a project has an impact on their subsequent feelings of involvement. All too often, adults do the initial planning in a project before bringing in children.

Such a move is likely to be a fatal flaw, making genuine child participation much more difficult to achieve. There may, of course, be instances wherein a project has been in existence for a long time, but it had not been clear that it was relevant to children or that they could participate. As long as this is made clear to the children, there should be no problem. The difficulty arises when adults think that children cannot or should not define goals for themselves. In this case, the children will quickly realize that this limited participation is no different from the typical classroom situation.

CHILDREN'S PARTICIPATION IN PRACTICE

Environmental Design and Planning in the Schools

Although environmental education grew remarkably in the schools of the United States in the late 1960s and 1970s, the emphasis was almost entirely upon natural environments. On those rare occasions when the built environment was considered, it was usually in terms of its visual aesthetic properties. A different tradition was growing at the same time in the United Kingdom. Although there remains an emphasis upon teaching about natural systems in British schools, there are now a large number of teachers, many of them trained in geography, who teach about the quality of the urban environment for its organisms—people. These teachers, both at the elementary and secondary level, are served by a unique journal. *The Bulletin of Environmental Education* (*B.E.E.*) is devoted to encouraging children's participation in environmental decision making as their democratic right and responsibility. Ward and Fyson, cofounders of *B.E.E.*, saw the journal as a means of achieving, through education and participation, the kinds of civic responsibility called for by the British planner Patrick Geddes. They have summarized their approach to environmental education in *Streetwork* (1976), a title meant to contrast with the past emphasis on fieldwork in environmental education and science classes.*

The articles published in the *B.E.E.* vary in the degree of participation described and reflect the lower six rungs of Arnstein's ladder of participation. There are occasional examples of partnership in which children co-design places, usually facilities for children such as classrooms, but consultation by planners with children is more common, and informing remains the most frequent kind of participation, even in this progressive journal. It is important to avoid applying these labels too quickly with children, however. Simulation exercises with adults would probably be

*Readers wishing to obtain a more complete understanding of the ideas behind Colin Ward's view of the importance of environmental education and children's participation in planning should turn to Ward (1978).

placed by Arnstein low on the second rung of her ladder, but with children simulation is often the only way of allowing them to understand some of the complexities of a project. If combined with other experiences it can be considered a valuable preparation for their participation as adults at the highest levels of the ladder. One very effective example from *B.E.E.* is the Houses Game (Jones, 1979). It requires only two standard sheets of paper and a little glue. Children are challenged to design a housing layout on one sheet of paper using cutout houses from the other sheet. The requirements for open space and areas such as parking are demanding, and the game is so fascinating that it is likely that children playing it will have a lasting awareness of the importance of careful environmental planning and design.

There are very few examples in the United States of children's participating in the planning and design of their local environment through their schools. There are a number of possible reasons for this. One is undoubtedly the avoidance by all public schools of field trips, a weakness that has been further aggravated by the fear of law suits. Another reason is that democratic participation by adults in local environmental planning in the United States is a less well organized affair. The *B.E.E.* approach, for example, received great impetus from the British government's Skeffington Report in the 1970s, which called for public participation in local government planning decisions. As a result of this, many counties have planners serving an educational liaison function with the schools. Some of these planners work hard to bring children and teachers from the relevant nearby schools directly into the different local planning issues that arise.

Many school teachers have seen the value of allowing children to build spaces and then play out dramas in them (e.g., Sprague-Mitchell, 1934). A recent example is the City Building Education Programs designed by Doreen Nelson and based in Los Angeles (Nelson, 1978). The physical building of a model city, only one part of a large, carefully sequenced curriculum, ignites interest and helps the children understand the complex social, political, and economic phenomena that make up a city. Although this simulated future city idea has the advantage of being exciting and flexible, it may not expose children in a sufficiently realistic way to the realities of urban environmental decision making. This is, of course, difficult for any simulation program to achieve well.

Real participatory planning projects have their own drawbacks. There is the danger of disappointment and disillusionment if the children work hard and see nothing come of their work. There is also the danger of pretense when some change by the children is guaranteed because it is set up by a teacher, or when their participation is touted as more meaningful than it really is. Classic examples of this are stories of waste lots transformed by children from rubble into beautiful gardens, when in truth children had no part in, or even awareness of, the legal, financial, or political maneuverings to obtain the space. Their contribution was the enjoyable but superficial task of planting the flowers.

One way of avoiding this dilemma is to realize that although children have limited ability to achieve physical change in their neighborhood, they can still do a great deal that is significant; they can study their environment and how it is changing, inform others of these changes, and communicate their own ideas for the future. The Environmental Exchange Program conducted with elementary and junior high schools in New York, New Jersey, Vermont, New Hampshire, nd and Massachusetts is one such project (Hart & Perez, 1981). In this project children studied sites selected by themselves and other members of their neighborhood community for a whole school year. They developed alternative possible plans for these sites and anticipated the positive and negative impact of their proposed changes. Their ideas were communicated to other members of the community through subway station murals, community newspapers, and child-led walking tours of their study sites. Throughout the year, children in each participating classroom exchanged what they were learning about their own community with pen pals in a contrasting "twin" community. In this way children focus on what they can best explore and understand, their own local environment. Moreover, they come to understand that in all types of communities environmental decisions have to be made by people and that the quality of these decisions affects the environment and the quality of life.

Playgrounds, Farms, and Gardens

Adventure playgrounds were conceived in Denmark during World War II and developed rapidly after the war, first in Scandinavia and subsequently throughout Western Europe, as places where children are able to build their own places with all kinds of loose parts (Bengtsson, 1972; Benjamin, 1974; Lambert & Pearson, 1974; *Landscape Architecture,* 1974). When they are properly run, these are probably the only institutionalized form of citizen control for children. Sometimes small "cities" are established. The functions of a good playleader are limited to arbitrating serious disputes, advising with building problems and other issues when asked, looking out for dangerous design elements, and occasionally administering first aid. Consequently, there are excellent opportunities for children to learn with one another how to create and manage environments. Adventure playgrounds have failed to develop to any large extent in the United States, probably because of the ugliness and anarchy that parents commonly believe they bring and the inaccurate belief that they are more dangerous (see Cooper, 1970). Nonetheless, there is a small but steadily growing literature on designing play environments with the collaboration of children and adults (e.g., Bengtsson, 1972; Benjamin, 1974; Frost & Klein, 1979; Hogan, 1974; Wilkinson, 1980).

City farms are another innovative idea that has grown rapidly in the past decade in the United Kingdom (*Childhood City Newsletter,* 1981/1982, Urban Farms). Created in the heart of dense urban areas, they are managed and visited by both children and adults of all ages (unlike adventure playground areas). Urban farms have not developed in the United States, but over the past 15 years there has been a remarkable expansion of community gardens, particularly in cities. Gardening has proved to be a very effective means of building community groups (see survey by Francis *et al.,* 1981). By first forming around the highly visible, straightforward, comprehensive idea of a garden, community residents often gain a sense of group cohesion and self-reliance that enables them to go on to more ambitious projects such as forming a formal community organization and rehabilitating old housing. Technical assistance groups to the hundreds of community gardens in New York City tell us that children and teenagers are always among the first and most energetic participants in these projects.

Urban Studies Centers

Just as *Streetwork* was word play on *fieldwork,* so the urban studies center concept draws its name from the nature study centers which have been visited by British schoolchildren for decades. Strongly promoted by Ward and Fyson, urban studies centers are intended to serve as bases from which children can explore and come to understand urban neighborhoods physically, socially, economically, and politically (*Bulletin for Environmental Education;* Ward & Fyson, 1976; Ward, 1978). Centers should be equipped with a rich array of maps, photographs, books, archives, and field research equipment which the children can learn to use in order to collect information useful not only to themselves but to the community under study. Data and reports prepared by the children can then in turn enter the archives to become a resource for other groups of children and adults who use the center. Notting Dale Urban Studies Center in a low-income area of West London fulfills the dreams of Ward and Fyson (Ward, 1978; Ward & Fyson, 1976). Not only does it serve children from the immediate neighborhood and from surrounding schools, but it is also an urban base for classes of suburban children who visit the center for a day or a week (the center has dormitory space for a class of children). In its archives are a large collection of meeting minutes, statistics, photographs, newspaper cuttings, and students' written documentaries, describing life changes in the community, why they are occurring, and how they could be improved. Over the years this center has established itself as such a valuable community resourse that it serves as the local political center for community meetings. In this way, it has become a valuable institution for democratic urban community planning. Notting Dale Urban Studies Center is a model of how valuable children's participation can be. Unfortunately, it is a rare phenomenon. In spite of the success of this center, the urban study center concept is not growing even in Britain.

CONCLUDING THOUGHTS

Developing a competent, participating citizenry is difficult. The long-term benefits to society are hard to observe and therefore easy to ignore, whereas the short-term inconvenience of involving children is all too obvious. Community participation is not appreciated by many planners or designers, for it slows down the process. Those of us who work with people in the creation and management of environments can contribute a great deal through demonstration and research to improve our understanding of how genuinely to involve children in the process. We must then work to convince others that this involvement is beneficial to both children and to society.

ACKNOWLEDGMENTS

Many of the ideas expressed in this chapter arose out of the Young People's Participation Project which I codirected with Robin Moore. Numerous people participated in this project and assisted in editing the three volumes of *Childhood City Quarterly* on participation, from which this chapter draws heavily. The Y.P.P.P. was developed at the request of the United States section of the International Association for the Child's Right to Play (I.P.A.) as their contribution to the International Year of the Child. Funding came from the National Endowment for the Arts and the Environmental Protection Agency.

REFERENCES

Arnstein, S. R. Eight rungs on the ladder of citizen participation. *Journal of The American Institute of Planners*, July, 1979.

Bengtsson, A. *Adventure playgrounds.* New York: Praeger, 1972.

Benjamin, J. *Grounds for play.* London: Bedford Square Press, 1974.

Boris, J., & Hirschler, G. Living space imagined and actualized by children. *Cahier Sandoz* No. 19, Edition Sandoz, 1971.

Boulding, E. *Children's rights and the wheel of life.* Transaction Books, 1979.

Bruner, J. S., Jolly, A., & Sylva, K. *Play: Its role in development and evolution.* New York: Penguin, 1976.

Bulletin for Environmental Education. Published ten times per year by Streetworks. BEE SUBS, c/o Notting Dale Urban Studies Centre, 189 Freston Road, London W10 6TH.

Buttimer, A. Grasping the dynamism of Lifeworld. *Annals of the Association of American Geographers,* 1976, *66,* 279–292.

Childhood City Newsletter. *Participation one: An introduction.* New York: Center for Human Environments of the City University of New York Graduate Center, 1981, No. 22. (a)

Childhood City Newsletter. *Participation two: A survey of projects, programs and organizations.* New York: Center for Human Environments of the City University of New York Graduate Center, 1981, No. 23. (b)

Childhood City Newsletter. *City farms.* New York: Center for Human Environments of the City University of New York, Graduate Center, Winter 1981/1982, No. 26.

Childhood City Quarterly. *Participation three: Techniques.* New York: Center for Human Environments of the City University of New York Graduate Center. Double Issue Vol. 9, No. 4 and Vol. 10 No. 1, 1982/1983.

Cooper, C. Adventure playgrounds. *Landscape Architecture,* 1970, *61* (1), 18–29 and 88–91.

Cooper, C. *The house as symbol of self.* Berkeley, CA: University of California Institute of Urban and Regional Planning, Working Paper #120, 1971.

Duncan, J. *Housing and identity.* London: Croom-Helm, 1981.

Eliade, M. *The sacred and the profane: The nature of religion.* New York: Harvest Books, 1965.

Erikson, E. H. Sex differences in the play configurations of pre-adolescents. *American Journal Orthopsychiatry,* 1951, *21,* 667–692.

Erikson, E. H. *Childhood and society* Toys and reasons,(pp. 209–246). New York: Norton, 1963.

Francis, M., Cashdan, L., & Paxson, L. *The making of neighborhood open spaces: Community design, development and management of open spaces.* New York: Center for Human Environments of the City University of New York Graduate School, 1981.

Frost, J., & Klein, B. L. *Children's play and playgrounds.* Chapter 5: Planning for play: Involving parents, children, and community groups. Boston: Allyn & Bacon, 1979.

Gesell, A., & Ilg, F. L. *The child from five to ten.* New York: Harper, 1946.

Goodman, P. *Growing up absurd.* New York: Vantage, 1956.

Halprin, L. *Taking part: A workshop approach for collective creativity.* Cambridge, MA: MIT Press, 1975.

Hart, R. A. *Children's experience of place.* New York: Irvington, 1979.

Hart, R. A., & Perez, C. The Environmental Exchange Program. In *Bulletin of Environmental Education.* London: Town and Country Planning Association, September 1981.

Hogan, P. *Playgrounds for free.* Cambridge, MA: MIT Press, 1974.

Isaacs, S. *Social development in young children.* New York: Harcourt Brace, 1933.

Jones, S. The houses game: Plan your own area. *Bulletin of Environmental Education,* 1979, *99,* 17–20.

Klein, M. *The psycho-analysis of children.* New York: Delacorte Press, 1975.

Lambert, J., & Pearson, J. *Adventure playgrounds.* Harmondsworth, Middlesex: Penguin, 1974.

Landscape Architecture (Special issue: *Children Know Best*), 1974, *65* (5).

Millar, S. *The psychology of play.* London: Penguin, 1968.

Muntanola-Thornberg, J. The child's conception of places to live in. *Proceedings of the Environmental Design Research Association, Fourth Annual Conference.* Stroudsberg, PA: Dowden, Hutchinson & Ross, 1973.

Muntanola-Thornberg, J. *La arquitectura como lugar.* Barcelona: Gustavo Gili, 1974.

Muntanola-Thornberg, J. *Strategies for the invention of architectural objects.* Unpublished, available from the author. School of Architecture, University of Barcelona, Barcelona, Spain, 1982.

Murphy, L. B. *Methods for the study of personality in young children* (pp. 9–101). New York: Basic Books, 1956.

Nelson, D. *City Building Education Programs: A way to learn.* Santa Monica, California: Center for City Building Education Programs, 1983.

Nicholson, S. Children as planners. *Bulletin of Environmental Education,* 1974, *36,*13–16.
Relph, E. C. *Place and placelessness.* London: Pion, 1976.
Rogoff, B., Sellers, J., Pirotta, S., Fox, N., & White, S. H. Age of assignment of roles and responsibilities to children: A cross-cultural survey. *Human Development,* 1976, *19.*
Rubin, K. H., Fein, G. G., & Vandenberg, B. Play. In Paul Mussen (Ed.), *Handbook of child psychology. Vol. 4: Socialization, personality and social development.* New York: Wiley, 1983.
Rudofsky, B. *Architecture without architects.* New York: Doubleday, 1964.
Saegert, S., & Hart, R. The development of environmental competence in boys and girls. *In* M. Salter (Ed.), *Play: Anthropological perspectives.* Cornwall, NY: Leisure Press, 1978.
Schwartzman, H. B. *Transformations: The anthropology of children's play.* New York: Plenum Press, 1978.
Seamon, D. *A geography of lifeworld.* London: Croom-Helm, 1979.
Selman, R. L. *The growth of interpersonal understanding: Developmental and clinical analysis.* (Developmental Psychology Series.) New York: Academic Press, 1980.
Spivak, M. Archetypal place. *Architecture Forum,* 1973, 44–50.
Sprague-Mitchell, L. *Young geographers.* New York: Bank Street College of Education, 1934.
Ward, C. *The child in the city.* New York: Pantheon, 1978.
Ward, C., & Fyson, T. *Streetwork: The exploding school.* London: Routledge and Kegan Paul, 1976.
Wilkinson, P. *Innovation in play environments.* London: Croom-Helm, 1980.
Winnicott, D. W. *Playing and reality.* London: Tavistock, 1971.
Zerner, C. *The Alligator Learning Experience: Children's Strategies and Approaches to a Design Problem.* Los Angeles: Proceedings of the third annual Conference of the Environmental Design Research Association, 1972.

Chapter 11

Imaging and Creating Alternative Environments with Children

CAROL BALDASSARI, SHEILA LEHMAN, AND MAXINE WOLFE

> Luis: What do you think about the people that make the buildings and they don't let people in because of their color and their age and all that?
>
> Will: Well, sometimes they think they're dirty and sometimes they think they're not. That's why. That's what I think.
>
> Luis: Well, I think that they will make a new law, or maybe they'll report that to the city—you know, the black people and the old people, *or maybe, the young people.*
>
> —Two boys, age 14, East Barton

INTRODUCTION

The Children Creating Alternative Futures project began in 1981 when a group of us with diverse professional experience, technical skills, and aca-

---

CAROL BALDASSARI, SHEILA LEHMAN, AND MAXINE WOLFE • Environmental Psychology Program, Graduate Center, City University of New York, New York, NY 10036. Our work was funded through a one-year grant from the National Endowment for the Arts (No. A-81-202175; M. Wolfe and R. Lorenzo, coprincipals) to develop, implement, and evaluate the project and to write a workbook–guide for teachers to replicate and/or adapt our work.

demic backgrounds initiated an environmentally focused, action-research process for children.

We understood that neighborhoods, cities, and societies change continuously—the result of short- and long-term, private and public planning, design, and policy making. Yet, the local community residents who are most affected by these changes are rarely involved in the decisions that bring them about. They may understand what problems exist in their neighborhoods and communities, but they do not necessarily know how to resolve them in ways that reflect their needs. Some put hope in the "next generation." However, children are not often taught that much of the world around us is the result of human decisions that could have been made differently. As Goodman and Goodman wrote in 1947:

> A child accepts the man-made background as the inevitable nature of things; he does not realize that somebody once drew some lines on a piece of paper who might have drawn otherwise. But now as engineer and architect once drew, people have to walk and live. (p. 3)

A basic assumption of this project was that if our children, as adults, are to contribute to creating a better quality of life, they will have to understand the relationship between environmental change and societal change. In other words, they will have to understand environmental change in terms of both its causes and consequences, intended and unintended. On the basis of this assumption, we developed a learning/teaching process through which children could come to understand the nature of environmental change in the past, present, and future by viewing themselves as, and indeed becoming, active participants in bringing about environmental change that would speak to their needs and the needs of their communities—a participatory planning and design process.

We implemented this process in three schools in three different neighborhoods in New York City, working with boys and girls who varied in academic level, age (9 to 16), socioeconomic level, race, and ethnic background. We met with each of the groups, ranging in size from 13 to 31 children, twice per week, two hours a session, over a four-month period. This chapter focuses on the work in two of the schools, highlighting similarities and differences between them and presenting the viewpoints of three facilitators who worked together throughout.

Conceptual Framework, Assumptions, and Goals

In the tradition of Freire (1970, 1973), the "futures" process is a process of "conscientization," having as its basis the everyday reality and actual life situations of the learners rather than the partial and manipulated experiences of school. We used the neighborhood environment as the primary learning place and resource, selecting schools in urban neighborhoods that were obviously undergoing processes of change (abandonment, gentrification, or both). This was to insure that the idea of environmental change would be relevant and visible to the children.

The focus on children's imaging, planning for, and direct involvement in alternative futures for their neighborhoods reflects both the traditions of alternative education and our own developmental and environmental psychological perspective on the growing child in the context of a material world of objects, places, and community settings. We drew many of the concepts of our work from the ecological and transactional emphases of the Vygotskian (1962, 1978) tradition of developmental studies, especially as continued by Bronfenbrenner (1979); the kind of urban environmental education pioneered in England and exemplified in Ward and Fyson's *Streetwork* (1973); and the emphasis on student-structured, small-group, hands-on learning typified by the work of Kohl (1969).

To help children discover how they could be active participants and creators of the future, the process addressing these issues had to allow them to have that role within it. Although the project was always formally about the future of neighborhoods, within this framework the unfolding of the process belonged to the children. Our role was that of facilitator and technical advisor. Kids identified their own problems and discovered their own alternative solutions, with varying amounts of support. By challenging their assumptions and stereotypes, raising questions about the information they obtained and the alternatives developed, we tried to help them become critical thinkers. Children worked together cooperatively in small groups, sharing ideas and images and developing common goals.

One of our particular goals was for children, through the development of their skills and creative/critical capabilities within a collaborative research process, to become active agents of change. In this respect our work has links to that of Lewin (1947, 1951a, 1951b) and his colleagues (Reissman & Miller, 1949; Seltiz & Wormser, 1949) who began to do participatory environmental research for community change in the mid-1940s, and to other participatory environmental research (Craddock, 1975; Wooley, 1977; Kassam & Mustafa, 1979, 1982) which is being done today. The Habermassian (1970, 1971) tradition of emancipatory research or research for freedom gave us a useful epistemological framework. Finally, we have a commitment to increased participation by nonexperts in enviromental change, which, in agreement with Chombart de Lauwe (1976), we see as inevitably linked to societal change. We believe that future change begins when individuals begin to alter the way they live in the present and that ultimately real change will depend on people's ability to act collectively in order to reshape basic societal institutions and perhaps to invent new ones. Yet, the ability to act for change will depend on the ability to image a range of future alternatives and understand their consequences (Polak, 1961).

Out of all of these concerns grew a way of working with children that initially focused on the development of nonstereotyped images of the generalized future and then shifted to the development of alternative neighborhood futures. The limited literature on children's divergent thinking has focused on "gifted" children. Boulding (1979, 1981, 1983) is among the few who have been concerned more broadly, both with images of alternative or discontinuous futures and the participation of a range of children and youth in their realization, and upon whose ideas we could build. Singer (1975) was another. As opposed to writers and researchers who contend that children have unique powers of imagination which they can use to create more humane worlds (Cobb, 1959; Masini, 1980a, 1980b; Nicholson, 1974; 1979), Singer does not see children as having qualities that make them essentially different from older people. Rather, he points out in his work on creativity, they may just not have been told the "proper" way to go about many things, especially if they are very young or when things are considered beyond their abilities. This, together with societally sanctioned exploratory tendencies of children, may, in certain circumstances, allow them more freedom to tackle problems creatively. Combining the ideas of Boulding and Singer, we provided children with the freedom to experiment with tools to create, understand, and communicate images—tools usually reserved for experts. The end result, we hoped, would demystify both the technology and expertise and facilitate the development of nonstereotypic images.

It was also part of the project's process to show children ways in which meaning can be constructed—and deconstructed as well—by creating, evaluating, and combining or transforming images, both visual and verbal, which are nonstereotyped and reflective of individual differences and preferences while at the same time having shared meaning. Communication within the group was encouraged as a way of facilitating the shared development and understanding of ideas and images. Our focus in this project was *collective image development,* and its process served as the basis for active and collaborative involvement in change.

Our Evaluation Process and Methods

Our evaluation process and methods reflected a combination of approaches drawing heavily from the models of action research (Stone, 1980), participatory action research (Kassam & Mustafa, 1979, 1982), and ethnographic and naturalistic responsive evaluation (Guba & Lincoln, 1981). Using a rigorous qualitative methodology, our evaluation was a continual process through which we examined the appropriateness of our goals as well as the extent to which they were being met. We used this information to resolve issues affecting implementation as they arose and to evaluate the project at its end.

One evaluation tool was a systematic process of detailed observation, documentation, discussion, and reflection. We met weekly to evaluate our activities and the children's, make necessary changes, and plan for the coming week's work.* A second tool was the recording and cataloguing of the children's work, including their photographic images, slides, and constructions and our photographs of the process and their images. We also transcribed and reviewed the children's audio tapes and those from large group sessions. These transcripts, which were also used by the children, provided an additional basis for our judgments and strategies during the process and for the final evaluation.

Evaluation was also obtained from (1) teachers and school staff, through meetings and interviews, during and at the end of the project; (2) children, who evaluated ongoing activities in a variety of ways, including interviewing one another and through group meetings; and (3) parents and community members.

In order to understand the outcome of such a project, implementation must also be evaluated. The implementation, the nature of the process, and its outcomes are clearly a function of the neighborhood, the particular school, and the particular children involved. These are not peripheral factors. In agreement with Singer (1975) as well as with process-oriented evaluation models, we believe that these factors are crucial to the outcomes since they profoundly affect the alternatives children can develop and/or implement.

TWO FUTURES GROUPS

We begin by describing the neighborhoods, the schools, and the children with whom we worked as a necessary basis for the descriptions and comparisons of the process as implemented in two settings. In each of these latter sections one school will be emphasized and the other used as contrast, in order to provide sufficient detail in a limited format. The last section of the chapter is an evaluation of the project as a whole and concludes with plans for future work.

The Neighborhoods, Schools, and Children

Port Hill, the neighborhood in which P.S. 94 is located, is ethnically and economically heterogeneous. Areas close to the park on which Port Hill

*This process was developed during the first phase. For each session, one facilitator took responsibility for recording (which included children and staff present, the details of the physical setting—which parts of the school and neighborhood were used, furniture arrangement, parts of room used, and so on—all the activities during the session, each child's activity and response, staff involvement, suggested evaluation, suggestions for change, questions). Each facilitator also kept a journal for recording experiences, evaluations, and impressions. At our weekly meeting we collaboratively reviewed the written document, adding or changing entries after discussion, and made decisions about the upcoming sessions.

borders were developed in the mid-1800s as an upper-class residential community of elegant brownstones and town houses. Farther from the park lived small shopowners and factor and waterfront workers. By the 1930s the neighborhood had become one of rooming houses or homes for working- and middle-class families, then Italian and Irish and, more recently, also Hispanic and black. During the last 10 years, changes in the city's economic base both eliminated blue-collar jobs and increased those for white-collar and professional workers. Many of Port Hill's large, once-elegant, but now relatively inexpensive brownstones have been bought and renovated by young professionals. As real estate speculators and developers come in, many long-term residents and shopkeepers continue to be displaced by inflated prices.

Although the dominant residents, now, are upper-middle-class white professionals, the neighborhood still has a core of working-class and middle-class Italian and Irish householders, many elderly, and younger poor or working-class Hispanics and blacks. Expensively renovated brownstones coexist with burned-out and boarded-up buildings, and expensive boutiques with "mom and pop" stores. Local action groups have worked to keep rents down, protect homes from arson, and create community gardens and safe play spaces for children. More recently, they have tried to convert, to tenant management and ownership, buildings taken by the city for nonpayment of taxes. Low-income housing for those displaced by gentrification has been planned and developed, but such plans have been opposed by other groups in the community which favor upper-middle-income housing and shops.

P.S. 94, a towering, well-kept, Victorian-style school over 100 years old, has an enrollment of 400 neighborhood children in grades 1–5. A traditional public school, its primary educational goals are that children read at grade level, that the stated curriculum be covered, and that order and decorum be maintained. The kids with whom we worked, like others in the school, usually sat in rows facing the front of the classroom and completed their tasks individually. Though the teacher volunteered to have the project in her classroom, she herself did not want to participate directly. She scheduled the project for free time and saw it in terms of enrichment. The project shared the regular classroom space since no other rooms were available.

The ethnic and socioeconomic diversity among the children, a group of 11 boys and 20 girls, reflected that of their neighborhood. Most were from working-class, lower-middle-class, or middle-class families. Everyone read at grade level or above, although abilities and talents ranged considerably, as did the social and physical maturity of these 10- or 11-years-olds.

East Barton, where the Alpha school is located, differs in several ways from Port Hill. It has always been a much more densely populated section of the city, and it is more homogeneous economically and ethnically. It has been the home of poor immigrants since the late 1800s and, since the Depression, mainly Puerto Rican. A very high percentage of households are below poverty level. Unemployment rates, always high, have been even higher for the past few years. City services are extremely poor here, and street crime and drug traffic are very high.

From the 1940s to the 1960s East Barton was a target for urban renewal. By 1972 13 high-rise projects had been constructed, mostly public housing. Yet, two-thirds of the population still live in deteriorating old and new-law tenements. Where tenements have been torn down, often rubble-filled lots remain. Most small businesses and factories have disappeared; empty storefronts mirror abandoned housing. Not far to the south are streets filled with expensive renovated buildings, boutiques, and cafes. The gentrification in this neighborhood, now "creeping into East Barton," as one community member commented, is already causing displacement of low-income families. Since the 1950s, when residents were galvanized by urban renewal activities, there have been active community groups responding to such threats.

Alpha, a self-contained minischool with 80 students, is located on the top floor of a junior high school near the gentrified border of East Barton. Alpha's internal physical condition is poor, and severe city budget cuts have meant a lack of materials and supplies. All Alpha students are there because they have been unable to "make it" in other schools in the district.

The basic premise of Alpha's program is that such "problem" kids "need structure." In accordance with this idea the entire day is programmed. There is no free time. Kids remain in their seats, in their room, except for lunch and gym. They may not get up or leave their classroom without permission. The classrooms can accommodate 30, but classes at Alpha are much smaller and desks are spaced at large distances to "prevent incidents." Kids are harshly reprimanded for any actions, however small, that are not dictated by the staff, and they are counseled when more serious infractions occur. Administrators feel these conditions provide kids with a mixture of structure and support.

The director welcomed the project and designated the art teacher as our administrative liaison. The project was slotted into both art and social studies times and had a large (25 feet by 40 feet) unused classroom for project space.

The sixth-grade class involved in the project consisted of 12 boys and one girl, ranging from 11 to 16 years old. Eight were Puerto Rican and four were American blacks. All were from low-income households; a few were living in circumstances of extreme poverty. Although they varied considerably in their personalities and their capabilities, all were in Alpha because they were defined as having problems in relation to school.

Initial Images and Questions about the Future

At both sites we first introduced the kids to the idea of the future, provided opportunities for them to create future images with a variety of materials, and then collaboratively explored and discussed the meaning of their images.

At P.S. 94, kids spent several weeks in this initial work. Early images were stereotypical and mainly pessimistic: "Sometimes I wish that it would be better, but I know it won't be." The future meant the intensification of present problems, the extension of existing technological trends, and the deterioration of human relationships. School was a centralized skyscraper superschool, or, alternatively, kids worked alone at home with robot teachers. Robots replaced humans as gas station attendants and personal servants too, but only the rich could afford them. When people lost their jobs to robots or computers, they danced to disco music while they waited in massive unemployment lines. Space wars were a reality; people drove fully armed space vehicles. In fact, the earth as we now know it had vanished. Everyone lived in space or underground.

When the images were hung up and discussed, no one could say what had happened. The world of the future just *was,* created by unnamed persons—*they.* How these changes occurred and what impact they had on people's lives were seldom expressed in the drawings. The future machine designed by one boy provided a frightening look into the future but no way to change what was seen. It was only during group discussion of these images and the questions they generated that kids began to articulate the implications of living in this imagined future world. A few questions were specific and personal—about family relationships, where they would live, or what they would do in their immediate future. Most were more general. They wondered about schools (Would people learn from computers in their homes? Who would have such computers? Would it still be important to get an education in the future?). They asked what life would be like (Would there still be enough food? Would people still work, or would machines take over the world and would people become useless?). They wanted to know how people would act in the face of all these changes (Would there be freedom or a return to prejudice and slavery? Who would use and control the machines? Would crime increase? Who would make the laws and enforce them?). Would people, and the earth, survive at all? They thought the future was unknowable or that knowing it might confirm their worst fears.

At Alpha, the project began differently, with our organizing the room together, unpacking, and finding storage space. Kids were especially drawn to construction materials and media equipment. Some immediately began to create things; others used cameras and tape recorders in mock television interviews—questioning teachers, us, one another, the principal. Kids used art and construction materials with exceptional ease and creativity, but they had had few experiences with planning their own work and working collaboratively. In fact, they were viewed as being unable to work on their own. Because the Alpha experience provided no such opportunities, kids had little confidence in their own ideas or respect for those of their classmates, within the school setting.

Despite this, kids did construct images of the future. Although they dreamed of decent housing in a safe, more attractive neighborhood, jobs, enough food, clothing, and a few luxuries, they acknowledged that such prospects were not especially likely. Several who said they could not imagine a world without war made swords, which in their view could not destroy the entire world in the way modern military technology could. They were "fair" weapons requiring facing your enemy. One boy thought we would need swords to kill animals for food because "food's going to run out by that time."

At the end of this phase, we displayed their constructions and transcribed interviews. Seeing their own words in print helped them to take themselves seriously and to know that we did, too. This process also paved the way for later group discussions and built confidence in skills as imagers, interviewers, and interviewees. At this point it was clear that similar issues were raised by kids at both schools, but in different ways. Kids at P.S. 94 feared the future in general; kids at Alpha felt things would have to change drastically in order for them to have any acceptable personal future at all.

Documenting the Neighborhood and Creating Alternative Environments

In this second phase, kids could document, research, and come to understand the process of development, change, and the future on a small scale, in surroundings familiar and important to them—their neighborhoods. They could discover the consequences of past changes, speculate about the impact of changes presently occurring, and image alternatives.

At P.S. 94, kids used their questions to find out what others thought about the future. They hung posters, distributed question booklets, and interviewed schoolmates; they found out that those interviewed knew no more about the abstract future than they themselves did. They made several informal trips into the neighborhood to buy materials, to distribute question books, and to interview local factory workers about their ideas of the future. The transition from the classroom and imaging of general futures to the community and researching the processes of neighborhood change was not an easy one. It was difficult for kids to move from their abstract, global questions to more concrete and local ones. To help them focus on their community, we began drawing route maps for a trip into the neighborhood. We found that kids could identify large institutions in their community but had little breadth or depth of experience with community life. They had a very limited home range and normally went directly home or to organized activities after school.

On our first formal trip into the neighborhood, kids brought cameras and tape recorders and interviewed people about the future of the neighborhood. We helped to focus conversations on local issues and identified changes taking place—a new hospital addition, abandoned buildings, burned houses, a community-created playground, and graffiti murals. Kids were asked to consider the roles neighbors had in these changes and what the positive and negative impacts for the community were and would be. We hoped the trip would encourage children to explore issues of neighborhood change, who created it, and how it happened.

The kids' photographs and street interviews were eventually transformed to create neighborhood alternatives. A street map was posted on a classroom wall, and some kids traced the trip route and placed photographs of places visited or persons interviewed (see Figure 1, top, p. 252). Using enlarged duplicated copies of their photographs, other kids made photocollages to transform the local institutions, abandoned houses, empty lots, and playgrounds they had visited or to identify local problems. The photocollages showed burning buildings, traffic accidents, and super heroes saving local people from crime. These images revealed both their hopes for the future and their fears of what it might become.

Alpha kids were more eager to move the project out into the neighborhood, where they were more comfortable than they were in school. Before going out into the neighborhood, we asked kids to draw maps, use collage techniques, or in some way create an image of the things they liked or did not like, the things that were important to them or just the places they wanted us to see on the trip. Most drew stores, houses, schools, rivers, parks, and plazas. Each described his or her drawing while other kids and staff made comments and asked questions. Places for our trip were chosen while kids became more aware of the similarities and differences in their neighborhood perceptions. These maps also gave us the opportunity to share the rich information the kids possessed about their neighborhood, to understand their positive and negative feelings about East Barton, and to raise questions about change.

We covered a 48-block area on our trip, mainly going to everyday places rather than institutions. Kids were at ease, met people they knew on the way, and talked about a range of things in the neighborhood and its connection to their own lives. Tanya, who wanted more flowers in the future, said as we passed a vacant lot: "This was a big lot . . . then it was a garden, but people don't use it no more." Kids interviewed people in stores about their jobs and businesses. In school, kids used their fluency in Spanish as a way to gain privacy from their teachers; in the neighborhood it became a skill allowing them to speak to people who could not communicate in English. In this way, for instance, we learned that a mural and memorial park had been made by neighborhood residents, in honor of four people who had been killed in a car accident. Kids found graffiti they thought were good, and not good ("wack"), and showed us their own "tags"—their graffiti signatures.

Research for Change

In the next phase of the project we asked kids to select local issues they would like to investigate further as a focus for change. A "crisis of confidence" occurred at this point at each school. At P.S. 94, kids discussed their own and their families' individual unsuccessful attempts to change things. They described unresolved problems with large institutions and unresponsive city service agencies. They concluded that real change was beyond their control. We pointed out that the problems they faced were ones they shared with one another and with others in their communities. We encouraged them to identify and investigate the specific problems which concerned them most and to seek information and strategies from people who had been successful in creating change.

Kids formed three groups, each approaching problems differently. Wanting to know "how change can happen," one group investigated local community action organizations. They developed an interview and met with Nancy, a long-time neighborhood resident, who had joined together with others more than seven years ago to fix up a local playground and had continued to work on other neighborhood issues. Nancy described her group's strategies, as well as the nature of some competing interest groups in the neighborhood. She explained that change, although difficult, was possible. Kids recorded the interview and, during a tour with her, photographed housing, parks, and commercial developments on which her group had worked.

A second group investigated tenant–landlord problems (Figure 3, top, p. 254), while the third group selected for their research an empty lot located on a block where several kids from the class lived. The lot had been an eyesore as long as the kids could remember, but no one had been successful in changing it. They photographed it, measured it so they could draw a site plan to scale, and tape-recorded interviews with residents on the block about how it had come to be this way, how people had tried to change it, why these efforts had failed, and how they, the neighbors, would like to see it transformed. Interviews revealed the different images various socioeconomic and racial/ethnic groups had for the future of Port Hill and how this prevented residents from working together as a group to solve a shared problem. Kids were realistic about the impediments to resolving the issue, but they began to create alternative designs for the lot. They also wrote to the landlord requesting his help and permission to clean up the lot.

The diversity of projects gave kids the opportunity to practice research, documentation, and communication skills acquired during earlier activities and also provided insights into how they could become involved in community change. Their interviews revealed community experiences with problems, provided information about approaches to creating change, and identified resources for support within the community. Kids examined the

FIGURE 1. Parts of the future process. Attaching photographs to a base map of the neighborhood to document our first trip (top). Documenting project activities (bottom).

FIGURE 2. "This is my lot, I invented it." Collage on duplicated photograph creating alternatives for an empty lot (top). Creating a quiet space for tape recording (bottom).

FIGURE 3. Street interviews (top and bottom).

information critically, considered the human consequences of current development practices, and created alternatives focusing on community collaboration. Although they had limited time within the project to make changes, they were eager to share their research with families, friends, and neighbors in the hope that the communication of these images and ideas would spur further community activity.

Like the kids at P.S. 94, Alpha kids also went through a crisis with us revolving around their ability to create change (it had other dimensions as well, as we shall explain later). Its resolution also allowed kids to continue the project. They worked in small groups or alone to tape-record their ideas or discussions about issues of concern to them in terms of their own futures and the future of the neighborhood: drugs, crime, fires, garbage, jobs, vacant lots, schools, housing, and graffiti. They voted to focus on housing and graffiti, and each student picked one of the two groups to work in during the rest of the project.

Kids then went out into the neighborhood, photographed examples of existing graffiti and housing, and interviewed people. They went on tours and visits to speak with people in neighborhood organizations, finding out what had been done and what was being done at present. They brought this material back and, using a variety of media techniques, developed two slide–tape shows.

Their work on graffiti revealed their own aesthetic criteria. They appreciated skilled "writers." They discovered that people in the neighborhood had a wide range of attitudes. No one was totally negative. They went to the Graffiti Hall of Fame, an entire school yard of graffiti where kids had permission to do their art, planned for it, and made quite elaborate designs. They discovered that a local community organization was arranging for kids to do a graffiti mural supervised by a local artist. Their slide–tape show focused on what people thought, gave a view of different types of graffiti in the neighborhood, and showed how kids viewed graffiti. It included acetate slides kids had made of their own tags and ended with a slide of the Graffiti Wall of 1990—the future of graffiti.

Kids who investigated housing issues interviewed people on the street and people who worked at housing projects or in the neighborhood (Figure 3, bottom, p. 254). In the gentrified areas they discovered that speculators were buying and renovating buildings, rents were increasing rapidly, and long-time residents were being forced out. One of the founders of a local community organization took them on a tour and visited the school. They learned that co-ops were coming in because there were no federal monies for low-cost housing. Interviews revealed that residents had positive attitudes toward the neighborhood and a commitment to it, despite the problems.

Kids created a slide–tape show called "Give a Hand," showing the state of present housing, the changes that were happening, and their own alternatives (see the opening quotation). The soundtrack included a narration and had dramatized interviews, though much of it was a rap song kids had written and sung about their future and the future of East Barton and how "they were going to make history."

Communicating: Presenting Our Work

Throughout the futures process there was continual discussion among kids in the group in ways ranging from an informal response to another's "what's that you're working on?" to a whole group discussion or viewing of a slide show in progress. In addition, every child, in some way, presented the project to the outside world and involved others in the work—going into other classrooms, stopping people on the street, talking with community activists, and so on.

About midway through the project, P.S. 94 kids made a trip to the university at which we worked. They presented their work in progress with great confidence and high spirits in a forum normally reserved for presentations by faculty and graduate students. At Alpha, one boy who had had difficulty "getting into" the project suggested we present our work to the kids at P.S. 94. The presentation, to which other kids agreed, included a display of photos kids had taken showing themselves unpacking materials, drawing, discussing, and interviewing; two slide shows based on their neighborhood trip; and collages and drawings showing alternative designs for the future—empty lots cleaned up and planted, houses built or repainted, storefronts repaired. The P.S. 94 kids were welcoming, attentive, and focused on the presentations. Kids talked about the similarities and differences in their neighborhoods and about issues that concerned them and also shared the less formal experiences of hanging around with each other before and after the presentation.

In each school the kids also decided to do a final presentation of their work. At Alpha it took place in our regular project room during school hours. This decision, made by the administration, meant that none of the parents were able to attend. However, other Alpha kids and teachers as well as school district staff were there. Kids arranged photos, site plans, constructions, collages, tape transcriptions, and other project materials around the room, set up chairs, and helped purchase food for a party afterwards. For each show, one kid handled the slide projector and another the tape recorder, while the others clustered around them. After the show, kids voted not to take their individual work home but to put it together into a portfolio for future Alpha kids to see.

At P.S. 94, kids invited school staff, families, and community members to the final presentation. Equipment filled the school cafeteria as kids borrowed or made props, designed a program guide, and lettered bilingual (English, Spanish) signs directing guests to the action.

Just before the presentation the kids received a letter from the landlord who owned the empty lot. In response to their request he had already made some initial changes—sweeping the sidewalk, removing some debris that filled the space, and attempting to repair the fence. There was the exciting possibility that he might appear at the presentation. He did not, but block association officers and other residents of the street were among the 150 guests.

Kids had devised different methods for sharing their findings and presenting their proposals for change. For example, the empty lot group had created a site plan with various pieces of model-size outdoor furniture, flowers, and shrubbery that could be moved around on it. They had a ballot and asked people to vote for one of the specified alternative uses (obtained from their interviews) or to write in their own alternatives. A second group dramatized events in the life of a family whose landlord refused to make repairs. Instead of resolving the situation, the kids called on the audience to form a conclusion. This "slice of life" vignette raised critical neighborhood issues and engaged the audience—which contained tenants, homeowners, and landlords—in negotiating a resolution.

EVALUATION OF THE PROJECT

Our overall goal was to help children to become active creators of and participants in the change processes affecting their future and to perceive themselves in this way. We set out to accomplish this by (1) facilitating children's participation in a collaborative planning process in which they had decision-making roles: (2) providing them with access to a range of skills and technology usually reserved for decision makers; (3) helping them to develop nonstereotypic images that would speak to their needs and the needs of their neighborhoods, and (4) directly involving them in the process of enviromental change.

Our ongoing evaluation process, described earlier, enabled us both to examine the appropriateness of our goals and to change our daily project work when we determined that goals were not being met. We also recognized that progress toward group and related individual goals might be uneven in different spheres, especially in a short-term project. Moreover, any participatory planning and design process exists within a political, social, and economic context; ours was no exception. We will discuss these factors before evaluating our objectives and their attainment in relation to the children.

Issues in Implementation

We had been invited to conduct the project in both schools after having fully described both its content and process to school administrators, all staff, parents, and, in one school, a public community school board. We made sustained efforts to communicate with school staff and to involve them in a variety of ways. Staff and administrators liked the focus on the issues of the future and neighborhoods because they saw that children were interested and motivated to work. Yet, both Alpha and P.S. 94 were institutions of hierarchical control. Despite differences in the expression of this institutional characteristic (Rivlin & Wolfe, 1985), both schools limited the project in similar ways. The attitudes of staff and administrators about the process and some specific content areas were often quite negative.

The process aspects of the project were viewed as especially inappropriate and unacceptable. We allowed children to direct their own learning and to decide what direction the project would take. They had free access to and could experiment with materials and equipment. It was a basic premise of the project that if kids could not become active decision makers in their own learning process or learn to experiment and test things out, the concepts of the future and neighborhood change would lose meaning. We believe that when children—or adults—are asked for input but have no power, they eventually are discouraged from being active participants altogether.

The definition of education, learning, and schooling shared by staff and administrators led them to categorize a project based on such assumptions to be, at best, peripheral to "real" learning and, at worst, as a waste of time and disruptive. School staff became seriously threatened by the role of children as active participants in the process. We were struck by the similarity between these attitudes and those associated with some planners, designers, and program administrators when discussing citizen participation. These attitudes, and their attendant behavior, had several impacts on the project.

The teacher at P.S. 94 did not want to be directly involved in the project, but she often remained in the room to monitor children's behavior, trying with eye contact to keep them "in line." When they behaved in a way she considered inappropriate she would ring her bell or reprimand them. But her definition of *appropriate* did not mesh with that of the project. For example, she severely admonished a girl who, in her excitement about an idea, tapdanced across the room. The other children were absorbed with their own tasks, but she was told to stop immediately because her behavior was "disruptive."

At Alpha, the staff liaison became the guardian of the school structure. On the first day, as children were unpacking equipment and supplies and trying things out, one, then another, took their tape recorders down the hall to interview staff in the office. Though we followed nearby and had the agreement of the classroom teacher, the staff liaison ordered them back to the room. When we intervened he said it was "his word that counted" and that the project "had to stay within the walls of the project room." In fact, the process was viewed as so antithetical to Alpha's structure that any and all of the children's "disruptive" behavior during the week was considered "spillover" from the project and we were asked to be accountable for it.

We found that we were challenging deep-seated assumptions about learning and about children's capabilities when we introduced media as a vehicle for children's serious independent and critical reflection and communication. The teacher at P.S. 94, for example, reprimanded kids when they used the tape recorder to record rap songs about the future or to record dramatized versions of their interviews. From her perspective they were not taking the project seriously. In both schools any time kids seemed to be enjoying themselves, laughing, or using humor in their work, the assumption was that they were not really working. It was a powerful statement, indeed, about what schools teach children about learning.

The use of media also raised issues about underlying power relationships between kids and teachers. Teachers and other school staff were uncomfortable with kids' making decisions about the allocation of resources, their free access to scarce and expensive equipment, and their assumption of expert roles *vis à vis* equipment. They attempted to control kids' use of tape recorders, cameras, and rexograph machines. At P.S. 94 kids were blamed for a broken rexograph machine, even though they had not been using it. In fact, they knew how to use it correctly and fixed it as well. We found we had to intervene fairly often with teachers in order for kids to be able to use the media freely.

Another issue was *content*. At P.S. 94 the classroom teacher did not want to be held responsible for the political implications of the kids' work. She told us she did not understand why they chose such controversial topics as tenant–landlord relations to research when crime was a much more important neighborhood problem. (Kids considered many landlord actions they heard people talk about, for example, arson, to be crimes.) She did not speak at the presentation and left quickly afterward. However, the principal was more supportive on this occasion, pointing out to parents that *he* did not censor children in *his* school.

At Alpha, the attitude that the children were essentially incompetent was pervasive. When kids began speaking out on controversial issues in group discussions this was dismissed as "neighborhood rhetoric." The implications were, first, that they were really incapable of dealing with such questions or of thinking for themselves about them; second, that we ought therefore to discourage them from bringing such issues up for discussion; and third, that children's personal experiences and local knowledge were invalid within the school context.

At both schools we worked hard to establish a dialogue with school staff, to accommodate to some of the issues they raised, and to work for constructive change. At Alpha, when the director expressed concerns that we were not controlling the kids and that the project was without structure, we agreed to submit lesson plans for each and every session. Since the sequence of events grew out of the process itself and kids' decisions, this meant finding time after each session to do the plan so it would reflect rather than direct the process. At P.S. 94, when the children were blamed for the broken rexograph machine we agreed to move it into the classroom so that, supposedly, we could monitor its use.

One problem we faced when dealing with the schools was that their requirements or complaints were always couched in pedagogic terms, although they were not necessarily pedagogically based. Stated goals did not necessarily match actions. At Alpha, for example, staff and administrators said they wanted kids to learn to listen to each other, share ideas, and work cooperatively. Yet, when kids demonstrated such behavior it was acceptable only in ways that the school defined and controlled. This became clear when, after the trip to P.S. 94, staff told us that the kids wanted to talk about "problems with the project." We were positive about their being active in their own behalf and hoped for a productive dialogue with them, their classroom teacher, and the staff liaison. Kids began by complaining that they had been told by staff that this would be free time but we were asking them to "do work." We discussed differences in expectations and how to work out a solution. When kids shifted to a critique of the school rather than the project—they had to sit all day in their seats; the only time they could move around was during gym and lunch; and they often lost what free time they did have for misbehavior—the staff response was to chastise the kids. Staff did nothing to support kids' issues nor did they show any willingness to enter a dialogue. They became extremely defensive and finally cut off the discussion.

Another problem with demands originating from school structure or staff is that they were backed by decision-making power. At P.S. 94 we were given less than a week's notice that the project would have to be suspended for a month so that kids could be drilled for citywide exams during this free time. At Alpha the administration decided that the children's presentation would be made in school to a limited audience. And when we invited P.S. 94 kids to the Alpha presentation their new teacher decided that they could not come. She admitted that she had judged, without consulting them, that kids' parents would not want them going to the dangerous Alpha neighborhood.

At times we stood our ground and took the chance that we would be asked to leave. At Alpha, for example, we were asked to "provide consistency" by structuring our time as other staff did and using a similar method of discipling children. We refused, pointing out that this would dramatically alter the very foundation of the project. They chose to let us remain.

We found that children often bore the brunt of the school's reaction to our process. They got into trouble for doing things that were part of it, even when those activities had been discussed and prearranged. They were threatened with punishment and sometimes actually punished for activities that were acceptable in the project, and not being allowed to be in the project itself became a punishment. We felt that we could not ethically expose children to these experiences, nor did we want to add to the negative definitions of children which could continue to follow them, especially if their past behavior had already been categorized as problem-ridden. Often we could not absorb or counter the abuses of power that we saw and the children experienced, exacerbated by bigoted reactions to their race, class, or sex. Such realities of doing work in these settings meant that we had to curtail some activities and parts of the process. In addition, it took a tremendous amount of our energy and time continually to respond to these barriers to implementation.

Children Changing

Within the limits of each setting, the children accomplished some significant things. They learned to use many of the traditional tools of neighborhood planners and architects: base maps and blue prints, scale drawings, T-squares and triangles. They learned to operate cameras and slide projectors, to work with contact sheets and slide mounts, and to use tape recorders and microphones, with assurance and competence (see Figure 1, bottom, p. 252). They used different media techniques. They grouped and regrouped their neighborhood images and ready-made images from magazines, used acetate overlays to show alternative possibilities (see Figure 2, top, p. 253), altered photographs with colored pens, and used multiple images produced by xerography and color xerography. They combined images and maps, images and music (for slide–tape presentations), or images and written text (in photomontages and other photographic displays).

Not all children gained experience with all media or acquired all skills. Everyone learned to do something that he or she had not done before and saw that other children could do such things too. The process was successful in its goal of demystifying technology and facilitating children's media skill development and knowledge. And the use of different media, alone and in combination, was successful in helping children develop images and alternatives rather than simply integrating images and meanings developed by others. The media supported collaboration and communication among the children and between children and adults and led to the development of shared ways of perceiving and understanding things.

Inevitably, however, issues of power and control were raised among kids, and between kids and teachers, in relation to media use. With variable amounts of intervention on our part, kids worked out their own solutions in sharing important yet limited media resources. We worked toward the children's own management of sharing and responsible use of materials but tried not to allow their own hierarchy of power to regulate the situation.

We were more successful at Alpha, where the group was more homogeneous economically, ethnically, and racially and where all of the kids had been defined as incompetent. Our major focus became helping children break out of their usual roles and relationships (for example, the monopolization of media based on physical power or initial technical competence). One boy who had never seen a camera before got the chance to use it and to help put together a slide show; another who was usually pushed out of the way because he was quiet and weighed more than the other kids not only had his slides used in a show but operated the slide projector during the final presentation. Yet another, who was used to being in control, learned to be an active participant without attempting to run things, and the only girl in the class with 13 boys broke out of her reactive role.

It was more difficult at P.S. 94, where the group was more heterogeneous and where the class, race, and sex differences were reinforced by the school structure and its definition of competence. The kids generally defined by the school as competent, mostly the white middle-class girls, were secure with traditional academic and verbal modes of expression. Since the project was viewed as an "extra," they avoided the risk of doing less well with hands-on media work. The kids generally defined by the school as incompetent, the black working-class boys, monopolized tape recorders, often using them to withdraw from the group process. Both of these groups of children did not welcome outsiders. In order to empower all of the children to act collaboratively, we needed to change these patterns of dominance to patterns of reciprocity. But, just as this has been an issue in participatory planning processes with adults, we found it was not easy to adopt a pluralistic ethic within a larger system in which kids had unequal power and unequal access to resources. Had we had more resources, we perhaps could have dealt more effectively with these issues of power and control, though the heterogeneous group would still have made it more difficult at P.S. 94.

Despite such difficulties, the use of the media, the communication possibilities, and the research process did indeed help kids break out of their usual roles, develop skills generally valued within the school context as well as those not usually supported, and work collaboratively. For example, in both schools there were children who were fluent Spanish speakers. In neither school was this perceived as a valuable skill; in fact, it was usually considered a negative attribute. But when we wanted to interview community people, Spanish-speaking ability became a vital resource. At P.S. 94, one girl arranged for a group to visit the sewing factory in which her mother worked and to interview the workers, all of whom spoke only Spanish. The bilingual kids did the interviewing. For many this was the first time their language skill had been relevant to "school work" and valued by themselves and other kids as a competence.

The use of media also enhanced children's sense of their own competence, even in relation to more traditional school objectives. When we transcribed interviews, the children were amazed that these printed words were ones they had spoken. They were anxious to read them and to use them as scripts for plays or presentations. They also saw transcripts as evidence that we took their ideas seriously enough to spend the time and effort involved in transcribing.

In fact, another effect of the use of media was to dissolve the traditional distinction between work and play that fosters the separation of critical and analytical from creative abilities, lumping art with play. Teachers, as described earlier, categorized the project as play, not real learning, a view that proved largely unchangeable. Children, in the school context, also first understood what they were doing as play—freedom from school's usual constraints on physical movement and noise and a much broader than usual range of choices—as in gym or art class.

However, through the presentations midway through the project, it became apparent that the project entailed possibilities for more serious involvement than kids had anticipated, along with, and inseparable from, the play elements. In each of these presentations, the use of media supported children's communication of ideas and provided the basis for thoughtful exchanges among children and between children and adults. With these new audiences listening to them, the kids began to listen to one another in a new way and to value their own and their peers' work. Their dialogues were genuine, not contrived and stereotyped. They experienced communication as an active, two-way process rather than as a passive absorption of messages. This was especially true at Alpha, where kids were ordinarily prevented from working collaboratively in any way. In fact, one visitor commented on their group cohesiveness as they sat "riveted on their slides" during their final presentation. Therefore, in contrast to the teachers, children in each group came to transcend the distinction between work and play, between the critical and the creative.

The research skills children acquired were another means by which they understood what collaborative work implied and the issues it raised. The research process provided validation of kids' ability to have and to express ideas and to question the ideas presented to them; this is something we believe truly moved and changed every child with whom we worked. The community research process allowed each of them to listen to one another and to listen to neighbors, family members, and community workers in a new way, as the experts to be taken seriously. They began to connect their own experiences in their households and communities with what they were learning about the history and processes of neighborhood change. This validated their own cultures and everyday lives and gave them a basis for the critical evaluation of received truths. Children went beyond their own original science-fiction or techno-utopian images of the future. They began to develop a conception of social and physical change, which would be a reflection of the needs of the community rather than an abstraction entered into for its own sake. The vague *they* of their initial images became specific, as they began to envision a role for themselves in the process of change.

How long-lasting this impact will be for individual children is hard to determine. Yet we have some indication that it lasted beyond the project. The semester after we worked at P.S. 94, the school ran a science fair, the theme of which was "The Future." Kids who had not participated in the project created mostly stereotypic images of the future similar to those produced in the project's early stages. There were robots, space vehicles, computers—all ruling the world. In contrast, many of the kids who had participated in the project created images depicting both technology and social institutions developing with the broader participation of people. For example, one boy created a model of a future school in which kids participated in all of the decisions. And, as much as 1½ years later, we would meet children in the neighborhood who discussed the project in relation to their current lives and activities.

Children Creating and Involved in Change

Children's actions and their critical reflections on those actions created a degree of change in their schools, even though such change was not the direct focus of the project and certainly was limited by the systemic structures and attitudes we have described earlier. On the most concrete level, kids learned to alter their classrooms to meet the needs of their activities—to push desks together, to use the floor, to adjust lighting, to put things on bulletin boards to be shared by others, to find and use alternative spaces to achieve quiet space and privacy (see Figure 2, bottom, p. 253). Rather than allowing the physical structure or regulations surrounding the classroom environment to limit their activities, they made it responsive to their needs and, within limits, the teachers and school authorities went along with their actions.

The project not only changed the use of the classroom environment but also extended learning beyond the classroom and the school. At both Alpha and P.S. 94, the neighborhood trip loosened the school's control over the kids and made that control less likely to limit the project. At Alpha, the director allowed kids into the neighborhood somewhat more freely after the successful first trip, seeing that once out in the neighborhood kids were more self-confident and behaved better than they did in school.

School staff also became more sensitive to the strengths of the bilingual children, who were able to make a unique contribution to the research project. Significantly, at P.S. 94, the bilingual teacher was the only teacher other than the children's own classroom teacher who attended the final presentation, even though several other classes and their teachers had directly participated in the children's work.

Judging what lasting impact the project may have had at Alpha is more difficult. Children's positive participation in the project brought into question the school's view of their capabilities. Throughout the process, the staff often openly expressed amazement at what the children were doing. The quality of their work at the final presentation and the sustained interest of the kids in the audience also were noticed and commented upon. Consequently the director and a consultant to the alternative schools in the city are presently developing a social studies curriculum on the future of East Barton. Whether this program will promote the project's process as well as its content or simply fit isolated aspects of the project into the business of school as usual remains a question.

The following semester at P.S. 94, as mentioned earlier, the school ran a science fair the theme of which was "The Future." The classroom teacher with whom we had worked used more group projects the following year and began to use some art materials in her regular teaching. The sixth-grade teacher applied for and received a small grant to continue her version of the project with the kids with whom we had worked, now in her class. However, she decided that the most important neighborhood problem was littering and focused the kids' attention on solving that.

The project was far less successful in enabling the children actually to implement changs in their communities. Within the context of Alpha, our limited access to parents and the focusing of the project within the school meant that there was, as far as we know, limited impact outside of the school. Yet, even at P.S. 94, only the empty lot project saw any real results—the landlord actually cleaned up part of the lot and the kids succeeded where adults had not in renewing neighborhood attempts to solve the problem. However, largely because the project operated within the school's time frame, it was over before kids could see whether and how their efforts would come to fruition.

Other kinds of change occurred. Parents and other adults began to listen when kids addressed them, and to one another as well. For the final presentation at P.S. 94 every event included a participatory component and a chance for dialogue. The members of the audience responded with great seriousness, and some later commented on the sophisticated ways in which children dealt with complex issues of neighborhood change and development. Parents spoke with pride of their children's confidence and knowledge and their ability to put together and manage the entire program.

One letter from a girl's mother and father described the widening impact the project had, first on their daughter, then on their family, then on their family's relationship to the community. In other cases, relationships within the family were altered. One father, himself a landlord, learned to respect his daughter's opinions and research about tenants' rights. For the first time, he viewed her as a thinking person rather than a dependent child.

One boy, interviewed one month after the project was over, related family responses when he decided to join a march against nuclear war.

> I was going down there, I thought I could change my future. I could stop them, at least one more hand could help stop the war. So I went on the walk. My mother didn't really want me to go, but my father said, "If he really wants to help his future, let him—let him change his future while he's still got a chance." He surprised me, because he doesn't usually go along with what I say.

FUTURE DIRECTIONS FOR THE PROJECT

Based on our work and evaluation we are writing a workbook–guide for teachers and others who may want to implement such a program, which we would prefer to base in a community rather than in the schools. The difficulties we encountered in the schools were one basis for this new direction. We also believe, however, that locating the project in the community, providing programs for kids after school and in the summer as well, would provide new possibilities for kids and for the outcome of their work. They would have more time to develop their skills and knowledge and, more importantly, to implement and evaluate change projects. Work done by one group of children could be followed through by another. A permanent community-based location would enable us to offer materials, equipment, and exposure to skills difficult to provide within the time, space, and organizational limits of the school environment. We would be able to reach kids of different ages and could support parents' involvement—for example, an open-door policy during the day would allow parents who could attend during this time to do so, bringing younger children with them if they wished. We could have workshops for adults in the evening and provide child care to enable parents to participate.

A location within the community would not prohibit schools from participating; children could come to this space for programs during school hours. In fact, we would be able to reach more schools. However, since we would take responsibility for children's activities, this would free the school and the teacher from having to consider possible issues of appropriate behavior or the political sensitivity of the content. Our physical location would also reinforce the educative function of the community.

If it were based in the community, we believe the program would have a greater impact on the children, the community, and eventually the schools. We would also implement an evaluation process. We believe that the integration of theory and practice through evaluation is vitual to the development of environmental change projects that speak to the needs of local communities and their residents.

REFERENCES

Boulding, E. *Children's rights and the wheel of life.* New Brunswick, NJ: Transaction Books, 1979.

Boulding, E. Learning about the future. *Bulletin of Peace, Proposals,* 1981, (Feb.), 173–177.

Boulding, E. *Familia faber:* The family as maker of the future. *Journal of Marriage and the Family,* 1983, *45*(2), 257–266.

Bronfenbrenner, U. *The ecology of human development: Experiments by nature and design.* Cambridge, MA, and London: Harvard University Press, 1979.

Chombart de Lauwe, P. H. Appropriation of space and social change. In P. K. Serfaty (Ed.), *Appropriation of space.* Strasbourg, France: Institut Louis Pasteur, 1977.

Cobb, E. *The ecology of imagination in childhood.* New York: Columbia University Press, 1977.

Craddock, K. *Council tenants' participation in housing management.* London: Association of London Housing Estates, 1975.

Freire, P. *Pedagogy of the oppressed.* [Trans. by M. Ramos.] New York: Herder and Herder, 1970.

Freire, P. *Education for critical consciousness.* [Trans. by M. Ramos.] New York: Continuum, 1973.

Goodman, P., & Goodman, P. *Communitas.* New York: Random House, 1947.

Guba, E. G., & Lincoln, Y. S. *Effective evaluation: Improving the usefulness of evaluation results through responsive and naturalistic approaches.* New York: Jossey-Bass, 1981.

Habermas, J. *Toward a rational society.* Boston: Beacon Press, 1970.

Habermas, J. *Knowledge and human interest.* Boston: Beacon Press, 1971.

Kassam, Y., & Mustafa, K. (Eds.). *Participatory research: An emerging alternative methodology in social science research.* Toronto: Participatory Research Group, 1979.

Kassam, Y., & Mustafa, K. (Eds.). *Annotated bibliography on participatory research and popular education.* Toronto: Participatory Research Group, 1982.

Kohl, H. R. *The open classroom: A practical guide to a new way of teaching.* New York: New York Review, 1969.

Lewin, K. Frontiers in group dynamics. Channel of group life: Social planning and action research. *Human Relations,* 1947, *1,* 143–153.

Lewin, K. *Resolving social conflicts: Selected papers on group dynamics.* New York: Harper, 1951. (a)

Lewin, K. *Field theory in social science: Selected theoretical papers.* New York: Harper, 1951. (b)

Masini, E. B. Human development and childhood. Unpublished paper prepared for the Human Development Meeting, UNU, Bariloche, Argentina, 1980. (a)

Masini, E. B. Women and children as builders of the future. Unpublished, 1980. (b)

Nicolson, S. Children as planners. *Bulletin of Environmental Education,* April, 1974.

Nicolson, S. Children imagining futures. *Alternative Futures: The Journal of Utopian Studies,* Summer, 1979.

Polak, F. L. *The Image of the future* (Vols 1 and 2). New York: Oceana Publications, 1961.

Reissman, F., & Miller, S. M. (Eds.). Participation, culture and personality. *Journal of Social Issues,* 1949, *5*(1), 2–55.

Rivlin, L. G., & Wolfe, M. *Institutional settings in children's lives.* New York: Wiley, 1985.

Seltiz, C., & Wormser, M. H. (Eds.). Community self-surveys: An approach to social change. *Journal of Social Issues,* 1949, *5*(2), 2–65.

Singer, J. Navigating the stream of consciousness: Research in day-dreaming and related inner experience. *American Psychologist,* 1975, *30,* 727–738.

Stone, F. A. Action research: A qualitative approach to educational studies. *Multicultural Research Guides Series,* No. 5. Storrs, CT: I. N. Thut World Center, 1980.

Vygotsky, L. S. *Thought and language,* Cambridge, MA: MIT Press, 1962.
Vygotsky, L. S. *Mind in society: The development of higher psychological processes.* Cambridge: MA: Harvard University Press, 1978.
Ward, C., & Fyson, A. *Streetwork: The exploding school.* London and Boston: Routledge and Kegan Paul, 1973.
Wooley, T. The politics of intervention. In J. Cowley, A. Kaye, M. Mayo, & M. Thompson (Eds.), *Community or class struggle.* London: Stage 1, 1977.

Chapter 12

Children's Spaces

Designing Configurations of Possibilities

MICHAEL BAKOS, RICHARD BOZIC,
AND DAVID CHAPIN

> We used every kind of space, every different environment available to us. The railing-bound area under the front porch, in which you could stand, though you had to stoop to get through the doorway, was the jail. We played in the bushes, too. Behind them, under them, we had names for each place. There were always "forts". Fort This and Fort That. We dug six-inch deep moats around a couple of them and tried to keep them filled with water, to the despair of my father to whose lot it fell to pay the monthly bill. We wore the grass clean off the backyard, which we used for a baseball diamond and miscellaneous scrimmaging, all-star games, etc. It took years to grow back.
>
> We played games in the apple tree behind the garage. In fact we each "owned" a tree, divided up by common consent, and had a "fort" beneath it. There was almost always a place you could go, depending on how you felt, depending on what you felt like doing. We used the grounds and every cranny of the house, including closets and the spaces under the stairs, thoroughly.
>
> When I was nineteen, and a visionary would-be poet in the grand tradition of Rimbaud and John Keats, I announced boldly one night to a group of friends, while we stood in the middle of a street under the thrashing trees, that a place was not simply where two roads meet, but a configuration of possibilities.
>
> —Dennis Dooley, the ARC group, 1972

MICHAEL BAKOS AND RICHARD BOZIC • The ARC Group, 1743 East 116th Place, Cleveland, OH 44106. DAVID CHAPIN • The ARC Group, 1743 East 116th Place, Cleveland, OH 44106 and Environmental Psychology Program, Graduate Center, City University of New York, NY 10036.

INTRODUCTION: BECOMING IMMERSED

Time is a luxury for a designer: only rarely does an architect have the time to become deeply involved with the users of a building. Yet, it is only by becoming immersed within a place (which takes time) that it is possible to create what we call "configurations of possibilities."

Since our work has often been supported with research grants, we have been able to take unusually long periods of time to do each of our projects. Doing research has accustomed us to having the time to practice architecture the way we choose (ARC, 1976).

Our approach has been to become immersed within the place where we are working, sometimes by moving in and setting up drafting tables and sometimes by building our own designs on site. Through participatory processes, we share the pleasure and work of doing good design (for example, see Bakos, Bozic, Chapin, & Neuman, 1980.) This open, empathic process has meant dropping some aspects of professionalized architectural practice, particularly the stance of knowing, always, the right answer. It has therefore meant making a more inclusive definition of who our client is, so that children—users—and housekeeping people also participate, along with administrators and professionals. It has, of course, also required the luxury of time.

Out of this process we have learned lessons, some to do with personal sensitivity, others to do with organizational relationships. Our thought is to pass some of this on, not as a substitute for immersion by others, but as an encouragement for others to become more immersed.

In this chapter we will describe two projects that we have worked on during the past few years: the Broadview playroom and the Heights playstructure. Both are spaces that suggest many possible uses by children; they both represent configurations of possibilities. (For a rich view of how children explore the possibilities of places, see Holt, 1974.) Both are settings for play and both accommodate special needs of physically and mentally disabled children. Otherwise, they are very different.

THE BROADVIEW PLAYROOM

The Playroom as We Found It

The Broadview playroom is part of one ward within a large state institution in Ohio for mentally retarded children. The institution was a former tuberculosis hospital, built, as they all were, to isolate inmates from society and, internally, from each other. The result is cellular living spaces in remote locations, which is destructive to human community, a configuration of nonpossibility. (An environmental history should be written of how these buildings were put to new uses, once penicillin made their original intent obsolete. They certainly qualify as the worst imaginable environment for all children, but particularly so for those who are mentally retarded.)

The ward, which was then home to 27 children, included cellular sleeping rooms, hard-surfaced corridors, a virtually unfurnished dayroom, gang toilets, several staff offices, and a playroom. The playroom had formerly been a nursing station. It was an empty room with a few toys—bleak, stuffy, stinky, and noisy—an undifferentiated space of about 480 square feet without even simple storage. There was no place for a child to get away to, to be quiet in, or from which to watch others; nor was there a space defined for active play. The room was so unaccommodating that one child was all that could be handled at a time. Unbelievable though it may seem, it was then the most stimulating environment available to the children; the dayroom was even more barren (see Rivlin & Wolfe, 1985).

A special play program had been operating in the playroom for about a year before we began our work to change the physical environment. Besides 9- to 16-year-old children, users of this place included line staff, teachers, psychologists, and volunteers. The play program worked toward advancing children up to a level of competence high enough so that they could get off the ward itself and begin to participate in other activities within the larger institution.

One component of the ongoing play program was evaluation of the children through use of a test adapted by center staff from standardized behavioral age tests. Staff were asked to rate children on items such as "puts socks on" and "produces individual speech sounds," using a four-point scale ranging from "never" to "always." Answers to these questions formed a behavioral profile for each child which was compared to standardized norms to determine behavioral age.

Children in the play program had a very low behavioral age. Just before the new playroom was ready for use, the children, whose mean chronological age was 159 months (13 years, 3 months), had a mean behavioral age of 13.5 months, or a generalized rate of growth of one month in 12 months. Even when they had the opportunity, they did not engage in either parallel or cooperative play. Although physically they were preteens or teenagers, they were disruptive and acted out, could not participate in regular group activities, and in many cases were not toilet-trained.

Of all the children in the institution, these had the greatest need for the regular activity therapy program; yet, because they were "problems" they were excluded. Before they could join the regular program, the children had to learn to play. To begin, many needed to work at the basic level of simply responding to stimulation—sounds, textures, shape, and color.

In the playroom as we found it, the children typically had three one-half-hour sessions a week. (More sessions and longer sessions were intended, but the room's inability to accommodate more than one person at a time and the lack of volunteers combined to limit this.) Here, in a one-to-one relationship, an adult volunteer placed importance on making eye contact, focusing attention, and creating trust. A lot of this took place across a table using games. Other activities included development of gross motor skills through climbing, swinging, and balancing, all done using ordinary manufactured play equipment.

The Finished Room

The room, at 480 square feet, is only about half the size of an ordinary classroom, but within it there are three small defined areas (one with a table) for play and testing and a larger, open area for more active play. The finished room is highly differentiated, with the whole made of parts defined by edges and boundaries, created through changes in levels and materials. Each of these differentiated parts has its own special qualities, each suggesting different activities, making the whole a configuration of possibilities. It is a lively, rich environment; there is nothing about it that would mark it as being for children with special needs. However, it is the process that produced the room, as much as the room itself, that bears description.

The Design Process

Even before work on the playroom began, the process was atypical because staff people were involved in the conception of the project itself. At our invitation, they "bid" on the project and it continued to evolve from their initiative. Available resources included an allocation of a few thousand dollars for an environmental change research project, in-kind support from the institution, and administrative support from the superintendent and staff.

The project got under way through workshops for all staff people involved in the program, giving a general orientation toward environmental issues and sounding out interest. After these initial sessions, a design team was formed, including line staff, psychologists, activity therapists, and members of the ARC group.

In order to learn more of daily routines and the abilities of the children, we spent a good deal of time observing and interacting with them in both the undifferentiated, unfurnished dayroom as well as in the existing play program. We played actively with the children, using corrugated cartons and packing material; it was striking to see how they would gravitate to small "cozy" spaces. Also, without interacting, we observed them and the limiting environment they were in, trying to sort out one from the other.

The design team used a simple cardboard model as a tool to begin to see possibilities within the room. Time was spent talking about the goals of the play program, activities that were expected to happen, who was involved when, and what the problems were in the existing room. The team considered many issues: making the room workable for more than one child at a time, inclusion of regular ward staff in use of the room, connection to the rest of the ward, and so on. Over a period of two months, the design team continued to explore possibilities. Gradually, a design was evolved that included everything that seemed possible within the limited budget.

Construction of the room was also part of our responsibility. We built the room ourselves, step by step, always inviting staff people and children in to see the progress and for us to see reactions. Having this ongoing involvement allowed us to learn and to make modifications to plans along the way. A half-circle-shaped rainbow painted on the wall was changed, for instance, after we saw the apparent confusion of children in identifying individual colors. A psychologist in the play program suggested that the children were confusing color and shape; simpler horizontal bars of color would be less confusing. This was evidently true since after the change some of the children were better able to identify colors. Another example: we had thought that having handles at two heights on a sliding door would accommodate different-sized people; in fact, when we tried them we found that everyone shoved the door by its edge and did not use the handles at all.

Informal Evaluation

Ten months after the new room was completed, about half the children "graduated" into at least some of the regular activity programs, whereas none had done so before completion, despite the fact that the same program was in effect. This, after all, accomplished the intent of the program: to let kids get off the ward into regular programs. As an explanation of this, staff people noted a reduction in those disruptive behaviors that had previously kept children from this ward out of the regular programs. Volunteers, who had been difficult to attract and keep in what had been an unpleasant, smelly place, were now more readily available; there were, after changes, more volunteers for the program than were needed. This, coupled with the new room's accommodation of several children at once, led to a dramatic increase in their participation in the program. The maintenance staff, who had also participated in the building process, took over care of the room with considerable pride. Whereas visitors had been steered away from the ward before, the new playroom became a regular stop on tours of the institution.

Changes in children's behavioral ages were remarkable. Five months after completion of the playroom, the mean behavioral age had increased from 13.5 months to 15.7 months. Ten months after completion, it was

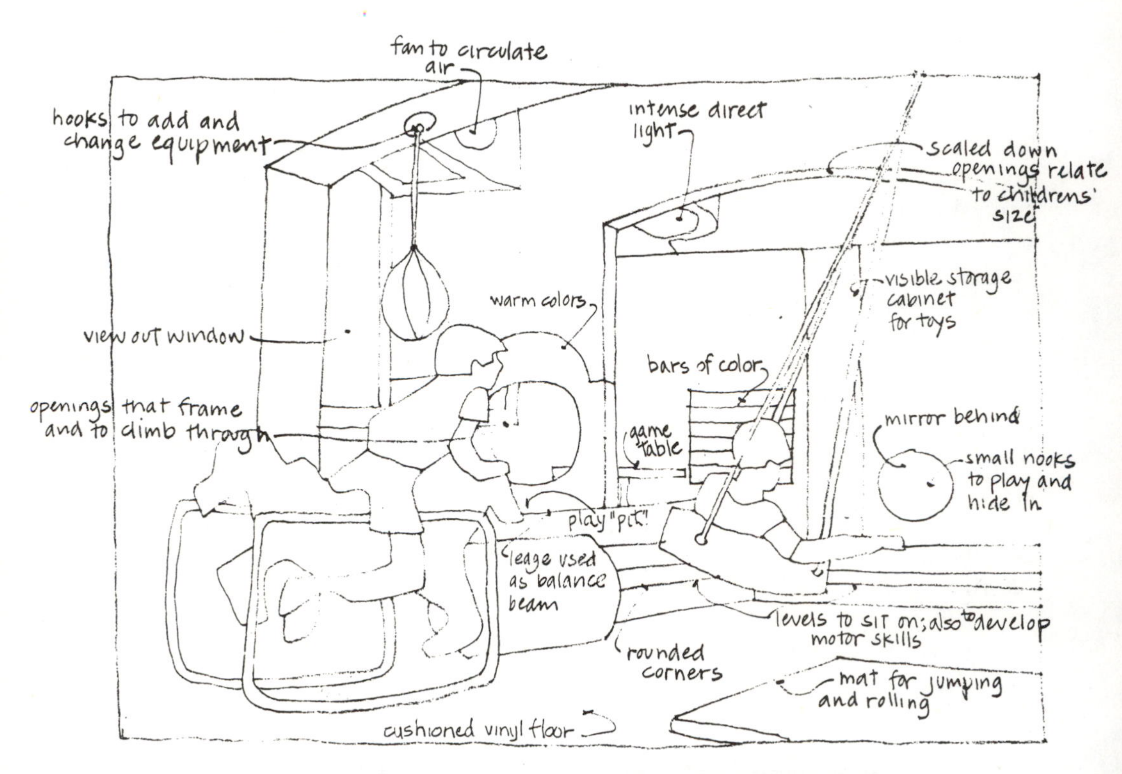

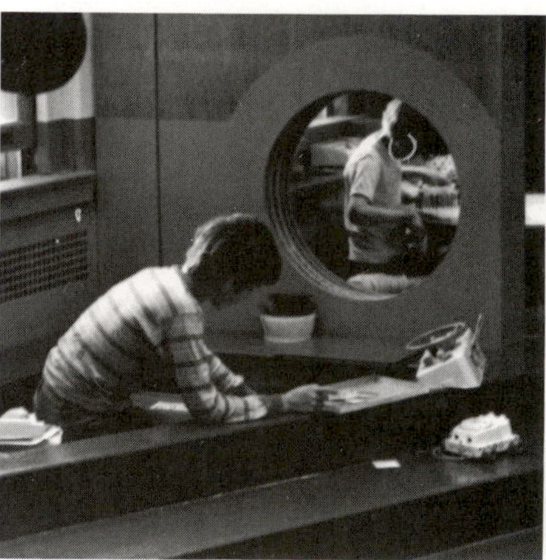

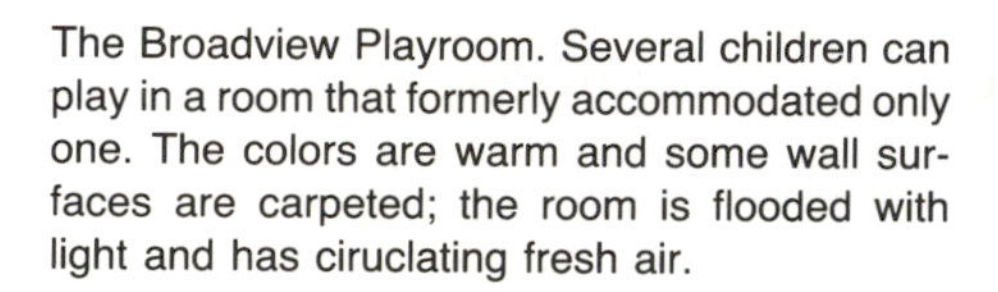

The Broadview Playroom. Several children can play in a room that formerly accommodated only one. The colors are warm and some wall surfaces are carpeted; the room is flooded with light and has ciruclating fresh air.

The play "pit" has easily perceived boundaries that give it a sense of place within the whole of the room. There is a "here" and a "there."

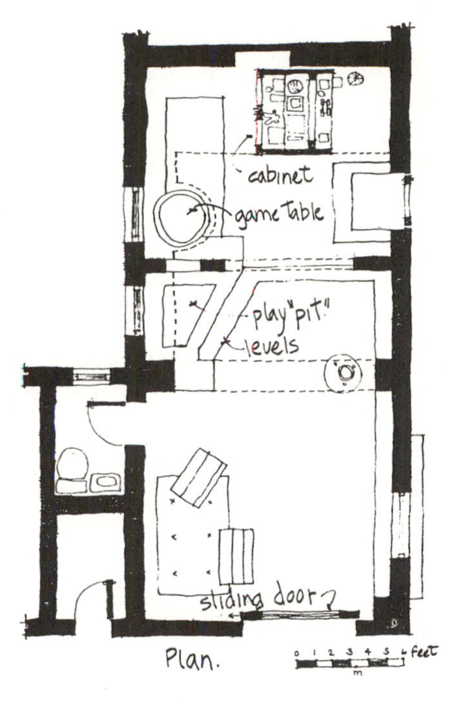

The round game table has a clearly defined edge; its single pedestal and bench accommodate both children and adults. The cabinet locks easily but keeps things always on display.

measured at 20.2 months. This represents a new generalized growth rate, during the period of measurement, of slightly over 6 months in 12 months. This is a clue to the general success of the playroom; but since the evaluation was not specifically targeted to characteristics of the room itself, it is not possible to sort cause and effect. The finished room facilitated an increase in the availability of volunteers and an increase in the time allocated to each child; this must have had an effect. We also assume that after their intimate involvement in the design process, the increased enthusiasm of the staff had a lot to do with these results.

THE HEIGHTS PLAYSTRUCTURE

A local high-school boosters group in Cleveland Heights, Ohio, received federal funding to install new night lighting, build a running track, and resurface the football field. Funding was made conditional on inclusion of an area for integrated play which could be used by all children, including physically and mentally disturbed children. Although this project had no research component at all, the design contract was written to allow our involvement over an extended period of time, long enough to become immersed. The playstructure was built through a conventional architectural process of preparing contract documents (working drawings and specifications), advertising for bids, and hiring a contractor.

The site is on the edge of the high-school grounds next to a busy intersection. It is not the location that most adults would pick, but it is in fact the very sort of lively corner most people—children and adults—gravitate toward as a hangout. The best measure of the playstructure's success, perhaps, is that it is indeed used by a large number of children, constantly.

The completed structure is a continuous wooden ramp winding up and around a large open center space with a climbing net over it (see p. 278). The four supporting corners, each defining several small, child-sized spaces, are fabricated from welded steel pipe. Overall, it is about 60 feet square and 16 feet high.

The playstructure works well as a framework for additions by users over time; in this sense it was intended that it never be finished. Users have taken in planks, ropes, and other scraps—and imagination—to add to the structure. The playstructure is truly a configuration of possibilities because (without dictating behavior) it suggests many different uses and also because it is added to and changed over time.

The Design Process

With the Broadview playroom, people who participated in the workshops were future users of the room and would benefit directly from the result of the process. With the playstructure there was no constituency, no committed user group; so, essentially, we created one.

To get participation by the local community (both to enhance the design itself and build a sense of community ownership), workshops were conducted in the local library. We gave ourselves a name—Playgroundwork—to convey to workshop participants the sense of being involved with something with momentum. We wrote to people who might, in turn, know other people who would be interested in participating.

To take these first steps, it was necessary to set enough direction for the project to make it interesting without setting so much of the direction that the workshops would not, in fact, have major decisions yet to make. Two decisions were fixed: the site and the budget. Beyond that, it was virtually true that the group could make any decisions it chose to make.

In every project involving participation, we have been amazed at the range of talented people, all available for the seeking. Workshop members included parents of disabled kids, special education classroom teachers, some children, and diverse individuals such as the city recreation director, a groundskeeper, a Ph.D. specializing in sports for disabled people, and a woman who testifies in playground accident cases. Participants in turn involved their neighbors and their children.

Some material was prepared ahead of time: a slide survey of all the play spaces then available for kids in the area; slide copies of various images of play including illustrations from a Sears catalog (as well as more inspirational sources—e.g., Lady Allen of Hurtwood, 1968; Dattner, 1974), and copies of some fairly accessible journal articles, all as food for thought.

Within the workshop sessions, an early exercise had each participant making sketches of memorable childhood play experiences. We did not ask for good experiences or for weird ones, but the results were some very lively images of kids at play: almost all included an element of risk or of the forbidden. Several people, for instance, described a game played by jumping from one garage roof to another from one end of the block to the other—the only rule being not to touch the ground. Since some garage roofs are quite a distance apart, this might require a great leap, the use of a handy tree branch, or even swinging on electrical wires; beside the risk of a nasty fall, being chased by police made it all even more exciting. One woman brought up almost primordial images of snakes in dark culverts. A boy drew a muddy ravine where he liked to ride his bike, an activity prohibited, of course, by his parents. This whole exercise was exciting because it appeared, at this point, that there would begin to be statements that would become part of the architectural program—statements about experiences and feelings that we could use to shape a design.

The Heights Playstructure. The continuous ramp spirals up 11 feet, forming a hollow "hill," limiting falls to short distances on the outside, and creating a "meeting place" on the inside.

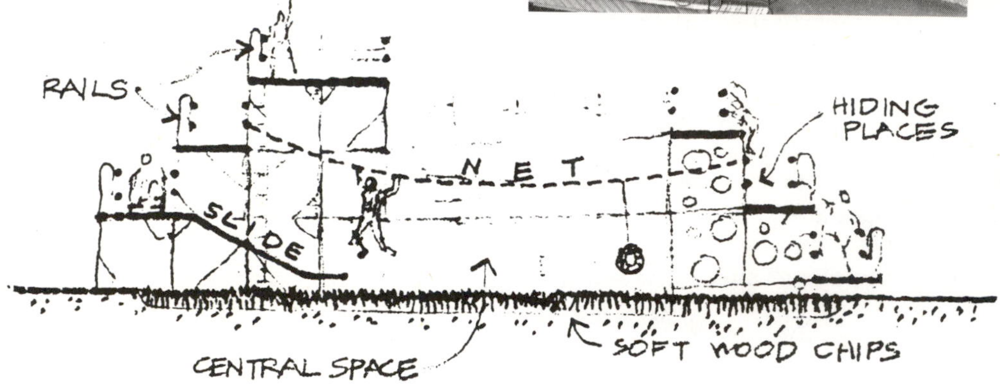

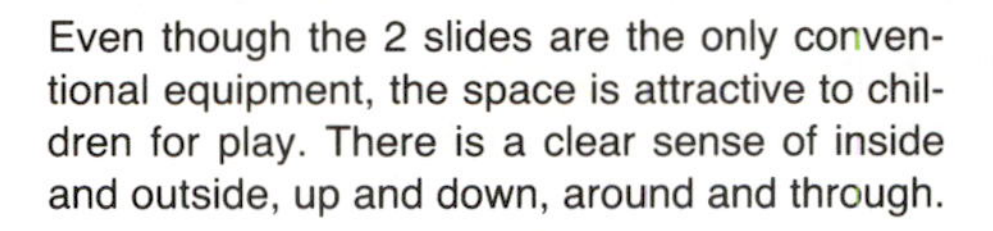

Even though the 2 slides are the only conventional equipment, the space is attractive to children for play. There is a clear sense of inside and outside, up and down, around and through.

WHAT HAPPENED IN THE TWO DESIGN PROCESSES

Even in a conventional process the perfect step-by-step design flow charts prepared ahead of time rarely represent reality. In a participatory process this is all the more true; there are invariably false assumptions about who has bought into what and there are always mistaken paths. The people who participate are likely to be a diverse group who may have very different experiences of working in a creative design process. In a bureaucratic organization in particular, proposals to change the setting may touch on usually hidden issues of rivalries, power, and turf, issues that may become as important to the project as the design itself. This is not all unpredictable, however; there are some typically recurring situations which may be prepared for.

Using Analogies instead of Conventional Images

In writing about the Heights playstructure, we related the excitement we felt when participants in the workshops began to draw out their memorable play experiences. Something remarkable happened, however, as soon as the same people were asked to use the same means of expression to say what might happen in the new playground. Suddenly there were dozens of sketches of swing sets and teeter-totters! As soon as people stopped bringing out their own memorable experiences as kids and began to think about what should happen *for* kids, conventional images took over. Yet, the garage roofs and muddy ravines talked about earlier were much more exciting than these conventional images.

It is not that conventional images are so bad—it is just that they are usually so limiting; they stifle insight. An exception, however, was one very nice image, which was conventional for the children who made drawings of it in this workshop and was called the "cheesehouse." The cheesehouse was a 3- or 4-foot cube-shaped playhouse—which had recently been torn down—named for the holes in its sides which resembled Swiss cheese. This turned out to be a much loved, "friendly object" (Prangnell, 1969) that many children recognized, had played on, and remembered fondly. A version of it was incorporated into the playstructure design, although it was later cut to meet the budget.

Sometimes, to keep from getting stuck in conventional images of swing sets and teeter-totters, we have asked people to speak in analogies (Hart, 1973): "This playroom ought to be like a circus. Three rings, each separate, but a lot of action." This is an experiential statement that, at the Broadview playroom, helped along the design process. "What we're really talking about here is a meeting place for children. This isn't a playground, it's a meeting place!" And, in fact, the central open space of the Heights playstructure is a meeting place, reinforced by the many small nooks ringing the central space.

Keep a sharp ear and you will hear people talking in analogies without prompting. After one playstructure workshop meeting had broken up, one man said, almost out of desperation, "You might just as well make a big hill. That's about all the kids would play on without getting hurt." In fact, this almost casual remark came right to the core of the matter. The complete design is like a big hill, getting smaller as it goes up and limiting the distance down that anyone can fall. It is interesting that this was said after a workshop meeting, as people were on their way out. The participatory workshop was a situation in which information evolved, but it did not evolve in a clearly predictable line. The process is certainly not linear, beginning to end.

Replacing "You Can't" Statements with Statements of Conflicts

At the Broadview playroom we heard this: "You can't have anything soft because the kids will eat it. We have to watch them all the time to make sure they don't unravel their socks and eat the thread." "You can't keep any toys out in the open because they'll be ripped off." "The volunteers can't work with more than one child at a time. With the noise and chaos around here, you wouldn't believe how wild the kids get."

At the Heights playstructure we were told, "Don't put in anything movable because there won't be any staff to supervise." "You can't have any cozy spaces since that will only attract rapists and dope smokers." "Safety is important above all else. We'll have a law suit over anything that isn't safe."

There is some institutional wisdom contained in each of these statements; on the fact of it, each one seems correct to those who have actually experienced similar situations. But there is also, within each, a hint of something awry. The logic seems strong but the results are truly absurd. Imagine what the world is like for an institutionalized child who unravels socks and from whom soft things are methodically removed.

It is hard, sometimes, to distinguish between a problem a person has and a problem that the environment has. Were the children "wild" because they had a problem—hyperactivity—or because the environment had a problem—too many hard, noise-reflecting (but, of course, easy to clean) surfaces? Calling the children wild without considering their environment is a really classic example of blaming the victim. Further, merely to view the children in their existing, barren, institutional environment is a failure to see how they might have been in a nurturing, stimulating, supportive environment.

Safety is, of course, a genuine concern, and even if it were not, the appearance of safety certainly is: during the design and construction of the playstructure, being sued was an often expressed concern of the school board, the booster committee, the workshop participants, the funding source, the general contractor, the subcontractor who built the welded pipe structure, and the fabricator who made the net. But at the same time, it is clear that children seek challenge and risk. If the playstructure were too safe, kids would play somewhere else, more fun but less safe. A perfectly safe—but unused—piece of equipment can be seen on almost any playground: a slide that is not steep enough to get up any speed is an example. What is not so easy to see is that, as a result of this stifling degree of safety, the children are somewhere else, seeking challenge. Risk is part of growth.

Given the situation, these "you can't" statements were true. Unquestioned, they would have served to limit the situation, *status quo.* Since part of our intent was to change the situation, these statements would have put unacceptable limits on the design work. (Although, unfortunately, the lack of any staff pressure at the Heights playstructure did remain a limit. It is not reasonable to build a place that is attractive to dozens of children without making provisions for some supervision. We argued but lost.)

Christopher Alexander has woven the idea of conflicts deeply into the concept of an environmental pattern language (Alexander, Ishikawa, Silverstein, *et al.,* 1977; we describe our use of Alexander's work—particularly the idea of conflict statements—in ARC, 1976.) Seeing the conflicts in a situation is one way of getting out of the trap that "you can't" statements set up.

The trouble with "you can't" statements is that they obscure the important forces that a designer must see. Change the statements with the assumption in mind that there are probably at least two opposing forces in conflict; "The children's need for tactile stimulation is in conflict with their tendency to eat anything available, regardless of the consequences." The problem can now be tackled by a designer: Design something that is tactilely stimulating but also will not be eaten by the children. There are many possible designs that fit this statement. In the Broadview playroom, we included fire-resistant carpet, wrapped at the edges to eliminate unravelling, on both walls and soffits. Carpet is an excellent absorber of sound, is colorful, and is easy to keep clean. Occasionally, a child would come into the room apparently just to feel the walls.

Public places and institutions are usually run according to the idea that "you can't keep anything out in the open." Truthfully, you cannot. Anything valuable and anything dangerous (which, taken together, includes almost everything that is interesting) will be locked away in the name of security. The result is dull, uninteresting institutional spaces, devoid of the stimulation and visual suggestivity inherent in visible, useful objects. A good-hearted designer might decide simply to forge ahead with the idea that things out in the open are a lot nicer than things stored out of sight. But the result will still be unsatisfactory. Those nice open shelves will soon be empty and everything interesting will again be locked away in some closed place. In the conflict between stimulation and security, security always wins.

If we change the statement so that it reflects a conflict of opposing forces, however, the problem becomes approachable: Design something that will keep objects secure and yet still also keep them as an integral, stimulating part of the space. Again, there are many possible designs that might result from this statement. One design is a display cabinet, not gigantic, with glazed openings on two sides, a light overhead, and a snap lock on the doors. That the contents can be seen suggests use, but the cabinet can be locked on a moment's notice.

Actually, in use, we have rarely seen one of these cabinets kept locked; they are usually open. In conventional spaces the possibility of something negative happening—no matter how infrequently—means that everything stimulating is kept put away. An awful sort of barrenness results. With the cabinets, the same negative event would lead only to more care in keeping the cabinets locked.

Getting the Questions Right by Being Aware of a Hierarchy of Needs

Before having any involvement with the Broadview play program, we had visited the ward. The dayroom was large and barren, without the sort of differentiation and human scale that comes from smaller parts making up a larger whole. There was occasional fighting. We were struck with the general sense that the children were adrift in space, afraid, and left to their own devices. (The noise alone was almost overwhelming. In addition to the noises of 27 children with nothing to do, there were also noises and intrusions of staff people on duty as well as those of visitors and volunteers.) This is the setting for a very significant portion of the early development of these children. It was, for many, the closest thing to home they had ever known.

A designer had attempted to humanize the unit by putting up a colorful mural and some large cartoon character cutouts high up on the walls; there were new, bright draperies, also high on the walls, out of reach. We were asked to look at the unit because the high hopes of the designer and staff had not been met; the children seemed not even to notice. Our reaction was, "Good answer; Wrong question!"

The environmental problems of the unit were deeper than what could be affected by cheery colors. We have found Maslow's "theory of human motivation" (Maslow, 1943) to be a useful analytical tool to see this more clearly. Essentially, Maslow says that individual needs can be ranked on a hierarchy from basic to advanced. Basic needs are prepotent to the more advanced needs; it is no good for a person to attempt to deal with the higher-level needs if the basic ones have not been met. (Maslow's work, of course, is not the only possible source for this view; see Erikson, 1963, or Spivak, 1984.)

Now, to apply this thinking to places, this leap is required: we have to agree that some environmental elements are generally supportive of individual attempts to satisfy particular needs; other elements can be generally associated with other levels of needs.

The cheery colors, for instance, are an environmental element that might enhance one's feeling of self-esteem. Yet, the self-esteem needs are close to the top of Maslow's hierarchy. In the ward, what reason was there to suppose that the children were dealing with esteem needs, at all? Knowing Maslow's view and, through empathy, imagining the fear and insecurity of the children, adrift in this undifferentiated space, one might consider a prepotent need: the need for *safety.*

With safety needs in mind, a designer would surely look for some alternative to the noise and chaos of the unit. Delving more deeply, it seems likely that the lack of any defined parts or personal territories in the room would result in each child's being preoccupied with the self-defense that the environment did not offer. Restructuring the unit into small groups in a bounded, stable physical setting is certainly a physical change more significant to consider than cheery colors.

When it came to working on the playroom, we had this experience of Broadview in mind. The scope of the work did not include restructuring the ward, of course, but within the playroom we did try to make many small, clearly defined parts. A child-sized hole was cut in the lower part of the cabinet and a small, solidly mounted plate glass mirror was installed inside. The space within is also child-sized and acts as a secure private place for a quiet time: a safe retreat, a "cave." The "balance beam" helped to define one boundary of a "pit." Even the formica surfaced testing table was affected. Its buff color was surrounded with a 4-inch red circle to distinguish the *center* from the *edge*—an otherwise difficult conceptualization for children at this level of development, the importance of which is clear to anyone who has tried to tell a child to keep the toys away from the edge so that they will not fall off.

Avoiding the Head Nurse by Involving All

Of course, it is not always the head nurse, but each time we have done a project somebody emerges who acts like a head nurse. It is someone who has been promoted up above the middle of the table of organization, who values job security and stability greatly, and reacts very negatively—but usually not directly—to any proposals for changing the turf. It usually is not someone at the bottom or the top, as they are more often open to innovation.

While working at Broadview, we had become quite comfortable in inviting kids into the playroom while we were building. For them it was an opportunity to run a vacuum cleaner or watch a saw being used close up. For us it was a chance to see day-by-day how kids were able to handle the steps without a railing or to be aware of how fascinated they were by their own mirror image.

The "head nurse" had shown no interest in participating in the planning workshops and was quite unaware of the safety measures we had taken to protect the children. The reaction was simply an order that the kids were to be kept in the dayroom during the day shift—the very hours we were working. The line staff people knew the purpose of this order and immediately subverted it. They simply agreed among themselves to spirit the kids back to the dayroom whenever this particular head nurse made one of his (fortunately) infrequent appearances.

The "head nurse" at the Heights playstructure is really not a fair example, since he was not hired until after the planning workshops were over and therefore could not have been involved in the planning process. Suddenly, a large number of youngsters were playing in one corner of a high-school athletic field—the athletic field that he had been hired to oversee. His reaction was to install a sign: "THIS AREA FOR HANDICAPPED ONLY"—exactly opposite the original purpose of the structure. Removal of this sign was instigated by a workshop participant.

The more thorough the job of involving users, the less the likelihood a head nurse will emerge. But keep in mind that dealing with space is always a case of dealing with someone's turf and for many people the right to control turf is a very important source of power. Particularly in a hierarchical organization, head nurses are easily threatened by proposals for change. On some projects, we have initiated a very small change—we have joined with users to wash the windows, for instance—to build trust and get the lay of the land. Our interest has been not so much to cut anyone out of control but to show that power can be shared. The idealized advantage of shared power is that there is also shared responsibility; everyone takes better care of spaces over which everyone feels control.

User involvement is an empowering process; it is a process that takes a lot of time. Some people have gotten used to the idea that their power to affect space is very limited. Building models, making full-sized mock-ups, drawing on the walls, or putting tape on the floor are all nonthreatening ways to get the point across that affecting space can be lively and exciting.

Making a Design: Integrating Images into Places

In this narrative, we have been moving forward and backward a bit through our process to try to describe common threads in the work. We want to focus now on the act of making a design. This occurs in any project; at some point designs happen. All this information and all these experiences become integrated into the design or else they do not.

Actually, we design in the same way as other designers. As others do, we float repeatedly between a process of analysis and a process of synthesis. An important difference in our process is that, early on, participation by users generates many more images of parts than conventional design processes are capable of generating. Finally, we sit down with a blank piece of paper, a pencil, and these many strong images. We start to draw these images, alone or in a group, sometimes layering one image over another, piecing parts together, always seeking to integrate disparate parts.

A clue to the success of design integration—a guidepost to look for as the design progresses—is that one part begins to contain many parts. Visually and functionally the design becomes very suggestive; meaning emerges. Ezra Pound said that literature is language charged with meaning. He went on to say, "Great literature is simply language charged with meaning to the utmost degree" (1960, p. 28). In the same way, what distinguishes architecture from lackadaisical design is that architecture is design charged with meaning. The design becomes charged from the layering of one image over another image, from integrating one part with many other parts. The result is that one thing does many things; again, the place becomes a configuration of possibilities.

At the Heights playstructure, for instance, we began to sketch out the image of a "big hill" that had come from one of the workshop sessions; this led to thinking about a spiral ramp; it began to look like a ziggurat. Then we sketched a "meeting place"—also from the workshop sessions. To put the two together, the big hill had to become hollow. We built a toothpick model of this and began to think and sketch how the many other images we had of parts could fit into this whole. There were other beginning points and some blind alleys, but it was from this toothpick model, where the hill and the meeting place came together, that the whole appeared.

We began to look at different ways of supporting the hill. The finished design is built of a highly indeterminate series of welded pipe frames, purposely designed as many small-diameter kids'-hand-sized parts rather than as few too-large-to-grasp parts. The pipes hold up the structure and also act as many handholds.

At the Broadview playroom, design happened openly in the design team sessions with much back and forth; it was a group effort. An issue early on in the process was the sense that many staff people expressed of wanting "a room with things in it." At this point, integration was lacking. For instance, staff people wanted a balance beam and a set of "practice" stairs, both intended to develop balance, coordination, motor skills, and muscles. Their idea was two conventional pieces of equipment, standing separate, each with a built in "right answer."

Together we worked with sketches and the cardboard model. Initially there was a we–they split; we would propose and they would react. But gradually everyone became more comfortable with the process and they also made proposals. "Take out that wall." "Add a platform here." "That opening seems too small." "It needs more little nooks." Ideas came from all sides as the group came to life and began to sense its own power. Our role became to show how all these various ideas could become integrated into physical space.

So the practice stairs became a series of levels incorporating the balance beam and defining a pit and became seating around the central-pedestal testing table (comfortable for both kids and volunteers) and raised kids up high enough to look out over the high window sills and defined parts within the whole that gave the spaces a sense of differentiation so that the concept of "here" and "there" was more meaningful and helped define the human scale of the room. What had been separate thoughts were now integrated into the design, giving it meaning and possibilities.

It is in some ways scary for an architect to do this design work with users involved, openly. It means taking the risk of giving up the professionalized stance of being the sole source; it means being more vulnerable. The attractive thing about trying to operate this way is that it demystifies how architecture is done, welcoming the creativity of many people.

A REFLECTION

The point of being immersed in a place is not, of course, to do the same sort of design as what would have happened anyway. An open, encompassing, informed participatory process is right at the heart of what makes the result different and special.

What is different and special about these designs, however, is not that they read as some odd contraption for kids of limited capacity. In fact, most people would have no idea that these two projects were designed for children with any sort of disability. The designs are richer and more suggestive for all children because they have taken into account the special needs of some children. To put it differently, designing with any particular group, whether the actual future users or not, is better than designing for an abstraction.

As architecture has become professionalized, architects and other designers find it far more difficult to know their clients intimately; this is "professional distancing." Large investment in larger and larger projects means more sweeping decisions based only on abstracted notions of client needs; complex technologies and sophisticated building processes result in less time for immersion. Opportunities are lost for fine tuning and adjustments.

Part of the problem is just the overwhelming size of decisions. Karl Popper has said: "Our main point is very simple: it is difficult enough to be critical of our own mistakes, but it must be nearly impossible for us to persist in a critical attitude towards those of our actions which involve the lives of many men. To put it differently, it is very hard to learn from very big mistakes" (1957, p. 88).

This professional distancing is especially true when the user of design is a child. Children do not pay for buildings or for architects' time. Even when kids are involved in the design process—which in itself must really be quite rare—control remains in the hands of some adult. Their needs are usually interpreted through a parent, a school administrator, a developer, or a warden: the "surrogate client" (Spivak, 1973). The result of this process is bad fit; its inadequacies are described in other parts of this book.

A good deal of material in the field of environmental psychology seems to be published—this book is an example—with the idea that architects (and administrators, among others) will make better buildings by using the results of the work of environmental psychologists. This presents an interesting dilemma. Using the results of studies suggests avoiding having to go directly through the process of study and particularly, from our point of view, the process of immersion. Surely there are many facts to be learned from environmental psychologists; more important than their facts, though, is their process of interacting directly with users over time. In this sense and to a limited degree, the existence of environmental psychology as a new field, striving for professional legitimacy, has the potential for imposing itself between architects and what they ought to experience directly.

ACKNOWLEDGMENTS

Along with the authors, several members of The ARC Group (Architecture Research Construction) were responsible for the described projects: Charles Craig, Kenneth Esposito, Barbara Hartford, Steven Kahn, and Robert Reeves. Philmore Hart, Architect, Cleveland, and Phyllis Brody of Creative Art Activities, Inc., Cleveland, both contributed to this writing.

REFERENCES

Alexander, A., Ishikawa, S., Silverstein, M., *et al. A pattern language* (New York: Oxford University Press, 1977.

Lady Allen of Hurtwood. *Planning for play.* Cambridge, MA: MIT Press, 1968.

Architecture Research Construction. Behavioral change on Ward 8. *Journal of Architectural Education,* 1976, *29*(4), 26–29.

Bakos, M., Bozic, R., Chapin, D., & Neuman, S. Effects of environmental change on elderly residents' behavior. *Hospital and Community Psychiatry,* 1980, *31*(1), 677–682.

Dattner, R. *Design for play.* Cambridge, MA: MIT Press, 1974.

Erikson, Erik. *Childhood and society* (pp. 247–261). New York: W. W. Norton, 1963.

Hart, P. J. "Humanizing architects: Feeling vs. object. *AIA Journal,* 1973, *59*(1), 41–43.

Holt, J. Children are sensitive to space. *School Review,* 1974, *82*(4), 667–70. (There are many other good articles in this issue on design with children.)

Maslow, A. H. A theory of human motivation. *Psychological Review,* 1943, *50,* 370–396.

Popper, K. R. *The poverty of historicism.* New York: Harper & Row, 1957.

Pound, E. *ABC of reading* (p. 28). New York: New Directions, 1960.

Prangnell, P. The friendly object. *Harvard Educational Review,* 1969, *39*(4), 36–41.

Rivlin, L. & Wolfe, M. Institutional settings in children's lives. New York: John Wiley & Sons, 1985.

Spivak, M. *Institutional settings: An environmental design approach* (pp. 35–52). New York: Human Sciences Press, 1984.

Part V

Conclusions

Chapter 13

Developmental Perspectives on Designing for Development

THEODORE D. WACHS

INTRODUCTION

In analyzing the nature and impact of the built environment one can approach the matter from many perspectives. By perspective I mean an organized set of principles, methods, and facts that help structure one's approach to specific problems, which help delineate the major questions to be addressed and help make sense of obtained results. Three major perspectives are addressed in this volume: the architectural, the educational, and that of the environmental psychologist. It is the major thesis of this chapter that an additional perspective may also be necessary. To the extent that one is interested in the developmental consequences of the built environment (as is implied by the title of the volume) the principles, methods, and data base used by environmentally oriented developmental researchers (that is, a developmental perspective) must also be considered as potentially relevant.

Advocating the relevance of a developmental perspective when looking at the relationship of the built environment to development does not in any way obviate the validity of other perspectives for other types of questions. The validity of a perspective is directly dependent upon the question that is being asked. Thus, if the question being addressed is how best to reconcile conflicting demands about safety needs of children versus the need to provide a stimulating environment, the most valid perspective for this question

THEODORE D. WACHS • Department of Psychological Sciences, Purdue University, West Lafayette, IN 47907.

would be that of the designer–architect, as elegantly demonstrated by Bakos, Bozic, and Chapin (Chapter 12, this volume). However, when the primary question concerns consequences of the built environment for children's development, our ability to answer this question will be enhanced if the principles, methods, and data base of the developmentalist are integrated into the contributions from other disciplines.

To promote this type of integration I will be considering the information presented in this volume within a developmental perspective across four areas: (1) the nature of questions required by a developmental perspective, (2) methodological considerations, (3) the use of the knowledge base gathered by environmentally oriented developmental researchers, and (4) the implications of existing models of environmental action.

THE BUILT ENVIRONMENT AND CHILDREN'S DEVELOPMENT: ARE WE ASKING THE RIGHT QUESTIONS?

Although the historical roots of the study of the relationship of experience to development can be traced back to the time of the Greek philosophers, empirical research on this question has been actively pursued for only about 50 years (Hunt, 1979). As I have pointed out in a previous paper (Wachs, 1983), over the past 50 years there has been a systematic shift in the types of questions being asked by developmental psychologists about the relation of experience to development. The initial stage of inquiry was characterized by efforts to show that the environment was, in fact, relevant to development. It appears clear that this question has been answered in the affirmative (Hunt, 1979; Wachs & Gruen, 1982). The second stage of inquiry, beginning in the early 1960s, was characterized by efforts to delineate which specific aspects of the environment are most relevant for development. On the basis of research done over the past 25 years we are now able to provide specific answers to this question as well (Gottfried, 1984; Wachs & Gruen, 1982). Currently, a number of environmentally oriented developmental researchers are now turning toward a third stage of inquiry, characterized by investigation of a different and more complex set of questions. These questions involve the generalizability of specific environmental influences across different developmental domains, and the mediation of environmental influences by individual, organismic characteristics: "What specific aspects of the environment are relevant for what specific aspects of development, at what specific ages, for what specific individuals?" (Wachs, 1983, p. 397).

What is the relevance of this systematic change in the nature of questions asked by environmentally oriented developmental researchers for understanding the relationship of the built environment to development? It seems fair to say that, in general, models describing the impact of the built environment upon development remain primarily at stage 1. Does this mean that researchers must first demonstrate that the built environment is actually relevant for development? Not necessarily. What is described in this volume as the "built environment" encompasses many of the dimensions used by environmentally oriented developmental psychologists interested in studying the relation of the physical environment to development. Available evidence (Wachs & Gruen, 1982; Wohlwill & Heft, in press) allows us to state with a high level of confidence that the question of whether the physical environment is relevant for children's development has been answered in the affirmative. Further, as noted in available reviews (Wachs & Gruen, 1982; Wohlwill & Heft, in press), we have made some progress on the stage 2 question of delineating what specific dimensions of the physical environment are most relevant for development.

Given this data base, it seems clear that further attempts simply to show that the built (physical) environment is relevant to development (stage 1 question) will not be very productive. The more appropriate stage 2 and stage 3 questions appear to consider what specific aspects of the built environment are relevant for what specific aspects of development for which children. To answer these stage 2 and stage 3 questions, researchers must begin to utilize appropriate stage 2 and stage 3 methodologies.

SOME CONSIDERATIONS FOR APPROPRIATE RESEARCH METHODOLOGY

The Use of Intervention and Institutional Studies

In general, intervention or institutional studies are most appropriate for answering stage 1 questions about the impact of the environment *per se*. Particularly for intervention studies our ability to conclude that the intervention has had the desired impact will depend on the researchers' ability to demonstrate that changes are due only to the intervention and not to extraneous factors. An example of this problem is seen in the intervention program described by Baldassari, Lehman, and Wolfe (Chapter 11, this volume). It may well be that the changes in children's behavior during the course of the intervention, as described by the authors, were due to the intervention. However, since the authors did not use any control groups, acceptance of their conclusions becomes an article of faith. It is equally plausible that any changes arose from random variations in children's behavior, maturation of the children, school influences on children's behavior, or a placebo effect (e.g., attention) having nothing at all to do with the content of the program. Without appropriate controls it is impossible to differentiate between these alternatives.

Obviously, finding appropriate control groups is more difficult in field research than in standard laboratory studies. However, in many cases potential no-treatment controls are available. For example, Baldassari *et al.* note the existence of other schools in the areas in which they were doing their research, which might have served as controls. Alternatively, use of cohort, regression change, or time series designs (Cook & Campbell, 1970) may also serve as quasi-controls, allowing some degree of estimation of the impact of treatment effects.

What of the researcher who wishes to use intervention or institutional studies to answer stage 2 questions? To do this it is necessary to specify what aspects of the built environment are involved, either by direct manipulation or by direct measurement. For example, researchers must go beyond simply assuming that certain environments (e.g., institutions) are inadequate, as do Wolfe and Rivlin (Chapter 5, this volume) and begin to define which specific institutional features predict which developmental outcomes for children. An appropriate model of a stage 2 strategy for institutional research would be the studies of Tizard (Tizard, Cooperman, Joseph, & Tizard, 1972) on specific institutional influences on young children's development. Similarly, for day-care interventions the researcher must specify which aspects of the built environment in the day-care setting predicted changes in childrens development, rather than collapsing specific environmental dimensions into a global measure such as "stimulus-rich." As an example, use of the Early Childhood Physical Environment Scale described by Moore (Chapter 3, this volume), would allow the researcher to determine which specific spatial–temporal dimensions of child-care centers relate to variability of outcomes in children's development across specific domains (a stage 3 question).

Utilization of Adequate Environmental Measures

Inadequate environmental measures leave open the question of what the relevant influences really were. This is particularly critical when the researcher is focusing on stage 2 questions, designed to specify what are the relevant aspects of the environment. Problems occur most often when the researcher utilizes measures that are not direct assessments of the environment. An example is seen in Chapter 7 by Johnson (this volume), where the author relies almost exclusively upon interview techniques as a measure of the environment. The use of interview techniques for this purpose has been criticized on a number of grounds, including unreliability of information (Wachs, in press; Yarrow, Campbell, & Burton, 1970) and caregiver bias in terms of what is reported (Wachs & Gruen, 1982). This is not to say that interview measures are not a useful technique for research questions derived from other perspectives. As illustrated in the chapter by Shaw (Chapter 9 of this volume), interviews may be very useful within a design perspective, as a means of obtaining information on what features of the environment children prefer. However, when the question is one about environmental influences on development, either direct assessments of the environment or multiple measures that include interviews as only one source of data are to be preferred.

Developmental versus Process Outcome Measures

One critical question that must be asked is whether the outcome measures chosen are appropriate, given the nature of the questions being asked. Within an educational perspective, the use of children's behavior in the classroom would be an appropriate outcome measure. However, if the researcher is interested in developmental outcomes these classroom process measures may not be particularly useful variables. As pointed out in a number of educational reviews (Lynn, 1981; MacTurk & Neisworth, 1978), changes in specific classroom behaviors or skills may have little salience in promoting critical developmental changes for the child. Specific classroom behaviors may be chosen for study because they are easily measured or because they relate to specific instructional objectives. This does not guarantee that the skills represent either the precursors or the critical mediators of important developmental processes (Robinson & Robinson 1975).

An example of this problem is seen in the chapter by Moore, in which he discusses the relevance of physical setting to children's use of "cognitive play activities." The implication of this term is that children who utilize this type of play activity will be cognitively advantaged, as compared to children who are low in their use of cognitive play activities. Nowhere are we given evidence, however, showing the relationship of cognitive play activities to cognitive development. The link between cognitive play and cognitive development is only an untested assumption. A similar point can be made when classroom features are changed (i.e., Weinstein, Chapter 8 herein). These changes may influence classroom behavior, but the relevance of these changes to development cannot be assessed unless appropriate developmental measures are used or a link is demonstrated between classroom behaviors and developmental outcomes.

Is there a way out of this problem? Happily, several studies reviewed in this volume offer a satisfactory model for future research on the relevance of setting to development. An example of a design-based study using outcome measures appropriate to both educational and developmental perspectives is seen in the paper by Nash (1981) cited by Weinstein. Looking at the impact of randomly organized versus spatially planned preschool classrooms, Nash utilized measures appropriate to answering educational questions (manipulative activities in the classroom with available material) as well as measures appropriate to answering developmental questions (Piagetian conservation tasks). The use of rate changes in children's level of behavioral functioning, as seen in the chapter by Bakos *et al.*, offers another potential alternative.

Ideally, design intervention studies should integrate across a variety of outcome measures, including measures of changes in teachers behavior, changes in child behavior, and appropriate developmental measures. Through the use of a variety of measures it becomes possible to assess whether developmental changes were directly due to design features (if the changes in developmental parameters were independent of changes in teacher behavior or child's classroom behavior) or were mediated by changes in teacher behavior or by the activities the child began to adopt in the classroom following the change. These types of studies, looking at how changes are mediated, would allow researchers on the built environment to move beyond the stage 1 question (is there an impact) to more sophisticated levels of model specification and model testing.

THE UTILIZATION OF EXISTING KNOWLEDGE

In utilizing available information it must be stressed that we are again talking in terms of perspectives. For persons working primarily within a design or educational perspective, knowledge of developmental research may not be particularly useful. However, when one is attempting to answer questions derived from a developmental perspective, as in the relation of the built environment to children's development, a knowledge of the available data base on this question can be very valuable.

The Problem of Assumptions

All researchers and intervention specialists make assumptions about the nature and etiology of the phenomena they work with. To the extent that these assumptions are spelled out, and are not contradicted by available data, their use is acceptable. In some situations, if assumptions are treated as questions, important research may result. As an example, Olds (Chapter 6, this volume) assumes that kinesthetic stimulation is directly related to the development of children's reading skills. This unverified assumption could be directly tested through comparing the reading skills of children in a kinesthetically rich environment with the reading skills shown by children encountering an equally rich built environment, but one that is centered on other dimensions such as visual-auditory rather then kinesthetic stimulus factors.

The prime danger in using assumptions occurs when assumptions presented as fact are actually contradicted by available data. One major problem with using incorrect assumptions is that in some cases their utilization may hinder the carrying out of appropriate research. For example, as in the chapter by Baldassari *et al.*, if one assumes that schools are repressive institutions then the researcher may choose not to use school record material such as grade retention, achievement tests, or disciplinary actions as a data source, when such data may be quite relevant to the research question being asked. The potential utility of this type of data is nicely seen in the chapter by Bakos *et al.*, who utilized existing information on the number of retarded children advancing into a regular activity group after an institutional playroom was redesigned, as one measure of change.

In addition, the use of invalid assumptions may hinder the implementation of appropriate intervention strategies for children at risk. For example, Wolfe and Rivlin assume that institutional settings are designed primarily to serve their own purposes rather then to help the child. This assumption ignores an impressive body of evidence indicating that schools may serve to promote satisfactory outcomes for children at risk for various developmental problems (Rutter, 1983). This assumption is also contradicted by evidence indicating that for children from disadvantaged home environments, a residential institution may be a better place for the child then its natural home environment (Tizard & Rees, 1976; Zigler & Balla, 1981). Although some institutions may be repressive, an assumption that all institutions are repressive increases the chances that institutional settings will not be used as interventions, even though they may be the best available treatment in some situations.

Weinstein has emphasized the need to use empirical data rather than intuition or bias when designing classroom environments. The same point must be considered when designing research studies and interventions on the impact of the built environment upon development.

Utilization of Available Knowledge on Environment and Development

Knowledge of the data base gathered by environmentally oriented developmental researchers can be useful in verifying the generalizability to development of concepts or findings formulated in other domains. For example, working within an architectural framework, Shaw noted that designing a variety of spaces and diverse paths in playgrounds led to rich patterns of play behavior. Similarly, Olds has suggested the need to rotate classroom material to maintain the child's interest. This emphasis by designers upon change and variety of spaces and materials receives support from environmentally oriented developmental researchers, who consistently report a positive relationship between variety of experience and subsequent development (Wachs & Gruen, 1982). Theoretically, variety is thought to promote development through allowing a greater probability of "match" between the child's interests and the parameters of the environment available to the child. For example, working with a design perspective Shaw notes the relevance of "defensible spaces" (a place where a child can observe group activities before deciding whether or not to join in). From a developmental perspective, defensible spaces provide an appropriate environmental match for a shy child, who may need this type of environmental prop to derive maximal benefit from a noisy, active playground situation.

Integration of knowledge across domains can also lead to testable hypotheses. For example, noting the high levels of noise in typical playroom situations for the retarded, Bakos *et al.* suggest building small spaces into which the child can retreat to avoid the noisy environment. The design solution in this case is paralleled by the concept of "stimulus shelter," which has been shown to enhance cognitive functioning in young children (Wachs, 1979). Integrating this data with the Bakos *et al.* design solution leads to the testable prediction that the highest rates of cognitive development would occur for those retarded children who make the most use of the small spaces (stimulus shelters) designed by Bakos and his colleagues.

Similarly, available data indicate higher cognitive development for children residing in homes with a higher rooms–people ratio (Wachs & Gruen, 1982). We would thus predict more rapid cognitive development for children in day-care settings characterized by a high play spaces–number of children ratio, as defined by Prescott (Chapter 4, this volume).

Utilization of available developmental knowledge can also offer alternative methodological approaches to research workers from other perspectives who are interested in dealing with developmental problems. For example, Proshansky and Fabian (Chapter 2) note the potential relevance of regularity of features in the home to development of place identity. One approach to testing this hypothesis would be to utilize existing home environment measurement instruments, which include observational codes measuring the regularity of features and scheduling in the home. Examples include the Caldwell HOME scale (Elardo & Bradley, 1981) or the Purdue Home Stimulation Inventory (Wachs, Francis, & McQuiston, 1979). Similarly, the difficulties noted by Prescott in coding conversations involving the child's asking about the world and people may be resolved through use of observational codes developed to measure these dimensions. Examples would include the referential speech code developed by Clarke-Stewart (1973) or the procedure for assessing referential communication developed by Dickson, Hess, Miyake, and Azuma (1979).

A knowledge of appropriate developmental research can also serve to point out the most appropriate types of intervention in a given area. An excellent example of this is seen in Weinstein's chapter, when she utilizes available developmental data on age changes in symbolic play as a means of formulating guidelines for the types of objects that should go into preschool dramatic play areas for children of different ages.

UNDERSTANDING THE NATURE OF ENVIRONMENTAL ACTION

In a paper on valid and invalid uses of reductionism, Anderson (1972) pointed out that inferences about causality at higher levels should be congruent with relationships found at fundamental levels. Generalizing this point to the present discussion suggests that models illustrating the role of the built environment upon development should be congruent with fundamental models of environmental action. A number of examples of this point are given below.

The Nature of the Relationship between the Physical and Social Environments

In a recent paper (Wachs, 1986) I delineated four potential relationships that could exist between the physical and social environments in terms of their impact upon development. These are shown in Figure 1. Several of the authors herein (Moore, Proshansky & Fabian) have stated that researchers must consider the relevance of setting to development. Although I would agree that researchers should always consider setting, Figure 1 suggests that the relevance of setting will depend upon the type of environmental action pattern operating. In the case of pattern A (independent influences) or pattern D (physical mediates social) it is correct to speak about setting influences upon development. However, when we are in a situation involving the operation of pattern B (covariance) or pattern C (social mediates physical), attributing variability in development to physical environmental influences *per se* is an overstatement. The operation of pattern B implies that the interrelationship between the social and physical environments is so intermingled that it is misleading to study them in isolation. Potential examples of the operation of pattern B are described in chapters by Hart, Moore, and Proshansky and Fabian, who note the possibility that characteristic parental attitudes may be mirrored by the types of physical surroundings that parents also provide for their offspring. Pattern C implies that any relationships between the physical environment and development will be indirect, since the impact of the physical environment will be mediated by the nature of social interactions between caregiver and child. Available evidence suggests that no single pattern of environmental action described above operates across all developmental parameters. Rather, the relevant form of environmental action will vary as a function of the developmental parameters under study (Wachs, 1986).

Given the above, the determination of whether setting influences development becomes an empirical question. The most appropriate means of testing this question is through the use of statistical techniques such as hierarchical multiple regression or path modeling, whereby order of entry of environmental dimensions into the prediction equation can be varied. Significant predictive variability associated with both social and physical environmental dimensions, regardless of order of entry, supports the validity of pattern A. If predictive variability associated with the physical environment vanishes when it is entered after the social environment dimension, this supports the validity of pattern C; similarly, if variability associated

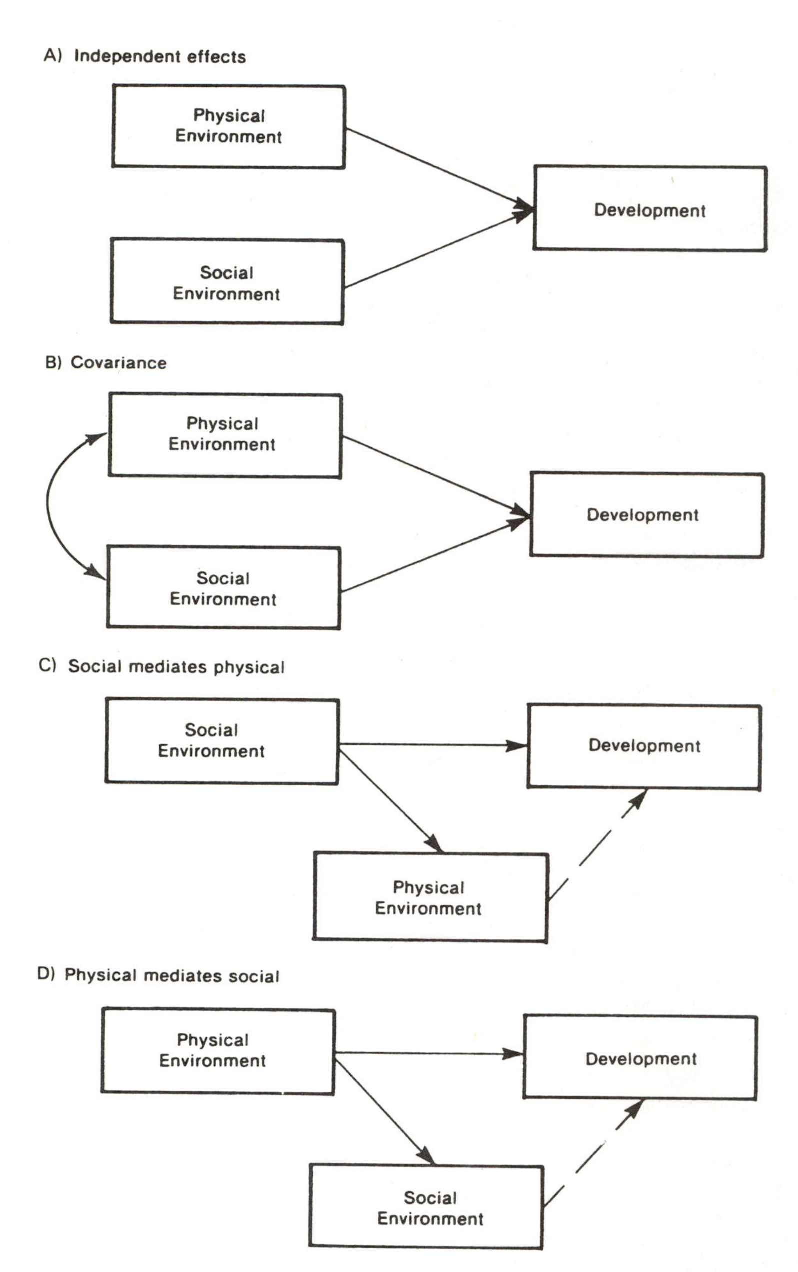

FIGURE 1. Models of the relationship between the physical and social environments.

with the social environment disappears when this dimension is entered after the physical environment dimension, this supports the validity of pattern D. A significant interaction term involving both physical and social environment dimensions supports the validity of pattern B. The point to remember is that one cannot automatically assume setting influences without making tests of this type.

Environmental Specificity

Environmental specificity refers to the fact that different aspects of development are influenced by different aspects of the environment (Wachs & Gruen, 1982; Wachs, 1986). The existence of environmental specificity is one reason why Moore's statement, that there is no theoretical reason to separate the physical environment from other aspects of the environment, must be questioned. Such separation is necessary because physical environmental parameters may have unique influences upon development that are not found for social environmental parameters. Similarly, the strong emphasis given to play activities as a means of facilitating development by authors in this volume (e.g., Prescott) must be tempered by the possibility that play may be salient only for certain aspects of development, with structured, nonplay experiences being equally salient for other aspects of development not influenced by play. The increasing amount of evidence on differential outcomes associated with different types of preschool programs (Miller & Medley, 1984) supports the caveat not to assume a uniform impact of physical environmental influences upon all aspects of development.

Organism–Environment Covariance

Passive Covariance (Polmin, DeFries, & Loehlin, 1977; Wachs & Mariotto, 1978). Passive covariance refers to a situation wherein parents transmit not only environment but also genes (and genetically mediated characteristics) to their offspring. Under these conditions it becomes very difficult to attribute variability in children's development solely to the environmental surroundings (Plomin, Loehlin, & DeFries, 1985). One can rule out passive covariance influences only when environmental surroundings and relevant parent characteristics are measured simultaneously, so as to test for the degree of association.

Reactive Covariance (Plomin *et al.*, 1977; Wachs & Mariotto, 1978). Reactive covariance refers to the fact that the relationship of the child to the environment is not unidirectional. Not only does the environment influence the child; the child can also influence the environment. Specifically, children with certain characteristics may pull certain types of reactions from their environments.

The relevance of reactive covariance to understanding environment–

development relationships is seen in the assumption by a number of authors in this volume (e.g., Baldassari *et al.*, Wolfe & Rivlin) that high levels of structure in institutional settings are causing child behavior problems, rather than considering the possibility that behaviorally disordered children cause their environments to increase structure. Examples of the potential operation of reactive covariance are seen in a number of the case studies given by these authors. For example, in the chapter by Baldassari *et al.* the reaction of the black, working-class male teenagers to an unstructured situation (monopolizing tape recorders and withdrawing from the group process) supports the hypothesis that imposition of a highly structured environment was a result and not a cause of the teenagers' behavior.

Without appropriate longitudinal observations it becomes very difficult to determine whether differences in environment are a result or a cause of children's behavior patterns. As Bakos *et al.* have correctly noted, it is often difficult to know if the locus of the problem is the environment or the child.

Active Organism Environment Covariance (Plomin *et al.*, 1977; Scarr & McCartney, 1983). This third type of covariance refers to individuals' selecting which aspects of the environment they respond to. The selection process appears to be rooted in biological and experientially determined preferences and tolerances. A number of authors in this volume, without using this concept, have addressed similar issues, as in the comment by Moore that the child is an agent of its own development and the observation by Hart that children may prefer different types of media depending upon the style of the child.

The major implication of active organism environment covariance for studies of the impact of the built environment is that simply redesigning the physical environment may not have the impact desired because the child may avoid the changes and seek out its own niche in the redesigned environment, a niche that may not correspond well with what the designer had in mind.

Given the possibility that the child may actively select which aspects of its environment it responds to, the suggestion by Bakos *et al.* on the necessity for observing children's routines and abilities prior to implementing design changes is very well considered. Alternatively, the designer can build in a high degree of short- and long-term variety in the setting, in hopes that each child encountering the setting will be able to find his or her preferred "stimulus niche."

Organismic Specificity

In contrast to a main effects model of environmental action, wherein environments are viewed as having the same impact upon all individuals encountering the environment, researchers have begun to move toward models of environmental action in which the impact of environment is mediated by individual, organismic characteristics (*organismic specificity*—Wachs, 1983). Data from a variety of sources, indicating nonuniform reactions of children to similar environmental circumstances, clearly support the necessity for this shift (Wachs & Gruen, 1982; Wachs, 1986).

This is not to deny the contributions of main effects research, particularly in areas like the study of the built environment in which there is still a lack of data on what specific aspects of the built environment are most salient for specific aspects of development. Ultimately, however, main effects questions like those raised by Proshansky and Fabian (What is the effect of the built environment on personal development?) must be revised to avoid the assumption that the impact of the built environment will be a cohort experience, with all individuals within the cohort reacting equally. Such an assumption can be supported only by evidence indicating that we have wide between-setting variance and low within-setting variance (i.e., most of the variability in development is due to differences between and not differences within settings). In fact, to use schools as an example, available evidence indicates high levels of variability associated both with between-school (Rutter, 1983) and within-school influences (Stevenson, Parke, Wilkins, Bonnevaux, & Gonzalez, 1978; Williams, 1977), even when differential treatment of children within individual schools was almost impossible (Stevenson *et al.*, 1978).

Given evidence supporting the need to consider individual differences when investigating influences of the built environment, what changes can be made in future research strategies or intervention efforts? What appears to be most critical is the utilization of methodologies that allow us to specify both the degree and the nature of the impact of individual differences. In terms of degree, besides reporting mean differences between children in different environmental settings, researchers could also report the range of reaction within settings. *Range of reaction* refers to the range of differences in children's performance before and after an intervention. Only when the between-setting range clearly outweighs the within-setting range of reaction can the investigator feel comfortable in discussing setting differences independently of individual differences in reaction to the setting.

If significant within-setting variability exists, the next critical step would be to identify individual children who responded differentially to setting changes. One approach would be that described by Prescott, characterizing children in day-care centers as thrivers, average, or nonthrivers. Once they are identified, the next and perhaps the most critical stage is to specify the individual, organismic characteristics that differentiate children who thrive in a particular built environment from those who do not. An excellent model for this type of approach is seen in the Dansky (1980) study cited by Weinstein. Prior to children's being placed under different treatment conditions, Dansky first characterized children as high or low in their spontaneous use of make-believe play. By using this design Dansky was able to demonstrate that variability in associative fluency, following experience with free play, was mediated by the amount of spontaneous make-believe play demonstrated by the children.

The results of the Dansky study strongly suggest the need for categorizing children on specific individual difference dimensions, *prior* to implementing environmental change. As Shaw has noted, the designer cannot decide which aspects of the environment present which levels of difficulty; this can be done only by those utilizing the environment. Obviously, our ability to categorize children requires either a theoretical or an empirical basis for deciding which individual, organismic characteristics are most likely to act as mediators within a particular type of environment. Fortunately, a number of the authors in this volume have suggested potential individual difference parameters that may mediate the impact of the built environment. These are noted in Table 1.

In addition to the above dimensions, other individual characteristics that may also serve to mediate the impact of the built environment have been noted by developmental researchers. These would include individual differences in stress tolerance (Garmezy & Rutter, 1983), the question whether the child is oriented primarily toward dealing with objects or per-

TABLE 1. Potential Individual Differences Factors Noted in this Volume

Author	Relevant organismic dimensions	Comments
Proshansky & Fabian	Differences in children's ability to screen out unwanted stimuli	See Mehrabian & Falander (1978) for one potential approach for measuring this dimension.
Proshansky & Fabian	Different requirements for children's aloneness–privacy	Need for privacy in classroom may be particularly salient for children who are less popular and more aggressive (see Chapter 8).
Prescott	Child's activity level	Highly active children may do poorly in highly focused settings (see Chapter 4).
Weinstein	Sex of child	Males show more cooperative play with toys in situation in which classes get extra environmental stimulation (see Chapter 8). Note also that males may be more sensitive than females to stress situations, such as ambient background noise (Wachs, 1979).

sons (Wachs, 1986), and individual differences in behavioral inhibition in strange situations (Coll, Kagan, & Reznick, 1984). Although all potential mediating characteristics cannot be integrated into a single investigation, careful consideration of the nature of the environment and the characteristics of individual difference dimensions will suggest to the researcher which organismic characteristics are most likely to mediate reactivity to the specific environmental influences being studied. For example, chapter authors have suggested the relevance of complexity of setting (Prescott, Weinstein) and arousal potential inherent in the setting (Olds) for development. Although specific aspects of the environment can be scaled on degree of complexity or degree of arousal potential, this does not mean that all children will react similarly to high versus low complex or arousing settings. Available evidence indicates that the impact upon development of physically defined measures of complexity are mediated by a variety of individual difference factors, including *age* and *sex* of child, child's *state* when encountering the stimuli, child's *biomedical status* and the child's prior *experiential history* (Wachs, 1977). Similarly, available evidence suggests that the arousal potential of a stimulus setting for a particular child will be governed by a variety of individual difference factors, including individual *biomedical status* and child's *temperament* (Wachs, 1986). Hence, what is a high-complexity or an over-arousing situation for one child may be low-complexity or under-arousing for a second child, in terms of the characteristics noted above.

The necessity for considering individual differences in reaction to the environment is also seen when designing intervention projects. Ideally, intervention specialists would attempt to tailor microinterventions for specific groups of children displaying common characteristics. However, such tailor-made interventions, although theoretically correct, are often difficult to implement. Until it becomes feasible to provide appropriate environments for specific children, the most useful strategy may be to provide a variety of environments in the hope that different children can respond to different aspects of the environment. An example of this is seen in the three-dimensional playground described by Shaw. In such a situation the socially oriented child may find a stage upon which to perform, while the behaviorally inhibited child may find a niche from which to observe. While such an approach has something of the shotgun in its orientation, in terms of hoping that the appropriate stimulus dimensions will affect the appropriate child, it is certainly preferable to providing a single set of environmental conditions that, it is assumed, will be right for all children. *The existence of organismic specificity means that there is no right environment for all children.* Utilizing the Dansky (1980) study cited earlier, free play experiences are a right environment only for children high in spontaneous use of make-believe. For children low in spontaneous use of make-believe other environmental interventions may have to be considered.

CONCLUSIONS

The necessity for interdisciplinary collaboration in projects involving the study or manipulation of children's environments has been called for by a number of authors in this volume (Moore, Weinstein). The evidence presented in this chapter also suggests the need for more interdisciplinary collaboration between designers, intervention specialists, and environmentally oriented developmental psychologists, all of whom can benefit from exposure to the methods, models, and knowledge of other disciplines. However, the main beneficiaries of such collaboration will undoubtedly be children, for whom such collaborations are more likely to lead to matching environment to child and thus to more favorable developmental outcomes.

REFERENCES

Anderson, P. More is different. *Science,* 1972, *177,* 393–396.

Clarke-Stewart, A. Interactions between mothers and their young children. *Monographs of the Society for Research in Child Development,* 1973, *38.*

Coll, C., Kagan, J., & Reznick, J. Behavioral inhibition in young children. *Child Development,* 1984, *55,* 1005–1019.

Cook, J., & Campbell, D. *Quasi-experimentation: Design and analysis issues for field settings.* Chicago: Rand McNally, 1970.

Dansky, J. Make believe: A mediation of the relation between play and associative fluency. *Child Development,* 1980, *51,* 576–579.

Dickson, W., Hess, R., Miyake, N., & Azuma, H. Referential communication accuracy between mother and child as a predictor of cognitive development in the United States and Japan. *Child Development,* 1979, *50,* 53–59.

Elardo, R., & Bradley, R. The HOME observation for measurement of the environment. *Developmental Review,* 1981, *1,* 113–145.

Garmezy, N., & Rutter, M. *Stress, coping, and development in children.* New York: McGraw-Hill, 1983.

Gottfried, A. *Home environment and early cognitive development.* New York: Academic Press, 1984.

Hunt, J. McV. Psychological development: Early experience. *Annual Review of Psychology,* 1979, *30,* 103–143.

Lynn, R. Issues of validity for criterion referenced measures. *Applied Psychological Measurement,* 1981, *4,* 547–561.

MacTurk, R., & Neisworth, J. Norm and criterion based measures with handicapped and non-handicapped preschoolers. *Exceptional Children,* 1978, 45, 34–39.

Mehrabian, A., & Falender, C. A questionnaire measure of individual differences in child stimulus screening. *Educational & Psychological Measurement,* 1978, *38,* 1119–1127.

Miller, L., & Medley, S. *Pre-school intervention: Fifteen years of research.* Paper presented to the American Psychological Association, Toronto, 1984.

Nash, B. The effects of classroom spatial organization on 4- and 5-year-old children's learning. *British Journal of Educational Psychology,* 1981, *51,* 144–155.

Plomin, R., DeFries, J., & Loehlin, J. Genotype–environment interaction and correlation in the analysis of human behavior. *Psychological Bulletin,* 1977, *84,* 309–322.

Plomin, R., Loehlin, J., & DeFries, J. Genetic and environmental components of "environmental influences." *Developmental Psychology,* 1985, *21,* 391–402.

Robinson, C., & Robinson, J. Sensory motor functions and cognitive development. In M. Snell (Ed.), *Systematic instruction of the moderately and severely handicapped.* Columbus, OH: Merrill, 1978.

Rutter, M. School effects on pupil progress. *Child Development,* 1983, *54,* 1–29.

Scarr, S., & McCartney, K. How people make their own environments. *Child Development,* 1983, *54,* 424–435.

Stevenson, H., Parke, T., Wilkons, A., Bonnevaux, B., & Gonzalez, M. Schooling, environment and cognitive development. *Monographs of the Society for Research in Child Development,* 1978, *175.*

Tizard, B., Cooperman, O., Joseph, P., & Tizard, J. Environmental effects on language development. *Child Development,* 1972, *43,* 337–358.

Tizard, B., & Rees, J. A comparison of the effect of adoption, restoration to the natural mother and continued institutionalization on the cognitive development of 4-year-old children. In A. Clarke & A. Clarke (Eds.), *Early experience: Myth and evidence.* London: Open Book, 1976.

Wachs, T. D. The optimal stimulation hypothesis and human development: Anybody got a match? In I. Uzgiris & F. Weizmann (Eds.), *The structure of experience.* New York: Plenum Press, 1977.

Wachs, T. D. Proximal experience and early cognitive-intellectual development: The physical environment. *Merrill-Palmer Quarterly,* 1979, *25,* 3–41.

Wachs, T. D. The use and abuse of environment in behavior genetic research. *Child Development,* 1983, *54,* 396–407.

Wachs, T. D. Models of physical environmental action: Implications for the study of play materials and parent–child interaction. In A. Gottfried (Ed.) *Play interactions: The contribution of play materials and parent involvement to child development.* New York: Lexington, 1986.

Wachs, T. D. Environmental assessment with developmentally disabled infants and preschoolers. In T. D. Wachs & R. Sheehan (Eds.), *Assessment of developmentally disabled children.* New York: Plenum Press, in press.

Wachs, T. D., Francis, J., & McQuiston, S. Psychological dimensions of the infant's physical environment. *Infant Behavior and Development,* 1979, *2,* 151–161.

Wachs, T. D., & Gruen, G. *Early experience and human development.* New York: Plenum Press, 1982.

Wachs, T. D., & Mariotto, M. Criteria for the assessment of organism–environment correlation in human development studies. *Human Development,* 1978, *21,* 268–288.

Williams, T. Infant development and supplemental care. *Human Development,* 1977, *20,* 1–30.

Wohlwill, J., & Heft, H. The physical environment and the development of the child. In D. Stokols & I. Altman (Eds.), *Handbook of environmental psychology,* New York: Wiley, in press.

Yarrow, M., Campbell, J., & Burton, R. Recollections of childhood: A study of the retrospective method. *Monographs of the Society for Research in Child Development,* 1970, *35.*

Zigler, E., & Balla, D. Issues in personality and motivation in retarded persons. In M. Begab, H. C. Haywood, & H. Garber (Eds.), *Psychosocial influences in retarded performance* (Vol. 1). Baltimore: University Park Press, 1981.

Chapter 14

Children's Environments

Implications for Design and Design Research

CRAIG ZIMRING AND RICHARD D. BARNES

INTRODUCTION

A glance at a newspaper or at any large city quickly reveals society's priorities: billions of dollars are spent on highways, yet almost nothing on playgrounds; over 50% of mothers in the United States work, but competent day care is expensive and difficult to find. The affluent white, male automobile driver remains the focus of most design, planning, and research (Zimring, Carpman, & Michelson, 1987).

Early work in environment and behavior studies attempted in some ways to counterbalance this emphasis. Whereas traditional social scientists have tended to study college sophomores in controlled laboratory settings, some environment and behavior researchers have examined environments for vulnerable populations. However, these researchers tended to focus on adults and adult facilities. Although a few studies looked at children in the 1960s and 1970s (Altman & Wohlwill, 1978, for example) the present intense concern with spaces for children is quite new. The current volume is a significant step toward directing attention to the environmental needs and concerns of children.

We approach the task of reviewing research on environments for children as active environmental researchers but not as experts in children's environments. To some extent, then, we present the views and opinions of

CRAIG ZIMRING • College of Architecture, Georgia Institute of Technology, Atlanta, GA 30329. RICHARD D. BARNES • Department of Psychology, Randolph-Macon Woman's College, Lynchburg, VA 24503.

outsiders to this field. However, in our view, this work faces many of the same problems confronted by researchers studying other environments.

A CHARACTERIZATION OF CURRENT RESEARCH

Content Issues: Who and What Are Being Studied?

Play is a ubiquitous, spontaneous activity of children that fosters physical, mental, and social development. During spontaneous play children actively become involved with their surroundings in order to develop and exercise skills in these domains. Berger (1983), for instance, suggests that children engage in *sensorimotor play* for the sheer joy of experiencing new sensations; *mastery play,* to expand their repertoire of cognitive and motor skills; *rough-and-tumble play,* in which they learn social cues to distinguish between playful intent and aggression; and *social and dramatic play,* to develop social interaction skills, play out social roles, and practice cooperation and conflict resolution. Through these forms of play a child builds a sense of trust in other people, a confidence in his or her own physical skills and abilities, and a sense of individual identity. In our view, research in this field has tended to focus on the cognitive aspects of play more than on the social and emotional aspects. Several contributions to this volume redress this imbalance (see particularly Johnson, Chapter 7; Olds, Chapter 6; Prescott, Chapter 4; and Weinstein, Chapter 8).

A second question concerns the differing functions and roles of day-care and home settings in children's development. In some work comparing home and day-care environments there seems to be the assumption that both serve (or should serve) the same functions for children. As Johnson points out, this assumption may not be valid. Children engage in very different forms of play when at home than when attending day-care centers. Research has focused on answering the question of whether day-care centers are "better or worse" than home environments in promoting cognitive development, with the weight of evidence suggesting that day care does not hinder, and may facilitate, cognitive development (Moore, Chapter 3 in this volume). It would be interesting to ask (as Prescott does) a slightly different question: What different developmental needs may day-care and home settings serve for children? Might it be that the former are best for furthering formal cognitive and social interaction skills, whereas home environments function more as places for the development of self-identity, including development of a system of personal values, trust in others, and self-esteem? In what ways, and perhaps in what different ways, do children experience home and day-care settings?

Traditionally, environment–behavior research on children's settings has focused on defining characteristics of the setting rather than characteristics of the children who use the setting. This lack of attention to individual differences is understandable, since this research in general has been a response to an overemphasis in psychology on internal personality factors and a relative neglect of the physical setting. However, in designing environments for children's development, attention to differences among children is critical. Children may play and develop differently depending not only on their age, but also on sex, ethnic and cultural background, and socioeconomic status. Children from different cultures may have very different scripts for how environments are to be used. For example, as Moore notes, high SES children do better in open classrooms than low SES children. Do they have a different set of norms and assumptions for use of open classrooms? It may not be valid to assume a "generic child" in research on children's environments. Attention is given in this volume to the particular needs of physically handicapped children (Olds; Shaw, Chapter 9), the institutionalized mentally retarded (Bakos, Bozic, & Chapin, Chapter 12), and the emotionally disturbed (Wolfe & Rivlin, Chapter 5). This direction should be continued and expanded to include other significant individual differences among children in the ways they use and perceive physical settings.

A final content issue concerns the scale of environments that have been studied. The primary focus of work on children's environments has been on the smaller-scale, near environment of children—homes, playgrounds, day-care settings, and schools. Proshansky and Fabian (Chapter 2 in this volume) suggest a broader approach. In a sense, development in children's knowledge and use of physical settings can be seen as an expansion of the child's world from his or her own home outwards. Children first experience their own home (and day-care setting), then the yard, the playground, the school, the neighborhood, the city, and so on as they grow in knowledge and confidence. However, relatively little work has explored how children use and experience larger-scale environments. How do neighborhoods contribute to a child's sense of self-identity? How can children's needs for exploration and for socializing be taken into account in the planning of residential neighborhoods?

Methodological Issues

As the above discussion suggests, the relationships between children's characteristics, environmental characteristics, and developmental goals and tasks are likely to be exceedingly complex. In order to capture meaningful patterns and relationships in this complexity, researchers in this area will have to employ multivariate designs to a greater degree than has been done to date. Reserach on children's environments (and developmental psychology research in general) has been characterized by the use of nonintrusive observational methods. However, if progress is to be made toward theory-based research on children's environments, more causal, manipulative approaches and quasi-experimental designs will have to be explored.

A characteristic of early work on children's environments has been its strong value perspective. Early research in this area justifiably attempted to redress the lack of attention to children's needs and concerns in design and so sometimes seemed ideological and confrontational in tone. However, children are rarely the exclusive users of a setting. Work in this volume suggests that a more balanced approach is emerging that takes into account the needs of all users and recognizes potential conflicts among children's needs, the needs of other users, and the programmatic needs of the organization. It is likely that such an approach will be more acceptable to design professionals, administrators, parents, and teachers who make decisions about children's environments than an approach that appears one-sided and polemical.

In summary, our perception of research on environments for children, as represented in this volume, is that a productive beginning has been made in examining the influence of environments on children's development. We feel that promising future directions for this research lie in continuing and extending work on the effects of settings on social and emotional development, exploring cultural and individual differences in the way children use environments, looking at the influence of larger-scale environments, and examining children's needs in the context of other demands on design.

WAYS OF DEFINING SETTINGS

Although the chapters herein represent considerable diversity in approach and in the backgrounds of the authors, who include architects, psychologists, and others, there is much similarity in how they view the environment, and particularly in what categories they use to describe it. Which categories are emphasized, such as open plan–closed plan or noisy–quiet, has considerable impact on how settings are studied and designed.

Environmental categories can be defined on at least three levels (Archea, 1984): properties, attributes, and types of setting. Properties are measurable, objective qualities of environments, such as intensity, weight, and color. Properties are basic elements of settings, out of which more complex attributes are constructed. Studies that look at the effect of noise levels on children's cognitive performance (e.g., Cohen, Glass, & Singer, 1973; Cohen & Weinstein, 1982; Wohlwill & Heft, 1977) tend to focus on properties of settings. Attributes of settings are combinations of properties that are chosen for practical or theoretical reasons because of their importance to the setting's occupants or to the operation of the setting. For example, a number of authors discuss the importance of boundaries in schools, homes, day-care centers, and playgrounds. Boundaries are not measurable, unidimensional properties as are noise levels; rather, they are combinations of properties (opacity, height, rigidity, etc.) that take on significance because of the activities they separate, the past experience of the setting's occupants (for example, in their interpretation of floor-paving change as a boundary), and the rules that operate in the setting.

Finally, a number of setting types have been defined and studied. At the most global level these are defined by spatial scale and by common social and legal definitions: house, school, day-care center, playground, neighborhood. Within these categories are subcategories: adventure playgrounds or traditional playgrounds, open-plan or traditional schools.

The choice of what properties, attributes, or settings to study, or what to use as the basis of design, has a clear and pervasive influence on the progress of the field to date. As we have discussed above, for reasons of interest, disciplinary background, and availability of subjects, researchers have tended to focus on cognitive development by middle-class children in school settings and have underrepresented social and emotional development, home and neighborhood settings, and children with other needs or cultural backgrounds. More generally, however, the choice of what to study appears to reflect a conceptual perspective on how people relate to their settings. With some exceptions, a focus on properties such as noise or illumination levels tends to reflect a unidirectional causal model: noise causes distraction, task decrement, stress, and so on. It seems to imply that the child is a responder to environmental change. Some properties such as noise and illumination, at least in their extreme, have been demonstrated to have fairly clear impacts on children's school performance (see Moore).

An attribute-oriented approach seems to reflect a more transactional model of person–environment relations. The notion of the importance of manipulability by children, for example, carries with it assumptions about how things can be manipulated, what children find interesting, and how they play and interact with the environment. This attribute approach has proved both useful and difficult in studying settings for adults. For example, a major study of offices has found that degree of enclosure, defined as number of walls, is a highly significant predictor of worker satisfaction and productivity (Brill, 1984). The value of this approach is that the issues it highlights are more like those considered by designers, building owners, and others. A designer of a day-care center seldom makes an isolated decision about the maximum noise level but may make decisions about the amount of enclosure in the setting (for example, whether it has a few large open spaces or a greater number of smaller areas).

The problem with studying attributes is with measurement and definition. For instance, how may *enclosure* be defined or measured? Should one use number of walls as Brill (1984) did, or transmission of noise, or how much one can see (Archea, 1984)? Some researchers are making promising starts. In a study reported herein, Moore used a 10-dimensional scale with items such as "degree of spatial definition and enclosure, degree of visual connections, degree of spatial separation, degree of connection between indoor and outdoor settings" to establish three levels of day-care center: open, modified open, and closed plan.

Archea's theory of access and exposure provides another approach to studying attributes (Archea, 1984). Briefly, Archea argues that environmental behavior can be understood, at least in part, by the visual opportunities the environment provides. High-exposure places, in which the environment potentially allows the individual to be seen by many other people (such as the center of a large open space) tend to attract people who want to display their activities; high-access places, from which people can potentially view many other people (such as the corner or edge of a space) tend to attract people who want to track what others are doing. This suggests, for example, why single, isolated children may pick the corner of the room to play and more social children may pick the center. In addition, Archea has developed a quantitative system for plotting visual access and exposure. This system, which reflects the placement of walls, doors, and other barriers, provides predictions about where people will situate themselves and what they will do. These predictions have been borne out in a series of small studies of a home for the elderly, banks, and airports (Archea, 1984). Systems for measuring other attributes have to be developed.

Some knotty problems are presented at the level of setting definition as well. Setting types often are used as independent variables, such as in studies comparing home settings to day care, but what dimensions should be used to define settings? Is a home in which three unrelated children are cared for during the day a home or a day-care center? Is it reasonable to separate schools into two categories (such as open-plan versus traditional), into three categories as Moore did or into a continuum? There is clearly no single answer; it depends on the issue being studied. However, the ambiguity of category definitions partly may account for conflicting findings so common in research on children's environments.

Furthermore, the method one uses to establish categories of settings, and the theoretical underpinnings of the method, have significant implications for research. For example, a study focusing on the impact of ambient noise on student attentiveness (e.g., Cohen, Evans, Krantz, & Stokols, 1980) may classify noise level and setting as continuous variables. An alternative view is to consider settings as fairly robust, discrete entities that generate certain scripts or schemas among occupants. For example, two classrooms at a local Atlanta school seem to generate different schemas. One classroom is 30 years old, is a narrow rectangle, and has student desks bolted to the floor in rows. The teacher's desk is on a 6-inch raised platform in the front of the room. The second room is 3 years old, is square, and has movable furniture. The rooms generate different scenarios about how one should behave. The first room generates structured lectures whereas the second seems to encourage group discussion. One can identify specific attributes of the room that encourage these activities, such as lack of eye contact among students in the first room, but perhaps a more interesting question is how assumptions about style of student–teacher interaction are imbedded in the rooms in ways that perpetuate those assumptions. Most people seem to recognize what is appropriate behavior immediately on entering the rooms. This approach generates a number of questions: How can one create a typology of settings? What are the most important factors that distinguish a setting type (such as relative freedom of motion and visual surveillance)? Do children use the same cues as adults do to recognize a setting? What are these cues? How are they learned? How are they perpetuated and changed? These questions are similar to those addressed by Barker and his colleagues (Barker, 1968; Wicker, 1979), by Stokols and Shumaker (1981), and by Hillier and Hanson (1984).

SUGGESTIONS FOR FURTHER RESEARCH

In light of this discussion, it is our impression that the following areas are potentially valuable directions for additional research:

1. Expand the range of settings, children's needs, and kinds of children studied. Study home environments, social and emotional development needs, and children who have been largely ignored, such as low-income and non-English-speaking children.
2. Clarify the use of categories in children's environment research. Consider the implications of categories of children, properties, and attributes.
3. Improve methodology; especially use multivariate research designs and consider self-selection factors. As opposed to the laboratory, real-world settings are complex and require complex causal schemes to capture them. Also, children or parents may select certain kinds of settings (adventure playgrounds, day-care centers) because they fit their needs and interests; these needs and interests must be considered in research.

IMPLICATIONS FOR DESIGN

The preceding chapters in this volume make a number of valuable suggestions for creating and improving environments for children. Although it is beyond the scope of this chapter to consider these suggestions in detail, it is important to consider how environments for children come about and how they are maintained.

These chapters help to clarify the varying settings and spatial scales within which children operate. The understandable focus of psychologists on institutions has given way to the realization that children deal with a variety of building types, such as schools, homes, and day-care centers, and also spend considerable time outdoors, both in playgrounds and streets and in other areas that can be considered the context within which buildings exist. This conceptual broadening of the child's domain also enlarges the audience at whom environmental design suggestions should be directed. Rather than focusing on architects and interior designers as the primary users of design research, this broader view suggests that design recommendations must consider the role of city planners and city officials, landscape architects, and other professionals.

Fundamentally, however, this more inclusive approach also requires a rethinking of the design and building delivery, or environment delivery, process. All too often this process is seen as a simple relationship between a client (such as a school or class) and a designer (either a professional architect, a teacher, or other person acting as a designer) with the outcome being a classroom or playground. This is clearly inadequate in view of the process by which environments are actually designed and created. Among other influences, the designs of children's environments are the result of a variety of codes and standards such as life-safety codes, handicapped accessibility standards, and institutional space standards. These often have a critical impact on the form, number, and size of environmental features but often are based on precedent or tradition. For instance, the time-honored requirement that window area be 10% of floor area is based on erroneous nineteenth-century notions that diseases are carried by airborne particles rather than an an analysis of occupants' needs (Archea & Connell, 1986). Similarly, accessibility standards are often based on limited research and seldom have addressed the physical or emotional needs of disabled children. The theory-based and empirically based recommendations in this volume can have a dramatic impact on design by addressing these codes and standards. For example, several authors propose that environments be "child-scale." What implications does this recommendation have for the design of accessible restrooms, emergency egress routes, signage, and other features in children's environments and also in environments that are used by children but are not primarily children's spaces?

Also, other groups, such as parents, school boards, and, increasingly, financial concerns and businesses, affect the design of environments for children. For example, the number of commercial day-care centers expands as the role of the private sector in child care grows. These groups have different needs, speak different languages, and have different value perspectives. Whereas parents may be highly child-oriented and demand environments that are conducive to children's exploration and manipulation, a day-care center operator may value control and durability of materials. Although some writers and researchers may reject such a view, recommendations will not be acted upon unless they acknowledge the needs of the actor. A design recommendation must help someone do their job better, as they perceive their job. (This raises the obvious point of helping decision makers become aware of alternate perspectives. This is important but is difficult to do without personal contact and long-term commitment by the researcher or designer.)

Rethinking how decisions are made may even be necessary for recommendations aimed at architects, a traditional target of design recommendations. Although initially there was great optimism in the 1960s and 1970s that environment and behavior research would provide considerable help to architects, those expectations have not fully borne fruit. This is partially due to the recent antirationalist trends in architecture (such as postmodernism), which have tended to emphasize the artistic and symbolic components of architecture. Fundamentally, however, those preparing recommendations for design may have misunderstood how architects use information.

Korobkin (1976) has suggested that architects design in three basic steps. First they *develop an image* of a project. This image is not simply visual; it is a whole network of ideas about what a building should be like. The image comes from personal experience, professional interactions and norms, architectural magazines, and (potentially) research. Second, they *represent* that image by drawing it or otherwise describing it. In representation, the image usually changes somewhat. Third, they *test* the image. The test is against some specific criterion such as cost, square footage, efficiency, and so on. Typically, the representation does not fully satisfy the test; for example, it may be discovered that a playground as represented is too expensive, and as a result the project must be reimaged, rerepresented, and retested until it satisfies the criteria.

Given this process, it is essential that information intended to be used by architects be presented in terms of image information, expressing what a setting should be like (for example, what a good elementary school classroom is like), as well as test information that provides specific criteria for testing a given design solution. Image information should be visual whenever possible. Test information may be in the form of design review questions, checklists, specifications, or other similar approaches. In this regard, work such as that of Bakos *et al.* is particularly valuable since it represents the active involvement of practitioners in research on environments for children and because it involves both evocative images and research-based design recommendations.

Unfortunately, research on children's environments is scattered among many publication outlets and is often mired in the turgid disciplinary jargon of the researcher. It has little impact on architects, teachers, parents, administrators, or others who design and manage settings for children. Two strategies are important for increasing the impact of research on the design of children's places. First, environmental research information must be published in accessible outlets—in trade journals and magazines, popular books, and as part of on-line computer search services. *Day Care U.S.A.*, for example, is a better vehicle to reach day-care operators than is *Environment and Behavior.* Second, environmental researchers should become involved with all levels of the building delivery process—in establishing codes and standards and in working with architects, school districts, owners of day-care centers, and parents' advocacy groups. In sum, there must be better communication among researchers, architects, and those who manage children's environments. This volume represents a significant step toward the achievement of this goal.

REFERENCES

Altman, I., & Wohlwill, J. F. (Eds.). *Children and the environment.* New York: Plenum Press, 1978.

Archea, J. C. *Visual access and exposure: An architectural basis for interpersonal behavior.* Unpublished doctoral dissertation, Pennsylvania State University, College Park, PA, 1984.

Archea, J. C., & Connell, B. R. Architecture as an instrument of public health: Mandating practice prior to the conduct of systematic inquiry. In J. Wineman, R. D. Barnes, & C. Zimring (Eds.), *The costs of not knowing: Proceedings of the Environmental Design Research Association.* Washington, DC: Environmental Design Research Association, 1986.

Barker, R. G. *Ecological psychology.* Palo Alto, CA: Stanford University Press, 1968.

Berger, K. S. *The developing person through the lifespan.* New York: Worth, 1983.

Brill, M. *Using office design to incerase productivity.* Buffalo, NY: Workplace Design and Productivity, 1984.

Cohen, S., & Weinstein, N. Non-auditory effects of noise on behavior and health. In G. W. Evans (Ed.), *Environmental stress.* New York: Cambridge University Press, 1982.

Cohen, S., Glass, D. C., & Singer, J. E. Apartment noise, auditory discrimination, and reading ability in children. *Journal of Experimental Social Psychology,* 1973, *9,* 407–422.

Cohen, S., Evans, G. W., Krantz, D. S., & Stokols, D. Physiological, motivational, and cognitive effects of aircraft noise on children: Moving from the lab to the field. *American Psychologist,* 1980, *35,* 231–243.

Hillier, B., & Hanson, J. *The social logic of space.* New York: Cambridge University Press, 1984.

Korobkin, B. J. *Images for design: Communicating social science research to architects.* Cambridge, MA: Architecture Research Office, Harvard Graduate School of Design, 1976.

Stokols, D., & Shumaker, S. A. People in places: A transactional view of settings. In J. H. Harvey (Ed.), *Cognition, social behavior, and the environment.* Hillsdale, NJ: Erlbaum, 1981.

Wicker, A. W. *An introduction to ecological psychology.* Monterey, CA: Brooks/Cole, 1979.

Wohlwill, J. F., & Heft, H. Environments fit for the developing child. In H. McGurk (Ed.), *Ecological factors in human development.* Amsterdam: New Holland Press, 1977.

Zimring, C. M., Carpman, J. R., & Michelson, W. Design for special populations: Mentally retarded persons, children, hospital visitors. In D. Stokols & I. Altman (Eds.), *Handbook of environmental psychology.* New York: Wiley, 1987.

Index